NIETZSCHE

Selections

THE GREAT PHILOSOPHERS

Paul Edwards, General Editor

NIETZSCHE
Selections

Edited, with Introduction, Notes, and
Bibliography, by
RICHARD SCHACHT
University of Illinois at Urbana-Champaign

A Scribner/Macmillan Book
Macmillan Publishing Company
  NEW YORK
Maxwell Macmillan Canada
  TORONTO

To Judy

Editor: Maggie Barbieri

Production Supervisor: Ann-Marie WongSam

Production Manager: Su Levine

Text and Cover Designer: Angela Foote

Cover illustration: The Bettmann Archive

This book was set in Benguiat Book by Carlisle Communications, and was printed and bound by Book Press. The cover was printed by New England Book Components.

Macmillan Publishing Company
866 Third Avenue, New York, New York 10022

Macmillan Publishing Company is part of
the Maxwell Communication Group of Companies.

Maxwell Macmillan Canada, Inc.
1200 Eglinton Avenue East
Suite 200
Don Mills, Ontario M3C 3N1

Library of Congress Cataloging-in-Publication Data

Nietzsche, Friedrich Wilhelm, 1844–1900.
    [Selections. English. 1993]
    Nietzsche selections / edited, with introduction, notes, and
bibliography, by Richard Schacht.
        p. cm. —(The Great philosophers)
    "A Scribner/Macmillan book."
    Includes bibliographical references.
    ISBN 0–02–406681–8 (paper)
    1. Philosophy. I. Schacht, Richard, 1941–   . II. Title.
III. Series.
B3302.E5S33 1993   92–38158
193 —dc20   CIP

Acknowledgments begin on page v, which constitutes a continuation of the copyright page.

Printing: 1 2 3 4 5 6 7 Year: 3 4 5 6 7 8 9

Acknowledgments

I am very grateful to the publishers of the translations of Nietzsche's writings from which the selections in this volume were taken for their permission to use these selections. Specific acknowledgments are made below. I also thank R. J. Hollingdale for his kindness in permitting me to use his translations published by Cambridge University Press. I am grateful to Paul Edwards and to Macmillan Publishing Company for the opportunity to compile this volume, and to Edwards for his many helpful suggestions concerning both the selections and my introductions. Thanks are also owing to the series of graduate assistants who helped me at various stages along the way: Nina Jarmolych Koski, Kevin Hill, David Blacker, James Janowski, and Alexandra Bradner.

I would like to take this occasion to express my gratitude to the many enthusiastic students who have taken my courses dealing with Nietzsche during my quarter-century of teaching; to the responsive audiences of the talks I have given on him over the years around this country and abroad; to my fellow Nietzsche scholars and other colleagues who have tuned in; to the appreciative readers of my *Nietzsche* and related writings; to the participants in my National Endowment for the Humanities summer seminars on Nietzsche's philosophical thought; and to the members of the North American Nietzsche Society. I am grateful to them one and all, both for their interest and for the inspiration their interest has been. And I must once again acknowledge my great and very special debt, personal as well as intellectual and educational, to Walter Kaufmann.

The following permissions for the selections indicated are gratefully acknowledged:

Selections from *The Birth of Tragedy:* from *The Birth of Tragedy and The Genealogy of Morals* by Friedrich Nietzsche, translated by Francis Golffing. Copyright © 1956 by Doubleday, a division of Bantam, Doubleday, Dell Publishing Group, Inc. Used by permission of Doubleday, a division of Bantam, Doubleday, Dell Publishing Group, Inc.

Selections from *On Truth and Lies in a Nonmoral Sense:* from *Philosophy and Truth*, edited and translated by Daniel Breazeale. Copyright © 1979 by Daniel Breazeale. Used by permission of Humanities Press International, Inc., Atlantic Highlands, N.J.

Selections from *On the Uses and Disadvantages of History for Life* and *Schopenhauer as Educator:* from *Untimely Meditations* by Friedrich Nietzsche, translated by R. J. Hollingdale. Copyright © Cambridge University Press, 1983. Reprinted by permission of Cambridge University Press.

Selections from *Human, All Too Human:* from *Human, All Too Human* by Friedrich Nietzsche, translated by R. J. Hollingdale. Copyright © Cambridge University Press, 1986. Reprinted by permission of Cambridge University Press.

Note on Excerpts

With the exception of Nietzsche's prefaces to his various writings, which are presented here in their entirety, all of the selections in this volume are excerpts rather than complete works. In some cases they amount to substantial portions of the essays and books from which they are taken, while in others the excerpts represent smaller fractions of their contents.

The section and paragraph numbers appearing in many of the selections are Nietzsche's own. In his early writings he used only section numbering; but from *Human, All Too Human* on, he numbered each of his reflections within sections or parts of his works as well. (This is how they are usually identified when cited.) Lines of asterisks mark breaks in the sequence of numbered sections or paragraphs excerpted from them. From the jumps in the numbering of the excerpts presented, one can get some idea of how much intervening material is between them. In the presentation of notebook material collected in *The Will to Power*, lines of asterisks separate the various notes selected. Ellipses in brackets indicate the deletion of portions of such sections, paragraphs, and notes. (Ellipses that are not bracketed are Nietzsche's.)

Richard Schacht

Contents

NIETZSCHE

Selections

Introduction

"God is dead!" This is only one of the many startling claims Friedrich Nietzsche made, for which he had already become both famous and notorious by the time of his own death in 1900. He may be the most controversial thinker in the entire history of philosophy—not only because he is so easily misunderstood, but also because he rejects so many commonly accepted beliefs and advances so many disturbing ideas in their place. The fact that the Nazis claimed him as their philosophical inspiration made it almost impossible for him to be given a fair hearing in the English-speaking world for many years. But even though their representation of his thought is now recognized to have been a travesty, he continues to be widely regarded with deep suspicion and to arouse strong opposition.

This is hardly surprising. Nietzsche not only proclaims the "death of God" but also attacks Christianity violently. He rejects both the religious idea of God as the source of all meaning and the humanistic idea of the intrinsic value of the human individual; and in their place he proposes the idea of the *Übermensch*—the "superman" or "overman"—as "the meaning of the earth." He denounces both democracy and socialism; and he challenges every point affirmed in the declaration: "We hold these truths to be self-evident: that all men are created equal; that they are endowed by their Creator with certain inalienable rights; and that among these rights are life, liberty, and the pursuit of happiness."

Nietzsche likewise is scathingly critical of conventional morality, calling it a morality fit only for "herd animals," and proposing to take his stand "beyond" its ideas of "good and evil." He celebrates competition and conflict, frequently avails himself of the language of "war" and "power," and advocates indifference to suffering. He questions every traditionally and commonly accepted value, calling for the "revaluation of all values." The new standard of value he proposes to employ derives from his seemingly strange and startling interpretation of all life and the world itself in terms of what he calls "will to power."

Nietzsche further rejects the idea that human beings are anything more to begin with than a peculiar species of animal that has emerged in the course of natural events. He considers the creative few to be a higher and more valuable type of human being than the great majority who lack creative powers. He dismisses the idea that there is anything like Divine Providence or long-term progress or even rationality, either in history or in the world. He is severely critical not only of traditional religious ways of thinking but of the efforts of most of his philosophical predecessors as well. He also disputes the rival claim of modern science to be able to deliver "the truth, the whole truth, and nothing but the truth" about the world and ourselves. He esteems art more highly than science, and cre-

1

ativity above reason. He even rejects traditional and ordinary ways of conceiving of truth and knowledge, claiming that "there are no facts, only interpretations." And these are only some of Nietzsche's radical and unsettling views.

It is small wonder that many people find all of this shocking and repelling and conclude that Nietzsche was either a madman or worse. Many philosophers have agreed; and the fact that he did not write and argue as most philosophers do has given many of them yet another reason to pay no serious attention to him. Bertrand Russell, one of the most prominent and influential English-speaking philosophers of this century, gave expression to this widespread dismissive view of him (in 1945, under the dark shadow of the Second World War) in his *History of Western Philosophy:*

> Nietzsche, though a professor, was a literary rather than an
> academic philosopher. . . . His general outlook . . . remained very
> similar to that of Wagner in the *Ring;* Nietzsche's superman is very
> like Siegfried, except that he knows Greek. This may seem odd,
> but that is not my fault. . . .
> He condemns Christian love because he thinks it is an outcome
> of fear. . . . His "noble" man—who is himself in his
> day-dreams—is a being wholly devoid of sympathy, ruthless,
> cunning, cruel, concerned only with his own power. King Lear, on
> the verge of madness, says: "I will do such things—what they are
> yet I know not—but they shall be the terror of the earth." This is
> Nietzsche's philosophy in a nutshell.[1]

Russell's harsh assessment has been shared by many British and American philosophers until recently. In Europe, on the other hand, Nietzsche has long been regarded as one of the greatest and most important thinkers in the history of modern philosophy, and has been profoundly influential. Martin Heidegger saw Nietzsche as the culmination of the entire history of Western philosophy before him. According to Heidegger, Nietzsche brought its long metaphysical tradition to a final end, signaling the necessity of turning philosophy in a radically new direction:

> What fundamental metaphysical position does Nietzsche's
> philosophy assume for itself on the basis of its response to the
> guiding question within Western philosophy, that is to say, within
> metaphysics?
> Nietzsche's philosophy is the end of metaphysics, inasmuch as it
> reverts to the very commencement of Greek thought, taking up
> such thought in a way that is peculiar to Nietzsche's philosophy
> alone. . . .
> Because Nietzsche's fundamental metaphysical position is the
> end of metaphysics, . . . it performs the grandest and most

---

[1](New York: Simon & Schuster, 1945), 760, 767.

profound gathering—that is, accomplishment—of all the
fundamental positions in Western philosophy since Plato and in the
light of Platonism.[2]

In the English-speaking world, Russell's low opinion of Nietzsche was
challenged and eventually overturned through the efforts of more sympathetic interpreters such as Walter Kaufmann. Kaufmann undertook his
influential 1950 study of Nietzsche's thought in the spirit of the appreciation expressed in his opening remarks:

> Nietzsche, more than any other philosopher of the past hundred
> years, represents a major historical event. His ideas are of concern
> not only to the members of one nation or community, nor alone to
> philosophers, but to men everywhere, and they have had
> repercussions in recent history and literature as well as in
> psychology and religious thought.[3]

Few would dissent from these remarks today. But there is little further
agreement either in the interpretation or in the assessment of Nietzsche's
thought—and the disagreements only seem to increase as his work re-
ceives more scholarly and philosophical attention. Who was this extraordinary iconoclastic and controversial figure?

1

Nietzsche's active life and career were lamentably brief. They ended
tragically when he was only forty-four with his complete physical and
mental collapse, from which he never recovered, though he lived on in
invalid insanity for another eleven years. But he packed a great deal into
the short few decades of his adult life before his collapse, under extraordinarily difficult conditions during much of that time.

Friedrich Wilhelm Nietzsche was born on October 15, 1844, in a small
town in the Prussian province of Saxony. His father died when he was
very young; and he and his sister were raised by their mother, their
father's mother, and two aunts. His childhood years in this all-female
household undoubtedly contributed to his troubled relations with women
in his later bachelor life, and reinforced the typically nineteenth-century
sexist views about women that mar his writings.

At the age of fourteen, the young Nietzsche was sent to a boarding
school specializing in classical languages and literatures, where he remained for six years and distinguished himself in his studies. He then

---

[2]*Nietzsche*, vol. 2, trans. David Krell (New York: Harper & Row, 1984), 199–200, 205.
Originally published in German in 1961.
[3]*Nietzsche: Philosopher, Psychologist, Antichrist*, 4th ed. (Princeton, NJ: Princeton University
Press, 1974), p. xiii. Original work published in 1950.

attended the universities of Bonn and Leipzig, where he continued his classical studies for another seven years. He performed so brilliantly that he received an appointment as professor of classical philology at the Swiss university of Basel before even earning his doctorate, at the astonishingly early age of twenty-four. This was quite unheard of in Europe at that time and would be extraordinary even today.

During his early years at Basel, Nietzsche was attracted to the circle of admirers of the composer Richard Wagner and became a frequent visitor at the Wagners' home. Although he later became one of Wagner's harshest critics, he revered Wagner during this period of his life, and celebrated Wagner's operas in several of his first published works. Nietzsche was also a talented musician in his own right. He played the piano very well and even composed a considerable amount of music. His compositions include works for one and two pianos, for piano and voice, for orchestra and chorus, and a sketch of an opera. He abandoned composing in his late twenties, but his life-long interest in music grew out of his early intimate involvement with it.

Nietzsche remained at Basel from 1869 until 1879, when he resigned from his professorship for reasons of poor health and changed interests. A mere ten years remained to him before his collapse and final illness. It was during that phenomenally productive final decade of activity that he wrote most of the works that established his claim to greatness.

Nietzsche the man could not have differed more from the robust and terrifying "blond Teutonic beast of prey" he conjures up in his depiction of presocial humanity, or from the magnificent figure he portrays in his descriptions of Zarathustra. Of modest physical stature and severely short-sighted, he was outwardly very reserved, soft-spoken, polite, and rather shy, especially with women. He was distinguished in his appearance only by an enormous moustache and by eyes that seemed piercing despite his near blindness. In his youth and early adulthood, he was vigorous and energetic, often making a striking impression on those who met him. But he was plagued by migraine headaches throughout his life, and his health deteriorated dramatically from his mid-twenties onward. The dysentery and diphtheria he contracted during his brief service as an orderly in the Franco-Prussian war of 1870 took a heavy toll on him; and he suffered for the rest of his life from a terrible variety of illnesses and afflictions, which only rarely gave him any respite.

In his early adult life, Nietzsche enjoyed many close and rewarding personal relationships. He was unable to sustain most of them as his condition worsened, however; and his relations with the few friends who stood by him became increasingly troubled in his later years. His family ties with his possessive mother and sister were more a source of stress than of satisfaction to him. He never married, although he had hopes of marriage on several occasions. He was chaste most of his life; and so it is bitterly ironic that the cause of his final physical and mental collapse was probably syphilis. (He is known to have visited brothels on a few early occasions, and may have contracted the disease in doing so.)

Following his resignation from his professorship at Basel, Nietzsche lived a lonely and very simple life in a succession of boarding houses in Switzerland and Italy, seeking relief from his nearly constant physical torments. During these years before his collapse, he devoted all the effort he could muster to his work, which obsessed him. Stefan Zweig vividly describes Nietzsche's later life:

> Carefully the myopic man sits down to a table; carefully, the man with the sensitive stomach considers every item on the menu; . . . for every mistake in his diet upsets his sensitive digestion, and every transgression in his nourishment wreaks havoc with his quivering nerves for days. . . .
>
> And up again into the small, narrow, modest, coldly furnished [room], where innumerable notes, pages, writings and proofs are piled up on the table, but no flower, no decoration, scarcely a book and rarely a letter. Back in a corner, a heavy and graceless wooden trunk, his only possession, with the two shirts and the other worn suit. Otherwise only books and manuscripts, and on a tray innumerable bottles and jars and potions: against the migraines, which often render him all but senseless for hours, against his stomach cramps, against spasmodic vomiting, against the slothful intestines, and above all the dreadful sedatives against his insomnia. . . . Wrapped in his overcoat and woolen scarf, . . . his fingers freezing, his double glasses pressed close to the paper, his hurried hand writes for hours—words the dim eyes can hardly decipher. For hours he sits like this and writes until his eyes burn.[4]

It is astonishing that this man, so sorely afflicted throughout the last dozen years of his active life, could have produced such a wealth of brilliant writings during this brief period and under these conditions. But Nietzsche did—and in doing so, he provided a most compelling example of the overcoming of human frailty, the hardness in the face of suffering, and the creative redemption of life, to which he attaches such importance in his writings. He knew all too well what he was talking about; and it was a part of his greatness that he was able to surmount his adversity and even turn what he learned from it to philosophical advantage.

Nietzsche's first book, *The Birth of Tragedy*, dealt with Greek tragedy and related aspects of Greek culture. Yet even in this early book, he was already concerned with the possibility of a rebirth of tragic art and culture in the modern world and with questions that are fundamentally philosophical rather than merely philological. He had discovered the work of

---

[4]Quoted by Walter Kaufmann in his preface to his translation of *Thus Spoke Zarathustra* (New York: Penguin Books, 1978), xiii–xiv.

the philosopher Arthur Schopenhauer while a student and had been greatly impressed. He was persuaded by Schopenhauer of the untenability of traditional philosophical and religious interpretations of reality and human nature and of the fundamental irrationality of life and the world. Yet he was repelled by Schopenhauer's darkly pessimistic conclusions and was determined to discover some way of avoiding them.

Even during his Basel years, Nietzsche was not content to devote himself to the kind of scholarship that was expected of him by his colleagues. By their standards he was a great disappointment. *The Birth of Tragedy* was a very unscholarly, imaginative, and tendentious reinterpretation of Greek art and culture. Its clear intent was to draw on this account of them to suggest what would be required in the modern world to endow life with new meaning, following the collapse of traditional religious and philosophical beliefs. It so outraged Nietzsche's fellow classical scholars that it made him a virtual outcast in the academic community.

Undeterred by their reaction, Nietzsche published a series of essays (his *Untimely Meditations*) that were even less scholarly than his first book, addressing himself ever more directly to his cultural concerns. He then turned to a different style of writing and published a series of books of aphorisms and short reflections dealing with human life in both its common and more exceptional forms, beginning with *Human, All Too Human* and culminating in *The Gay Science* (or *Joyful Wisdom*, as its title is also translated). It was during this period, in the years just before and after his retirement from his professorship at Basel, that he discovered his true vocation as a philosopher.

But Nietzsche's next work was far removed from anything resembling a philosophical treatise. It was his great literary–philosophical experiment, *Thus Spoke Zarathustra*. Having arrived at a new outlook on life, which he hoped would replace traditional religious and philosophical ways of thinking, he chose the figure of Zarathustra to proclaim it, in an almost Biblical fashion. He selected this figure because he associated the early Persian religious thinker and prophet Zarathustra (a variant on the name of Zoroaster) with the emergence of these fateful illusions, and therefore chose to have a new Zarathustra announce their demise and replacement.

In this work the artist in Nietzsche, earlier expressed in his musical efforts, found a new literary expression. He subsequently continued to avail himself of it, in verse as well as in his penchant for vivid language and metaphor in his philosophical writings. But he realized that he needed to write in a more prosaic manner to pursue his philosophical tasks more adequately and to express himself more clearly and precisely. In such later works as *Beyond Good and Evil, On the Genealogy of Morals*, and *Twilight of the Idols*, and also in voluminous notebooks he kept, he addressed a wide range of philosophical issues. He seldom dealt with them systematically, but offered a wealth of reflections on them that remain of value to this day. He was little known at the time of his collapse in 1889; but by the time of his death eleven years later, he had already begun to attract the attention and controversy that continue today.

2

Few philosophers have had a more impassioned driving concern than Nietzsche did; and few have felt that more depended on their philosophical enterprises. He believed that our entire civilization—and indeed humanity generally—is moving toward a profound and dangerous crisis. We have come to a fateful period, in which the fundamental assumptions about ourselves and the world that have given structure and meaning to life for the past 2500 years in the Western world can no longer be sustained, and are on the verge of collapse. This is what he meant by "the death of God" and the looming advent of "nihilism." He feared that unless something could be done, humanity would cease to flourish and develop and would instead sink into a degenerate and ultimately moribund condition. He saw Schopenhauer as the first modern European to give clear and powerful philosophical expression to this development; and while Schopenhauer was not taken seriously by a great many of his contemporaries, Nietzsche regarded him as a herald of things to come, unless someone could show another way.

Nietzsche viewed this situation with great alarm—comparable to the alarm with which Plato viewed the collapse of traditional values in the Greece of his day. He sensed impending disaster; and this is reflected in the increasing urgency with which he wrote and the relentlessness with which he drove himself. He felt that there was a profound need he had to try to meet, and that therefore a tremendous responsibility rested on his shoulders. He could grant that weak souls like Schopenhauer would quite naturally lack the stomach to jump into the fray and try to make something of life despite its agonies. But he was far from indifferent to the possibility that the whole of humanity might become as weak and as hostile to life as Schopenhauer had been. He was not content simply to observe that the strong will be able to take the hardships of life in their stride while the weak will not—and that if no one is strong then humanity will cease to flourish and ultimately will atrophy or simply wither away. Rather, he felt that this must not be allowed to happen and so must somehow be resisted and countered.

The year before Nietzsche's birth, Kierkegaard had written vividly of what seemed to him to be at stake along with the religious faith he believed to be so essential:

> If there were no eternal consciousness in man, if at the
> foundation of all there lay only a wildly seething power which

> writhing with obscure passions produced everything that is great
> and everything that is insignificant, if a bottomless void never
> satiated lay hidden beneath all—what then would life be but
> despair? If such were the case, . . . if one generation replaced the
> other like the song of birds in the forest, if the human race passed
> through the world as the ship goes through the sea, like the wind
> through the desert, a thoughtless and fruitless activity . . . how
> empty then and comfortless life would be![5]

This description of what life would amount to in the absence of God expresses the way things actually are for Schopenhauer, for whom there is no Kierkegaardian God to redeem the situation. For Kierkegaard, however, God is a higher reality transcending this world, in relation to whom human life in this world can become something positive and meaningful—as it would not be in the absence of such a God-relationship. Kierkegaard had an underlying basic concern no less impassioned than Nietzsche's, which informed his writings. It is expressed in his question: How is an eternal happiness possible? That is, how can it be possible, given the way the world and our condition in it are, to achieve a happiness that is great enough and unshakable enough to render human life meaningful and worth living? And Kierkegaard's answer, conditioned by 1800 years of Christianity, was: only through a relation to a God who transcends this world.

The great "crime" of Christianity for Nietzsche, and of other-worldly religions generally, is to have taught us to think in precisely this way. It and they have taught us to think that without God the world and our existence in it would be meaningless and wretched, and that only belief in God can fend off despair and enable one to find life endurable and worth living. This dichotomy—faith or despair—was in effect accepted by Schopenhauer, who refused to make Kierkegaard's leap of faith. Schopenhauer viewed the world as Kierkegaard says one would have to view it if one did not believe in God. Persuaded that life as Kierkegaard described it is utterly without meaning, and unwilling to concede that there is any transcendent God in relation to whom human life can become meaningful, Schopenhauer concluded that life is nothing but pointless striving and suffering and therefore is not worth affirming and actively pursuing.

Schopenhauer too had an underlying basic concern: to show that the only sensible thing to do is to refuse to play the game. To live is to suffer, in far greater measure than any possible amount of pleasure can ever offset. Suffering pointlessly is a negative value and is the only value of any consequence associated with life. The most one can hope for, for Schopenhauer, and what one ought to strive for, is the elimination of

---

[5]Soren Kierkegaard, *Fear and Trembling*, trans. Walter Lowrie (Princeton, NJ: Princeton University Press, 1968), 30.

suffering. This can be done in a conclusive way, however, only by denying and eradicating the irrational "will to live." The best state of affairs would be one in which suffering no longer exists; but this would be possible only if life itself were to disappear. The bottom line for Schopenhauer thus is not that life is simply life, utterly without value. Rather, it is that life *has* a value—and that its value is *negative*.

This for Nietzsche is the final and disastrous legacy of Christianity, which has blinded us to the meaning life has (or might have) in its own right. It has taught us to think and fear that, if there were no God, life would not be worth living. If one then comes to be convinced that there is no God, Schopenhauer's conclusion—that life is not worth living— follows quite logically. Kierkegaard would reject this conclusion by accepting the first point but rejecting the second. Nietzsche avoids this conclusion by in effect accepting the second premise but rejecting the first. Half of his polemic is directed against Kierkegaard's way of avoiding Schopenhauer's conclusion; but the other half is intended to avoid Schopenhauer's conclusion itself, by persuading us to reject the first premise and to see that life on its own terms—or at least life at its best—is worthy of affirmation, even if all that Schopenhauer says against it is granted.

Nietzsche thus came to be concerned with a cluster of related problems he discerned in contemporary Western culture and society, which he believed were becoming increasingly acute, and for which he considered it imperative to try to find new solutions. He sought both to diagnose these ills and to discover some way of avoiding Schopenhauer's pessimistic conclusions. Traditional religious and philosophical thought were for him deeply implicated in the problems and so could not be looked to for their solution. The way to cultural renewal thus had to be sought elsewhere. He at first (in *The Birth of Tragedy*) looked to the ancient Greeks for clues and to Wagner for inspiration, believing that their art held the key to human flourishing in this fundamentally Schopenhauerian world. In his subsequent series of *Untimely Meditations*, he expanded on his theme of the need to reorient human thought and endeavor in a manner more conducive to the creativity and vitality of human life. In the early 1880s, when he conceived and wrote *Thus Spoke Zarathustra*, he arrived at a conception of human life and possibility—and with it, a new approach to value and meaning—that he believed could more than fill the void left by the collapse of traditional modes of interpretation and so overcome the nihilism attendant on their collapse.

Nietzsche prophesied the advent of a period of nihilism—characterized by the radical repudiation of the very possibility of truth and value— following the collapse of traditional modes of interpretation and valuation. He considered it inevitable in the aftermath of "the death of God" and the demise of metaphysics, and the discovery of the inability of science to

yield anything like absolute knowledge. But this prospect deeply dis-
tressed him. He was firmly convinced of the untenability of the "God-
hypothesis" and associated religious interpretations of the world and our
existence and likewise of their metaphysical variants. Having also become
persuaded of the fundamentally nonrational character of the world, life,
and history, he took the basic challenge of philosophy to be that of overcoming not only traditional ways of thinking but also the nihilism resulting
from their abandonment. This led him to undertake to reinterpret life and
the world along lines that would be more tenable and would also enable
us to arrive at a new sense of value by means of which we might live.

What Nietzsche called "the death of God" was both a cultural event—
the waning and impending demise of the "Christian-moral" interpretation
of life and the world—and a philosophical development: the abandonment of the "God-hypothesis" as a notion deserving to be taken seriously.
As a cultural event, it was a phenomenon to be reckoned with and a source
of profound concern. He feared the "nihilistic rebound" that was sure to
follow in its wake and worried about the consequences for human life and
culture if no countermovement to it were forthcoming. As a philosophical
development, on the other hand, it was his point of departure, which he
took to call for a radical reconsideration of everything—from the world,
human existence, and knowledge to value and morality. The "de-
deification of nature," the "translation of man back into nature," the
"revaluation of values," the tracing of the "genealogy of morals" and their
critique, and the elaboration of "naturalistic" accounts of knowledge,
value, morality, and our entire "spiritual" nature thus came to be among
the main tasks with which he took himself and the "new philosophers" he
called for to be confronted.

3

It is a matter of controversy, even among those who have a high regard
for Nietzsche, whether it is appropriate to regard him as having attempted
to work out positions on philosophical issues bearing any resemblance to
the efforts and concerns of other philosophers before and after him. He
was harshly critical of most of his predecessors and contemporaries; and he
considered it necessary to break fundamentally with them and their ways
of thinking, calling into question many of their basic ideas and procedures. His own writings, moreover, both before and after *Thus Spoke
Zarathustra* (not to mention that work itself), are quite unlike those of
most other philosophers—with a few notable exceptions, such as those of
the later Wittgenstein.

The writings that Nietzsche himself published (as well as his reflections
in his notebooks) do not systematically set out and develop views on these

and other issues in clearly discernible lines of argument cast in dry and measured prose. Rather, they consist for the most part in collections of short paragraphs and sets of aphorisms, often only loosely if at all connected. Many deal with philosophical topics but in very unconventional ways; and because his remarks about these topics are scattered through many different works, they are all too easily taken in isolation and misunderstood. Much of what he wrote on some topics, moreover, is to be found only in his notebooks, which he did not intend for publication (although much of what he did publish was derived from ideas he developed in them). His language, furthermore, is by turns coolly analytical, heatedly polemical, sharply critical, and highly metaphorical. He seldom indicates clearly the scope of his claims or what he means by the terms he uses. And he frequently intersperses his philosophical reflections with remarks on a wide variety of topics ranging over the multitude of his cultural, social, political, literary, and other interests. (These remarks, while often insightful, are frequently idiosyncratic, and are sometimes appallingly prejudiced and ill-considered.)

It is not surprising, therefore, that many philosophers have found it difficult to know what to make of Nietzsche and to take him seriously. It also is not surprising that there is great disagreement about his intent. Some interpreters have taken him to repudiate altogether the traditional philosophical enterprise of trying to arrive at reasoned conclusions with respect to the questions with which philosophers have long been concerned. They regard him as heralding the "death" not only of religious and metaphysical thinking but also of philosophy itself. Others read him very differently, as having sought rather to effect a fundamental reorientation of philosophical thinking and to indicate by both precept and example how philosophical inquiry might better be pursued.

Those who regard Nietzsche as repudiating philosophy altogether take his criticisms of his philosophical predecessors and contemporaries to apply to any possible attempt to address the issues generally identified as "the problems of philosophy." They seize on and construe some of his more sweeping negative pronouncements with respect to truth and knowledge (e.g., in his early unfinished essay "On Truth and Lies" and in his notebooks of this period) as indicating that he believed it to be impossible for anything we might come up with along these lines to amount to more than fictions and merely expedient perspectival expressions of our needs and desires, as groups or as individuals. They thus take him to have been a radical nihilist himself, seeking to subvert the entire philosophical enterprise and to replace it with a kind of thinking more akin to the literary exploration of human possibilities in the service of life—a kind of artistic play liberated from all concern with truth and knowledge.

Those who view him as attempting to reorient philosophical thinking take seriously his professed desire and determination to find a way of *overcoming* the nihilism he believed to be the consequence of traditional ways of thinking. They also make much of his retention of recast notions of truth and knowledge and his evident concern (especially in his later writings) to contribute to the comprehension of a broad range of phenomena. This way of understanding him, no less than the former, has been and remains controversial; but it permits an interpretation of his writings that is philosophically more fruitful, yielding results that are of considerable interest.

Nietzsche indisputably insisted on the *interpretive* character of all human thought and so of all philosophical thinking. He called for "new philosophers" who would follow him in engaging in more self-conscious and intellectually responsible attempts to assess prevailing interpretations of human life and affairs and to improve on them. He also was deeply concerned with the ways in which these matters have been and might better be *evaluated* and with the differing *values* by which human beings live and alternatively might live. So he made much of the need for a "revaluation" of all received values and for attention to the problems of the nature, status, and standards of value and evaluation. One form of inquiry he took to be of great utility in connection with these tasks is "genealogical" inquiry—inquiry into the conditions under which various modes of interpretation and evaluation have come to be established and embraced. This is only one of the kinds of inquiry he considered to be needed, however, serving merely to prepare the way for others that must be brought to bear before any conclusions are warranted.

Nietzsche further emphasized the "perspectival" character of all thinking and the merely provisional character of all knowing, rejecting the idea of the very possibility of absolute knowledge transcending all perspectives. Precisely because he also rejected the idea that things (and values) have any absolute existence "in themselves" apart from the relations serving to make them what they are, however, he held that by availing oneself of a multiplicity of perspectives from which many of these relations come to light, they admit of a significant measure of comprehension. His "perspectivism" thus does not exclude the possibility of any sort of knowledge deserving of the name, but rather indicates the manner in which it is to be conceived and achieved. His kind of philosophy, which he characterizes as *die fröhliche Wissenschaft* (in one of his book titles, perhaps best translated as "the joyful pursuit of knowledge"), proceeds by way of a variety of such "perspectival" approaches to the various matters with which he deals.

Thus, for Nietzsche there is no "truth" in the sense of a correspondence to some absolute reality of anything we might think or say (and, indeed, no such "true world" of "being" to which it may even be imagined to *fail* to correspond); no "knowledge" conceived in terms of any such truth; and further, no knowledge at all—even of ourselves and the world of which we are a part—that is absolute, nonperspectival, and certain. But that, he came to realize, does not leave us entirely empty-handed. For example, there are ways of thinking that may be more or less well warranted in relation to differing sorts of interest and practice, not only within the context of social life but also in our dealings with our environing world. Nietzsche's reflections on the reconceptualization of truth and knowledge along these lines thus point in the direction of a *naturalistic epistemology* with which he would replace the conceptions of truth and knowledge of his predecessors and fill the nihilistic void seemingly left by their bankruptcy.

One common misunderstanding of Nietzsche in this connection involves the assimilation of his thinking about the possibility of knowledge (reconceived along these lines) to another point he makes and emphasizes in a variety of contexts. This point is that many sorts of concepts and beliefs are highly useful and even indispensable for practical purposes in human life but are "fictions," "errors," "lies," and "illusions," whose only warrant is their practical usefulness or indispensability. We have developed them and retain them because we cannot get along without them (or get along better with them), despite—or indeed owing in part precisely to—their fictitious and illusory character.

This theme was taken up by Nietzsche from Schopenhauer and F. A. Lange (whose *History of Materialism* he regarded highly) and has affinities with both Plato's notion of the "noble lie" and Kant's conception of the status and function of the "ideas of reason"; and it figures prominently in Nietzsche's writings from *The Birth of Tragedy* and "On Truth and Lies" onward. Not only religion and art but also morality, science, ordinary language, and social life are held to depend crucially on such devices, which he seeks both to expose for what they are and to reassess—in terms of their bottom-line "value for life," rather than their accordance with reality.

The fact that Nietzsche emphasized the ubiquity of such fictions and illusions and the many needs and interests they serve, however, does not mean that he deems all thinking to be incapable of amounting to anything more than this. The necessity of illusions (in some contexts and respects) does not preclude the possibility of genuine comprehension. And Nietzsche clearly took this possibility to be a real one. He accorded great importance to it in his own case and for others with the ability and courage to meet the challenges it presents—even while emphasizing its dangers as well as its difficulties and limitations, and suggesting that fictions and illusions very often have a greater "value for life."

There is, moreover, a good deal about ourselves and our world that Nietzsche became convinced we are capable of comprehending. Our comprehension may be restricted to what life and the world show themselves to be and involve in our experience; but if they are the only reality, there is no longer any reason to divorce the notions of truth, knowledge, and the

value from them. The question then becomes how best to go about
interpreting and assessing what we find as we proceed to explore them. It
is to these tasks of interpretation and "revaluation" that Nietzsche devoted his main efforts in his later writings. They led him beyond his
analysis and reassessment of truth and knowledge to a reconsideration of
our own nature and possibilities—and of life and the world more generally. It was as he pursued this reconsideration that he was led to propose
his interpretation of the basic character of both ourselves and the world in
terms of the "will to power."

4

The status of this comprehensive interpretation is much disputed.
Some interpreters regard it as Nietzsche's new and different type of metaphysics, while others consider it to be his attempt to develop a nonmetaphysical philosophical cosmology, biology, and anthropology. Still others
contend that his critiques of language, truth, and knowledge rule out the
viability of any philosophical enterprise of either sort. They hold that
Nietzsche advances this interpretation merely for its purported "life-
enhancing" value, or as the generalized expression of his conviction that all
ways of thinking are only symptoms or projections of the needs and
desires of those who initially developed or now embrace them.

Nietzsche certainly was relentlessly critical of the entire metaphysical
tradition. He regarded it as fundamentally allied with religions that in-
vidiously contrast this life and world to some imagined higher form of
existence and ultimate reality transcending them. He considered both to
be ill-motivated expressions of profound dissatisfaction with the conditions of life in this world and to be incapable of withstanding critical
scrutiny; and he waged his campaign—his "war"—against them on both
of these levels. So he sought to subvert and demolish not only the "God-
hypothesis" and the related "soul-hypothesis," but also the very idea of
"things-in-themselves" and the rest of the entire inventory of the history
of metaphysics (including Schopenhauer's "world as will" as well as Hegel's *Weltgeist* and matter-in-motion materialism). He deemed all such
notions to be warrantless fictions owing their invention and appeal entirely
to naivete, error, the seductiveness of language, practical needs, and ulterior motivation.

According to the last-mentioned group of Nietzsche's interpreters, that
for him is—or should be—the end of the matter: Metaphysics is to be
"deconstructed" and demolished rather than reformed or replaced by any
alternative attempt to comprehend our human reality and the world of
which we are a part. Yet Nietzsche himself at least seems to have gone
further. In place of all metaphysical schemes cast in terms of notions of the

sorts he inventoried and dismissed, he suggested an interpretation of the world as a dynamic affair without any inherent structure or final end: an interplay of forces ceaselessly organizing and reorganizing itself, as the fundamental assertive disposition he took to be characteristic of all such forces gives rise to successive arrays of power-relationships among the forms it takes (as "dynamic quanta" and systems of such "quanta"). He called this ubiquitous disposition the "will to power"; and he invoked it to convey the basic character of all that goes on in the world, our lives included. "This world is the will to power—and nothing besides! And you yourselves are also this will to power—and nothing besides!" Like most of what he wrote about the world and life along these lines, this passage occurs in one of his notebooks; but he did also tentatively advance this interpretation in his later published writings as what he considered to be the best way (in terms of economy, warrant, explanatory power, and adequacy) of making comprehensive sense of the world and what goes on in it.

Nietzsche seems to have believed that this interpretation is better off than the metaphysical schemes of which he is so critical; but it is a matter of dispute whether this is so, in view of the vagueness of the notion of the "will to power" and the difficulty of seeing what sorts of evidence might count for or against the interpretation he frames in terms of it. Such considerations prompt some to suppose that he cannot have been seriously committed to this interpretation, and lead others to conclude that he turns out to be a metaphysician himself despite his repudiation of metaphysics, with a metaphysical theory that is no less objectionable—even on his own critical grounds—than the others he dismisses. It is also arguable, however, that neither of these verdicts does justice to his thinking here, and that he can be regarded as making an attempt to sketch the outlines of a nonmetaphysical account of the basic character of life and the world to which evidence is relevant, and the merits of which can be meaningfully debated. The issue of what to make of this interpretation is much discussed in the literature; and the selections in this volume provide readers with the opportunity to consider it for themselves.

The status of Nietzsche's thought of "eternal recurrence" (the idea that all events recur eternally) is more problematic. Versions of this idea have been advanced since ancient times, and probably first came to his attention during his philological studies of the Presocratics. At least a part of its attraction for him undoubtedly had to do with its vividness as an emblem of the radically "de-deified" conception of nature he was seeking to work out and foster. It figures centrally in *Thus Spoke Zarathustra* but is rarely mentioned elsewhere in Nietzsche's published writings; and while its importance to him in connection with the challenge of life-affirmation is clear, his commitment to it as a cosmological theory was tentative at most.

In a few late entries in his notebooks, Nietzsche experimented with the possibility of arguing for the "eternal recurrence" as an actual cosmological hypothesis, applying quite literally even to particular events and their succession. Some of his notes suggest that he believed that physics supports this strong version of the idea, according to which everything that happens must happen infinitely many times in the same sequence of events; and at one point his interest in it even led him to contemplate pursuing studies in the natural sciences with a view to gathering scientific evidence for it. Nietzsche initially introduced and employed the idea, however, merely as a hypothetical extreme-case test of one's ability to affirm life without recourse to any appeal beyond life and the world as they are. Can one affirm them if one envisions them as remaining ever the same—even in all of the respects and details that one may find most disagreeable—with no prospect of their transformation or transcendence? This idea can serve its testing function well enough, even if it is regarded not as a cosmological hypothesis but rather as a kind of thought-experiment in mythical guise, the literal "truth" of which is beside the point.

Nietzsche devoted far more effort to his attempt to reorient and contribute to our understanding of ourselves. He was concerned not only to criticize others' conceptions of our nature but also to advance and develop a more tenable alternative to them. Beginning with the recognition that human life is a form of animal life, he proceeded to reinterpret our attained humanity accordingly, attentive both to its emergent general features and to the differences it exhibits. He thus sought to replace traditional metaphysical conceptions of the self and philosophies of *Geist* (spirit) and mind with a kind of naturalistic philosophical anthropology, in which a multiplicity of perspectives on human life are drawn on in an attempt to do justice to it.

As he pursued this task, Nietzsche persistently brought two basic and complementary ideas into play. On the one hand, everything about ourselves must be the outcome of developments of an entirely mundane sort, relating to our evolution, history, and life-circumstances. Yet on the other, justice must be done to the wealth of human phenomena discerned by diverse observations and investigations of the human scene. His many scattered particular comments and reflections pertaining to human life typically express thoughts along only one or the other of these lines; but it is only if they are taken together that one-sided misunderstandings of his thinking can be avoided. When this is done, it becomes clear that Nietzsche's naturalistic philosophical anthropology is "emergentist" rather than "reductionist," and that it emphasizes the significance of the respects in which our original animality has been transformed in various ways and along differing lines—which in turn have set the stage for further actual and possible transformations.

Nietzsche thus construed our human nature and existence *naturalistically*, in terms of the "will to power" and its ramifications in the establishment and expression of the kinds of complex systems of dynamic quanta in which human beings consist. "The soul is only a word for something about the body," he has Zarathustra say, and the body is fundamentally a configuration of natural forces and processes. At the same time, however, he insisted on the importance of social arrangements and interactions in the development of human forms of awareness and activity. He also made much of the possibility of the emergence of exceptional human beings capable of an independence and creativity elevating them beyond the level of the general human rule. So he stressed the difference between "higher men" and "the herd." Through Zarathustra, he further proclaimed the "overman" *(Übermensch)* to be "the meaning of the earth," employing this image to convey the ideal of the overcoming of the "all-too-human" and the fullest possible creative "enhancement of life." Far from seeking to diminish our humanity as he stressed our animality, he sought to direct our attention and efforts to the emergence of a "higher humanity" capable of endowing existence with a human redemption and justification—above all through the enrichment of cultural life.

5

Notwithstanding his frequent characterization as a nihilist, therefore, Nietzsche actually sought to counter and overcome the nihilism he expected to become prevalent in the aftermath of the collapse and abandonment of traditional religious and metaphysical modes of interpretation and evaluation. Although he was highly critical of the latter, it was not his intention merely to oppose and subvert them. He further not only attempted to make out the possibility of forms of truth and knowledge to which philosophical interpreters of life and the world might after all aspire, but also espoused a "Dionysian value-standard" in place of all nonnaturalistic modes of valuation.

In keeping with his interpretation of life and the world in terms of his conception of the "will to power," Nietzsche framed his basic standard of value and evaluation in terms of this interpretation. The only tenable alternative to nihilism, he maintained, must be based on a recognition and affirmation of the world's fundamental character. For him this meant positing as a general standard of value the attainment of a kind of life in which the "will to power" as the creative transformation of existence is raised to its highest possible intensity and qualitative expression. This in turn led him to take the "enhancement of life" and creativity to be the guiding ideas of his "revaluation of values" and development of a naturalistic value-theory.

This way of thinking carried over into Nietzsche's thinking with respect to morality as well. Insisting that moralities along with other traditional modes of valuation ought to be understood and assessed "in the perspective of life," he argued that most of them were contrary rather than conducive to the enhancement of life, reflecting the all-too-human needs and weaknesses and fears of less-favored human groups and types. Distinguishing between "master-" and "slave-moralities," he suggested that the latter has eclipsed the former in human history, and has become the dominant type of morality in the modern world.

Nietzsche regarded present-day morality as a form of "herd-animal morality," well suited to the requirements and vulnerabilities of the mediocre who are the human rule, but stultifying and detrimental to the development of potential exceptions to it. Accordingly, he sought to draw attention to the origins and functions of this type of morality (as a social-control mechanism and device by means of which the weak defend and revenge and assert themselves against the actually or potentially stronger). He further suggested the possibility and desirability of a "higher morality" for the exceptions. In this "higher" type of morality, the content and contrast of the basic "slave-" and "herd-morality" categories of "good and evil" would be replaced by categories more akin to the "good and bad" contrast characteristic of "master-morality." Yet it would have a revised (and variable) content better attuned to the conditions and attainable qualities of the enhanced forms of life that such exceptional human beings have it in them to achieve.

The strongly creative flavor of Nietzsche's notions of such a "higher humanity" and associated "higher morality" reflects his linkage of both to his conception of art, to which he attached great importance. Art, for Nietzsche, is a fundamentally creative (rather than cognitive) affair, serving to prepare the way for the emergence of a sensibility and manner of life reflecting the highest potentiality human beings may possess. Art—as the creative transformation of the world as we find it (and of ourselves thereby) on a small scale and in particular media—affords us a glimpse of the possibility of a kind of life that would be lived more fully in this manner, and constitutes a step in the direction of its emergence. In this way, Nietzsche's mature thought thus expanded on the idea of the basic connection between art and the justification of life, which was his general theme in his first major work, *The Birth of Tragedy*.

6

I have chosen the selections contained in this volume in an attempt to make possible an understanding of the development, manner, and substance of Nietzsche's thinking. Included are selections from his published and unpublished writings both before and after the three-year period in the early 1880s when he published only *Thus Spoke Zarathustra*, as well as a portion of that remarkable literary-philosophical work. The greater part of this volume consists of substantial selections from his writings from 1882 on (including some of the material from his notebooks that was gathered together and published after his death under the title *The Will to Power*). During this final period, his intellectual and philosophical development of the previous decade bore its most significant fruits. His earlier writings are of no little interest and value; but in these later writings, one can best encounter the thought of the philosopher Nietzsche became.

Nietzsche has had many interpreters—among whom the most notable was Nietzsche himself. Few philosophers have reflected on their own efforts in print as extensively as he did, first in the remarkable set of prefaces to most of his pre-*Zarathustra* works, which he wrote in 1886; and then in his prefaces to each of his subsequent works; and once again in his last completed book, *Ecce Homo*. It may be that no author's self-interpretation can be taken to be decisive in the interpretation of his thought. Yet such self-interpretations are of no little interest and deserve to be taken seriously. This is especially true in the case of Nietzsche, in view of the unconventional nature of his writings and the controversies about how they are to be viewed; for his own statements about what he took himself to have been doing in them are obviously highly relevant to their understanding.

All of his prefaces have therefore been included in this volume, in their entirety. Because they all were written during the last years of his active life—many in the same stock-taking year (1886) just before his final burst of writing—they warrant and reward being read together. They certainly make for interesting reading and are quite helpful in making sense of the preceding sections.

With the exception of these prefaces (which are reserved to the final section), the contents of this volume are arranged more or less chronologically. So, for example, the excerpts from the first four parts of the work variously translated as *Joyful Wisdom* and *The Gay Science*, which were written just before *Thus Spoke Zarathustra*, are placed before the excerpt from it; the excerpts from the fifth part, which Nietzsche added when he published its second edition half a dozen years later (after writing both *Thus Spoke Zarathustra* and *Beyond Good and Evil*), are in a subsequent section appropriate to its date. On the other hand, the excerpts from *Beyond Good and Evil* have been separated to place those dealing with morality together with the excerpts from *On the Genealogy of Morals*.

One other departure from chronology is in the grouping of the second set of selections from the material gathered from Nietzsche's notebooks of 1883–1888 and published as *The Will to Power* after his death. In that volume, its compilers not only arranged the notes they chose to include by topic but also completely disregarded chronology. The selections here have been restored to their approximate chronological order. Thus, those deriving from the several years (1884–1886) when Nietzsche was turning from *Thus Spoke Zarathustra* to his "Prelude to a Philosophy of the Future" (*Beyond Good and Evil*) are presented separately from the notes written during his last three active years (1886–1888).

I have divided the latter into groups of notes on four of the large topics with which Nietzsche concerned himself in his notebooks in this final period: the problem of nihilism, the reconsideration of reason and knowledge, the reinterpretation of the world and life, and the revaluation of values. These topics had been dealt with to some extent in his earlier notes and works; but in these last years, they were given much more intensive scrutiny, and his thinking with respect to them underwent considerable development. Within these various groupings of notes, however, I have for the most part placed them in their notebook ordering to make the development of his thinking with respect to them more readily discernible.

The status and value of this material from Nietzsche's notebooks are much debated and disputed by Nietzsche scholars. I have included some of it to show how Nietzsche initially set down his thoughts and ideas and worked on them, before writing what he did (and as he did) in his published writings. I have also done so because this material shows that he was at least tentatively thinking about some things he had only begun to address in the works he completed before his active life abruptly ended. The writings he completed for publication obviously have a status that these notes lack, but the notes still have value for the insights they afford into his thinking. One should not make too much of them; but there is no good reason to ignore them completely.

It should be kept in mind, however, that the notebook selections presented here constitute only a small fraction of the 1,067 notes gathered together in *The Will to Power*—and that they in turn represent only a small fraction of the great mass of material in the notebooks themselves, which fill literally thousands of pages in the critical edition of Nietzsche's writings. The notes I have selected pertain to only a few of the many matters on which Nietzsche reflected in his notebooks, and I have chosen them largely with a view to supplementing what one can find in his published works. More of this material can be found in *The Will to Power*, of which there are several complete English translations.[6] At present, however, there is no English translation of the entire contents of the notebooks. An excellent critical edition of them, along with all of Nietzsche's other writings, now exists[7]; but it is likely to be many years before an English translation of it appears.

---

[6]*The Will to Power*, ed. Walter Kaufmann, trans. Walter Kaufmann and R. J. Hollingdale (New York: Vintage, 1967); also trans. Anthony M. Ludovici as vols. 14 and 15 of *The Complete Works of Friedrich Nietzsche*, ed. Oscar Levy, first published 1909–1911 (Reissued, New York: Russell & Russell, 1964).

[7]*Nietzsche Werke: Kritische Gesamtausgabe*, eds. Giorgio Colli and Mazzino Montinari (Berlin and New York: DeGruyter), Parts VII and VIII (1970–1974).

The translations of the two sets of these notes in this volume are my own.[8] The original compilers and editors of *The Will to Power* (and its translators) smoothed out the roughness of many of Nietzsche's notes and often took liberties with their wording—presumably in the interest of style and readability. I have been more literal in my translations, to be more faithful to both the "notebook" character and actual wording of this material—incomplete sentences and all.

The other selections in this volume are from translations of Nietzsche's writings by a variety of different translators. This was both inevitable—because no one has translated all of his writings—and also unavoidable for practical reasons. I have used the translations made by Walter Kaufmann and R. J. Hollingdale to the extent that I could; but in the cases of a number of Nietzsche's works, I was obliged to use others. One result is a certain unevenness of style; and another is the occasional occurrence of alternate spellings, as well as alternate renderings (e.g., both *Joyful Wisdom* and *The Gay Science* are alternate versions of the title of *Die fröhliche Wissenschaft*). This mix of translations serves well enough, however, and even has certain advantages; for it not only introduces the reader to different available translations and translators, but also should help to counter the tendency to identify Nietzsche too closely with the language and style of any one of them.

7

The developments of the past several decades have dramatically transformed Nietzsche's relation to the philosophical community in the English-speaking world; and this transformation has affected the way in which he figures in the study of philosophy as well as in the history and ongoing endeavor of philosophy itself. It was not long ago—at least in this part of the world—that Nietzsche was not taken at all seriously by most philosophers, and was not even considered to have been of any significance in the history of philosophy (except in the dubious role of precursor of existentialism). Little was being written about him, and he was rarely included in philosophy courses. Today all of this is changing. Nietzsche's historical importance and contemporary significance—far transcending his relation to existential philosophy—are coming to be widely recognized, as old orthodoxies with respect to the history of philosophy and philosophical

---

[8]In making my translations of these selections from the collection of this material published as *The Will to Power*, my points of departure were the long-standard German text to be found in the second edition of *Nietzsche Werke* (Leipzig: Alfred Kroner Verlag)—the so-called *"Grossoktavausgabe"*—in vols. XV (1911) and XVI (1922), together with Kaufmann's datings in his edition. (See note 6.) However, I have also consulted the new critical edition (see note 7) and have followed it in cases of divergence with respect to dating, emphasis, wording, and the way in which the text is set out.

inquiry give way and a maturing body of Nietzsche scholarship emerges. Interest in him is growing in other disciplines as well. These developments are reflected in the increasingly common inclusion of Nietzsche in a variety of courses in philosophy and related areas. All of this is most welcome and long overdue.

But where is one to start? None of his various books alone is a satisfactory introduction to the range and development of his philosophical thought. The present volume is intended to meet this need. It provides such an introduction and also shows where to look for more. There is more to Nietzsche's thinking than his philosophical thought—and more to his philosophical thought than is to be found here. But for those who seek to become acquainted with Nietzsche as a philosopher, these selections should amply serve the purpose. They do not form a systematic presentation of "Nietzsche's philosophy," nor could they do so; for he was not a systematic writer, any more than he was a systematic thinker. But they do unfold and hang together in a way that is roughly and loosely coherent in their basic concerns and general themes, as he pursued and developed them.

The extent to which this is so, however, and, indeed, the interpretation of these concerns and themes, as well as the understanding and assessment of the more specific positions Nietzsche takes and cases he tries to make, are all matters of dispute. Students as well as scholars thus have their work cut out for them in coming to terms with these texts. But that is part of what makes taking Nietzsche seriously so interesting and rewarding.

There is no such thing as *the* correct way of interpreting Nietzsche—although there are many ways of distorting and misunderstanding him, as the past century has amply demonstrated. As Nietzsche himself might put it, some interpretations can be better than others, but there is and can be none that would be "the truth, the whole truth and nothing but the truth" about his thought. Yet it would be misguided in dealing with him—as misguided as he helps us to see it would be in dealing with human life and the world—to be so impressed by the latter point that one loses sight of real possibility of better and worse interpretations. And there may be no better way of developing the abilities involved in genuine philosophical thinking of the kind Nietzsche calls for than to encounter *his* thinking seriously, making the effort to try to figure out what to make of it and how to deal with it.

I

From Philology to Philosophy
(1872–1877)

Excerpts from

The Birth of Tragedy

Homer's Contest

On Truth and Lies in a Nonmoral Sense

On the Uses and Disadvantages of History for Life
(Second Untimely Meditation)

Schopenhauer as Educator
(Third Untimely Meditation)

EARLY WRITINGS

Introduction

Nietzsche's first book and essays are not the writings of a philosopher, although they venture into philosophical territory. They are the writings of a brilliant young scholar of classical languages and literatures, devoted friend and disciple of Richard Wagner, admirer of Arthur Schopenhauer, and maverick intellectual, whose interests could not be confined to the kind of scholarship typical of his discipline. Yet these early writings are well worth reading, both for what they are and for the insights they provide into the basic interests and concerns of the young Nietzsche that impelled him toward philosophy.

They also are Nietzsche's first attempts to express some of the ideas he later would rework and incorporate into his philosophical thinking. As he gradually emancipated himself from the spell of Wagner and Schopenhauer, attained greater intellectual maturity, and developed the analytical and interpretive abilities his later writings display, his early interests and ideas changed significantly. One can best understand his thinking as the philosopher he subsequently became, however, if one sees where he began.

Nietzsche did not come to philosophy through the formal study of its history and various areas of inquiry. He discovered and read Schopenhauer on his own during his student years.[1] The Greek and Roman philosophers were familiar to him, because their writings were a part of the body of classical literature in his chosen area of study and discipline; but he had only a general acquaintance with the history of modern philosophy before his migration toward philosophy in the course of his brief academic career.

The initial attempts made in his first book and essays to address philosophical questions were thus a part of Nietzsche's own philosophical self-education. They were stimulated and strongly influenced by his encounter with Schopenhauer's thought and by his knowledge of the Greeks and Romans, but by little else—other than his own sense of problems that somehow had to be dealt with.[2] That these early writings are nonetheless of considerable philosophical interest testifies to the extraordinary mind from which they sprang.

[1]Nietzsche came across a copy of Schopenhauer's most important work, *The World as Will and Representation*, in a bookstore one day, quite by chance.

[2]What Nietzsche knew about Kant at this time, for example, he got chiefly from his reading of Schopenhauer, who had been greatly influenced by Kant and considered himself to be fundamentally Kantian.

This section begins with selections from Nietzsche's first book, *The Birth of Tragedy*. The basic topic—the relation of the kind of drama that came to be called "tragedy," as it emerged in ancient Greece, to the other and earlier main art forms of Greece—was an appropriate choice for a classical scholar. Nietzsche's concern in writing the book, however, was by no means merely scholarly. His interpretation of the nature and significance of these art forms, and of tragedy in particular, was motivated by his conviction that something similar was needed once again—and that Wagner was in the process of providing it. The book's primary thesis is that the Greeks had been saved from despair by their art. It was their art (Nietzsche contends) that enabled them to respond affirmatively to life despite "the terror and horrors of existence" without benefit of the illusions of religious, metaphysical, or scientific faith—though by means of the different sorts of illusions engendered by their various forms of art themselves. But the main message of the book is a more contemporary one: that our predicament today is similar to theirs, and that a similar salvation might be found in Wagner's kind of art,[3] in which (the young Nietzsche believed) the power of tragedy to inspire an affirmation of life without religious or rationalistic illusions was being reborn.

Nietzsche very soon began to back away from this great overestimation of art and of Wagner. Yet the basic problem that had led him to look to them remained of deep concern to him. In the next selections, from two essays he began writing shortly thereafter (but never completed or published), one can see the two directions in which the development of his thinking led him. In "Homer's Contest," he took a much broader look at Greek culture, reflecting on the way it worked more generally, rather than focusing so narrowly on its art forms. The role of culture in the enhancement of human life—conceived in terms of the attainment of excellence—now became his theme, as he considered the remarkable results in the lives of the Greeks of the kinds of institutions and practices they developed.

In "On Truth and Lies in a Nonmoral Sense," on the other hand, Nietzsche made a first attempt to sketch out the stark view of the human condition and of the merely conventional and artificial character of language within which human thinking is confined, to which his interest in culture was conjoined. The essay clearly reflects the influence of his reading of Schopenhauer (and of Schopenhauer's reading of Kant) and is no more than the point of departure for his later thinking on these matters. Yet it shows that he was interested from the outset in larger philosophical questions, even while he was still preoccupied with problems relating to the flourishing of human life and culture. And it also indicates

---

[3]I.e., Wagner's new kind of opera.

the basic picture of the human condition with which he was operating as he raised and sought to deal with these problems.

The next writings Nietzsche published were four essays he later gathered together in one volume under the title *Untimely Meditations (Unzeitgemässe Betrachtungen)*. He chose this title for them to indicate that they went against the current of the time. They were his only publications after *The Birth of Tragedy* until his last year as a professor of classical philology at Basel, when the first volume of *Human, All Too Human* appeared. Unlike his first book, these "meditations" had nothing at all to do with classical languages and literatures. Like that book, however, they had very much to do with his developing interest in what was conducive and detrimental to the enhancement of human life in the context of modern culture. Selections from two of them—*The Uses and Disadvantages of History for Life* and *Schopenhauer as Educator*—conclude this section. *David Strauss, the Confessor and Writer*, 1873, the first of the four, is a critique of both Strauss[4] and the cultural conditions that enabled him to achieve great popularity. The last of them, *Richard Wagner in Bayreuth*, 1876, is an overtly, but less than wholeheartedly, favorable discussion of Wagner's enterprise and its cultural significance.[5]

All four of these "meditations" were written after the "On Truth and Lies" essay—and in all of them, Nietzsche addressed himself to "quality of life" issues. He thus obviously felt that such issues could and should be taken seriously despite (or perhaps precisely because of) his view of the human condition as it is described in that essay. In *On the Uses and Disadvantages of History for Life*, moreover, Nietzsche does not doubt that at least one kind of knowledge—namely, knowledge *of historical phenomena*—is humanly possible. On the contrary: he grants that it is possible, but questions whether it is either necessary or sufficient for human life and culture to flourish. And in *Schopenhauer as Educator*, he does not dispute the worth of philosophical inquiry, despite his doubts about the attainability of anything deserving of the name of absolute knowledge of reality. His basic point rather is that its worth, and the importance of encountering a philosopher like Schopenhauer, have to do above all with the impetus thereby given to one's commitment to the further enhancement of cultural life—and so of the quality of human life itself, as one lives it and contributes to it.

These essays thus show that Nietzsche's initial response to the understanding of the human condition expressed in "On Truth and Lies" was not merely to dwell on the limitations of our abilities and the contingency

---

[4]David Strauss (1808–1874) was a popular writer and one of the leading critics of Christianity in the nineteenth century.

[5]Nietzsche later became one of Wagner's most severe critics. See the excerpts from his *The Case of Wagner* (1888) in Parts VII and VIII of this volume.

of our existence. Rather, it was to turn to a consideration of how we might make the most of them. And here, as subsequently, this meant for him that what matters most in human life is what transpires in the realm of culture, rather than what we are in and by ourselves or what we can (and cannot) do as merely natural or purely rational beings.

The Birth of Tragedy[1] (1872)
(Excerpts)

1

Much will have been gained for esthetics once we have succeeded in apprehending directly—rather than merely *ascertaining*—that art owes its continuous evolution to the Apollonian-Dionysiac[2] duality, even as the propagation of the species depends on the duality of the sexes, their constant conflicts and periodic acts of reconciliation. I have borrowed my adjectives from the Greeks, who developed their mystical doctrines of art through plausible *embodiments*, not through purely conceptual means. It is by those two art-sponsoring deities, Apollo and Dionysos, that we are made to recognize the tremendous split, as regards both origins and objectives, between the plastic, Apollonian arts and the non-visual art of music inspired by Dionysos. The two creative tendencies developed alongside one another, usually in fierce opposition, each by its taunts forcing the other to more energetic production, both perpetuating in a discordant concord that agon which the term *art* but feebly denominates: until at last, by the thaumaturgy of an Hellenic act of will, the pair accepted the yoke of marriage and, in this condition, begot Attic tragedy, which exhibits the salient features of both parents.

To reach a closer understanding of both these tendencies, let us begin by viewing them as the separate art realms of *dream* and *intoxication*, two physiological phenomena standing toward one another in much the same relationship as the Apollonian and Dionysiac. [. . .]

---

[1]The full title of the first edition was *The Birth of Tragedy from the Spirit of Music*. When Nietzsche brought out a new edition in 1886, he changed the title to *The Birth of Tragedy, or: Hellenism and Pessimism*. He supplied the later edition with a remarkable self-critical preface, which is included with his other prefaces of 1886–1888 in the final section of this volume.

[2]In some translations of this and other writings of Nietzsche, one will find "Apollinian" instead of "Apollonian" and "Dionysian" instead of "Dionysiac."

The fair illusion of the dream sphere, in the production of which every man proves himself an accomplished artist, is a precondition not only of all plastic art, but even, as we shall see presently, of a wide range of poetry. Here we enjoy an immediate apprehension of form, all shapes speak to us directly, nothing seems indifferent or redundant. Despite the high intensity with which these dream realities exist for us, we still have a residual sensation that they are illusions; [. . . but] our innermost being, the common substratum of humanity, experiences dreams with deep delight and a sense of real necessity. This deep and happy sense of the necessity of dream experiences was expressed by the Greeks in the image of Apollo. Apollo is at once the god of all plastic powers and the soothsaying god. He who is etymologically the "lucent" one, the god of light, reigns also over the fair illusion of our inner world of fantasy. The perfection of these conditions in contrast to our imperfectly understood waking reality, as well as our profound awareness of nature's healing powers during the interval of sleep and dream, furnishes a symbolic analogue to the soothsaying faculty and quite generally to the arts, which make life possible and worth living. [. . .] In an eccentric way one might say of Apollo what Schopenhauer says, in the first part of *The World as Will and Idea*, of man caught in the veil of Maya: "Even as on an immense, raging sea, assailed by huge wave crests, a man sits in a little rowboat trusting his frail craft, so, amidst the furious torments of this world, the individual sits tranquilly, supported by the *principium individuationis* and relying on it." One might say that the unshakable confidence in that principle has received its most magnificent expression in Apollo, and that Apollo himself may be regarded as the marvelous divine image of the *principium individuationis*,[3] whose looks and gestures radiate the full delight, wisdom, and beauty of "illusion."

In the same context Schopenhauer has described for us the tremendous awe which seizes man when he suddenly begins to doubt the cognitive modes of experience, in other words, when in a given instance the law of causation seems to suspend itself. If we add to this awe the glorious transport which arises in man, even from the very depths of nature, at the shattering of the *principium individuationis*, then we are in a position to apprehend the essence of Dionysiac rapture, whose closest analogy is furnished by physical intoxication. Dionysiac stirrings arise either through the influence of those narcotic potions of which all primitive races speak in their hymns, or through the powerful approach of spring, which penetrates with joy the whole frame of nature. So stirred, the individual forgets himself completely. [. . .]

---

[3]Principle of individuation.

Not only does the bond between man and man come to be forged once more by the magic of the Dionysiac rite, but nature itself, long alienated or subjugated, rises again to celebrate the reconciliation with her prodigal son, man. The earth offers its gifts voluntarily, and the savage beasts of mountain and desert approach in peace. The chariot of Dionysos is bedecked with flowers and garlands; panthers and tigers stride beneath his yoke. If one were to convert Beethoven's "Paean to Joy"[4] into a painting, and refuse to curb the imagination when that multitude prostrates itself reverently in the dust, one might form some apprehension of Dionysiac ritual. Now the slave emerges as a freeman; all the rigid, hostile walls which either necessity or despotism has erected between men are shattered. Now that the gospel of universal harmony is sounded, each individual becomes not only reconciled to his fellow but actually at one with him—as though the veil of Maya had been torn apart and there remained only shreds floating before the vision of mystical Oneness. Man now expresses himself through song and dance as the member of a higher community; he has forgotten how to walk, how to speak, and is on the brink of taking wing as he dances. Each of his gestures betokens enchantment; through him sounds a supernatural power, the same power which makes the animals speak and the earth render up milk and honey. He feels himself to be godlike and strides with the same elation and ecstasy as the gods he has seen in his dreams. No longer the *artist*, he has himself become a *work of art:* the productive power of the whole universe is now manifest in his transport, to the glorious satisfaction of the primordial One. The finest clay, the most precious marble—man—is here kneaded and hewn, and the chisel blows of the Dionysiac world artist are accompanied by the cry of the Eleusinian mystagogues: "Do you fall on your knees, multitudes, do you divine your creator?"

2

So far we have examined the Apollonian and Dionysiac states as the product of formative forces arising directly from nature without the mediation of the human artist. At this stage artistic urges are satisfied directly, on the one hand through the imagery of dreams, whose perfection is quite independent of the intellectual rank, the artistic development of the individual; on the other hand, through an ecstatic reality which once

[4]Normally translated "Ode to Joy."

again takes no account of the individual and may even destroy him, or else
redeem him through a mystical experience of the collective. In relation to
these immediate creative conditions of nature every artist must appear as
"imitator," either as the Apollonian dream artist or the Dionysiac ecstatic
artist, or, finally (as in Greek tragedy, for example) as dream and ecstatic
artist in one. We might picture to ourselves how the last of these, in a state
of Dionysiac intoxication and mystical self-abrogation, wandering apart
from the reveling throng, sinks upon the ground, and how there is then
revealed to him his own condition—complete oneness with the essence of
the universe—in a dream similitude. [. . .]

   Yet there is [. . . a] profound gap separating the Dionysiac Greeks from
the Dionysiac barbarians. Throughout the range of ancient civilization
(leaving the newer civilizations out of account for the moment) we find
evidence of Dionysiac celebrations which stand to the Greek type in
much the same relation as the bearded satyr, whose name and attributes
are derived from the hegoat, stands to the god Dionysos. The central
concern of such celebrations was, almost universally, a complete sexual
promiscuity overriding every form of established tribal law; all the savage
urges of the mind were unleashed on those occasions until they reached
that paroxysm of lust and cruelty which has always struck me as the
"witches' cauldron" *par excellence*. It would appear that the Greeks were
for a while quite immune from these feverish excesses which must have
reached them by every known land or sea route. What kept Greece safe
was the proud, imposing image of Apollo, who in holding up the head of
the Gorgon to those brutal and grotesque Dionysiac forces subdued them.
Doric art has immortalized Apollo's majestic rejection of all license. But
resistance became difficult, even impossible, as soon as similar urges
began to break forth from the deep substratum of Hellenism itself. Soon
the function of the Delphic god developed into something quite different
and much more limited: all he could hope to accomplish now was to wrest
the destructive weapon, by a timely gesture of pacification, from his
opponent's hand. That act of pacification represents the most important
event in the history of Greek ritual; every department of life now shows
symptoms of a revolutionary change. The two great antagonists have been
reconciled. Each feels obliged henceforth to keep to his bounds, each will
honor the other by the bestowal of periodic gifts, while the cleavage
remains fundamentally the same. And yet, if we examine what happened
to the Dionysiac powers under the pressure of that treaty we notice a great
difference: in the place of the Babylonian Sacaea, with their throwback of
men to the condition of apes and tigers, we now see entirely new rites

celebrated: rites of universal redemption, of glorious transfiguration. Only now has it become possible to speak of nature's celebrating an *esthetic* triumph; only now has the abrogation of the *principium individuationis* become an esthetic event. That terrible witches' brew concocted of lust and cruelty has lost all power under the new conditions. Yet the peculiar blending of emotions in the heart of the Dionysiac reveler—his ambiguity if you will—seems still to hark back (as the medicinal drug harks back to the deadly poison) to the days when the infliction of pain was experienced as joy while a sense of supreme triumph elicited cries of anguish from the heart. [. . .] It is not difficult to imagine the awed surprise with which the Apollonian Greek must have looked on him. And that surprise would be further increased as the latter realized, with a shudder, that all this was not so alien to him after all, that his Apollonian consciousness was but a thin veil hiding from him the whole Dionysiac realm.

3

In order to comprehend this we must take down the elaborate edifice of Apollonian culture stone by stone until we discover its foundations. At first the eye is struck by the marvelous shapes of the Olympian gods who stand upon its pediments, and whose exploits, in shining bas-relief, adorn its friezes. [. . .] But what was the radical need out of which that illustrious society of Olympian beings sprang?

Whoever approaches the Olympians with a different religion in his heart, seeking moral elevation, sanctity, spirituality, loving-kindness, will presently be forced to turn away from them in ill-humored disappointment. Nothing in these deities reminds us of asceticism, high intellect, or duty: we are confronted by luxuriant, triumphant *existence*, which deifies the good and the bad indifferently. And the beholder may find himself dismayed in the presence of such overflowing life and ask himself what potion these heady people must have drunk in order to behold, in whatever direction they looked, Helen laughing back at them, the beguiling image of their own existence. But we shall call out to this beholder, who has already turned his back: Don't go! Listen first to what the Greeks themselves have to say of this life, which spreads itself before you with such puzzling serenity. An old legend has it that King Midas hunted a long time in the woods for the wise Silenus, companion of Dionysos, without being able to catch him. When he had finally caught him the king asked him what he considered man's greatest good. The daemon remained sullen and uncommunicative until finally, forced by the king, he broke into a shrill laugh and spoke: "Ephemeral wretch, begotten by accident and toil, why do you force me to tell you what it would be your greatest boon not to hear? What would be best for you is quite beyond your reach: not to have been born, not to *be*, to be *nothing*. But the second best is to die soon.''

What is the relation of the Olympian gods to this popular wisdom? It is that of the entranced vision of the martyr to his torment.

Now the Olympian magic mountain opens itself before us, showing us its very roots. The Greeks were keenly aware of the terrors and horrors of existence; in order to be able to live at all they had to place before them the shining fantasy of the Olympians. Their tremendous distrust of the titanic forces of nature: *Moira*, mercilessly enthroned beyond the knowable world; the vulture which fed upon the great philanthropist Prometheus; the terrible lot drawn by wise Oedipus; the curse on the house of Atreus which brought Orestes to the murder of his mother: that whole Panic philosophy,[5] in short, with its mythic examples, by which the gloomy Etruscans perished, the Greeks conquered—or at least hid from view—again and again by means of this artificial Olympus. In order to live at all the Greeks had to construct these deities. The Apollonian need for beauty had to develop the Olympian hierarchy of joy by slow degrees from the original titanic hierarchy of terror, as roses are seen to break from a thorny thicket. How else could life have been borne by a race so hypersensitive, so emotionally intense, so equipped for suffering? The same drive which called art into being as a completion and consummation of existence, and as a guarantee of further existence, gave rise also to that Olympian realm which acted as a transfiguring mirror to the Hellenic will. The gods justified human life by living it themselves—the only satisfactory theodicy ever invented. To exist in the clear sunlight of such deities was now felt to be the highest good, and the only real grief suffered by Homeric man was inspired by the thought of leaving that sunlight, especially when the departure seemed imminent. Now it became possible to stand the wisdom of Silenus on its head and proclaim that it was the worst evil for man to die soon, and second worst for him to die at all. Such laments as arise now arise over short-lived Achilles, over the generations ephemeral as leaves, the decline of the heroic age. It is not unbecoming to even the greatest hero to yearn for an afterlife, though it be as a day laborer. So impetuously, during the Apollonian phase, does man's will desire to remain on earth, so identified does he become with existence, that even his lament turns to a song of praise.

It should have become apparent by now that the harmony with nature which we late-comers regard with such nostalgia, and for which Schiller has coined the cant term *naïve*, is by no means a simple and inevitable

---

[5] I.e., philosophy of (the Greek god) Pan, whom Nietzsche associates with a Dionysian orientation.

condition to be found at the gateway to every culture, a kind of paradise. Such a belief could have been endorsed only by a period for which Rousseau's Emile was an artist and Homer just such an artist nurtured in the bosom of nature. Whenever we encounter "naïveté" in art, we are face to face with the ripest fruit of Apollonian culture—which must always triumph first over titans, kill monsters, and overcome the somber contemplation of actuality, the intense susceptibility to suffering, by means of illusions strenuously and zestfully entertained. But how rare are the instances of true naïveté, of that complete identification with the beauty of appearance! It is this achievement which makes Homer so magnificent— Homer, who, as a single individual, stood to Apollonian popular culture in the same relation as the individual dream artist to the oneiric capacity of a race and of nature generally. The naïveté of Homer must be viewed as a complete victory of Apollonian illusion. Nature often uses illusions of this sort in order to accomplish its secret purposes. The true goal is covered over by a phantasm. We stretch out our hands to the latter, while nature, aided by our deception, attains the former. In the case of the Greeks it was the will wishing to behold itself in the work of art, in the transcendence of genius; but in order so to behold itself its creatures had first to view themselves as glorious, to transpose themselves to a higher sphere, without having that sphere of pure contemplation either challenge them or upbraid them with insufficiency. It was in that sphere of beauty that the Greeks saw the Olympians as their mirror images; it was by means of that esthetic mirror that the Greek will opposed suffering and the somber wisdom of suffering which always accompanies artistic talent. As a monument to its victory stands Homer, the naïve artist.

* * * *

7

At this point we need to call upon every esthetic principle so far discussed, in order to find our way through the labyrinthine origins of Greek tragedy. I believe I am saying nothing extravagant when I claim that the problem of these origins has never even been posed, much less solved, no matter how often the elusive rags of ancient tradition have been speculatively sewn together and ripped apart. That tradition tells us in no uncertain terms that tragedy arose out of the tragic chorus and was, to begin with, nothing but chorus. [. . .]

[. . .] Perhaps we can gain a starting point for this inquiry by claiming that the satyr, that fictive nature sprite, stands to cultured man in the same relation as Dionysiac music does to civilization. Richard Wagner has said of the latter that it is absorbed by music as lamplight by daylight. In the same manner, I believe, the cultured Greek felt himself absorbed into the satyr chorus, and in the next development of Greek tragedy state and society, in fact all that separated man from man, gave way before an overwhelming sense of unity which led back into the heart of nature. The metaphysical solace (with which, I wish to say at once, all true tragedy sends us away) that, despite every phenomenal change, life is at bottom indestructibly joyful and powerful, was expressed most concretely in the chorus of satyrs, nature beings who dwell behind all civilization and pre-serve their identity through every change of generations and historical movement.

With this chorus the profound Greek, so uniquely susceptible to the subtlest and deepest suffering, who had penetrated the destructive agen-cies of both nature and history, solaced himself. Though he had been in danger of craving a Buddhistic denial of the will, he was saved by art, and through art life reclaimed him.

While the transport of the Dionysiac state, with its suspension of all the ordinary barriers of existence, lasts, it carries with it a Lethean element in which everything that has been experienced by the individual is drowned. This chasm of oblivion separates the quotidian reality from the Dionysiac. But as soon as that quotidian reality enters consciousness once more it is viewed with loathing, and the consequence is an ascetic, abulic state of mind. In this sense Dionysiac man might be said to resemble Hamlet: both have looked deeply into the true nature of things, they have *under-stood* and are now loath to act. They realize that no action of theirs can work any change in the eternal condition of things, and they regard the imputation as ludicrous or debasing that they should set right the time which is out of joint. Understanding kills action, for in order to act we require the veil of illusion; such is Hamlet's doctrine, not to be con-founded with the cheap wisdom of John-a-Dreams, who through too much reflection, as it were a surplus of possibilities, never arrives at action. What, both in the case of Hamlet and of Dionysiac man, overbal-ances any motive leading to action, is not reflection but understanding, the apprehension of truth and its terror. Now no comfort any longer avails, desire reaches beyond the transcendental world, beyond the gods them-selves, and existence, together with its gulling reflection in the gods and an immortal Beyond, is denied. The truth once seen, man is aware ev-erywhere of the ghastly absurdity of existence, comprehends the symbol-ism of Ophelia's fate and the wisdom of the wood sprite Silenus: nausea invades him.

Then, in this supreme jeopardy of the will, art, that sorceress expert in healing, approaches him; only she can turn his fits of nausea into imagi-nations with which it is possible to live. These are on the one hand the spirit of the *sublime*, which subjugates terror by means of art; on the other hand the *comic* spirit, which releases us, through art, from the tedium of absurdity. The satyr chorus of the dithyramb was the salvation of Greek art; the threatening paroxysms I have mentioned were contained by the intermediary of those Dionysiac attendants.

*   *   *   *   *

18

In age after age the same phenomenon recurs. Over and over the avid will finds means to maintain and perpetuate its creatures in life by spreading over existence the blandishments of illusion. One man is enthralled by the Socratic zest for knowledge and is persuaded that he can staunch the eternal wound of being with its help. Another is beguiled by the veil of art which flutters, tantalizing, before his eyes. Yet another is buoyed up by the metaphysical solace that life flows on, indestructible, beneath the whirlpool of appearances. Not to mention even commoner and more powerful illusions which the will holds in readiness at any moment. The three kinds of illusion I have named answer only to noble natures, who resent the burden of existence more deeply than the rest and who therefore require special beguilements to make them forget this burden. What we call culture is entirely composed of such beguilements. Depending on the proportions of the mixture, we have a culture that is principally Socratic, or artistic, or tragic. [. . .]

The blight which threatens theoretical culture has only begun to frighten modern man, and he is groping uneasily for remedies out of the storehouse of his experience, without having any real conviction that these remedies will prevail against disaster. In the meantime, there have arisen certain men of genius who, with admirable circumspection and consequence, have used the arsenal of science to demonstrate the limitations of science and of the cognitive faculty itself. They have authoritatively rejected science's claim to universal validity and to the attainment of universal goals and exploded for the first time the belief that man may plumb the universe by means of the law of causation. The extraordinary courage and wisdom of Kant and Schopenhauer have won the most difficult victory, that over the optimistic foundations of logic, which form the underpinnings of our culture. Whereas the current optimism had treated the universe as knowable, in the presumption of eternal truths, and space, time, and causality as absolute and universally valid laws, Kant showed how these supposed laws serve only to raise appearance—the work of Maya—to the status of true reality, thereby rendering impossible a genuine understanding of that reality: in the words of Schopenhauer, binding the dreamer even faster in sleep. This perception has initiated a culture which I dare describe as tragic. Its most important characteristic is that wisdom is put in the place of science as the highest goal. This wisdom, unmoved by the pleasant distractions of the sciences, fixes its gaze on the total constellation of the universe and tries to comprehend sympathetically the suffering of that universe as its own. [. . .]

*   *   *   *   *

24

When speaking of the peculiar effects of musical tragedy we laid stress on that Apollonian illusion which saves us from the direct identification with Dionysiac music and allows us to discharge our musical excitement on an interposed Apollonian medium. At the same time we observed how, by virtue of that discharge, the medium of drama was made visible and understandable from within to a degree that is outside the scope of Apollonian art *per se*. We were led to the conclusion that when Apollonian art is elevated by the spirit of music it reaches its maximum intensity; thus the fraternal union of Apollo and Dionysos may be said to represent the final consummation of both the Apollonian and Dionysiac tendencies. [. . .]

The genesis of tragedy cannot be explained by saying that things happen, after all, just as tragically in real life. Art is not an imitation of nature but its metaphysical supplement, raised up beside it in order to overcome it. Insofar as tragic myth belongs to art, it fully shares its transcendent intentions. Yet what is transcended by myth when it presents the world of phenomena under the figure of the suffering hero? Certainly not the "reality" of that phenomenal world, for myth tells us on the contrary: "Just look! Look closely! This is your life. This is the hour hand on the clock of your existence." Is this the life that myth shows us in order to transcend it? And if not, how are we to account for the delight we feel in viewing these images? I am speaking of *esthetic* delight, being at the same time fully aware that many of these images yield a moral delight as well, in the form of compassion or ethical triumph. But whoever tries to trace the tragic effect solely to these moral sources, as has been the custom among estheticians for so long, need not think that he is doing art a service. Art must insist on interpretations that are germane to its essence. In examining the peculiar delight arising from tragedy, we must look for it in the esthetic sphere, without trespassing on the areas of pity, terror, or moral grandeur. How can ugliness and disharmony, which are the content of tragic myth, inspire an esthetic delight?

At this point we must take a leap into the metaphysics of art by reiterating our earlier contention that this world can be justified only as an esthetic phenomenon. On this view, tragic myth has convinced us that even the ugly and discordant are merely an esthetic game which the will, in its utter exuberance, plays with itself. In order to understand the difficult phenomenon of Dionysiac art directly, we must now attend to the supreme significance of *musical dissonance*. The delight created by tragic myth has the same origin as the delight dissonance in music creates. That primal Dionysiac delight, experienced even in the presence of pain, is the source common to both music and tragic myth.

Now that we have touched upon the musical relation of dissonance we have perhaps come an important step nearer to the solution of the problem of tragedy. For now we can really grasp the significance of the need to look and yet go beyond that look. The auditory analogue of this experience is musical dissonance, as used by a master, which makes us need to hear and at the same time to go beyond that hearing. This forward propulsion, notwithstanding our supreme delight in a reality perceived in all its features, reminds us that both conditions are aspects of one and the same Dionysiac phenomenon, of that spirit which playfully shatters and rebuilds the teeming world of individuals—much as, in Heracleitus, the plastic power of the universe is compared to a child tossing pebbles or building in a sand pile and then destroying what he has built. [. . .]

25

Music and tragic myth are equally expressive of the Dionysiac talent of a nation and cannot be divorced from one another. Both have their origin in a realm of art which lies beyond the Apollonian; both shed their transfiguring light on a region in whose rapt harmony dissonance and the horror of existence fade away in enchantment. Confident of their supreme powers, they both toy with the sting of displeasure, and by their toying they both justify the existence of even the "worst possible world." Thus the Dionysiac element, as against the Apollonian, proves itself to be the eternal and original power of art, since it calls into being the entire world of phenomena. Yet in the midst of that world a new transfiguring light is needed to catch and hold in life the stream of individual forms. If we could imagine an incarnation of dissonance—and what is man if not that?—that dissonance, in order to endure life, would need a marvelous illusion to cover it with a veil of beauty. This is the proper artistic intention of Apollo, in whose name are gathered together all those countless illusions of fair semblance which at any moment make life worth living and whet our appetite for the next moment.

But only so much of the Dionysiac substratum of the universe may enter an individual consciousness as can be dealt with by that Apollonian transfiguration: so that these two prime agencies must develop in strict proportion, conformable to the laws of eternal justice. Whenever the Dionysiac forces become too obstreperous, as is the case today, we are safe in assuming that Apollo is close at hand, though wrapped in a cloud, and that the rich effects of his beauty will be witnessed by a later generation. [. . .]

Homer's Contest (1872)
(Excerpts)

When one speaks of *humanity*, the idea is fundamental that this is something which separates and distinguishes man from nature. In reality, however, there is no such separation: "natural" qualities and those called truly "human" are inseparably grown together. Man, in his highest and noblest capacities, is wholly nature and embodies its uncanny dual character. Those of his abilities which are terrifying and considered inhuman may even be the fertile soil out of which alone all humanity can grow in impulse, deed, and work.

Thus the Greeks, the most humane men of ancient times, have a trait of cruelty, a tigerish lust to annihilate—a trait that is also very distinct in that grotesquely enlarged mirror image of the Hellenes, in Alexander the Great, but that really must strike fear into our hearts throughout their whole history and mythology, if we approach them with the flabby concept of modern "humanity." When Alexander has the feet of Batis, the brave defender of Gaza, pierced, and ties him, alive, to his carriage, to drag him about while his soldiers mock, that is a revolting caricature of Achilles, who maltreats Hector's corpse in a similar fashion at night; and even this trait is offensive to us and makes us shudder. Here we look into the abyss of hatred. With the same feeling we may also observe the mutual laceration, bloody and insatiable, of two Greek parties, for example, in the Corcyrean revolution. When the victor in a fight among the cities executes the entire male citizenry in accordance with the laws of war, and sells all the women and children into slavery, we see in the sanction of such a law that the Greeks considered it an earnest necessity to let their hatred flow forth fully; in such moments crowded and swollen feeling relieved itself: the tiger leaped out, voluptuous cruelty in his terrible eyes. Why must the Greek sculptor give form again and again to war and combat in innumerable repetitions: distended human bodies, their sinews tense with hatred or with the arrogance of triumph; writhing bodies, wounded; dying bodies, expiring? Why did the whole Greek world exult over the combat scenes of the *Iliad?* I fear that we do not understand these in a sufficiently "Greek" manner; indeed, that we should shudder if we were ever to understand them "in Greek."

But what lies *behind* the Homeric world, as the womb of everything Hellenic? For *in* that world the extraordinary artistic precision, calm, and purity of the lines raise us above the mere contents: through an artistic deception the colors seem lighter, milder, warmer; and in this colorful warm light the men appear better and more sympathetic. But what do we behold when, no longer led and protected by the hand of Homer, we stride back into the pre-Homeric world? Only night and terror and an imagination accustomed to the horrible. What kind of earthly existence do these revolting, terrible theogonic myths reflect? A life ruled only by the children of Night: strife, lust, deceit, old age, and death. Let us imagine the atmosphere of Hesiod's poem, already hard to breathe, made still denser and darker, and without all the mollifications and purifications that streamed over Hellas from Delphi and from numerous abodes of the gods; let us mix this thickened Boeotian atmosphere with the gloomy volup-tuousness of the Ètruscans; then such a reality would wring from us a world of myth in which Uranos, Cronos, Zeus, and the wars with the Titans would seem like a relief: in this brooding atmosphere, combat is salvation; the cruelty of victory is the pinnacle of life's jubilation.

Further, it was in truth from murder and the expiation of murder that the conception of Greek law developed; so, too, the nobler culture takes its first wreath of victory from the altar of the expiation of murder. After the wave of that bloody age comes a trough that cuts deep into Hellenic history. The names of Orpheus, Musaeus, and their cults reveal the con-sequences to which the uninterrupted spectacle of a world of struggle and cruelty was pressing: toward a disgust with existence, toward the concep-tion of this existence as a punishment and penance, toward the belief in the identity of existence and guilt. But it is precisely these consequences that are not specifically Hellenic: in this respect, Greece is at one with India and the Orient in general. The Hellenic genius was ready with yet another answer to the question, "What is a life of struggle and victory for?" and it gave that answer through the whole breadth of Greek history.

To understand it, we must start with the point that the Greek genius tolerated the terrible presence of this urge and considered it *justified;* while the Orphic movement contained the idea that a life with such an urge as its root was not worth living. Struggle and the joy of victory were recognized—and nothing distinguishes the Greek world from ours as much as the coloring, so derived, of individual ethical concepts, for ex-ample, *Eris*[1] and envy. . . .

And not only Aristotle but the whole of Greek antiquity thinks differ-ently from us about hatred and envy, and judges with Hesiod, who in one

---

[1]"Discord" (trans.).

place calls one Eris evil—namely, the one that leads men into hostile fights of annihilation against one another—while praising another Eris as good—the one that, as jealousy, hatred, and envy, spurs men to activity: not to the activity of fights of annihilation but to the activity of fights which are *contests*. The Greek is envious, and he does not consider this quality a blemish but the gift of a *beneficent* godhead. What a gulf of ethical judgment lies between us and him! . . .

*   *   *   *   *

Every talent must unfold itself in fighting: that is the command of Hellenic popular pedagogy, whereas modern educators dread nothing more than the unleashing of so-called ambition. . . . And just as the youths were educated through contests, their educators were also engaged in contests with each other. The great musical masters, Pindar and Simonides, stood side by side, mistrustful and jealous; in the spirit of contest, the sophist, the advanced teacher of antiquity, meets another sophist; even the most universal type of instruction, through the drama, was meted out to the people only in the form of a tremendous wrestling among the great musical and dramatic artists. How wonderful! "Even the artist hates the artist." Whereas modern man fears nothing in an artist more than the emotion of any personal fight, the Greek knows the artist *only as engaged in a personal fight*. Precisely where modern man senses the weakness of a work of art, the Hellene seeks the source of its greatest strength. What, for example, is of special artistic significance in Plato's dialogues is for the most part the result of a contest with the art of the orators, the sophists, and the dramatists of his time, invented for the purpose of enabling him to say in the end: "Look, I too can do what my great rivals can do; indeed, I can do it better than they. No Protagoras has invented myths as beautiful as mine; no dramatist such a vivid and captivating whole as my *Symposion;* no orator has written orations like those in my *Gorgias*—and now I repudiate all this entirely and condemn all imitative art. Only the contest made me a poet, a sophist, an orator." What a problem opens up before us when we inquire into the relationship of the contest to the conception of the work of art!

However, when we remove the contest from Greek life we immediately look into that pre-Homeric abyss of a terrifying savagery of hatred and the lust to annihilate. This phenomenon unfortunately appears quite frequently when a great personality is suddenly removed from the contest by an extraordinarily brilliant deed and becomes *hors de concours*[2] in his own judgment, as in that of his fellow citizens. The effect is almost without exception a terrifying one; and if one usually infers from this that the

[2]Out of the action.

Greek was incapable of enduring fame and happiness, one should say more precisely that he was unable to endure fame without any further contest, or the happiness at the end of the contest. There is no clearer example than the last experiences of Miltiades. Placed on a solitary peak and elevated far above every fellow fighter by his incomparable success at Marathon, he feels a base, vengeful craving awaken in him against a Parian citizen with whom he has long had a feud. To satisfy this craving he misuses fame, state property, civic honor—and dishonors himself. . . . An ignominious death sets its seal on his brilliant heroic career and darkens it for all posterity. After the battle of Marathon the envy of the heavenly powers seized him. And this divine envy is inflamed when it beholds a human being without a rival, unopposed, on a solitary peak of fame. Only the gods are beside him now—and therefore they are against him. They seduce him to a deed of *hybris*,[3] and under it he collapses.

Let us note well that, just as Miltiades perishes, the noblest Greek cities perish too, when through merit and good fortune they arrive at the temple of Nike from the racecourse. Athens, who had destroyed the independence of her allies and then severely punished the rebellions of her subjects; Sparta, who expressed her domination over Hellas after the battle of Aegospotamoi, in yet much harsher and crueler ways, have also, after the example of Miltiades, brought about their own destruction through deeds of *hybris*, as proof that without envy, jealousy, and ambition in the contest, the Hellenic city, like the Hellenic man, degenerates. He becomes evil and cruel; he becomes vengeful and godless; in short, he became "pre-Homeric." . . .

---

[3]"Overbearing" (trans.), or "overweening pride."

On Truth and Lies in a Nonmoral Sense (1873)
(Excerpts)

1

Once upon a time, in some out of the way corner of that universe which is dispersed into numberless twinkling solar systems, there was a star upon which clever beasts invented knowing. That was the most arrogant and mendacious minute of "world history," but nevertheless, it was only a minute. After nature had drawn a few breaths, the star cooled and congealed, and the clever beasts had to die. —One might invent such a fable, and yet he still would not have adequately illustrated how miserable, how shadowy and transient, how aimless and arbitrary the human intellect looks within nature. There were eternities during which it did not exist. And when it is all over with the human intellect, nothing will have happened. For this intellect has no additional mission which would lead it beyond human life. Rather, it is human, and only its possessor and begetter takes it so solemnly—as though the world's axis turned within it. But if we could communicate with the gnat, we would learn that he likewise flies through the air with the same solemnity, that he feels the flying center of the universe within himself. There is nothing so reprehensible and unimportant in nature that it would not immediately swell up like a balloon at the slightest puff of this power of knowing. And just as every porter wants to have an admirer, so even the proudest of men, the philosopher, supposes that he sees on all sides the eyes of the universe telescopically focused upon his action and thought.

It is remarkable that this was brought about by the intellect, which was certainly allotted to these most unfortunate, delicate, and ephemeral beings merely as a device for detaining them a minute within existence. For without this addition they would have every reason to flee this existence as quickly as Lessing's son.[1] The pride connected with knowing and

---

[1] A reference to the infant born to the German writer Gotthold Ephraim Lessing (1729–1781) and Eva König, who died on the day of his birth. Lessing's writings were widely read, and his reflections on the incident made it a well-known study of a life of the utmost brevity—which those inclined to pessimism consider to be second in good fortune only to never existing at all.

sensing lies like a blinding fog over the eyes and senses of men, thus deceiving them concerning the value of existence. For this pride contains within itself the most flattering estimation of the value of knowing. Deception is the most general effect of such pride, but even its most particular effects contain within themselves something of the same deceitful character.

As a means for the preserving of the individual, the intellect unfolds its principal powers in dissimulation, which is the means by which weaker, less robust individuals preserve themselves—since they have been denied the chance to wage the battle for existence with horns or with the sharp teeth of beasts of prey. This art of dissimulation reaches its peak in man. Deception, flattering, lying, deluding, talking behind the back, putting up a false front, living in borrowed splendor, wearing a mask, hiding behind convention, playing a role for others and for oneself—in short, a continuous fluttering around the *solitary* flame of vanity—is so much the rule and the law among men that there is almost nothing which is less comprehensible than how an honest and pure drive for truth could have arisen among them. They are deeply immersed in illusions and in dream images; their eyes merely glide over the surface of things and see "forms." Their senses nowhere lead to truth; on the contrary, they are content to receive stimuli and, as it were, to engage in a groping game on the backs of things. Moreover, man permits himself to be deceived in his dreams every night of his life. His moral sentiment does not even make an attempt to prevent this, whereas there are supposed to be men who have stopped snoring through sheer will power. What does man actually know about himself? Is he, indeed, ever able to perceive himself completely, as if laid out in a lighted display case? Does nature not conceal most things from him—even concerning his own body—in order to confine and lock him within a proud, deceptive consciousness, aloof from the coils of the bowels, the rapid flow of the blood stream, and the intricate quivering of the fibers! She threw away the key. And woe to that fatal curiosity which might one day have the power to peer out and down through a crack in the chamber of consciousness and then suspect that man is sustained in the indifference of his ignorance by that which is pitiless, greedy, insatiable, and murderous—as if hanging in dreams on the back of a tiger. Given this situation, where in the world could the drive for truth have come from?

Insofar as the individual wants to maintain himself against other individuals, he will under natural circumstances employ the intellect mainly for dissimulation. But at the same time, from boredom and necessity, man wishes to exist socially and with the herd; therefore, he needs to make peace and strives accordingly to banish from his world at least the most flagrant *bellum omni contra omnes.*[2] This peace treaty brings in its wake

[2]War of all against all.

something which appears to be the first step toward acquiring that puzzling truth drive: to wit, *that* which shall count as "truth" from now on is established. That is to say, a uniformly valid and binding designation is invented for things, and this legislation of language likewise establishes the first laws of truth. For the contrast between truth and lie arises here for the first time. The liar is a person who uses the valid designations, the words, in order to make something which is unreal appear to be real. He says, for example, "I am rich," when the proper designation for his condition would be "poor." He misuses fixed conventions by means of arbitrary substitutions or even reversals of names. If he does this in a selfish and moreover harmful manner, society will cease to trust him and will thereby exclude him. What men avoid by excluding the liar is not so much being defrauded as it is being harmed by means of fraud. Thus, even at this stage, what they hate is basically not deception itself, but rather the unpleasant, hated consequences of certain sorts of deception. It is in a similarly restricted sense that man now wants nothing but truth: he desires the pleasant, life-preserving consequences of truth. He is indifferent toward pure knowledge which has no consequences; toward those truths which are possibly harmful and destructive he is even hostilely inclined. And besides, what about these linguistic conventions themselves? Are they perhaps products of knowledge, that is, of the sense of truth? Are designations congruent with things? Is language the adequate expression of all realities?

It is only by means of forgetfulness that man can ever reach the point of fancying himself to possess a "truth" of the grade just indicated. If he will not be satisfied with truth in the form of tautology, that is to say, if he will not be content with empty husks, then he will always exchange truths for illusions. What is a word? It is the copy in sound of a nerve stimulus. But the further inference from the nerve stimulus to a cause outside of us is already the result of a false and unjustifiable application of the principle of sufficient reason. If truth alone had been the deciding factor in the genesis of language, and if the standpoint of certainty had been decisive for designations, then how could we still dare to say "the stone is hard," as if "hard" were something otherwise familiar to us, and not merely a totally subjective stimulation! We separate things according to gender, designating the tree as masculine and the plant as feminine. What arbitrary assignments! How far this oversteps the canons of certainty! We speak of a "snake": this designation touches only upon its ability to twist itself and could therefore also fit a worm. What arbitrary differentiations! What one-sided preferences, first for this, then for that property of a thing! The various languages placed side by side show that with words it is never a question of truth, never a question of adequate expression; otherwise, there would not be so many languages. The "thing in itself" (which is precisely what the pure truth, apart from any of its consequences, would be) is likewise something quite incomprehensible to the creator of language and something not in the least worth striving for. This creator only designates the relations of things to men, and for expressing these relations he lays hold of the boldest metaphors. To begin with, a nerve stimulus is transferred into an image: first metaphor. The image, in turn, is imitated in a sound: second metaphor. And each time there is a complete over-leaping of one sphere, right into the middle of an entirely new and different one. One can imagine a man who is totally deaf and has never had a sensation of sound and music. Perhaps such a person will gaze with astonishment at Chladni's sound figures; perhaps he will discover their causes in the vibrations of the string and will now swear that he must know what men mean by "sound." It is this way with all of us concerning language: we believe that we know something about the things themselves when we speak of trees, colors, snow, and flowers; and yet we possess nothing but metaphors for things—metaphors which correspond in no way to the original entities. In the same way that the sound appears as a sand figure, so the mysterious X of the thing in itself first appears as a nerve stimulus, then as an image, and finally as a sound. Thus the genesis of language does not proceed logically in any case, and all the material within and with which the man of truth, the scientist, and the philosopher later work and build, if not derived from never-never land, is at least not derived from the essence of things.

In particular, let us further consider the formation of concepts. Every word instantly becomes a concept precisely insofar as it is not supposed to serve as a reminder of the unique and entirely individual original experience to which it owes its origin; but rather, a word becomes a concept insofar as it simultaneously has to fit countless more or less similar cases—which means, purely and simply, cases which are never equal and thus altogether unequal. Every concept arises from the equation of unequal things. Just as it is certain that one leaf is never totally the same as another, so it is certain that the concept "leaf" is formed by arbitrarily discarding these individual differences and by forgetting the distinguishing aspects. This awakens the idea that, in addition to the leaves, there exists in nature the "leaf": the original model according to which all the leaves were perhaps woven, sketched, measured, colored, curled, and painted—but by incompetent hands, so that no specimen has turned out to be a correct, trustworthy, and faithful likeness of the original model. We call a person "honest," and then we ask "why has he behaved so honestly today?" Our usual answer is, "on account of his honesty." Honesty! This in turn means that the leaf is the cause of the leaves. We know nothing whatsoever about an essential quality called "honesty"; but we do know of countless individualized and consequently unequal actions which we equate by omitting the aspects in which they are unequal and which we now designate as "honest" actions. Finally we formulate from them a *qualitas occulta*[3] which has the name "honesty." We obtain the concept, as we do the form, by overlooking what is individual and actual; whereas nature is acquainted with no forms and no concepts, and likewise with no species, but only with an X which remains inaccessible and undefinable for us. For even our contrast between individual and species is something anthropomorphic and does not originate in the essence of things; although we should not presume to claim that this contrast does not correspond to the essence of things: that would of course be a dogmatic assertion and, as such, would be just as indemonstrable as its opposite.

What then is truth? A movable host of metaphors, metonymies, and anthropomorphisms: in short, a sum of human relations which have been poetically and rhetorically intensified, transferred, and embellished, and which, after long usage, seem to a people to be fixed, canonical, and binding. Truths are illusions which we have forgotten are illusions; they are metaphors that have become worn out and have been drained of sensuous force, coins which have lost their embossing and are now considered as metal and no longer as coins.

We still do not yet know where the drive for truth comes from. For so far we have heard only of the duty which society imposes in order to exist: to be truthful means to employ the usual metaphors. Thus, to express it morally, this is the duty to lie according to a fixed convention, to lie with the herd and in a manner binding upon everyone. Now man of course forgets that this is the way things stand for him. Thus he lies in the manner indicated, unconsciously and in accordance with habits which are centuries' old; and precisely *by means of this unconsciousness* and forgetfulness he arrives at his sense of truth. From the sense that one is obliged to designate one thing as "red," another as "cold," and a third as "mute," there arises a moral impulse in regard to truth. The venerability, reliability, and utility of truth is something which a person demonstrates for himself from the contrast with the liar, whom no one trusts and everyone excludes. As a *"rational"* being, he now places his behavior under the control of abstractions. He will no longer tolerate being carried away by sudden impressions, by intuitions. First he universalizes all these impressions into less colorful, cooler concepts, so that he can entrust the guidance of his life and conduct to them. Everything which distinguishes man from the animals depends upon this ability to volatilize perceptual metaphors in a schema, and thus to dissolve an image into a concept. For something is possible in the realm of these schemata which could never be achieved with the vivid first impressions: the construction of a pyramidal order according to castes and degrees, the creation of a new world of laws, privileges, subordinations, and clearly marked boundaries—a new world, one which now confronts that other vivid world of first impressions as

[3]Occult quality.

more solid, more universal, better known, and more human than the immediately perceived world, and thus as the regulative and imperative world. Whereas each perceptual metaphor is individual and without equals and is therefore able to elude all classification, the great edifice of concepts displays the rigid regularity of a Roman columbarium,[4] and exhales in logic that strength and coolness which is characteristic of mathematics. Anyone who has felt this cool breath [of logic] will hardly believe that even the concept—which is as bony, foursquare, and transposable as a die—is nevertheless merely the *residue of a metaphor,* and that the illusion which is involved in the artistic transference of a nerve stimulus into images is, if not the mother, then the grandmother of every single concept. But in this conceptual crap game "truth" means using every die in the designated manner, counting its spots accurately, fashioning the right categories, and never violating the order of caste and class rank. [. . .]

[. . .] As a genius of construction man raises himself far above the bee in the following way: whereas the bee builds with wax that he gathers from nature, man builds with the far more delicate conceptual material which he first has to manufacture from himself. In this he is greatly to be admired, but not on account of his drive for truth or for pure knowledge of things. When someone hides something behind a bush and looks for it again in the same place and finds it there as well, there is not much to praise in such seeking and finding. Yet this is how matters stand regarding seeking and finding "truth" within the realm of reason. If I make up the definition of a mammal, and then, after inspecting a camel, declare "look, a mammal," I have indeed brought a truth to light in this way, but it is a truth of limited value. That is to say, it is a thoroughly anthropomorphic truth which contains not a single point which would be "true in itself" or really and universally valid apart from man. At bottom, what the investigator of such truths is seeking is only the metamorphosis of the world into man. He strives to understand the world as something analogous to man, and at best he achieves by his struggles the feeling of assimilation. Similar to the way in which astrologers considered the stars to be in man's service and connected with his happiness and sorrow, such an investigator considers the entire universe in connection with man: the entire universe as the infinitely fractured echo of one original sound—man; the entire universe as the infinitely multiplied copy of one original picture—man. His method is to treat man as the measure of all things, but in doing so he

---

[4]A columbarium is a vault with niches for funeral urns containing the ashes of cremated bodies (trans.).

again proceeds from the error of believing that he has these things [which he intends to measure] immediately before him as mere objects. He forgets that the original perceptual metaphors are metaphors and takes them to be the things themselves.

Only by forgetting this primitive world of metaphor can one live with any repose, security, and consistency: only by means of the petrification and coagulation of a mass of images which originally streamed from the primal faculty of human imagination like a fiery liquid, only in the invincible faith that *this* sun, *this* window, *this* table is a truth in itself, in short, only by forgetting that he himself is an *artistically creating* subject, does man live with any repose, security, and consistency. If but for an instant he could escape from the prison walls of this faith, his "self consciousness" would be immediately destroyed. It is even a difficult thing for him to admit to himself that the insect or the bird perceives an entirely different world from the one that man does, and that the question of which of these perceptions of the world is the more correct one is quite meaningless, for this would have to have been decided previously in accordance with the criterion of the *correct perception*, which means, in accordance with a criterion which is *not available*. But in any case it seems to me that "the correct perception"—which would mean "the adequate expression of an object in the subject"—is a contradictory impossibility. For between two absolutely different spheres, as between subject and object, there is no causality, no correctness, and no expression; there is, at most, an *aesthetic* relation: I mean, a suggestive transference, a stammering translation into a completely foreign tongue—for which there is required, in any case, a freely inventive intermediate sphere and mediating force. "Appearance" is a word that contains many temptations, which is why I avoid it as much as possible. For it is not true that the essence of things "appears" in the empirical world. A painter without hands who wished to express in song the picture before his mind would, by means of this substitution of spheres, still reveal more about the essence of things than does the empirical world. Even the relationship of a nerve stimulus to the generated image is not a necessary one. But when the same image has been generated millions of times and has been handed down for many generations and finally appears on the same occasion every time for all mankind, then it acquires at last the same meaning for men it would have if it were the sole necessary image and if the relationship of the original nerve stimulus to the generated image were a strictly causal one. In the same manner, an eternally repeated dream would certainly be felt and judged to be reality. But the hardening and congealing of a metaphor guarantees absolutely nothing concerning its necessity and exclusive justification. [. . .]

2

We have seen how it is originally *language* which works on the construction of concepts, a labor taken over in later ages by *science*. Just as the bee
simultaneously constructs cells and fills them with honey, so science
works unceasingly on this great columbarium of concepts, the graveyard of
perceptions. It is always building new, higher stories and shoring up,
cleaning, and renovating the old cells; above all, it takes pains to fill up
this monstrously towering framework and to arrange therein the entire
empirical world, which is to say, the anthropomorphic world. Whereas the
man of action binds his life to reason and its concepts so that he will not
be swept away and lost, the scientific investigator builds his hut right next
to the tower of science so that he will be able to work on it and to find
shelter for himself beneath those bulwarks which presently exist. And he
requires shelter, for there are frightful powers which continuously break in
upon him, powers which oppose scientific "truth" with completely different kinds of "truths" which bear on their shields the most varied sorts
of emblems.

The drive toward the formation of metaphors is the fundamental human drive, which one cannot for a single instant dispense with in thought,
for one would thereby dispense with man himself. This drive is not truly
vanquished and scarcely subdued by the fact that a regular and rigid new
world is constructed as its prison from its own ephemeral products, the
concepts. It seeks a new realm and another channel for its activity, and it
finds this in *myth* and in *art* generally. This drive continually confuses the
conceptual categories and cells by bringing forward new transferences,
metaphors, and metonymies. It continually manifests an ardent desire to
refashion the world which presents itself to waking man, so that it will be
as colorful, irregular, lacking in results and coherence, charming, and
eternally new as the world of dreams. Indeed, it is only by means of the
rigid and regular web of concepts that the waking man clearly sees that he
is awake; and it is precisely because of this that he sometimes thinks that
he must be dreaming when this web of concepts is torn by art. [. . .]

There are ages in which the rational man and the intuitive man stand
side by side, the one in fear of intuition, the other with scorn for abstraction. The latter is just as irrational as the former is inartistic. They both
desire to rule over life: the former, by knowing how to meet his principal
needs by means of foresight, prudence, and regularity; the latter, by
disregarding these needs and, as an "overjoyed hero," counting as real
only that life which has been disguised as illusion and beauty. Whenever,

as was perhaps the case in ancient Greece, the intuitive man handles his weapons more authoritatively and victoriously than his opponent, then, under favorable circumstances, a culture can take shape and art's mastery over life can be established. [. . .]

On the Uses and Disadvantages of History for Life (Second Untimely Meditation) (1874)
(Excerpts)

1

Consider the cattle, grazing as they pass you by: they do not know what is meant by yesterday or today, they leap about, eat, rest, digest, leap about again, and so from morn till night and from day to day, fettered to the moment and its pleasure or displeasure, and thus neither melancholy nor bored. This is a hard sight for man to see; for, though he thinks himself better than the animals because he is human, he cannot help envying them their happiness—what they have, a life neither bored nor painful, is precisely what he wants, yet he cannot have it because he refuses to be like an animal. A human being may well ask an animal: "Why do you not speak to me of your happiness but only stand and gaze at me?" The animal would like to answer, and say: "The reason is I always forget what I was going to say"—but then he forgot this answer too, and stayed silent: so that the human being was left wondering. [. . .]

[. . .] Thus the animal lives *unhistorically:* for it is contained in the present, like a number without any awkward fraction left over; it does not know how to dissimulate, it conceals nothing and at every instant appears wholly as what it is; it can therefore never be anything but honest. Man, on the other hand, braces himself against the great and ever greater pressure of what is past: it pushes him down or bends him sideways, it encumbers his steps as a dark, invisible burden which he would like to disown and which in traffic with his fellow men he does disown, so as to excite their envy. That is why it affects him like a vision of a lost paradise to see the herds grazing or, in closer proximity to him, a child which, having as yet nothing of the past to shake off, plays in blissful blindness between the hedges of past and future. Yet its play must be disturbed; all too soon it will be called out of its state of forgetfulness. Then it will learn to understand the phrase "it was": that password which gives conflict, suffering and satiety access to man so as to remind him what his existence fundamentally is—an imperfect tense that can never become a perfect one. If death at last brings the desired forgetting, by that act it at the same time extinguishes the present and all being and therewith sets the seal on the knowledge that being is only an uninterrupted has-been, a thing that lives by negating, consuming and contradicting itself.

If happiness, if reaching out for new happiness, is in any sense what fetters living creatures to life and makes them go on living, then perhaps no philosopher is more justified than the Cynic: for the happiness of the animal, as the perfect Cynic, is the living proof of the rightness of Cynicism. The smallest happiness, if only it is present uninterruptedly and makes happy, is incomparably more happiness than the greatest happiness that comes only as an episode, as it were a piece of waywardness or folly, in a continuum of joylessness, desire and privation. In the case of the smallest or of the greatest happiness, however, it is always the same thing that makes happiness happiness: the ability to forget or, expressed in more scholarly fashion, the capacity to feel *unhistorically* during its duration. He who cannot sink down on the threshold of the moment and forget all the past, who cannot stand balanced like a goddess of victory without growing dizzy and afraid, will never know what happiness is—worse, he will never do anything to make others happy. Imagine the extremest possible example of a man who did not possess the power of forgetting at all and who was thus condemned to see everywhere a state of becoming: such a man would no longer believe in his own being, would no longer believe in himself, would see everything flowing asunder in moving points and would lose himself in this stream of becoming: like a true pupil of Heraclitus, he would in the end hardly dare to raise his finger. Forgetting is essential to action of any kind, just as not only light but darkness too is essential for the life of everything organic. A man who wanted to feel historically through and through would be like one forcibly deprived of sleep, or an animal that had to live only by rumination and ever repeated rumination. Thus: it is possible to live almost without memory, and to live happily moreover, as the animal demonstrates; but it is altogether impossible to *live* at all without forgetting. Or, to express my theme even more simply: *there is a degree of sleeplessness, of rumination, of the historical sense, which is harmful and ultimately fatal to the living thing, whether this living thing be a man or a people or a culture.*

To determine this degree, and therewith the boundary at which the past has to be forgotten if it is not to become the gravedigger of the present, one would have to know exactly how great the *plastic power* of a man, a people, a culture is: I mean by plastic power the capacity to develop out of oneself in one's own way, to transform and incorporate into oneself what is past and foreign, to heal wounds, to replace what has been lost, to recreate broken moulds. There are people who possess so little of this power that they can perish from a single experience, from a single painful event, often and especially from a single subtle piece of injustice, like a man bleeding to death from a scratch; on the other hand, there are those who are so little affected by the worst and most dreadful disasters, and even by their own wicked acts, that they are able to feel tolerably well and be in possession of a kind of clear conscience even in the midst of them or at any rate very soon afterwards. The stronger the innermost roots of a man's nature, the more readily will he be able to assimilate and appropriate the things of the past; and the most powerful and tremendous nature would be characterized by the fact that it would know no boundary at all at which the historical sense began to overwhelm it; it would draw to itself and incorporate into itself all the past, its own and that most foreign to it, and as it were transform it into blood. That which such a nature cannot subdue it knows how to forget; it no longer exists, the horizon is rounded and closed, and there is nothing left to suggest there are people, passions, teachings, goals lying beyond it. And this is a universal law: a living thing can be healthy, strong and fruitful only when bounded by a horizon; if it is incapable of drawing a horizon around itself, and at the same time too self-centred to enclose its own view within that of another, it will pine away slowly or hasten to its timely end. Cheerfulness, the good conscience, the joyful deed, confidence in the future—all of them depend, in the case of the individual as of a nation, on the existence of a line dividing the bright and discernible from the unilluminable and dark; on one's being just as able to forget at the right time as to remember at the right time; on the possession of a powerful instinct for sensing when it is necessary to feel historically and when unhistorically. This, precisely, is the proposition the reader is invited to meditate upon: *the unhistorical and the historical are necessary in equal measure for the health of an individual, of a people and of a culture.*

First of all, there is an observation that everyone must have made: a man's historical sense and knowledge can be very limited, his horizon as narrow as that of a dweller in the Alps, all his judgments may involve injustice and he may falsely suppose that all his experiences are original to him—yet in spite of this injustice and error he will nonetheless stand there in superlative health and vigour, a joy to all who see him; while close beside him a man far more just and instructed than he sickens and collapses because the lines of his horizon are always restlessly changing, because he can no longer extricate himself from the delicate net of his judiciousness and truth for a simple act of will and desire. On the other hand we have observed the animal, which is quite unhistorical, and dwells within a horizon reduced almost to a point, and yet lives in a certain degree of happiness, or at least without boredom and dissimulation; we shall thus have to account the capacity to feel to a certain degree unhistorically as being more vital and more fundamental, inasmuch as it constitutes the foundation upon which alone anything sound, healthy and great, anything truly human, can grow. The unhistorical is like an atmosphere within which alone life can germinate and with the destruction of which it must vanish. It is true that only by imposing limits on this unhistorical element by thinking, reflecting, comparing, distinguishing, drawing conclusions, only through the appearance within that encompassing cloud of a vivid flash of light—thus only through the power of employing the past for the purposes of life and of again introducing into history that which has been done and is gone—did man become man: but with an excess of history man again ceases to exist, and without that envelope of the unhistorical he would never have begun or dared to begin. What deed would man be capable of if he had not first entered into that vaporous region of the unhistorical? Or, to desert this imagery and illustrate by example: imagine a man seized by a vehement passion, for a woman or for a great idea: how different the world has become to him! Looking behind him he seems to himself as though blind, listening around him he hears only a dull, meaningless noise; whatever he does perceive, however, he perceives as he has never perceived before—all is so palpable, close, highly coloured, resounding, as though he apprehended it with all his senses at once. All his valuations are altered and disvalued; there are so many things he is no longer capable of evaluating at all because he can hardly feel them any more: he asks himself why he was for so long the fool of the phrases and opinions of others; he is amazed that his memory revolves unwearyingly in a circle and yet is too weak and weary to take even a single leap out of this circle. It is the condition in which one is the least capable of being just; narrow-minded, ungrateful to the past, blind to dangers, deaf to warnings, one is a little vortex of life in a dead sea of darkness and oblivion: and yet this condition—unhistorical, anti-historical through and through—is the womb not only of the unjust but of every just deed too; and no painter will paint his picture, no general achieve his victory, no people attain its freedom without having first desired and striven for it in an unhistorical condition such as that described. As he who acts is, in Goethe's words, always without a conscience, so is he also always without knowledge; he forgets most things so as to do one thing, he is unjust towards what lies behind him, and he recognizes the rights only of that which is now to come into being and no other rights whatever. Thus he who acts loves his deed infinitely more than it deserves to be loved: and the finest deeds take place in such a superabundance of love that, even if their worth were incalculable in other respects, they must still be unworthy of this love.

If, in a sufficient number of cases, one could scent out and retrospectively breathe this unhistorical atmosphere within which every great historical event has taken place, he might, as a percipient being, raise himself to a *suprahistorical* vantage point such as Niebuhr once described as the possible outcome of historical reflection. "History, grasped clearly and in detail," he says, "is useful in one way at least: it enables us to recognize how unaware even the greatest and highest spirits of our human race have been of the chance nature of the form assumed by the eyes through which they see and through which they compel everyone to see—compel, that is, because the intensity of their consciousness is exceptionally great. He who has not grasped this quite definitely and in many instances will be subjugated by the appearance of a powerful spirit who brings to a given form the most impassioned commitment." We may use the word "suprahistorical" because the viewer from this vantage point could no longer feel any temptation to go on living or to take part in history; he would have recognized the essential condition of all happenings—this blindness and injustice in the soul of him who acts; he would, indeed, be cured for ever of taking history too seriously, for he would have learned from all men and all experiences, whether among Greeks or Turks, from a single hour of the first or of the nineteenth century, to answer his own question as to how or to what end life is lived. If you ask your acquaintances if they would like to relive the past ten or twenty years, you will easily discover which of them is prepared for this suprahistorical standpoint: they will all answer No, to be sure, but they will have different reasons for answering No. Some may perhaps be consoling themselves: "but the next twenty will be better"; they are those of whom David Hume says mockingly:

> *And from the dregs of life hope to receive*
> *What the first sprightly running could not give.*

Let us call them historical men; looking to the past impels them towards the future and fires their courage to go on living and their hope that what they want will still happen, that happiness lies behind the hill they are advancing towards. These historical men believe that the meaning of existence will come more and more to light in the course of its *process*, and they glance behind them only so that, from the process so far, they can learn to understand the present and to desire the future more vehemently; they have no idea that, despite their preoccupation with history, they in fact think and act unhistorically, or that their occupation with history stands in the service, not of pure knowledge, but of life.

But our question can also be answered differently. Again with a No— but with a No for a different reason: with the No of the suprahistorical man, who sees no salvation in the process and for whom, rather, the world is complete and reaches its finality at each and every moment. What could ten more years teach that the past ten were unable to teach! [. . .] The suprahistorical thinker beholds the history of nations and of individuals from within, clairvoyantly divining the original meaning of the various hieroglyphics and gradually even coming wearily to avoid the endless stream of new signs: for how should the unending superfluity of events not reduce him to satiety, over-satiety and finally to nausea! [. . .]

But let us leave the suprahistorical men to their nausea and their wisdom: today let us rejoice for once in our unwisdom and, as believers in deeds and progress and as honourers of the process, give ourselves a holiday. Our valuation of the historical may be only an occidental prejudice: but let us at least make progress within this prejudice and not stand still! Let us at least learn better how to employ history for the purpose of *life!* Then we will gladly acknowledge that the suprahistorical outlook possesses more wisdom than we do, provided we can only be sure that we possess more life: for then our unwisdom will at any rate have more future than their wisdom will. And in order to leave no doubt as to the meaning of this antithesis of life and wisdom, I shall employ an ancient, tried-and-tested procedure and straightway propound a number of theses.

A historical phenomenon, known clearly and completely and resolved into a phenomenon of knowledge, is, for him who has perceived it, dead: for he has recognized in it the delusion, the injustice, the blind passion, and in general the whole earthly and darkening horizon of this phenomenon, and has thereby also understood its power in history. This power has now lost its hold over him insofar as he is a man of knowledge: but perhaps it has not done so insofar as he is a man involved in life.

History become pure, sovereign science would be for mankind a sort of conclusion of life and a settling of accounts with it. The study of history is something salutary and fruitful for the future only as the attendant of a mighty new current of life, of an evolving culture for example, that is to say only when it is dominated and directed by a higher force and does not itself dominate and direct.

Insofar as it stands in the service of life, history stands in the service of an unhistorical power, and, thus subordinate, it can and should never become a pure science such as, for instance, mathematics is. The question of the degree to which life requires the service of history at all, however, is one of the supreme questions and concerns in regard to the health of a man, a people or a culture. For when it attains a certain degree of excess, life crumbles and degenerates, and through this degeneration history itself finally degenerates too. [. . .]

5

The oversaturation of an age with history seems to me to be hostile and dangerous to life in five respects: such an excess creates that contrast between inner and outer which we have just discussed, and thereby weakens the personality; it leads an age to imagine that it possesses the rarest of virtues, justice, to a greater degree than any other age; it disrupts the instincts of a people, and hinders the individual no less than the whole in the attainment of maturity; it implants the belief, harmful at any time, in the old age of mankind, the belief that one is a latecomer and epigone; it leads an age into a dangerous mood of irony in regard to itself and subsequently into the even more dangerous mood of cynicism: in this mood, however, it develops more and more a prudent practical egoism through which the forces of life are paralyzed and at last destroyed.

And now back to our first proposition: modern man suffers from a weakened personality. As the Roman of the imperial era became unRoman in relation to the world which stood at his service, as he lost himself in the flood of foreigners which came streaming in and degenerated in the midst of the cosmopolitan carnival of gods, arts and customs, so the same must happen to modern man who allows his artists in history to go on preparing a world exhibition for him; he has become a strolling spectator and has arrived at a condition in which even great wars and revolutions are able to influence him for hardly more than a moment. The war is not even over before it is transformed into a hundred thousand printed pages and set before the tired palates of the history-hungry as the latest delicacy. It seems that the instrument is almost incapable of producing a strong and full note, no matter how vigorously it is played: its tones at once die away and in a moment have faded to a tender historical echo. Expressed morally: you are no longer capable of holding on to the sublime, your deeds are shortlived explosions, not rolling thunder. Though the greatest and most miraculous event should occur—it must nonetheless descend, silent and unsung, into Hades. For art flees away if you immediately conceal your deeds under the awning of history. He who wants to understand, grasp and assess in a moment that before which he ought to stand long in awe as before an incomprehensible sublimity may be called reasonable, but only in the sense in which Schiller speaks of the rationality of the reasonable man: there are things he does not see which even a child sees, there are things he does not hear which even a child hears, and these things are precisely the most important things: because he does not understand these things, his understanding is more childish than the child and more simple than simplicity—and this in spite of the many cunning folds of his parchment scroll and the virtuosity of his fingers in unravelling the entangled. The reason is that he has lost and destroyed his instincts and, having lost his trust in the "divine animal," he can no longer let go the reins when his reason falters and his path leads him through deserts. Thus the individual grows fainthearted and unsure and dares no longer believe in himself: he sinks into his own subjective depths, which here means into the accumulated lumber of what he has learned but which has no outward effect, of instruction which does not become life. If one watches him from outside, one sees how the expulsion of the instincts by history has transformed man almost into mere *abstractis* and shadows: no one dares to appear as he is, but masks himself as a cultivated man, as a scholar, as a poet, as a politician. If, believing all this to be in earnest and not a mere puppet-play—for they all affect earnestness—one takes hold of these masks, one suddenly has nothing but rags and tatters in one's hands. That is why one should no longer let oneself be deceived, that is why one should order them: "Off with your coats or be what you seem!" It can no longer be borne that everyone of a noble seriousness should become a Don Quixote, since he has better things to do than to buffet about with such false realities. But he must nonetheless keep a sharp lookout, whenever he encounters a mask cry his "Halt! Who goes there?" and tear the mask from its face. Strange! One would think that history would encourage men to be *honest*—even if only honest fools; and hitherto this has indeed been its effect, only now it is no longer! Historical education and the identical bourgeois coat rule at the same time. While the "free personality" has never before been commended so volubly, there are no personalities to be seen, let alone free personalities—nothing but anxiously muffled up identical people. Individuality has withdrawn within: from without it has become invisible; a fact which leads one to ask whether indeed there could be causes without effects. Or is a race of eunuchs needed to watch over the great historical world-harem? Pure objectivity would certainly characterize such a race. For it almost seems that the task is to stand guard over history to see that nothing comes out of it except more history, and certainly no real events!—to take care that history does not make any personality "free," that is to say truthful towards itself, truthful towards others, in both word and deed. It is only through such truthfulness that the distress, the inner misery, of modern man will come to light, and that, in place of that anxious concealment through convention and masquerade, art and religion, true ancillaries, will be able to combine to implant a culture which corresponds to real needs and does not, as present-day universal education teaches it to do, deceive itself as to these needs and thereby become a walking lie. [. . .]

[. . .] And so let my proposition be understood and pondered: *history can be borne only by strong personalities, weak ones are utterly extinguished by it.* The reason is that history confuses the feelings and sensibility when these are not strong enough to assess the past by themselves. He who no longer dares to trust himself but involuntarily asks of history "How ought I to feel about this?" finds that his timidity gradually turns him into an actor and that he is playing a role, usually indeed many roles and therefore playing them badly and superficially. [. . .]

If the personality is emptied in the manner described and has become eternally subjectless or, as it is usually put, objective, nothing can affect it any longer; good and right things may be done, as deeds, poetry, music: the hollowed-out cultivated man at once looks beyond the work and asks about the history of its author. If he has already several other works behind him, he is at once obliged to have explained to him the previous and possible future progress of his development, he is at once compared with other artists, criticized as to his choice of subject and his treatment of it, dissected, carefully put together again, and in general admonished and set on the right path. The most astonishing thing may come to pass—the host of the historically neutral is always there ready to supervise the author of it even while he is still far off. The echo is heard immediately: but always as a "critique," though the moment before the critic did not so much as dream of the possibility of what has been done. The work never produces an effect but only another "critique"; and the critique itself produces no effect either, but again only a further critique. There thus arises a general agreement to regard the acquisition of many critiques as a sign of success, of few or none as a sign of failure. At bottom, however, even given this kind of "effect" everything remains as it was: people have some new thing to chatter about for a while, and then something newer still, and in the meantime go on doing what they have always done. The historical culture of our critics will no longer permit any effect at all in the proper sense, that is an effect on life and action: their blotting-paper at once goes down even on the blackest writing, and across the most graceful design they smear their thick brush-strokes which are supposed to be regarded as corrections: and once again that is the end of that. But their critical pens never cease to flow, for they have lost control of them and instead of directing them are directed by them. It is precisely in this immoderation of its critical outpourings, in its lack of self-control, in that which the Romans call *impotentia*, that the modern personality betrays its weakness. [. . .]

Schopenhauer as Educator (Third Untimely Meditation) (1874) (Excerpts)

1

A traveller who had seen many lands and peoples and several of the earth's continents was asked what quality in men he had discovered everywhere he had gone. He replied: "They have a tendency to laziness." To many it will seem that he ought rather to have said: "They are all timid. They hide themselves behind customs and opinions." In his heart every man knows quite well that, being unique, he will be in the world only once and that no imaginable chance will for a second time gather together into a unity so strangely variegated an assortment as he is: he knows it but he hides it like a bad conscience—why? From fear of his neighbour, who demands conventionality and cloaks himself with it. But what is it that constrains the individual to fear his neighbour, to think and act like a member of a herd, and to have no joy in himself? Modesty, perhaps, in a few rare cases. With the great majority it is indolence, inertia, in short that tendency to laziness of which the traveller spoke. He is right: men are even lazier than they are timid, and fear most of all the inconveniences with which unconditional honesty and nakedness would burden them. Artists alone hate this sluggish promenading in borrowed fashions and appropriated opinions and they reveal everyone's secret bad conscience, the law that every man is a unique miracle; they dare to show us man as he is, uniquely himself to every last movement of his muscles, more, that in being thus strictly consistent in uniqueness he is beautiful, and worth regarding, and in no way tedious. When the great thinker despises mankind, he despises its laziness: for it is on account of their laziness that men seem like factory products, things of no consequence and unworthy to be associated with or instructed. The man who does not wish to belong to the mass needs only to cease taking himself easily; let him follow his conscience, which calls to him: "Be your self! All you are now doing, thinking, desiring, is not you yourself."

Every youthful soul hears this call day and night and trembles when he hears it; for the idea of its liberation gives it a presentiment of the measure

of happiness allotted it from all eternity—a happiness to which it can by
no means attain so long as it lies fettered by the chains of fear and
convention. And how dismal and senseless life can be without this liberation! There exists no more repulsive and desolate creature in the world
than the man who has evaded his genius and who now looks furtively to
left and right, behind him and all about him. In the end such a man
becomes impossible to get hold of, since he is wholly exterior, without
kernel, a tattered, painted bag of clothes, a decked-out ghost that cannot
inspire even fear and certainly not pity. And if it is true to say of the lazy
that they kill time, then it is greatly to be feared that an era which sees its
salvation in public opinion, that is to say private laziness, is a time that
really will be killed: I mean that it will be struck out of the history of the
true liberation of life. How reluctant later generations will be to have
anything to do with the relics of an era ruled, not by living men, but by
pseudo-men dominated by public opinion; for which reason our age may
be to some distant posterity the darkest and least known, because least
human, portion of human history. I go along the new streets of our cities
and think how, of all these gruesome houses which the generation of public
opinion has built for itself, not one will be standing in a hundred years'
time, and how the opinions of these house-builders will no doubt by then
likewise have collapsed. On the other hand, how right it is for those who
do not feel themselves to be citizens of this time to harbour great hopes;
for if they were citizens of this time they too would be helping to kill their
time and so perish with it—while their desire is rather to awaken their time
to life and so live on themselves in this awakened life.

But even if the future gave us no cause for hope—the fact of our
existing at all in this here-and-now must be the strongest incentive to us
to live according to our own laws and standards: the inexplicable fact that
we live precisely today, when we had all infinite time in which to come
into existence, that we possess only a shortlived today in which to demonstrate why and to what end we came into existence now and at no other
time. We are responsible to ourselves for our own existence; consequently
we want to be the true helmsman of this existence and refuse to allow our
existence to resemble a mindless act of chance. One has to take a somewhat bold and dangerous line with this existence: especially as, whatever
happens, we are bound to lose it. Why go on clinging to this clod of earth,
this way of life, why pay heed to what your neighbour says? It is so
parochial to bind oneself to views which are no longer binding even a
couple of hundred miles away. Orient and Occident are chalk-lines drawn
before us to fool our timidity. I will make an attempt to attain freedom,
the youthful soul says to itself; and is it to be hindered in this by the fact
that two nations happen to hate and fight one another, or that two continents are separated by an ocean, or that all around it a religion is taught
which did not yet exist a couple of thousand years ago. All that is not you,

it says to itself. No one can construct for you the bridge upon which precisely you must cross the stream of life, no one but you yourself alone. There are, to be sure, countless paths and bridges and demi-gods which would bear you through this stream; but only at the cost of yourself: you would put yourself in pawn and lose yourself. There exists in the world a single path along which no one can go except you: whither does it lead? Do not ask, go along it. Who was it who said: "a man never rises higher than when he does not know whither his path can still lead him"?[1]

But how can we find ourselves again? How can man know himself? He is a thing dark and veiled; and if the hare has seven skins, man can slough off seventy times seven and still not be able to say: "this is really you, this is no longer outer shell." Moreover, it is a painful and dangerous undertaking thus to tunnel into oneself and to force one's way down into the shaft of one's being by the nearest path. A man who does it can easily so hurt himself that no physician can cure him. And, moreover again, what need should there be for it, since everything bears witness to what we are, our friendships and enmities, our glance and the clasp of our hand, our memory and that which we do not remember, our books and our handwriting. This, however, is the means by which an inquiry into the most important aspect can be initiated. Let the youthful soul look back on life with the question: what have you truly loved up to now, what has drawn your soul aloft, what has mastered it and at the same time blessed it? Set up these revered objects before you and perhaps their nature and their sequence will give you a law, the fundamental law of your own true self. Compare these objects one with another, see how one completes, expands, surpasses, transfigures another, how they constitute a stepladder upon which you have clambered up to yourself as you are now; for your true nature lies, not concealed deep within you, but immeasurably high above you, or at least above that which you usually take yourself to be. Your true educators and formative teachers reveal to you what the true basic material of your being is, something in itself ineducable and in any case difficult of access, bound and paralysed: your educators can be only your liberators. And that is the secret of all culture: it does not provide artificial limbs, wax noses or spectacles—that which can provide these things is, rather, only sham education. Culture is liberation, the removal of all the weeds, rubble and vermin that want to attack the tender buds of the plant, an outstreaming of light and warmth, the gentle rustling of nocturnal rain, it is imitation and worship of nature where nature is in her motherly and merciful mood, it is the perfecting of nature when it deflects her cruel and merciless assaults and turns them to good, and when it draws a veil over the expressions of nature's stepmotherly mood and her sad lack of understanding.

---

[1] Oliver Cromwell, as quoted by Cardinal de Retz in his *Memoirs* (trans.).

Certainly there may be other means of finding oneself, of coming to oneself out of the bewilderment in which one usually wanders as in a dark cloud, but I know of none better than to think on one's true educators. And so today I shall remember one of the teachers and taskmasters of whom I can boast, *Arthur Schopenhauer*—and later on I shall recall others.

*   *   *   *   *

5

But I have undertaken to exhibit my experience of Schopenhauer as an *educator*, and it is thus not nearly sufficient for me to paint, and to paint imperfectly, that ideal man who, as his Platonic ideal as it were, holds sway in and around him. The hardest task still remains: to say how a new circle of duties may be derived from this ideal and how one can proceed towards so extravagant a goal through a practical activity—in short, to demonstrate that this ideal *educates*. One might otherwise think it nothing but an intoxicating vision granted us only for moments at a time, and then leaving us all the more painfully in the lurch and prey to an even deeper dissatisfaction. It is also indisputable that that is how we *begin* our association with this ideal—with a sudden contrast of light and darkness, intoxication and nausea—and that this is a repetition of an experience which is as old as ideals themselves. But we ought not to stand long in the doorway, we ought soon to get through the beginning. And so we have seriously to ask the definite question: is it possible to bring that incredibly lofty goal so close to us that it educates us while it draws us aloft?—that Goethe's mighty words may not be fulfilled in us: "Man is born to a limited situation; he is able to understand simple, accessible, definite goals, and he accustoms himself to employing the means that happen to lie close at hand; but as soon as he oversteps his limits he knows neither what he wants nor what he ought to do, and it is all one whether he is distracted by the multiplicity of the things he encounters or whether his head is turned by their loftiness and dignity. It is always a misfortune when he is induced to strive after something which he cannot proceed towards through a practical activity."[2] The Schopenhauerean man appears to be singularly open to this objection: his dignity and loftiness can only turn our heads and thereby exclude us from any participation in the world of action; coherent duties, the even flow of life are gone. One man perhaps at last accustoms himself to living discontentedly according to two different rules of conduct, that is to say in conflict with himself, uncertain of how to act and therefore daily more feeble and unfruitful: while another may even renounce all action on principle and almost cease to pay any

[2]From *Wilhelm Meister's Lehrjahre*, Book 4 (trans.).

attention to the actions of others. The dangers are always great when things are made too difficult for a man and when he is incapable of *fulfilling* any duties at all; stronger natures can be destroyed by it, the weaker, more numerous natures decline into a reflective laziness and in the end forfeit through laziness even their ability to reflect.

Now, in face of such objections I am willing to concede that in precisely this respect our work has hardly begun and that from my own experience I am sure of only one thing: that from that ideal image it is possible to fasten upon ourselves a chain of fulfillable duties, and that some of us already feel the weight of this chain. But before I can conscientiously reduce this new circle of duties to a formula I must offer the following preliminary observations.

More profoundly feeling people have at all times felt sympathy for the animals because they suffer from life and yet do not possess the power to turn the goad of life against themselves and understand their existence metaphysically; one is, indeed, profoundly indignant at the sight of sense-less suffering. That is why there has arisen in more than one part of the earth the supposition that the bodies of animals contain the guilt-laden souls of men, so that this suffering which at first sight arouses indignation on account of its senselessness acquires meaning and significance as pun-ishment and atonement before the seat of eternal justice. And it is, truly, a harsh punishment thus to live as an animal, beset by hunger and desire yet incapable of any kind of reflection on the nature of this life; and no harder fate can be thought of than that of the beast of prey pursued through the wilderness by the most gnawing torment, rarely satisfied and even then in such a way that satisfaction is purchased only with the pain of lacerating combat with other animals or through inordinate greed and nauseating satiety. To hang on to life madly and blindly, with no higher aim than to hang on to it; not to know that or why one is being so heavily punished but, with the stupidity of a fearful desire, to thirst after precisely this punishment as though after happiness—that is what it means to be an animal; and if all nature presses towards man, it thereby intimates that man is necessary for the redemption of nature from the curse of the life of the animal, and that in him existence at last holds up before itself a mirror in which life appears no longer senseless but in its metaphysical signifi-cance. Yet let us reflect: where does the animal cease, where does man begin?—man, who is nature's sole concern! As long as anyone desires life as he desires happiness he has not yet raised his eyes above the horizon of the animal, for he only desires more consciously what the animal seeks through blind impulse. But that is what we all do for the greater part of our lives: usually we fail to emerge out of animality, we ourselves are the animals whose suffering seems to be senseless.

But there are moments *when we realize this:* then the clouds are rent asunder, and we see that, in common with all nature, we are pressing towards man as towards something that stands high above us. In this sudden illumination we gaze around us and behind us with a shudder: we behold the more subtle beasts of prey and there we are in the midst of them. The tremendous coming and going of men on the great wilderness of the earth, their founding of cities and states, their wars, their restless assembling and scattering again, their confused mingling, mutual imitation, mutual outwitting and downtreading, their wailing in distress, their howls of joy in victory—all this is a continuation of animality: as though man was to be deliberately retrogressed and defrauded of his metaphysical disposition, indeed as though nature, after having desired and worked at man for so long, now drew back from him in fear and preferred to return to the unconsciousness of instinct. Nature needs knowledge and it is terrified of the knowledge it has need of; and so the flame flickers restlessly back and forth as though afraid of itself and seizes upon a thousand things before it seizes upon that on account of which nature needs knowledge at all. [. . .]

[. . .] It is already much that we should raise our head above the water at all, even if only a little, and observe what stream it is in which we are so deeply immersed. And even this momentary emerging and awakening is not achieved through our own power, we have to be lifted up—and who are they who lift us?

They are those true *men, those who are no longer animal, the philosophers, artists and saints;* nature, which never makes a leap, has made its one leap in creating them, and a leap of joy moreover, for nature then feels that for the first time it has reached its goal—where it realizes it has to unlearn having goals and that it has played the game of life and becoming with too high stakes. This knowledge transfigures nature, and a gentle evening-weariness, that which men call "beauty," reposes upon its face. That which it now utters with this transfigured countenance is the great *enlightenment* as to the character of existence; and the supreme wish that mortals can wish is lastingly and with open ears to participate in this enlightenment. If we think of how much Schopenhauer for instance must have *heard* during the course of his life, then we might well say to ourselves afterwards: "Alas, your deaf ears, your dull head, your flickering understanding, your shrivelled heart, all that I call mine, how I despise you! Not to be able to fly, only to flutter! To see what is above you but not to be able to reach it! To know the way that leads to the immeasurable open prospect of the philosopher, and almost to set foot on it, but after a few steps to stagger back! And if that greatest of all wishes were fulfilled for only a day, how gladly one would exchange for it all the rest of life! To climb as high into the pure icy Alpine air as a philosopher ever climbed, up to where all the mist and obscurity cease and where the fundamental constitution of things speaks in a voice rough and rigid but ineluctably comprehensible! . . . And what a fate, on the other hand, to sense sufficient of the certainty and happiness of the philosopher to be able to feel the whole uncertainty and unhappiness of the non-philosopher, of him who desires without hope! To know oneself a fruit on the tree which can never become ripe because one is too much in the shadow, and at the same time to see close at hand the sunshine that one lacks!"

There is enough torment here to make a man who is mis-talented in such a way malicious and envious, if he is capable of malice and envy at all; probably, however, he will at last turn his soul in another direction so that it shall not consume itself in vain longing—and now he will *discover* a new circle of duties.

Here I have arrived at an answer to the question whether it is possible to pursue the great ideal of the Schopenhauerean man by means of a practical activity. One thing above all is certain: these new duties are not the duties of a solitary; on the contrary, they set one in the midst of a mighty community held together, not by external forms and regulations, but by a fundamental idea. It is the fundamental idea of *culture*, insofar as it sets for each one of us but one task: *to promote the production of the philosopher, the artist and the saint within us and without us and thereby to work at the perfecting of nature.* For, as nature needs the philosopher, so does it need the artist, for the achievement of a metaphysical goal, that of its own self-enlightenment, so that it may at last behold as a clear and finished picture that which it could see only obscurely in the agitation of its evolution—for the end, that is to say, of self-knowledge. It was Goethe who declared, in an arrogant but profound assertion, that nature's experiments are of value only when the artist finally comes to comprehend its stammerings, goes out to meet it halfway, and gives expression to what all these experiments are really about. "I have often said," he once exclaimed, "and I shall often repeat, that the *causa finalis* of the activities of men and the world is dramatic poetry. For the stuff is of absolutely no other use." And so nature at last needs the saint, in whom the ego is completely melted away and whose life of suffering is no longer felt as his own life—or is hardly so felt—but as a profound feeling of oneness and identity with all living things: the saint in whom there appears that miracle of transformation which the game of becoming never hits upon, that final and supreme becoming-human after which all nature presses and urges for its redemption from itself. It is incontestable that we are all related and allied to the saint, just as we are related to the philosopher and artist; there are moments and as it were bright sparks of the fire of love in whose light we cease to understand the word "I," there lies something beyond our being which at these moments moves across into it, and we are thus possessed of a heartfelt longing for bridges between here and there. It is true that, as we usually are, we can contribute nothing to the production of the man of redemption: that is why we *hate* ourselves as we usually are, and it is this hatred which is the root of that pessimism which Schopenhauer had again to teach our age, though it has existed for as long as the longing for culture has existed. Its root, not its flower; its bottom floor, so to speak, not its roof; the commencement of its course, not its goal: for at some time or other we shall have to learn to hate something else, something more universal, and cease to hate our own individuality and its wretched limitations, changeableness and restlessness: it will be in that elevated condition in which we shall also love something else, something we are now unable to love. Only when, in our present or in some future incarnation, we ourselves have been taken into that exalted order of philosophers, artists and saints, shall we also be given a new goal for our love and hate—in the meantime we have our task and our circle of duties, our hate and our love. For we know what culture is. Applied to the Schopenhauerean man, it demands that we prepare and promote his repeated production by getting to know what is inimical to it and removing it—in short, that we unwearyingly combat that which would deprive *us* of the supreme fulfilment of our existence by preventing us from becoming such Schopenhauerean men ourselves. —

6

Sometimes it is harder to accede to a thing than it is to see its truth; and that is how most people may feel when they reflect on the proposition: "Mankind must work continually at the production of individual great men—that and nothing else is its task." How much one would like to apply to society and its goals something that can be learned from observation of any species of the animal or plant world: that its only concern is the individual higher exemplar, the more uncommon, more powerful, more complex, more fruitful—how much one would like to do this if inculcated fancies as to the goal of society did not offer such tough resistance! We ought really to have no difficulty in seeing that, when a species has arrived at its limits and is about to go over into a higher species, the goal of its evolution lies, not in the mass of its exemplars and their wellbeing, let alone in those exemplars who happen to come last in point of time, but rather in those apparently scattered and chance existences which favourable conditions have here and there produced; and it ought to be just as easy to understand the demand that, because it can arrive at a conscious awareness of its goal, mankind ought to seek out and create the favourable conditions under which those great redemptive men can come into existence. But everything resists this conclusion: here the ultimate goal is seen to lie in the happiness of all or of the greatest number, there in the development of great communities; and though one may be ready to sacrifice one's life to a state, for instance, it is another matter if one is asked to sacrifice it on behalf of another individual. It seems to be an absurd demand that one man should exist for the sake of another man; "for the sake of all others, rather, or at least for as many as possible!" O worthy man! as though it were less absurd to let number decide when value and significance are at issue! For the question is this: how can your life, the individual life, receive the highest value, the deepest significance? How can it be least squandered? Certainly only by your living for the good of the rarest and most valuable exemplars, and not for the good of the majority, that is to say those who, taken individually, are the least valuable exemplars. And the young person should be taught to regard himself as a failed work of nature but at the same time as a witness to the grandiose and marvellous intentions of this artist: nature has done badly, he should say to himself; but I will honour its great intentions by serving it so that one day it may do better.

By coming to this resolve he places himself within the circle of *culture;* for culture is the child of each individual's self-knowledge and dissatisfaction with himself. Anyone who believes in culture is thereby saying: "I see above me something higher and more human than I am; let everyone help me to attain it, as I will help everyone who knows and suffers as I do: so that at last the man may appear who feels himself perfect and boundless in knowledge and love, perception and power, and who in his completeness is at one with nature, the judge and evaluator of things." It is hard to create in anyone this condition of intrepid self-knowledge because it is impossible to teach love; for it is love alone that can bestow on the soul, not only a clear, discriminating and self-contemptuous view of itself, but also the desire to look beyond itself and to seek with all its might for a higher self as yet still concealed from it. Thus only he who has attached his heart to some great man is by that act *consecrated to culture;* the sign of that consecration is that one is ashamed of oneself without any accompanying feeling of distress, that one comes to hate one's own narrowness and shrivelled nature, that one has a feeling of sympathy for the genius who again and again drags himself up out of our dryness and apathy and the same feeling in anticipation for all those who are still struggling and evolving, with the profoundest conviction that almost everywhere we encounter nature pressing towards man and again and again failing to achieve him, yet everywhere succeeding in producing the most marvellous beginnings, individual traits and forms: so that the men we live among resemble a field over which is scattered the most precious fragments of sculpture where everything calls to us: come, assist, complete, bring together what belongs together, we have an immeasurable longing to become whole.

This sum of inner states is, I said, the first sign that one is consecrated to culture; now, however, I have to describe the *further* stage of this consecration, and I realize that here my task is more difficult. For now we have to make the transition from the inward event to an assessment of the outward event; the eye has to be directed outwards so as to rediscover in the great world of action that desire for culture it recognized in the experiences of the first stage just described; the individual has to employ his own wrestling and longing as the alphabet by means of which he can now read off the aspirations of mankind as a whole. But he may not halt even here; from this stage he has to climb up to a yet higher one; culture demands of him, not only inward experience, not only an assessment of the outward world that streams all around him, but finally and above all an act, that is to say a struggle on behalf of culture and hostility towards those influences, habits, laws, institutions in which he fails to recognize his goal: which is the production of the genius. [. . .]

*   *   *   *   *

II
Free-Spirited Reflections
(1878–1882)

Excerpts from

Human, All Too Human
(Volumes One and Two)

Daybreak

Joyful Wisdom (or The Gay Science)
(Books One to Four)

THE "FREE SPIRIT" SERIES

Introduction

Nietzsche's publications in the years between his *Untimely Meditations* and the first part of *Thus Spoke Zarathustra* were very different from either of them. They consisted in a number of volumes of collections of brief reflections on various topics, distilled from the notebooks he kept. They began with the first volume of *Menschliches, Allzumenschliches* (*Human, All Too Human*) in 1878 and concluded with the first four parts of *Die fröhliche Wissenschaft* (translated both as *The Gay Science* and as *Joyful Wisdom*) in 1882. By the time he published the last of them, he had come to think of them as a series, writing of them on the back cover of its original edition:

> This book marks the conclusion of a series of writings by Friedrich Nietzsche, whose common goal is to erect *a new image and ideal of the free spirit*.[1]

This "series" also included two further collections of reflections that became the two parts of the second volume of *Human, All Too Human*[2] and another such collection entitled *Morganröte* (*Daybreak* or *Dawn*). In their form these works were modeled on volumes of this sort published by a number of earlier writers Nietzsche admired, such as Pascal[3] and Lichtenberg.[4] He found the style of the aphorism (a polished, pithy sentence or two expressing some insight or observation) and the reflection (a self-contained paragraph succinctly discussing some particular topic, usually indicated in a heading of a word or phrase) to be very congenial during this period. It suited both his emerging disposition and the intellectual ferment and turmoil he was experiencing. (Many of his later writings have much the same character.)

These were years of multiple crises for Nietzsche. His academic career came to an end shortly after he published the first volume of *Human, All Too Human*, as he was both compelled by poor health and impelled by

---

[1]See *The Gay Science,* trans. Walter Kaufmann (New York: Vintage, 1974), 30.

[2]*Mixed Opinions and Aphorisms* (initially added as an appendix to an expanded version of the first volume in 1879 and subsequently made Part One of the second volume of *Human, All Too Human* when Nietzsche published a new edition in two volumes, with prefaces to both, in 1886); and *The Wanderer and His Shadow* (initially published separately in 1880 and subsequently incorporated as Part Two of the second volume).

[3]Blaise Pascal (1623–1662), *Pensées,* trans. John Warrington (New York: E. P. Dutton, 1960). The title means "*Thoughts.*"

[4]Georg Christoph Lichtenberg (1742–1799), *Aphorisms,* trans. R. J. Hollingdale (London: Penguin, 1990).

changed interests to resign from his professorship in classical philology at Basel.[5] This book completed the alienation of most of his erstwhile colleagues and supporters. It also strained his formerly close relationship with Wagner almost to the breaking point, increasing his spiritual isolation and estrangement. Coping with his ever more debilitating physical problems further became a major and constant challenge.

Perhaps most important of all, Nietzsche had become profoundly disillusioned with virtually every aspect of modern life and the cultural and intellectual traditions associated with it. Everywhere he looked, what he saw seemed "all too human." Radical, disillusioning enlightenment became his task; and the "free spirit," whose liberation from all illusions was complete and whose intellectual honesty was uncompromising, became for him the only ideal worth aspiring to. His inspirations now were thinkers like Voltaire and the new natural sciences; and his "new image and ideal of the free spirit" had affinities with both the crusading humanistic spirit of the Enlightenment and the boldly positivistic spirit animating these new sciences. Yet it also stood at a distance from them; for Nietzsche regarded the optimism they shared, owing to their common faith in the power of reason, as naive and superficial. Indeed, he was for a time drawn strongly in the direction of the Schopenhauerian pessimism he wanted to resist and toward the nihilism it foreshadowed.

Nietzsche subsequently came to see this as only a "transitional stage,"[6] between disillusionment and the discovery of the possibility of a new and different affirmation of life, to which he soon would give powerful and eloquent expression in *Thus Spoke Zarathustra*. Yet it also was a very important period in his intellectual life, in which he developed the means of carrying out his emerging tasks as the philosopher he was becoming. He strengthened and refined his powers of observation and analysis, his psychological and historical sensitivity, his ability to probe beneath the surface to diagnose and comprehend underlying processes, his capacity to identify the connections and larger significance of many seemingly diverse and unrelated phenomena, and his flair for coming up with new and illuminating interpretations and characterizations of things obscured by conventional ways of thinking and speaking.

By the time he came to write the last of the works in this series, *Die fröhliche Wissenschaft*, Nietzsche had reached the threshold of his philosophical maturity, of which it is in many respects the first fruit. As its title was no doubt meant to suggest, it is fundamentally affirmative in spirit[7]

---

[5]In 1879.

[6]See the notes on nihilism in the second set of selections from his notebooks in Part VI of this volume.

[7]Hence the use of the adjective *fröhlich*, "gay" or "joyful"—in contrast to the grimness of a purely pessimistic way of thinking.

and constructive in intent.[8] The "death of God" is its point of departure, and the pervasiveness of the "all too human" remains one of its themes. Yet a strong counterpoint theme is repeatedly sounded in it as well, of the promising character of exceptional human possibilities with respect to the attainment of both knowledge and enhanced forms of human life. Here Nietzsche thus began to explore and emphasize what we *can* come to comprehend and make of our human existence, despite what human knowledge and human life all too often merely are, and what they are not and can never be. And in the course of his seemingly disconnected reflections along these lines, he has much of interest to say in this book—about a great many matters of philosophical importance—which in fact has an underlying coherence: as the beginnings of a comprehensive reinterpretation of our human nature and capacities.

While this work overshadows and in a sense supersedes *Human, All Too Human* and *Daybreak* in these respects, they too warrant attention; for they contain a wealth of reflections that are often insightful and invariably thought provoking. It is mainly Nietzsche the critic who speaks in these earlier volumes in this series; but he is unsurpassed *as* a critic—particularly of things we tend to take for granted, overestimate, and mystify. The fire of his criticisms scorches virtually everything in sight and, like the "refiner's fire," burns away everything that is not true metal. One owes it to oneself to see how much of what one holds dear can emerge intact from it.

The selections from *Human, All Too Human* and *Daybreak* with which this section begins are but a small sampling of the rich contents of these remarkable works. If Nietzsche had never written anything else, his reputation and significance certainly would have been very different; but these works would have sufficed to earn him laurels as a writer—and, more importantly, a place of honor among the heirs of Voltaire and warriors of the Enlightenment.

---

[8]*Wissenschaft* connotes the disciplined pursuit of knowledge, in contrast to a nihilistic denial of its value and very possibility.

Human, All Too Human
Volume One (1878)
(Excerpts)

1

Chemistry of concepts and sensations.—Almost all the problems of philosophy once again pose the same form of question as they did two thousand years ago: how can something originate in its opposite, for example rationality in irrationality, the sentient in the dead, logic in unlogic, disinterested contemplation in covetous desire, living for others in egoism, truth in error? Metaphysical philosophy has hitherto surmounted this difficulty by denying that the one originates in the other and assuming for the more highly valued thing a miraculous source in the very kernel and being of the "thing in itself." Historical philosophy, on the other hand, which can no longer be separated from natural science, the youngest of all philosophical methods, has discovered in individual cases (and this will probably be the result in every case) that there are no opposites, except in the customary exaggeration of popular or metaphysical interpretations, and that a mistake in reasoning lies at the bottom of this antithesis: according to this explanation there exists, strictly speaking, neither an unegoistic action nor completely disinterested contemplation; both are only sublimations, in which the basic element seems almost to have dispersed and reveals itself only under the most painstaking observation. All we require, and what can be given us only now the individual sciences have attained their present level, is a *chemistry* of the moral, religious and aesthetic conceptions and sensations, likewise of all the agitations we experience within ourselves in cultural and social intercourse, and indeed even when we are alone: what if this chemistry would end up by revealing that in this domain too the most glorious colours are derived from base, indeed from despised materials? Will there be many who desire to pursue such researches? Mankind likes to put questions of origins and beginnings out of its mind: must one not be almost inhuman to detect in oneself a contrary inclination?—

2

Family failing of philosophers. —All philosophers have the common failing of starting out from man as he is now and thinking they can reach their goal through an analysis of him. They involuntarily think of "man" as an *aeterna veritas*,[1] as something that remains constant in the midst of all flux, as a sure measure of things. Everything the philosopher has declared about man is, however, at bottom no more than a testimony as to the man of a *very limited* period of time. Lack of historical sense is the family failing of all philosophers; many, without being aware of it, even take the most recent manifestation of man, such as has arisen under the impress of certain religions, even certain political events, as the fixed form from which one has to start out. They will not learn that man has become, that the faculty of cognition has become; while some of them would have it that the whole world is spun out of this faculty of cognition. Now, everything *essential* in the development of mankind took place in primeval times, long before the four thousand years we more or less know about; during these years mankind may well not have altered very much. But the philosopher here sees "instincts" in man as he now is and assumes that these belong to the unalterable facts of mankind and to that extent could provide a key to the understanding of the world in general: the whole of teleology is constructed by speaking of the man of the last four millennia as of an *eternal* man towards whom all things in the world have had a natural relationship from the time he began. But everything has become: there are *no eternal facts*, just as there are no absolute truths. Consequently what is needed from now on is *historical philosophizing*, and with it the virtue of modesty.

3

Estimation of unpretentious truths. —It is the mark of a higher culture to value the little unpretentious truths which have been discovered by means of rigorous method more highly than the errors handed down by metaphysical and artistic ages and men, which blind us and make us happy. At first the former are regarded with scorn, as though the two things could not possibly be accorded equal rights: they stand there so modest, simple, sober, so apparently discouraging, while the latter are so fair, splendid, intoxicating, perhaps indeed enrapturing. Yet that which has been attained by laborious struggle, the certain, enduring and thus of significance for any further development of knowledge is nonetheless the

[1]Eternal truth.

higher; to adhere to it is manly and demonstrates courage, simplicity and abstemiousness. Gradually not only the individual but all mankind will be raised to this manliness, when they have finally become accustomed to valuing viable, enduring knowledge more highly and lost all faith in inspiration and the acquisition of knowledge by miraculous means. — Worshippers of *form*, with their standards of the beautiful and sublime, will, to be sure, at first have good ground for mockery once estimation of unpretentious truths and the scientific spirit begins to dominate: but only because either their eye has not yet discovered the charm of the *simplest* form or because those raised in that spirit are as yet very far from being thoroughly permeated by it, so that they still thoughtlessly imitate old forms (and do so badly, as does everyone to whom a thing no longer matters very much). Formerly the spirit was not engaged in rigorous thinking, its serious occupation was the spinning out of forms and symbols. That has now changed; serious occupation with the symbolic has become a mark of a lower culture. As our arts themselves grow ever more intellectual, our senses more spiritual, and as for example we now adjudge what is pleasant sounding quite differently from the way we did a hundred years ago: so the forms of our life will grow ever more *spiritual*, perhaps to the eye of earlier ages *uglier*, but only because it is incapable of seeing how the realm of inner, spiritual beauty is continually growing deeper and wider, and to what extent we may all now accord the eye of insight greater value than the fairest structure or the sublimest edifice.

4

Astrology and what is related to it. — It is probable that the objects of the religious, moral and aesthetic sensations belong only to the surface of things, while man likes to believe that here at least he is in touch with the world's heart; the reason he deludes himself is that these things produce in him such profound happiness and unhappiness, and thus he exhibits here the same pride as in the case of astrology. For astrology believes the starry firmament revolves around the fate of man; the moral man, however, supposes that what he has essentially at heart must also constitute the essence and heart of things.

5

Misunderstanding of the dream. — The man of the ages of barbarous primordial culture believed that in the dream he was getting to know a *second real world:* here is the origin of all metaphysics. Without the dream one would have had no occasion to divide the world into two. The dissection into soul and body is also connected with the oldest idea of the dream, likewise the postulation of a life of the soul, thus the origin of all belief in spirits, and probably also of the belief in gods. "The dead live on, *for* they appear to the living in dreams": that was the conclusion one formerly drew, throughout many millennia.

*   *   *   *   *

11

Language as putative science. —The significance of language for the evolution of culture lies in this, that mankind set up in language a separate world beside the other world, a place it took to be so firmly set that, standing upon it, it could lift the rest of the world off its hinges and make itself master of it. To the extent that man has for long ages believed in the concepts and names of things as in *aeternae veritates* he has appropriated to himself that pride by which he raised himself above the animal: he really thought that in language he possessed knowledge of the world. The sculptor of language was not so modest as to believe that he was only giving things designations, he conceived rather that with words he was expressing supreme knowledge of things; language is, in fact, the first stage of the occupation with science. Here, too, it is the *belief that the truth has been found* out of which the mightiest sources of energy have flowed. A great deal later—only now—it dawns on men that in their belief in language they have propagated a tremendous error. Happily, it is too late for the evolution of reason, which depends on this belief, to be again put back. —*Logic* too depends on presuppositions with which nothing in the real world corresponds, for example on the presupposition that there are identical things, that the same thing is identical at different points of time: but this science came into existence through the opposite belief (that such conditions do obtain in the real world). It is the same with *mathematics*, which would certainly not have come into existence if one had known from the beginning that there was in nature no exactly straight line, no real circle, no absolute magnitude.

*   *   *   *   *

16

Appearance and thing in itself. —Philosophers are accustomed to station themselves before life and experience—before that which they call the world of appearance—as before a painting that has been unrolled once and for all and unchangeably depicts the same scene: this scene, they believe, has to be correctly interpreted, so as to draw a conclusion as to the nature

of the being that produced the picture: that is to say, as to the nature of
the thing in itself, which it is customary to regard as the sufficient reason
for the existence of the world of appearance. As against this, more rigorous
logicians, having clearly identified the concept of the metaphysical as that
of the unconditioned, consequently also unconditioning, have disputed
any connection between the unconditioned (the metaphysical world) and
the world we know: so that what appears in appearance is precisely *not* the
thing in itself, and no conclusion can be drawn from the former as to the
nature of the latter. Both parties, however, overlook the possibility that
this painting—that which we humans call life and experience—has gradually *become*, is indeed still fully in course of *becoming*, and should thus not
be regarded as a fixed object on the basis of which a conclusion as to the
nature of its originator (the sufficient reason) may either be drawn or
pronounced undrawable. Because we have for millennia made moral, aesthetic, religious demands on the world, looked upon it with blind desire,
passion or fear, and abandoned ourselves to the bad habits of illogical
thinking, this world has gradually *become* so marvellously variegated,
frightful, meaningful, soulful, it has acquired colour—but we have been
the colourists: it is the human intellect that has made appearance appear
and transported its erroneous basic conceptions into things. Late, very
late—it has reflected on all this: and now the world of experience and the
thing in itself seem to it so extraordinarily different from one another and
divided apart that it rejects the idea that the nature of one can be inferred
from the nature of the other—or invites us in a chillingly mysterious
fashion to *abandon* our intellect, our personal will: so as to attain to the real
by *becoming real* oneself. Others again have assembled all the characteristic
traits of our world of appearance—that is to say, the idea of the world spun
out of intellectual errors we have inherited—and, *instead of indicting the
intellect as the guilty party*, have charged the essence of things with being the
cause of the very uncanny character this world in fact possesses and have
preached redemption from being.—With all these conceptions the steady
and laborious process of science, which will one day celebrate its greatest
triumph in a *history of the genesis of thought*, will in the end decisively have
done; for the outcome of this history may well be the conclusion: That
which we now call the world is the outcome of a host of errors and
fantasies which have gradually arisen and grown entwined with one another in the course of the overall evolution of the organic being, and are
now inherited by us as the accumulated treasure of the entire past—as
treasure: for the value of our humanity depends upon it. Rigorous science
is capable of detaching us from this ideational world only to a limited
extent—and more is certainly not to be desired—inasmuch as it is incapable of making any essential inroad into the power of habits of feeling
acquired in primeval times: but it can, quite gradually and step by step,
illuminate the history of the genesis of this world as idea—and, for brief

periods at any rate, lift us up out of the entire proceeding. Perhaps we shall then recognize that the thing in itself is worthy of Homeric laughter: that it appeared to be so much, indeed everything, and is actually empty, that is to say empty of significance.

*   *   *   *   *

33

Error regarding life necessary to life. —Every belief in the value and dignity of life rests on false thinking; it is possible only through the fact that empathy with the universal life and suffering of mankind is very feebly developed in the individual. Even those rarer men who think beyond themselves at all have an eye, not for this universal life, but for fenced-off portions of it. If one knows how to keep the exceptions principally in view, I mean the greatly gifted and pure of soul, takes their production for the goal of world-evolution and rejoices in the effects they in turn produce, one may believe in the value of life, because then one is *overlooking* all other men: thinking falsely, that is to say. And likewise if, though one does keep in view all mankind, one accords validity only to *one* species of drives, the less egoistical, and justifies them in face of all the others, then again one can hope for something of mankind as a whole and to this extent believe in the value of life: thus, in this case too, through falsity of thinking. Whichever of these attitudes one adopts, however, one is by adopting it an *exception* among men. The great majority endure life without complaining overmuch; they *believe* in the value of existence, but they do so precisely because each of them exists for himself alone, refusing to step out of himself as those exceptions do: everything outside themselves they notice not at all or at most as a dim shadow. Thus for the ordinary, everyday man the value of life rests solely on the fact that he regards himself more highly than he does the world. The great lack of imagination from which he suffers means he is unable to feel his way into other beings and thus he participates as little as possible in their fortunes and sufferings. *He,* on the other hand, who really could participate in them would have to despair of the value of life; if he succeeded in encompassing and feeling within himself the total consciousness of mankind he would collapse with a curse on existence—for mankind has as a whole *no* goal, and the individual man when he regards its total course cannot derive from it any support or comfort, but must be reduced to despair. If in all he does he has before him the ultimate goallessness of man, his actions acquire in his own eyes the character of useless squandering. But to feel thus *squandered,* not merely as an individual but as humanity as a whole, in the way we behold the individual fruits of nature squandered, is a feeling beyond

all other feelings. — But who is capable of such a feeling? Certainly only a
poet: and poets always know how to console themselves.

34

In mitigation. — But will our philosophy not thus become a tragedy? Will
truth not become inimical to life, to the better man? A question seems to
lie heavily on our tongue and yet refuses to be uttered: whether one *could*
consciously reside in untruth? or, if one were *obliged* to, whether death
would not be preferable? For there is no longer any "ought"; for morality,
insofar as it was an "ought," has been just as much annihilated by our
mode of thinking as has religion. Knowledge can allow as motives only
pleasure and pain, utility and injury: but how will these motives come to
terms with the sense for truth? For they too are in contact with errors
(insofar as inclination and aversion and their very unjust assessments are,
as we said, the essential determinants of pleasure and pain). The whole
of human life is sunk deeply in untruth; the individual cannot draw it up
out of this well without thereby growing profoundly disillusioned about
his own past, without finding his present motives, such as that of honour,
absurd, and pouring mockery and contempt on the passions which reach
out to the future and promise happiness in it. Is it true, is all that remains
a mode of thought whose outcome on a personal level is despair and on a
theoretical level a philosophy of destruction? — I believe that the nature of
the after-effect of knowledge is determined by a man's *temperament:* in
addition to the after-effect described I could just as easily imagine a
different one, quite possible in individual instances, by virtue of which a
life could arise much simpler and emotionally cleaner than our present life
is: so that, though the old motives of violent desire produced by inherited
habit would still possess their strength, they would gradually grow weaker
under the influence of purifying knowledge. In the end one would live
among men and with oneself as in *nature*, without praising, blaming,
contending, gazing contentedly, as though at a spectacle, upon many
things for which one formerly felt only fear. One would be free of emphasis, and no longer prodded by the idea that one is only nature or more
than nature. For this to happen one would, to be sure, have to possess the
requisite temperament, as has already been said: a firm, mild and at
bottom cheerful soul, a temper that does not need to be on its guard
against malice or sudden outbursts and in whose utterances there is nothing of snarling and sullenness — those familiar tedious qualities of old dogs
and men who have long been kept on the leash. A man from whom the
ordinary fetters of life have fallen to such an extent that he continues to
live only so as to know better must, rather, without envy or vexation be
able to forgo much, indeed almost everything upon which other men

place value; that free, fearless hovering over men, customs, laws and the traditional evaluations of things must *suffice* him as the condition he considers most desirable. He is happy to communicate his joy in this condition, and he *has*, perhaps, nothing else to communicate—which involves, to be sure, one more privation and renunciation. If more is nonetheless desired of him, he will, with a benevolent shake of the head, point to his brother, the free man of action, and perhaps not conceal a certain mockery in doing so: for of his "freedom" there is a curious tale still to be told.

*   *   *   *   *

107

Unaccountability and innocence. —The complete unaccountability of man for his actions and his nature is the bitterest draught the man of knowledge has to swallow if he has been accustomed to seeing in accountability and duty the patent of his humanity. All his evaluations, all his feelings of respect and antipathy have thereby become disvalued and false: his profoundest sentiment, which he accorded to the sufferer, the hero, rested upon an error; he may no longer praise, no longer censure, for it is absurd to praise and censure nature and necessity. As he loves a fine work of art but does not praise it since it can do nothing for itself, as he stands before the plants, so must he stand before the actions of men and before his own. He can admire their strength, beauty, fullness, but he may not find any merit in them: the chemical process and the strife of the elements, the torment of the sick man who yearns for an end to his sickness, are as little merits as are those states of distress and psychic convulsions which arise when we are torn back and forth by conflicting motives until we finally choose the most powerful of them—as we put it (in truth, however, until the most powerful motive chooses us). But all these motives, whatever exalted names we may give them, have grown up out of the same roots as those we believe evilly poisoned; between good and evil actions there is no difference in kind, but at the most one of degree. Good actions are sublimated evil ones; evil actions are coarsened, brutalized good ones. It is the individual's sole desire for self-enjoyment (together with the fear of losing it) which gratifies itself in every instance, let a man act as he can, that is to say as he must: whether his deeds be those of vanity, revenge, pleasure, utility, malice, cunning, or those of sacrifice, sympathy, knowledge. Degrees of intelligent judgement decide whither each person will let his desire draw him; every society, every individual always has present an order of rank of things considered good, according to which he determines his own actions and judges those of others. But this standard is continually changing, many actions are called evil but are only stupid, because the degree of intelligence which decided for them was very low. Indeed, in a certain sense *all* present actions are stupid, for the highest degree of human intelligence which can now be attained will certainly be exceeded in the future: and then all our actions and judgements will seem in retrospect as circumscribed and precipitate as the actions and judgements of still existing primitive peoples now appear to us. To perceive all this can be very painful, but then comes a consolation: such pains are birth-pangs. The butterfly wants to get out of its cocoon, it tears at it, it breaks it open: then it is blinded and confused by the unfamiliar light, the realm of freedom. It is in such men as are *capable* of that suffering—how few they will be!—that the first attempt will be made to see whether mankind could *transform itself from a moral to a knowing mankind.* The sun of a new gospel is casting its first beam on the topmost summits in the soul of every individual: there the mists are gathering more thickly than ever, and the brightest glitter and the gloomiest twilight lie side by side. Everything is necessity—thus says the new knowledge; and this knowledge itself is necessity.

*   *   *   *   *

222

What is left of art.—It is true, certain metaphysical presuppositions bestow much greater value upon art, for example when it is believed that the character is unalterable and that all characters and actions are a continual expression of the nature of the world: then the work of the artist becomes an image of the *everlastingly steadfast,* while with our conceptions the artist can bestow upon his images validity only for a time, because man as a whole has become and is changeable and even the individual man is not something firm and steadfast.—The same would be so in the case of another metaphysical presupposition: supposing our visible world were only appearance, as the metaphysicians assume, then art would come to stand quite close to the real world, for there would then be only too much similarity between the world of appearance and the illusory world of the artist; and the difference remaining would even elevate the significance of art above the significance of nature, because art would represent the uniform, the types and prototypes of nature.—These presuppositions are, however, false: after this knowledge what place still remains for art? Above all, it has taught us for thousands of years to look upon life in any of its forms with interest and pleasure, and to educate our sensibilities so far that we at last cry: "life, however it may be, is good!" This teaching imparted by art to take pleasure in life and to regard the human life as a piece of nature, as the object of regular evolution, without being too violently involved in it—this teaching has been absorbed into us, and it now reemerges as an almighty requirement of knowledge. One could give up art, but would not thereby relinquish the capacity one has learned from it: just as one has given up religion but not the enhancement of feeling and exaltations one has acquired from it. As the plastic arts and music are the measure of the wealth of feelings we have actually gained and obtained through religion, so if art disappeared the intensity and multifariousness of the joy in life it has implanted would still continue to demand satisfaction. The scientific man is the further evolution of the artistic.

*   *   *   *   *

292

Forward.—And with that, forward on the path of wisdom with a bold step and full of confidence! However you may be, serve yourself as your own source of experience! Throw off discontent with your nature, forgive yourself your own ego, for in any event you possess in yourself a ladder with a hundred rungs upon which you can climb to knowledge. The age in which with regret you feel yourself thrown counts you happy on account of this good fortune; it calls to you to participate in experiences that men of a later age will perhaps have to forgo. Do not underestimate the value of having been religious; discover all the reasons by virtue of which you have still had a genuine access to art. Can you not, precisely with aid of these experiences, follow with greater understanding tremendous stretches of the paths taken by earlier mankind? Is it not on precisely *this* soil, which you sometimes find so displeasing, the soil of unclear thinking, that many of the most splendid fruits of more ancient cultures grew up? One must have loved religion and art like mother and nurse—otherwise one cannot grow wise. But one must be able to see beyond them, outgrow them; if one remains under their spell, one does not understand them. You must likewise be on familiar terms with history and with playing the cautious game with the scales "on one hand—on the other hand." Turn back and trace the footsteps of mankind as it made its great sorrowful way through the desert of the past: thus you will learn in the surest way whither all later mankind can and may not go again. And by your desiring with all your strength to see ahead how the knot of the future is going to be tied, your own life will acquire the value of an instrument and means of knowledge. You have it in your hands to achieve the absorption of all you experience—your experiments, errors, faults, delusions, passions, your love and your hope—into your goal without remainder. This goal is yourself to become a necessary chain of rings of culture and from this necessity to recognize the necessity inherent in the course of culture in general. When your gaze has become strong enough to see to the bottom of the dark well of your nature and your knowledge, perhaps you will also behold in its mirror the distant constellations of future cultures. Do you believe that such a life with such a goal is too laborious, too much lacking in everything pleasant? Then you have not yet learned that no honey is sweeter than that of knowledge, or that the clouds of affliction hovering over you will yet have to serve you as udders from which you will milk the milk for your refreshment. Only when you grow old will you come to realize how you have given ear to the voice of nature, that nature which rules the whole world through joy: the same life that has its apex in old age also has its apex in wisdom, in that gentle sunshine of a constant spiritual joyousness; both of them, old age and wisdom, you will encounter on the *same* mountain ridge of life: so did nature will it. Then it is time, and no cause for anger, that the mists of death should approach. Towards the light—your last motion; a joyful shout of knowledge—your last sound.

*   *   *   *   *

Human, All Too Human
Volume Two

Part One
Assorted Opinions and Maxims[1] (1879)
(Excerpts)

1

To the disappointed of philosophy. — If you have hitherto believed that life was one of the highest value and now see yourselves disappointed, do you at once have to reduce it to the lowest possible price?

2

Spoiled. — It is possible to be spoiled even in regard to clarity of concepts: how repulsive one then finds it to traffic with the half-obscure, hazy, aspiring, portentous! How ludicrous and yet not at all cheering an effect is produced by their everlasting fluttering and snatching while being unable to fly or to capture!

*   *   *   *   *

284

The means to real peace. — No government nowadays admits that it maintains an army so as to satisfy occasional thirsts for conquest; the army is supposed to be for defence. That morality which sanctions self-protection is called upon to be its advocate. But that means to reserve morality to oneself and to accuse one's neighbour of immorality, since he has to be thought of as ready for aggression and conquest if our own state is obliged to take thought of means of self-defence; moreover, when our neighbour denies any thirst for aggression just as heatedly as our state does, and protests that he too maintains an army only for reasons of legitimate

---

[1]This collection of 408 aphorisms and reflections was originally published separately (under this title) in 1879, a year after the appearance of what subsequently became vol. 1 of *Human, All Too Human*, as an appendix and continuation of it. (See Nietzsche's preface to vol. 2 of this work in the concluding section of this text.)

self-defence, our declaration of why we require an army declares our neighbour a hypocrite and cunning criminal who would be only too happy to *pounce upon* a harmless and unprepared victim and subdue him without a struggle. This is how all states now confront one another: they presuppose an evil disposition in their neighbour and a benevolent disposition in themselves. This presupposition, however, is a piece of *inhumanity* as bad as, if not worse than, a war would be; indeed, fundamentally it already constitutes an invitation to and cause of wars, because, as aforesaid, it imputes immorality to one's neighbour and thereby seems to provoke hostility and hostile acts on his part. The doctrine of the army as a means of self-defence must be renounced just as completely as the thirst for conquest. And perhaps there will come a great day on which a nation distinguished for wars and victories and for the highest development of military discipline and thinking, and accustomed to making the heaviest sacrifices on behalf of these things, will cry of its own free will: *"we shall shatter the sword"* —and demolish its entire military machine down to its last foundations. *To disarm while being the best armed*, out of an *elevation* of sensibility—that is the means to *real* peace, which must always rest on a disposition for peace: whereas the so-called armed peace such as now parades about in every country is a disposition to fractiousness which trusts neither itself nor its neighbour and fails to lay down its arms half out of hatred, half out of fear. Better to perish than to hate and fear, and *twofold better to perish than to make oneself hated and feared*—this must one day become the supreme maxim of every individual state! —As is well known, our liberal representatives of the people lack the time to reflect on the nature of man: otherwise they would know that they labour in vain when they work for a "gradual reduction of the military burden." On the contrary, it is only when this kind of distress is at its greatest that the only kind of god that can help here will be closest at hand. The tree of the glory of war can be destroyed only at a single stroke, by a lightning-bolt: lightning, however, as you well know, comes out of a cloud and from on high. —

Part Two
The Wanderer and His Shadow[2] (1880)
(Excerpt)

350

The golden watchword.—Many chains have been laid upon man so that he should no longer behave like an animal: and he has in truth become gentler, more spiritual, more joyful, more reflective than any animal is. Now, however, he suffers from having worn his chains for so long, from being deprived for so long of clear air and free movement:—these chains, however, I shall never cease from repeating, are those heavy and pregnant errors contained in the conceptions of morality, religion and metaphysics. Only when this *sickness from one's chains* has also been overcome will the first great goal have truly been attained: the separation of man from the animals.—We stand now in the midst of our work of removing these chains, and we need to proceed with the greatest caution. Only the *ennobled man may be given freedom of spirit;* to him alone does *alleviation of life* draw near and salve his wounds; only he may say that he lives for the sake of *joy* and for the sake of no further goal; and in any other mouth his motto would be perilous: *Peace all around me and goodwill to all things closest to me.*—With this motto for individuals he recalls an ancient great and moving saying intended for *all* which has remained hanging over all mankind as a sign and motto by which anyone shall perish who inscribes it on his banner too soon—by which Christianity perished. The time has, it seems, still *not yet come* when *all* men are to share the experience of those shepherds who saw the heavens brighten above them and heard the words: "On earth peace, good will toward men."—It is still *the age of the individual.*

---

[2]Originally published separately (under this title) in 1880, as a second continuation of *Human, All Too Human.* The single excerpt from it included here is the final numbered reflection in it.

Daybreak (1881)
(Excerpts)

1

Supplemental rationality. —All things that live long are gradually so saturated with reason that their origin in unreason thereby becomes improbable. Does not almost every precise history of an origination impress our feelings as paradoxical and wantonly offensive? Does the good historian not, at bottom, constantly *contradict?*

2

Prejudice of the learned. —The learned judge correctly that people of all ages have believed they *know* what is good and evil, praise- and blameworthy. But it is a prejudice of the learned that *we now know better* than any other age.

*   *   *   *   *

9

Concept of morality of custom. —In comparison with the mode of life of whole millennia of mankind we present-day men live in a very immoral age: the power of custom is astonishingly enfeebled and the moral sense so rarefied and lofty it may be described as having more or less evaporated. That is why the fundamental insights into the origin of morality are so difficult for us latecomers, and even when we have acquired them we find it impossible to enunciate them, because they sound so uncouth or because they seem to slander morality! This is, for example, already the case with the *chief proposition:* morality is nothing other (therefore *no more!*) than obedience to customs, of whatever kind they may be; customs, however, are the *traditional* way of behaving and evaluating. In things in which no tradition commands there is no morality; and the less life is determined by tradition, the smaller the circle of morality. The free human being is immoral because in all things he is *determined* to depend upon himself and not upon a tradition: in all the original conditions of mankind, "evil" signifies the same as "individual," "free," "capricious," "unusual," "unforeseen," "incalculable." Judged by the standard of these conditions, if an action is performed *not* because tradition commands it but for other motives (because of its usefulness to the individual, for example), even indeed for precisely the motives which once founded the tradition, it is called immoral and is felt to be so by him who performed it: for it was not performed in obedience to tradition. What is tradition? A higher authority which one obeys, not because it commands what is *useful* to us, but because it *commands*. —What distinguishes this feeling in the presence of tradition from the feeling of fear in general? It is fear in the presence of a higher intellect which here commands, of an incomprehensible, indefinite power, of something more than personal—there is *superstition* in this fear. —Originally all education and care of health, marriage, cure of sickness, agriculture, war, speech and silence, traffic with one another and with the gods belonged within the domain of morality: they demanded one observe prescriptions *without thinking of oneself* as an individual. Originally, therefore, everything was custom, and whoever wanted to elevate himself above it had to become lawgiver and medicine man and a kind of demi-god: that is to say, he had to *make customs*—a dreadful, mortally dangerous thing! Who is the most moral man? *First*, he who obeys the law most frequently: who, like the Brahmin, bears a consciousness of the law with him everywhere and into every minute division of time, so that he is continually inventive in creating opportunities for obeying the law. *Then*, he who obeys it even in the most difficult cases. The most moral man is he who *sacrifices* the most to custom: what, however, are the greatest sacrifices? The way in which this question is answered determines the development of several divers kinds of morality; but the most important distinction remains that which divides the morality of *most frequent obedience* from that of the *most difficult* obedience. Let us not deceive ourselves as to the motivation of that morality which demands difficulty of obedience to custom as the mark of morality! Self-overcoming is demanded, *not* on account of the useful consequences it may have for the individual, but so that the hegemony of custom, tradition, shall be made evident in despite of the private desires and advantages of the individual: the individual is to sacrifice himself—that is the commandment of morality of custom. —Those moralists, on the other hand, who, following in the footsteps of Socrates, offer the *individual* a morality of self-control and temperance as a means to his own *advantage*, as his personal key to happiness, *are the exceptions*—and if it seems otherwise to us that is because we have been brought up in their after-effect: they all take a new path under the highest disapprobation of all advocates of morality of custom—they cut themselves off from the community, as immoral men, and are in the profoundest sense evil. Thus to a virtuous Roman of the old stamp every *Christian* who "considered first of all his *own* salvation" appeared— evil. —[. . .]

*   *   *   *   *

19

Morality makes stupid. —Custom represents the experiences of men of earlier times as to what they supposed useful and harmful—but the *sense for custom* (morality) applies, not to these experiences as such, but to the age, the sanctity, the indiscussability of the custom. And so this feeling is a hindrance to the acquisition of new experiences and the correction of customs: that is to say, morality is a hindrance to the creation of new and better customs: it makes stupid.

*   *   *   *   *

23

What we are most subtle in. —Because for many thousands of years it was thought that *things* (nature, tools, property of all kinds) were also alive and animate, with the power to cause harm and to evade human purposes, the feeling of impotence has been much greater and much more common among men than it would otherwise have been: for one needed to secure oneself against things, just as against men and animals, by force, constraint, flattering, treaties, sacrifices—and here is the origin of most superstitious practices, that is to say, of a considerable, *perhaps preponderant* and yet wasted and useless constituent of all the activity hitherto pursued by man! —But because the feeling of impotence and fear was in a state of almost continuous stimulation so strongly and for so long, the *feeling of power* has evolved to such a degree of *subtlety* that in this respect man is now a match for the most delicate gold-balance. It has become his strongest propensity; the means discovered for creating this feeling almost constitute the history of culture.

*   *   *   *   *

43

The many forces that now have to come together in the thinker. —To abstract oneself from sensory perception, to exalt oneself to contemplation of abstractions—that was at one time actually felt as *exaltation:* we can no longer quite enter into this feeling. To revel in pallid images of words and things, to sport with such invisible, inaudible, impalpable beings, was, out of contempt for the sensorily tangible, seductive and evil world, felt as a life in another *higher* world. "These *abstracta* are certainly not seductive, but they can offer us guidance!"—with that one lifted oneself upwards. It is not the content of these sportings of spirituality, it is they themselves which constituted "the higher life" in the prehistoric ages of science. Hence Plato's admiration for dialectics and his enthusiastic belief that dialectics necessarily pertained to the good, unsensory man. It is not only knowledge which has been discovered gradually and piece by piece, the means of knowing as such, the conditions and operations which precede knowledge in man, have been discovered gradually and piece by piece too. And each time the newly discovered operation or the novel condition seemed to be, not a means to knowledge, but in itself the content, goal and sum total of all that was worth knowing. The thinker needs imagination, self-uplifting, abstraction, desensualization, invention, presentiment, induction, dialectics, deduction, the critical faculty, the assemblage of material, the impersonal mode of thinking, contemplativeness and comprehensiveness, and not least justice and love for all that exists—but all these means to knowledge once counted individually in the history of the *vita contemplativa* as goals, and final goals, and bestowed on their inventors that feeling of happiness which appears in the human soul when it catches sight of a *final* goal.

44

Origin and significance. —Why is it that this thought comes back to me again and again and in ever more varied colours?—*that formerly*, when investigators of knowledge sought out the origin of things they always believed they would discover something of incalculable significance for all later action and judgment, that they always *presupposed*, indeed, that the *salvation* of man must depend on *insight into the origin of things:* but that now, on the contrary, the more we advance towards origins, the more our interest diminishes; indeed, that all the evaluations and "interestedness" we have implanted into things begin to lose their meaning the further we go back and the closer we approach the things themselves. *The more insight we possess into an origin the less significant does the origin appear:* while *what is nearest to us*, what is around us and in us, gradually begins to display colours and beauties and enigmas and riches of significance of which earlier mankind had not an inkling. Formerly, thinkers prowled around angrily like captive animals, watching the bars of their cages and leaping against them in order to smash them down: and *happy* seemed he who

through a gap in them believed he saw something of what was outside, of
what was distant and beyond.

45

A tragic ending for knowledge. —Of all the means of producing exaltation,
it has been human sacrifice which has at all times most exalted and
elevated man. And perhaps every other endeavour could still be thrown
down by *one* tremendous idea, so that it would achieve victory over the
most victorious—the idea of *self-sacrificing mankind.* But to whom should
mankind sacrifice itself? One could already take one's oath that, if ever
the constellation of this idea appears above the horizon, the knowledge of
truth would remain as the one tremendous goal commensurate with such
a sacrifice, because for this goal no sacrifice is too great. In the meantime,
the problem of the extent to which mankind can as a whole take steps
towards the advancement of knowledge has never yet been posed; not to
speak of what drive to knowledge could drive mankind to the point of
dying with the light of an anticipatory wisdom in its eyes. Perhaps, if one
day an alliance has been established with the inhabitants of other stars for
the purpose of knowledge, and knowledge has been communicated from
star to star for a few millennia: perhaps enthusiasm for knowledge may
then rise to such a high-water mark!

*   *   *   *   *

47

Words lie in our way!—Wherever primitive mankind set up a word, they
believed they had made a discovery. How different the truth is!—they
had touched on a problem, and by supposing they had *solved* it they had
created a hindrance to its solution. —Now with every piece of knowledge
one has to stumble over dead, petrified words, and one will sooner break
a leg than a word.

*   *   *   *   *

93

What is truth?—Who would not acquiesce in the *conclusion* the faithful
like to draw: "Science cannot be true, for it denies God. Consequently it
does not come from God; consequently it is not true—for God is the
truth." It is not the conclusion but the premise which contains the error:

how if God were *not* the truth and it were precisely this which is proved?
if he were the vanity, the lust for power, the impatience, the terror, the
enraptured and fearful delusion of men?

*   *   *   *   *

95

Historical refutation as the definitive refutation. — In former times, one
sought to prove that there is no God — today one indicates how the belief
that there is a God could *arise* and how this belief acquired its weight and
importance: a counter-proof that there is no God thereby becomes
superfluous. — When in former times one had refuted the "proofs of the
existence of God" put forward, there always remained the doubt whether
better proofs might not be adduced than those just refuted: in those days
atheists did not know how to make a clean sweep.

*   *   *   *   *

103

There are two kinds of deniers of morality. — "To deny morality" — this can
mean, *first:* to deny that the moral motives which men *claim* have inspired
their actions really have done so — it is thus the assertion that morality
consists of words and is among the coarser or more subtle deceptions
(especially self-deceptions) which men practise, and is perhaps so especially in precisely the case of those most famed for virtue. *Then* it can
mean: to deny that moral judgments are based on truths. Here it is
admitted that they really are motives of action, but that in this way it is
errors which, as the basis of all moral judgment, impel men to their moral
actions. This is *my* point of view: though I should be the last to deny that
in very many cases there is some ground for suspicion that the other point
of view — that is to say, the point of view of La Rochefoucauld and others
who think like him — may also be justified and in any event of great
general application. — Thus I deny morality as I deny alchemy, that is, I
deny their premises: but I do *not* deny that there have been alchemists
who believed in these premises and acted in accordance with them. — I
also deny immorality: *not* that countless people *feel* themselves to be
immoral, but there is any *true* reason so to feel. It goes without saying that
I do not deny — unless I am a fool — that many actions called immoral
ought to be avoided and resisted, or that many called moral ought to be
done and encouraged — but I think the one should be encouraged and the
other avoided *for other reasons than hitherto.* We have to *learn to think*

differently—in order at last, perhaps very late on, to attain even more: *to feel differently.*

*   *   *   *   *

106

Against the definitions of the goal of morality.—Everywhere today the goal of morality is defined in approximately the following way: it is the preservation and advancement of mankind; but this definition is an expression of the desire for a formula, and nothing more. Preservation *of what?* is the question one immediately has to ask. Advancement *to what?* Is the essential thing—the answer to this *of what?* and *to what?*—not precisely what is left out of the formula? So what, then, can it contribute to any teaching of what our duty is that is not already, if tacitly and thoughtlessly, regarded in advance as fixed? Can one deduce from it with certainty whether what is to be kept in view is the longest possible existence of mankind? Or the greatest possible deanimalisation of mankind? How different the means, that is to say the practical morality, would have to be in these two cases! Suppose one wanted to bestow on mankind the highest degree of rationality possible to it: this would certainly not guarantee it the longest period of duration possible to it! Or suppose one conceived the attainment of mankind's "highest happiness" as being the *to what* and *of what* of morality: would one mean the highest degree of happiness that individual men could gradually attain to? Or a—necessarily incalculable—average-happiness which could finally be attained to by all? And why should the way to that have to be morality? Has morality not, broadly speaking, opened up such an abundance of sources of displeasure that one could say, rather, that with every refinement of morals mankind has hitherto become *more discontented* with himself, his neighbour and the lot of his existence? Did the hitherto most moral man not entertain the belief that the only justified condition of mankind in the face of morality was the *profoundest misery?*

*   *   *   *   *

117

In prison.—My eyes, however strong or weak they may be, can see only a certain distance, and it is within the space encompassed by this distance that I live and move, the line of this horizon constitutes my immediate fate, in great things and small, from which I cannot escape. Around every being there is described a similar concentric circle, which has a mid-point and is peculiar to him. Our ears enclose us within a comparable circle, and so does our sense of touch. Now, it is by these horizons, within which each of us encloses his senses as if behind prison walls, that we *measure* the world, we say that this is near and that far, this is big and that small, this is hard and that soft: this measuring we call sensation—and it is all of it an error! According to the average quantity of experiences and excitations possible to us at any particular point of time one measures one's life as being short or long, poor or rich, full or empty: and according to the average human life one measures that of all other creatures—all of it an error! If our eyes were a hundredfold sharper, man would appear to us tremendously tall; it is possible, indeed, to imagine organs by virtue of which he would be felt as immeasurable. On the other hand, organs could be so constituted that whole solar systems were viewed contracted and packed together like a single cell: and to beings of an opposite constitution a cell of the human body could present itself, in motion, construction and harmony, as a solar system. The habits of our senses have woven us into lies and deception of sensation: these again are the basis of all our judgments and "knowledge"—there is absolutely no escape, no backway or bypath into the *real world!* We sit within our net, we spiders, and whatever we may catch in it, we can catch nothing at all except that which allows itself to be caught in precisely *our* net.

*   *   *   *   *

134

To what extent one has to guard against pity. —Pity *(Mitleiden),* insofar as it really causes suffering *(Leiden)*—and this is here our only point of view—is a weakness, like every losing of oneself through a *harmful* affect. It *increases* the amount of suffering in the world: if suffering is here and there indirectly reduced or removed as a consequence of pity, this occasional and on the whole insignificant consequence must not be employed to justify its essential nature, which is, as I have said, harmful. Supposing it was dominant even for a single day, mankind would immediately perish of it. In itself, it has as little a good character as any other drives: only where it is demanded and commended—and this happens where one fails to grasp that it is harmful but discovers a *source of pleasure* in it—does a good conscience adhere to it, only then does one gladly succumb to it and not hesitate to demonstrate it. Under other conditions, where the fact of its harmfulness is grasped, it counts as weakness: or, as with the Greeks, as a morbid recurring affect the perilousness of which can be removed by periodical deliberate discharge. —He who for a period of time made the experiment of intentionally pursuing occasions for pity in his everyday life and set before his soul all the misery available to him in his surroundings would inevitably grow sick and melancholic. He, however, whose desire it is to serve mankind as a physician *in any sense whatever* will have to be very much on his guard against that sensation—it will paralyse him at every decisive moment and apply a ligature to his knowledge and his subtle helpful hand.

Joyful Wisdom (or The Gay Science) Books One to Four (1882)
(Excerpts)

Book One

1

The Teachers of the Object of Existence. —Whether I look with a good or an evil eye upon men, I find them always at one problem, each and all of them: to do that which conduces to the conservation of the human species. And certainly not out of any sentiment of love for this species, but simply because nothing in them is older, stronger, more inexorable and more unconquerable than that instinct, —because it is precisely *the essence* of our race and herd. Although we are accustomed readily enough, with our usual short-sightedness, to separate our neighbours precisely into useful and hurtful, into good and evil men, yet when we make a general calculation, and reflect longer on the whole question, we become distrustful of this defining and separating, and finally leave it alone. Even the most hurtful man is still perhaps, in respect to the conservation of the race, the most useful of all; for he conserves in himself, or by his effect on others, impulses without which mankind might long ago have languished or decayed. Hatred, delight in mischief, rapacity and ambition, and whatever else is called evil—belong to the marvellous economy of the conservation of the race; to be sure a costly, lavish, and on the whole very foolish economy: —which has, however, hitherto preserved our race, *as is demonstrated to us.* I no longer know, my dear fellow-man and neighbour, if thou *canst* at all live to the disadvantage of the race, and therefore, "unreasonably" and "badly"; that which could have injured the race has perhaps died out many millenniums ago, and now belongs to the things which are no longer possible even to God. Indulge thy best or thy worst desires, and above all, go to wreck!—in either case thou art still probably the furtherer and benefactor of mankind in some way or other, and in that respect thou mayest have thy panegyrists—and similarly thy mockers! But thou wilt never find him who would be quite qualified to mock at thee, the individual, at thy best, who could bring home to thy conscience its limitless, buzzing and croaking wretchedness so as to be in accord with truth! To laugh at oneself as one would have to laugh in order to laugh *out of the veriest truth,* —to do this, the best have not hitherto had enough of the sense of truth, and the most endowed have had far too little genius! There is perhaps still a future even for laughter! When the maxim, "The race is all, the individual is nothing,"—has incorporated itself in humanity, and when access stands open to every one at all times to this ultimate emancipation and irresponsibility.—Perhaps then laughter will have united with wisdom, perhaps then there will be only "joyful wisdom." Meanwhile, however, it is quite otherwise, meanwhile the comedy of existence has not yet "become conscious" of itself, meanwhile it is still the period of tragedy, the period of morals and religions. What does the ever new appearing of founders of morals and religions, of instigators of struggles for moral valuations, of teachers of remorse of conscience and religious war, imply? What do these heroes on this stage imply? For they have hitherto been the heroes of it, and all else, though solely visible for the time being, and too close to one, has served only as preparation for these heroes, whether as machinery and coulisse, or in the rôle of confidants and valets. (The poets, for example, have always been the valets of some morality or other.)—It is obvious of itself that these tragedians also work in the interest of the *race*, though they may believe that they work in the interest of God, and as emissaries of God. They also further the life of the species, *in that they further the belief in life.* "It is worth while to live"—each of them calls out,—"there is something of importance in this life; life has something behind it and under it; take care!" That impulse, which rules equally in the noblest and the ignoblest, the impulse to the conservation of the species, breaks forth from time to time as reason and passion of spirit; it has then a brilliant train of motives about it, and tries with all its power to make us forget that fundamentally it is just impulse, instinct, folly and baselessness. Life *should* be loved, *for . . . !* Man *should* benefit himself and his neighbour, *for . . . !* And whatever all these *shoulds* and *fors* imply, and may imply in future! In order that that which necessarily and always happens of itself and without design, may henceforth appear to be done by design, and may appeal to men as reason and ultimate command,—for that purpose the ethiculturist comes forward as the teacher of design in existence; for that purpose he devises a second and different existence, and by means of this new mechanism he lifts the old common existence off its old common hinges. No! he does not at all want us to *laugh* at existence, nor even at ourselves—nor at himself; to him an individual is always an individual, something first and last and immense, to him there are no species, no sums, no noughts. However foolish and fanatical his inventions and valuations may be, however much he may misunderstand the course of nature and deny its conditions—and all systems of ethics hitherto have been foolish and anti-natural to such a degree that mankind would have been ruined by any one of them had it got the upper hand,—at any rate, every time that "the hero" came upon the stage something new was attained: the frightful counterpart of laughter, the profound convulsion of many individuals at the thought, "Yes, it is worth while to live! yes, I am worthy to live!"—life, and thou, and I, and all of us together became for a while *interesting* to ourselves once more.—It is not to be denied that hitherto laughter and reason and nature have *in the long run* got the upper hand of all the great teachers of design: in the end the short tragedy always passed over once more into the eternal comedy of existence; and the "waves of innumerable laughters"—to use the expression of Æschylus—must also in the end beat over the greatest of these tragedies. But with all this corrective laughter, human nature has on the whole been changed by the ever new appearance of those teachers of the design of existence,—human nature has now an additional requirement, the very requirement of the ever new appearance of such teachers and doctrines of "design." Man has gradually become a visionary animal, who has to fulfil one more condition of existence than the other animals: man *must* from time to time believe that he knows *why* he exists; his species cannot flourish without periodically confiding in life! Without the belief in *reason in life!* And always from time to time will the human race decree anew that "there is something which really may not be laughed at." And the most clairvoyant philanthropist will add that "not only laughing and joyful wisdom, but also the tragic with all its sublime irrationality, counts among the means and necessities for the conservation of the race!"—And consequently! Consequently! Consequently! Do you understand me, oh my brothers? Do you understand this new law of ebb and flow? We also shall have our time!

2

The Intellectual Conscience.—I have always the same experience over again, and always make a new effort against it; for although it is evident to me I do not want to believe it: *in the greater number of men the intellectual conscience is lacking;* indeed, it would often seem to me that in demanding such a thing, one is as solitary in the largest cities as in the desert. Everyone looks at you with strange eyes, and continues to make use of his scales, calling this good and that bad; and no one blushes for shame when you remark that these weights are not the full amount,—there is also no indignation against you; perhaps they laugh at your doubt. I mean to say that *the greater number of people* do not find it contemptible to believe this or that, and live according to it, *without* having been previously aware of the ultimate and surest reasons for and against it, and without even giving themselves any trouble about such reasons afterwards,—the most gifted men and the noblest women still belong to this "greater number." But what is kind-heartedness, refinement and genius to me, if he who has these virtues harbours indolent sentiments in belief and judgment, if *the longing for certainty* does not rule in him, as his innermost desire and profoundest need—as that which separates higher from lower men!

*   *   *   *   *

4

That which Preserves the Species. —The strongest and most evil spirits have hitherto advanced mankind the most: they always rekindled the sleeping passions—all orderly arranged society lulls the passions to sleep; they always reawakened the sense of comparison, of contradiction, of delight in the new, the adventurous, the untried; they compelled men to set opinion against opinion, ideal plan against ideal plan. By means of arms, by up-setting boundary-stones, by violations of piety most of all: but also by new religions and morals! The same kind of "wickedness" is in every teacher and preacher of the *new*—which makes a conqueror infamous, although it expresses itself more refinedly, and does not immediately set the muscles in motion (and just on that account does not make so infamous!). The new, however, is under all circumstances the *evil*, as that which wants to conquer, which tries to upset the old boundary-stones and the old piety; only the old is the good! The good men of every age are those who go to the roots of the old thoughts and bear fruit with them, the agriculturists of the spirit. But every soil becomes finally exhausted, and the plough-share of evil must always come once more. —There is at present a fundamentally erroneous theory of morals which is much celebrated, especially in England: according to it the judgments "good" and "evil" are the accumulation of the experiences of that which is "expedient" and "inexpedient"; according to this theory, that which is called good is conservative of the species, what is called evil, however, is detrimental to it. But in reality the evil impulses are just in as high a degree expedient, indispensable, and conservative of the species as the good: — only, their function is different.

*   *   *   *   *

54

The Consciousness of Appearance. —How wonderfully and novelly, and at the same time how awfully and ironically, do I feel myself situated with respect to collective existence, with my knowledge! I have *discovered* for myself that the old humanity and animality, yea, the collective primeval age, and the past of all sentient being, continues to meditate, love, hate, and reason in me, — I have suddenly awoke in the midst of this dream, but merely to the consciousness that I just dream, and that I *must* dream on in order not to perish; just as the sleep-walker must dream on in order not to tumble down. What is it that is now "appearance" to me! Verily, not the antithesis of any kind of essence, — what knowledge can I assert of any kind of essence whatsoever, except merely the predicates of its appearance! Verily not a dead mask which one could put upon an unknown X, and which to be sure one could also remove! Appearance is for me the operating and living thing itself; which goes so far in its self-mockery as to make me feel that here there is appearance, and Will o' the Wisp, and spirit-dance, and nothing more, — that among all these dreamers, I also, the "thinker," dance my dance, that the thinker is a means of prolonging further the terrestrial dance, and in so far is one of the masters of ceremony of existence, and that the sublime consistency and connectedness of all branches of knowledge is perhaps, and will perhaps, be the best means for *maintaining* the universality of the dreaming, the complete, mutual understandability of all those dreamers, and thereby *the duration of the dream.*

*   *   *   *   *

Book Two

57

To the Realists. — Ye sober beings, who feel yourselves armed against passion and fantasy, and would gladly make a pride and an ornament out of your emptiness, ye call yourselves realists, and give to understand that the world is actually constituted as it appears to you; before you alone reality stands unveiled, and ye yourselves would perhaps be the best part of it, — oh, ye dear images of Sais![1] But are not ye also in your unveiled condition still extremely passionate and dusky beings compared with the fish, and still all too like an enamoured artist? — and what is "reality" to an enamoured artist! Ye still carry about with you the valuations of things which had their origin in the passions and infatuations of earlier centuries! There is still a secret and ineffaceable drunkenness embodied in your sobriety! Your love of "reality," for example — oh, that is an old, primitive "love"! In every feeling, in every sense-impression, there is a portion of this old love: and similarly also some kind of fantasy, prejudice, irrationality, ignorance, fear,

[1] A reference to Friedrich Schiller's ballad "The Veiled Image at Sais."

and whatever else has become mingled and woven into it. There is that mountain! There is that cloud! What is "real" in them? Remove the phantasm and the whole human *element* therefrom, ye sober ones! Yes, if ye could do *that!* If ye could forget your origin, your past, your preparatory schooling, — your whole history as man and beast! There is no "reality" for us — nor for you either, ye sober ones, — we are far from being so alien to one another as ye suppose; and perhaps our good-will to get beyond drunkenness is just as respectable as your belief that ye are altogether *incapable* of drunkenness.

58

Only as Creators! — It has caused me the greatest trouble, and for ever causes me the greatest trouble, to perceive that unspeakably more depends upon *what things are called*, than on what they are. The reputation, the name and appearance, the importance, the usual measure and weight of things — each being in origin most frequently an error and arbitrariness thrown over the things like a garment, and quite alien to their essence and even to their exterior — have gradually, by the belief therein and its continuous growth from generation to generation, grown as it were on-and-into things and become their very body; the appearance at the very beginning becomes almost always the essence in the end, and *operates* as the essence! What a fool he would be who would think it enough to refer here to this origin and this nebulous veil of illusion, in order to *annihilate* that which virtually passes for the world — namely, so-called "reality"! It is only as creators that we can annihilate! — But let us not forget this: it suffices to create new names and valuations and probabilities, in order in the long run to create new "things."

*   *   *   *   *

Book Three

108

New Struggles. — After Buddha was dead people showed his shadow for centuries afterwards in a cave, — an immense frightful shadow. God is dead: but as the human race is constituted, there will perhaps be caves for millenniums yet, in which people will show his shadow. —And we —we have still to overcome his shadow!²

109

Let us be on our Guard. —Let us be on our guard against thinking that the world is a living being. Where could it extend itself? What could it nourish itself with? How could it grow and increase? We know tolerably well what the organic is; and we are to reinterpret the emphatically derivative, tardy, rare and accidental, which we only perceive on the crust of the earth, into the essential, universal and eternal, as those do who call the universe an organism? That disgusts me. Let us now be on our guard against believing that the universe is a machine; it is assuredly not constructed with a view to *one* end; we invest it with far too high an honour with the word "machine." Let us be on our guard against supposing that anything so methodical as the cyclic motions of our neighbouring stars obtains generally and throughout the universe; indeed a glance at the Milky Way induces doubt as to whether there are not many cruder and more contradictory motions there, and even stars with continuous, rectilinearly gravitating orbits, and the like. The astral arrangement in which we live is an exception; this arrangement, and the relatively long durability which is determined by it, has again made possible the exception of exceptions, the formation of organic life. The general character of the world, on the other hand, is to all eternity chaos; not by the absence of necessity, but in the sense of the absence of order, structure, form, beauty, wisdom, and whatever else our aesthetic humanities are called. Judged by our reason, the unlucky casts are far oftenest the rule, the exceptions are not the secret purpose; and the whole musical box repeats eternally its air, which can never be called a melody, —and finally the very expression, "unlucky cast" is already an anthropomorphising which involves blame. But how could we presume to blame or praise the universe! Let us be on our guard against ascribing to it heartlessness and unreason, or their opposites; it is neither perfect, nor beautiful, nor noble; nor does it seek to be anything of the kind, it does not at all attempt to imitate man! It is altogether unaffected by our aesthetic and moral judgments! Neither has it any self-preservative instinct, nor instinct at all; it also knows no law. Let us be on our guard against saying that there are laws in nature. There are only necessities: there is no one who commands, no one who obeys, no one who transgresses. When you know that there is no design, you know also that there is no chance: for it is only where there is a world of design that

²This is the first time Nietzsche uses the phrase "God is dead."

the word "chance" has a meaning. Let us be on our guard against saying that death is contrary to life. The living being is only a species of dead being, and a very rare species. — Let us be on our guard against thinking that the world eternally creates the new. There are no eternally enduring substances; matter is just another such error as the God of the Eleatics. But when shall we be at an end with our foresight and precaution! When will all these shadows of God cease to obscure us? When shall we have nature entirely undeified! When shall we be permitted to *naturalise* ourselves by means of the pure, newly discovered, newly redeemed nature?

110

Origin of Knowledge. — Throughout immense stretches of time the intellect produced nothing but errors; some of them proved to be useful and preservative of the species: he who fell in with them, or inherited them, waged the battle for himself and his offspring with better success. Those erroneous articles of faith which were successively transmitted by inheritance, and have finally become almost the property and stock of the human species, are, for example, the following: — that there are enduring things, that there are equal things, that there are things, substances, and bodies, that a thing is what it appears, that our will is free, that what is good for me is also good absolutely. It was only very late that the deniers and doubters of such propositions came forward, — it was only very late that truth made its appearance as the most impotent form of knowledge. It seemed as if it were impossible to get along with truth, our organism was adapted for the very opposite; all its higher functions, the perceptions of the senses, and in general every kind of sensation, co-operated with those primevally embodied, fundamental errors. Moreover, those propositions became the very standards of knowledge according to which the "true" and the "false" were determined — throughout the whole domain of pure logic. The *strength* of conceptions does not, therefore, depend on their degree of truth, but on their antiquity, their embodiment, their character as conditions of life. Where life and knowledge seemed to conflict, there has never been serious contention; denial and doubt have there been regarded as madness. The exceptional thinkers like the Eleatics, who, in spite of this, advanced and maintained the antitheses of the natural errors, believed that it was possible also *to live* these counterparts: it was they who devised the sage as the man of immutability, impersonality and universality of intuition, as one and all at the same time, with a special faculty for that reverse kind of knowledge; they were of the belief that their knowledge was at the same time the principle of *life*. To be able to affirm all this, however, they had to *deceive* themselves concerning their own condition: they had to attribute to themselves impersonality and unchanging permanence, they had to mistake the nature of the philosophic individual, deny the force of the impulses in cognition, and conceive of reason generally as an entirely free and self-originating activity; they kept their eyes shut to the fact that they also had reached their doctrines in contradiction to valid methods, or through their longing for repose or for exclusive possession or for domination. The subtler development of sincerity and of scepticism finally made these men impossible; their life also, and their judgments, turned out to be dependent on the primeval impulses and fundamental errors of all sentient being. — The subtler sincerity and scepticism arose wherever two antithetical maxims appeared to be *applicable* to life, because both of them were compatible with the fundamental errors; where, therefore, there could be contention concerning a higher or lower degree of *utility* for life; and likewise where new maxims proved to be, not necessarily useful, but at least not injurious, as expressions of an intellectual impulse to play a game that was like all games innocent and happy. The human brain was gradually filled with such judgments and convictions; and in this tangled skein there arose ferment, strife and lust for power. Not only utility and delight, but every kind of impulse took part in the struggle for "truths": the intellectual struggle became a business, an attraction, a calling, a duty, an honour—: cognizing and striving for the true finally arranged themselves as needs among other needs. From that moment, not only belief and conviction, but also examination, denial, distrust and contradiction became *forces;* all "evil" instincts were subordinated to knowledge, were placed in its service, and acquired the prestige of the permitted, the honoured, the useful, and finally the appearance and innocence of the *good.* Knowledge thus became a portion of life itself, and as life it became a continually growing power: until finally the cognitions and those primeval, fundamental errors clashed with each other, both as life, both as power, both in the same man. The thinker is now the being in whom the impulse to truth and those life-preserving errors wage their first conflict, now that the impulse to truth has also *proved* itself to be a life-preserving power. In comparison with the importance of this conflict everything else is indifferent; the final question concerning the conditions of life is here raised, and the first attempt is here made to answer it by experiment. How far is truth susceptible of embodiment? — that is the question, that is the experiment.

111

Origin of the Logical. — Where has logic originated in men's heads? Undoubtedly out of the illogical, the domain of which must originally have been immense. But numberless beings who reasoned otherwise than we do at present, perished; albeit that they may have come nearer to truth than we! Whoever, for example, could not discern the "like" often enough with regard to food, and with regard to animals dangerous to him, whoever, therefore, deduced too slowly, or was too circumspect in his deductions, had smaller probability of survival than he who in all similar cases immediately divined the equality. The preponderating inclination, however, to deal with the similar as the equal—an illogical inclination, for there is nothing equal in itself—first created the whole basis of logic. It was just so (in order that the conception of substance should originate, this being indispensable to logic, although in the strictest sense nothing actual corresponds to it) that for a long period the changing process in things had to be overlooked, and remain unperceived; the beings not seeing correctly had an advantage over those who saw everything "in flux." In itself every high degree of circumspection in conclusions, every sceptical inclination, is a great danger to life. No living being might have been preserved unless the contrary inclination—to affirm rather than suspend judgment, to mistake and fabricate rather than wait, to assent rather than deny, to decide rather than be in the right—had been cultivated with extraordinary assiduity.—The course of logical thought and reasoning in our modern brain corresponds to a process and struggle of impulses, which singly and in themselves are all very illogical and unjust; we experience usually only the result of the struggle, so rapidly and secretly does this primitive mechanism now operate in us.

112

Cause and Effect.—We say it is "explanation"; but it is only in "description" that we are in advance of the older stages of knowledge and science. We describe better,—we explain just as little as our predecessors. We have discovered a manifold succession where the naïve man and investigator of older cultures saw only two things, "cause" and "effect," as it was said; we have perfected the conception of becoming, but have not got a knowledge of what is above and behind the conception. The series of "causes" stands before us much more complete in every case; we conclude that this and that must first precede in order that that other may follow—but we have not *grasped* anything thereby. The peculiarity, for example, in every chemical process seems a "miracle," the same as before, just like all locomotion; nobody has "explained" impulse. How could we ever explain! We operate only with things which do not exist, with lines, surfaces, bodies, atoms, divisible times, divisible spaces—how can explanation ever be possible when we first make everything a *conception*, our conception! It is sufficient to regard science as the exactest humanising of things that is possible; we always learn to describe ourselves more accurately by describing things and their successions. Cause and effect: there is probably never any such duality; in fact there is a *continuum* before us, from which we isolate a few portions;—just as we always observe a motion as isolated points, and therefore do not properly see it, but infer it. The abruptness with which many effects take place leads us into error; it is however only an abruptness for us. There is an infinite multitude of processes in that abrupt moment which escape us. An intellect which could see cause and effect as a *continuum*, which could see the flux of events not according to our mode of perception, as things arbitrarily separated and broken—would throw aside the conception of cause and effect, and would deny all conditionality.

113

The Theory of Poisons.—So many things have to be united in order that scientific thinking may arise, and all the necessary powers must have been devised, exercised, and fostered singly! In their isolation, however, they have very often had quite a different effect than at present, when they are confined within the limits of scientific thinking and kept mutually in check:—they have operated as poisons; for example, the doubting impulse, the denying impulse, the waiting impulse, the collecting impulse, the disintegrating impulse. Many hecatombs of men were sacrificed ere these impulses learned to understand their juxtaposition and regard themselves as functions of one organising force in one man! And how far are we still from the point at which the artistic powers and the practical wisdom of life shall co-operate with scientific thinking, so that a higher organic system may be formed, in relation to which the scholar, the physician, the artist, and the lawgiver, as we know them at present, will seem sorry antiquities!

*   *   *   *   *

115

The Four Errors.—Man has been reared by his errors: firstly, he saw himself always imperfect; secondly, he attributed to himself imaginary qualities; thirdly, he felt himself in a false position in relation to the animals and nature; fourthly, he always devised new tables of values, and accepted them for a time as eternal and unconditioned, so that at one time this, and at another time that human impulse or state stood first, and was ennobled in consequence. When one has deducted the effect of these four errors, one has also deducted humanity, humaneness, and "human dignity."

116

Herd-Instinct.—Wherever we meet with a morality we find a valuation and order of rank of the human impulses and activities. These valuations and orders of rank are always the expression of the needs of a community or herd: that which is in the first place to *its* advantage—and in the second place and third place—is also the authoritative standard for the worth of every individual. By morality the individual is taught to become a function of the herd, and to ascribe to himself value only as a function. As the conditions for the maintenance of one community have been very different from those of another community, there have been very different moralities; and in respect to the future essential transformations of herds and communities, states and societies, one can prophesy that there will still be very divergent moralities. Morality is the herd-instinct in the individual.

*   *   *   *   *

120

Health of the Soul.—The favourite medico-moral formula (whose originator was Ariston of Chios), "Virtue is the health of the soul," would, for all practical purposes, have to be altered to this: "Thy virtue is the health of thy soul." For there is no such thing as health in itself, and all attempts to define a thing in that way have lamentably failed. It is necessary to know thy aim, thy horizon, thy powers, thy impulses, thy errors, and especially the ideals and fantasies of thy soul, in order to determine *what* health implies even for thy *body.* There are consequently innumerable kinds of physical health; and the more one again permits the unique and unparalleled to raise its head, the more one unlearns the dogma of the "Equality of men," so much the more also must the conception of a normal health, together with a normal diet and a normal course of disease, be abrogated by our physicians. And then only would it be time to turn our thoughts to the health and disease of the *soul,* and make the special virtue of everyone consist in its health; but, to be sure, what appeared as health in one person might appear as the contrary of health in another. In the end the great question might still remain open:—Whether we could *do without* sickness for the development of our virtue, and whether our thirst for knowledge and self-knowledge would not especially need the sickly soul as well as the sound one; in short, whether the mere will to health is not a prejudice, a cowardice, and perhaps an instance of the subtlest barbarism and unprogressiveness?

121

Life no Argument. —We have arranged for ourselves a world in which we can live—by the postulating of bodies, lines, surfaces, causes and effects, motion and rest, form and content: without these articles of faith no one could manage to live at present! But for all that they are still unproved. Life is no argument; error might be among the conditions of life.

*   *   *   *   *

123

Knowledge more than a Means. —Also *without* this passion—I refer to the passion for knowledge—science would be furthered: science has hitherto increased and grown up without it. The good faith in science, the prejudice in its favour, by which States are at present dominated (it was even the Church formerly), rests fundamentally on the fact that the absolute inclination and impulse has so rarely revealed itself in it, and that science is regarded *not* as a passion, but as a condition and an "ethos." Indeed, *amour-plaisir*[3] of knowledge (curiosity) often enough suffices, *amour-vanité*[4] suffices, and habituation to it, with the afterthought of obtaining honour and bread; it even suffices for many that they do not know what to do with a surplus of leisure, except to continue reading, collecting, arranging, observing and narrating; their "scientific impulse" is their ennui. Pope Leo X. once (in the brief to Beroaldus) sang the praise of science; he designated it as the finest ornament and the greatest pride of our life, a noble employment in happiness and in misfortune; "without it," he says finally, "all human undertakings would be without a firm basis,—even with it they are still sufficiently mutable and insecure!" But this rather sceptical Pope, like all other ecclesiastical panegyrists of science, suppressed his ultimate judgment concerning it. If one may deduce from his words what is remarkable enough for such a lover of art, that he places science above art, it is after all, however, only from politeness that he omits to speak of that which he places high above all science: the "revealed truth," and the "eternal salvation of the soul,"—what are ornament, pride, entertainment and security of life to him, in comparison thereto? "Science is something of secondary rank, nothing ultimate or unconditioned, no object of passion"—this judgment was kept back in Leo's soul: the truly Christian judgment concerning science! In antiquity its dignity and appreciation were lessened by the fact that, even among its most eager disciples, the striving after *virtue* stood foremost, and that

[3]Pleasure-love.
[4]Vanity-love.

people thought they had given the highest praise to knowledge when they celebrated it as the best means to virtue. It is something new in history that knowledge claims to be more than a means.

*   *   *   *   *

125

The Madman. — Have you ever heard of the madman who on a bright morning lighted a lantern and ran to the market-place calling out unceasingly: "I seek God! I seek God!" — As there were many people standing about who did not believe in God, he caused a great deal of amusement. Why! is he lost? said one. Has he strayed away like a child? said another. Or does he keep himself hidden? Is he afraid of us? Has he taken a seavoyage? Has he emigrated? — the people cried out laughingly, all in a hubbub. The insane man jumped into their midst and transfixed them with his glances. "Where is God gone?" he called out. "I mean to tell you! *We have killed him,* — you and I! We are all his murderers! But how have we done it? How were we able to drink up the sea? Who gave us the sponge to wipe away the whole horizon? What did we do when we loosened this earth from its sun? Whither does it now move? Whither do we move? Away from all suns? Do we not dash on unceasingly? Backwards, sideways, forewards, in all directions? Is there still an above and below? Do we not stray, as through infinite nothingness? Does not empty space breathe upon us? Has it not become colder? Does not night come on continually, darker and darker? Shall we not have to light lanterns in the morning? Do we not hear the noise of the grave-diggers who are burying God? Do we not smell the divine putrefaction? — for even Gods putrefy! God is dead! God remains dead! And we have killed him! How shall we console ourselves, the most murderous of all murderers? The holiest and the mightiest that the world has hitherto possessed, has bled to death under our knife, — who will wipe the blood from us? With what water could we cleanse ourselves? What lustrums, what sacred games shall we have to devise? Is not the magnitude of this deed too great for us? Shall we not ourselves have to become Gods, merely to seem worthy of it? There never was a greater event, — and on account of it, all who are born after us belong to a higher history than any history hitherto!" — Here the madman was silent and looked again at his hearers; they also were silent and looked at him in surprise. At last he threw his lantern on the ground, so that it broke in pieces and was extinguished. "I come too early," he then said, "I am not yet at the right time. This prodigious event is still on its way, and is travelling, — it has not yet reached men's ears. Lightning and thunder need time, the light of the stars needs time, deeds need time, even after they are done, to be seen and heard. This deed is as yet further from them than the furthest star, —*and yet they have done it!*"—It is further stated that the madman made his way into different churches on the same day, and there intoned his *Requiem aeternam deo.* When led out and called to account, he always gave the reply: "What are these churches now, if they are not the tombs and monuments of God?"—

126

Mystical Explanations. —Mystical explanations are regarded as profound; the truth is that they do not even go the length of being superficial.

*   *   *   *   *

Book Four

333

What does Knowing Mean?—*Non ridere, non lugere, neque detestari, sed intelligere!*[5]—says Spinoza, so simply and sublimely, as is his wont. Nevertheless, what else is this *intelligere* ultimately, but just the form in which the three other things become perceptible to us all at once? A result of the diverging and opposite impulses of desiring to deride, lament and execrate? Before knowledge is possible each of these impulses must first have brought forward its one-sided view of the object or event. The struggle of these one-sided views occurs afterwards, and out of it there occasionally arises a compromise, a pacification, a recognition of rights on all three sides, a sort of justice and agreement: for in virtue of the justice and agreement all those impulses can maintain themselves in existence and retain their mutual rights. We, to whose consciousness only the closing reconciliation scenes and final settling of accounts of these long processes manifest themselves, think on that account that *intelligere* is something conciliating, just and good, something essentially antithetical to the impulses; whereas it is only *a certain relation of the impulses to one another.* For a very long time conscious thinking was regarded as the only thinking: it is now only that the truth dawns upon us that the greater part of our intellectual activity goes on unconsciously and unfelt by us; I believe, however, that the impulses which are here in mutual conflict understand rightly how to make themselves felt by *one another,* and how to cause

[5]"Not to laugh, not to lament, nor to detest, but rather to understand." Benedict de Spinoza, *Tractatus Politicus* (1670), Part I, Section 4.

pain:—the violent, sudden exhaustion which overtakes all thinkers, may have its origin here (it is the exhaustion of the battle-field). Aye, perhaps in our struggling interior there is much concealed *heroism*, but certainly nothing divine, or eternally-reposing-in-itself, as Spinoza supposed. *Conscious* thinking, and especially that of the philosopher, is the weakest, and on that account also the relatively mildest and quietest mode of thinking: and thus it is precisely the philosopher who is most easily misled concerning the nature of knowledge.

334

One must Learn to Love.—This is our experience in music: we must first *learn* in general *to hear*, to hear fully, and to distinguish a theme or a melody, we have to isolate and limit it as a life by itself; then we need to exercise effort and good-will in order *to endure* it in spite of its strangeness, we need patience towards its aspect and expression, and indulgence towards what is odd in it:—in the end there comes a moment when we are *accustomed* to it, when we expect it, when it dawns upon us that we should miss it if it were lacking; and then it goes on to exercise its spell and charm more and more, and does not cease until we have become its humble and enraptured lovers, who want it, and want it again, and ask for nothing better from the world.—It is thus with us, however, not only in music: it is precisely thus that we have *learned to love* everything that we love. We are always finally recompensed for our good-will, our patience, reasonableness and gentleness towards what is unfamiliar, by the unfamiliar slowly throwing off its veil and presenting itself to us as a new, ineffable beauty:—that is its *thanks* for our hospitality. He also who loves himself must have learned it in this way: there is no other way. Love also has to be learned.

335

Cheers for Physics!—How many men are there who know how to observe? And among the few who do know,—how many observe themselves? "Everyone is furthest from himself"—all the "triers of the reins" know that to their discomfort; and the saying, "Know thyself," in the mouth of a God and spoken to man, is almost a mockery. But that the case of self-observation is so desperate, is attested best of all by the manner in which *almost everybody* talks of the nature of a moral action, that prompt, willing, convinced, loquacious manner, with its look, its smile, and its pleasing eagerness! Everyone seems inclined to say to you: "Why, my dear Sir, that is precisely *my* affair! You address yourself with your question to him who *is authorised* to answer, for I happen to be wiser with regard to this matter than in anything else. Therefore, when a man decides that *'this is right,'* when he accordingly concludes that *'it must therefore be done,'* and thereupon *does* what he has thus recognised as right and designated as necessary—then the nature of his action is *moral!''* But, my friend, you are talking to me about three actions instead of one: your deciding, for instance, that "this is right," is also an action,—could one not judge either morally or immorally? *Why* do you regard this, and just this, as right? "Because my conscience tells me so; conscience never speaks immorally, indeed it determines in the first place what shall be moral!"—But why do you *listen* to the voice of your conscience? And in how far are you justified in regarding such a judgment as true and infallible? This *belief*—is there no further conscience for it? Do you know nothing of an intellectual conscience? A conscience behind your "conscience"? Your decision, "this is right," has a previous history in your impulses, your likes and dislikes, your experiences and non-experiences; *"how* has it originated?" you must ask, and afterwards the further question: *"what* really impels me to give ear to it?" You can listen to its command like a brave soldier who hears the command of his officer. Or like a woman who loves him who commands. Or like a flatterer and coward, afraid of the commander. Or like a blockhead who follows because he has nothing to say to the contrary. In short, you can give ear to your conscience in a hundred different ways. But *that* you hear this or that judgment as the voice of conscience, consequently, *that* you feel a thing to be right—may have its cause in the fact that you have never thought about your nature, and have blindly accepted from your childhood what has been designated to you as *right:* or in the fact that hitherto bread and honours have fallen to your share with that which you call your duty,—it is "right" to you, because it seems to be *your* "condition of existence" (that you, however, have a *right* to existence seems to you irrefutable!). The *persistency* of your moral judgment might still be just a proof of personal wretchedness or impersonality; your "moral force" might have its source in your obstinacy—or in your incapacity to perceive new ideals! And to be brief: if you had thought more acutely, observed more accurately, and had learned more, you would no longer under all circumstances call this and that your "duty" and your "conscience": the knowledge *how moral judgments have in general always originated* would make you tired of these pathetic words,—as you have already grown tired of other pathetic words, for instance "sin," "salvation," and "redemption."—And now, my friend, do not talk to me about the categorical imperative! That word tickles my ear, and I must laugh in spite of your presence and your seriousness. In this connection I recollect old Kant, who, as a punishment for having *gained possession surreptitiously* of the "thing in itself"—also a very ludicrous affair!—was imposed upon by the categorical imperative, and with that in his heart *strayed back again* to "God," the "soul," "freedom," and "immortality," like a fox which strays back into its cage: and it had been *his* strength and shrewdness which had *broken open* this cage!—What? You admire the categorical imperative in you? This "persistency" of your so-called moral judgment? This absoluteness of the feeling that "as I think on this matter, so must everyone think"? Admire rather your *selfishness* therein! And the blindness, paltriness, and modesty of your selfishness! For it is selfishness in a person to regard *his* judgment as universal law, and a blind, paltry and modest selfishness besides, because it betrays that you have not yet discovered yourself, that you have not yet created for yourself any personal, quite personal ideal:—for this could never be the ideal of another, to say nothing of all, of every one!— —He who still thinks that "each would have to act in this manner in this case," has not yet advanced half a dozen paces in self-knowledge: otherwise he would know that there neither are, nor can be, similar actions,—that every action that has been done, has been done in an entirely unique and inimitable manner, and that it will be the same with regard to all future actions; that all precepts of conduct (and even the most esoteric and subtle precepts of all moralities up to the present), apply only to the coarse exterior,—that by means of them, indeed, a semblance of equality can be attained, *but only a semblance,*—that in outlook and retrospect, *every* action is, and remains, an impenetrable affair,—that our opinions of the "good," "noble" and "great" can never be proved by our actions, because no action is cognisable,—that our opinions, estimates, and tables of values are certainly among the most powerful levers in the mechanism of our actions, that in every single case, nevertheless, the law of their mechanism is untraceable. Let us *confine* ourselves, therefore, to the purification of our opinions and appreciations, and to the *construction of new tables of value of our own:*—we will, however, brood no longer over the "moral worth of our actions"! Yes, my friends! As regards the whole moral twaddle of people about one another, it is time to be disgusted with it! To sit in judgment morally ought to be opposed to our taste! Let us leave this nonsense and this bad taste to those who have nothing else to do, save to drag the past a little distance further through time, and who are never themselves the present,— consequently to the many, to the majority! We, however, *would seek to become what we are,*[6]—the new, the unique, the incomparable, making laws for ourselves and creating ourselves! And for this purpose we must become the best students and discoverers of all the laws and necessities in the world. We must be *physicists* in order to be *creators* in that sense,—whereas hitherto all appreciations and ideals have been based on *ignorance* of physics, or in *contradiction* thereto. And therefore, three cheers for physics! And still louder cheers for that which *impels* us thereto—our honesty.

*   *   *   *   *

[6]This is the first time Nietzsche uses this phrase.

337

Future "Humanity."—When I look at this age with the eye of a distant future, I find nothing so remarkable in the man of the present day as his peculiar virtue and sickness called "the historical sense." It is a tendency to something quite new and foreign in history: if this embryo were given several centuries and more, there might finally evolve out of it a marvellous plant, with a smell equally marvellous, on account of which our old earth might be more pleasant to live in than it has been hitherto. We moderns are just beginning to form the chain of a very powerful, future sentiment, link by link,—we hardly know what we are doing. It almost seems to us as if it were not the question of a new sentiment, but of the decline of all old sentiments:—the historical sense is still something so poor and cold, and many are attacked by it as by a frost, and are made poorer and colder by it. To others it appears as the indication of stealthily approaching age, and our planet is regarded by them as a melancholy invalid, who, in order to forget his present condition, writes the history of his youth. In fact, this is one aspect of the new sentiment. He who knows how to regard the history of man in its entirety as *his own history*, feels in the immense generalisation all the grief of the invalid who thinks of health, of the old man who thinks of the dream of his youth, of the lover who is robbed of his beloved, of the martyr whose ideal is destroyed, of the hero on the evening of the indecisive battle which has brought him wounds and the loss of a friend. But to bear this immense sum of grief of all kinds, to be able to bear it, and yet still be the hero who at the commencement of a second day of battle greets the dawn and his happiness, as one who has an horizon of centuries before and behind him, as the heir of all nobility, of all past intellect, and the obligatory heir (as the noblest) of all the old nobles; while at the same time the first of a new nobility, the equal of which has never been seen nor even dreamt of: to take all this upon his soul, the oldest, the newest, the losses, hopes, conquests, and victories of mankind: to have all this at last in one soul, and to comprise it in one feeling:—this would necessarily furnish a happiness which man has not hitherto known,—a God's happiness, full of power and love, full of tears and laughter, a happiness which, like the sun in the evening, continually gives of its inexhaustible riches and empties into the sea,—and like the sun, too, feels itself richest when even the poorest fisherman rows with golden oars! This divine feeling might then be called—humanity!

*   *   *   *   *

341

The Heaviest Burden. —What if a demon crept after thee into thy loneliest loneliness some day or night, and said to thee: "This life, as thou
livest it at present, and hast lived it, thou must live it once more, and also
innumerable times; and there will be nothing new in it, but every pain
and every joy and every thought and every sigh, and all the unspeakably
small and great in thy life must come to thee again, and all in the same
series and sequence—and similarly this spider and this moonlight among
the trees, and similarly this moment, and I myself. The eternal sand-glass
of existence will ever be turned once more, and thou with it, thou speck
of dust!" —Wouldst thou not throw thyself down and gnash thy teeth, and
curse the demon that so spake? Or hast thou once experienced a tremendous moment in which thou wouldst answer him: "Thou art a God, and
never did I hear anything so divine!" If that thought acquired power over
thee as thou art, it would transform thee, and perhaps crush thee; the
question with regard to all and everything: "Dost thou want this once
more, and also for innumerable times?" would lie as the heaviest burden
upon thy activity! Or, how wouldst thou have to become favourably inclined to thyself and to life, so as *to long for nothing more ardently* than for
this last eternal sanctioning and sealing? —[7]

*   *   *   *   *

---

[7]This is the first appearance in Nietzsche's published writings of the thought of the eternal
recurrence, which figures importantly in the third part of *Thus Spoke Zarathustra*, his next
work.

III
Zarathustra and Beyond
(1883–1886)

Excerpts from

Thus Spoke Zarathustra

Selections from

The Will to Power:
Notebooks of 1884–1886

THUS SPOKE ZARATHUSTRA
(1883–1885)

Introduction

Thus Spoke Zarathustra is certainly Nietzsche's best-known work today; and it was this work above all that initially made him famous in the decades following his collapse and death. The first three parts of it that were published in 1883 and 1884, however, attracted little attention at the time—to Nietzsche's profound disappointment. (The fourth part, written in 1885, was only printed privately and distributed to a few friends during his active life; it was not published with the other three parts until some years later.)

Nietzsche might have been gratified by its great eventual success—but it is doubtful whether he would have been pleased by the ways in which it was understood by many of those who came to respond to it with such enthusiasm. He regarded it as his most profound and significant work, and as his greatest gift to humanity; for he took it to show the way to a new and genuine affirmation of life beyond all otherworldly religious and metaphysical faiths, and also beyond the pessimism and nihilistic despair that he considered to be the inevitable consequences of the "death of God" and collapse of all such faiths. His own later praise of it (particularly in his discussion of it in *Ecce Homo*[1]) is wildly excessive. But it is extraordinarily rich and suggestive and is widely regarded as a work of philosophical and literary genius.

While the literary style and quasi-biblical idiom of *Thus Spoke Zarathustra* make it easily readable, its understanding is a very different matter. Its subtitle—"A Book for All and None"—is well chosen; for while it is accessible to all, Nietzsche suspected that there would be few if any among his contemporaries who would be ready, willing, and able to hear and grasp its meaning and take it to heart. He therefore should not have been surprised that it did not meet with the kind of reception and response he would have wished. He poured his heart and all of his hard-won wisdom into it; but there were few who shared and could appreciate his pathos, and who also could see their way past the surface of the work to comprehend it. And there were fewer still who were prepared to embrace what he was trying to express, as the best way of coming to terms with this life in this world that remains available to us in the post-Christian and postmodern age that was then just dawning.

---

[1] *Ecce Homo*, Part 3 ("Why I Write Such Good Books"), "Thus Spoke Zarathustra," in *On the Genealogy of Morals/Ecce Homo*, trans. Walter Kaufmann (New York: Vintage, 1967).

"God is dead; so where do we go from here?" This is Nietzsche's point of departure in *Thus Spoke Zarathustra*, as in his thinking more generally. He had already made this explicit in *The Gay Science*, in which he raised the questions and posed the challenges to which *Thus Spoke Zarathustra* indicates his response. This great literary-philosophical effort marked what (in a Nietzschean manner of speaking) might be called the "high noon" of his thinking, with respect to the things that mattered most to him from first to last. It was in it, and at this time in his intellectual life, that (as he puts it in *Ecce Homo*), "the Yes-saying part of my task had been solved."[2]

The following excerpt provides only an introduction to this work. It consists of the Prologue and first five "speeches" of Zarathustra in the first of its four parts. The Prologue and first speeches are important and illustrate the nature of the work; but they do not begin to indicate many of the themes and thoughts developed in the rest of it. The First Part as a whole is devoted to a reconsideration of many particular matters in the light of "the death of God," proclaimed by Zarathustra near the outset. Here the themes of the "overman" as "the meaning of the earth," "overcoming," "sublimination," and the "creation of new values" are sounded. In the Second Part, Nietzsche turns to the need for a fundamental reorientation of our thinking, requiring both reinterpretation and revaluation. The themes of the "will to power" and "creativity"—the guiding ideas in terms of which these tasks are to be carried out—are introduced, along with that of the "enhancement of life"; and various traditional "values" are "revalued."

In the Third Part the basic challenge of a fundamental life-affirming spiritual renewal is more directly confronted; and it is here that thought of "eternal recurrence" comes to the fore. This thought, which Nietzsche regarded as "the fundamental conception of the work" and the "highest formulation of affirmation that is at all attainable,"[3] is presented initially as profoundly dismaying before it eventually comes to be celebrated. Its celebration culminates in two love-songs to life. The first ("The Other Dancing Song") is sung as the midnight bell strikes:

> *One!*
> Oh man, take care!
> *Two!*
> What does the deep midnight declare?
> *Three!*
> "I was asleep—

---

[2]*Ecce Homo*, Part 3, "Beyond Good and Evil," Section 1, in *Genealogy/Ecce Homo*, trans. Kaufmann.

[3]*Ecce Homo*, Part 3, "Thus Spoke Zarathustra," Section 1, in *Geneaology/Ecce Homo*, trans. Kaufmann.

Four!
"From a deep sleep I awoke and swear;
 Five!
"The world is deep,
 Six!
"Deeper than the day had been aware.
 Seven!
"Deep is its woe;
 Eight!
"Joy—deeper yet than agony:
 Nine!
"Woe implores: Go!
 Ten!
"But all joy wants eternity—
 Eleven!
"Wants deep, wants deep eternity."
 Twelve![4]

The refrain of the second song ("The Yes and Amen Song") is: "*For I love you, O eternity!*"[5]

Nietzsche may have intended at the time to end the work here, at the end of the Third Part, which was the last he published. Soon thereafter, however, he added the privately printed Fourth Part, which consists of yet another reconsideration—this time of some of the ideas of the first three parts. It is heavily ironic, and far more sobering, emphasizing how "all too human" and vulnerable even the "higher" types of humanity remain. Yet it ends with another refrain of the midnight song, Zarathustra's renunciation of the temptation to feel pity for the sufferings even of the highest types (his "final sin") and his resolute re-entry into the fray of seeking to contribute to the enhancement of this life in this world, warts and all:

"My suffering and my pity for suffering—what does it matter? Am I concerned with *happiness?* I am concerned with my *work*.

"Well then! . . . Zarathustra has ripened, my hour has come: this is *my* morning, *my* day is breaking; *rise now*, rise, thou great noon!"

Thus spoke Zarathustra, and he left his cave, glowing and strong as a morning sun that comes out of dark mountains.[6]

---

[4]*Thus Spoke Zarathustra*, in *The Portable Nietzsche*, ed. and trans. Walter Kaufmann (New York: Viking Press, 1954), Third Part, Chapter 15.
[5]*Thus Spoke Zarathustra*, in *The Portable Nietzsche*, ed. and trans. Kaufmann, Third Part, Chapter 16.
[6]*Thus Spoke Zarathustra*, in *The Portable Nietzsche*, ed. and trans. Kaufmann, Fourth Part, Chapter 20.

Thus Spoke Zarathustra
First Part (1883)
(*Excerpts*)

Zarathustra's Prologue

1

When Zarathustra was thirty years old he left his home and the lake of his home and went into the mountains. Here he enjoyed his spirit and his solitude, and for ten years did not tire of it. But at last a change came over his heart, and one morning he rose with the dawn, stepped before the sun, and spoke to it thus:

"You great star, what would your happiness be had you not those for whom you shine?

"For ten years you have climbed to my cave: you would have tired of your light and of the journey had it not been for me and my eagle and my serpent.

"But we waited for you every morning, took your overflow from you, and blessed you for it.

"Behold, I am weary of my wisdom, like a bee that has gathered too much honey; I need hands outstretched to receive it.

"I would give away and distribute, until the wise among men find joy once again in their folly, and the poor in their riches.

"For that I must descend to the depths, as you do in the evening when you go behind the sea and still bring light to the underworld, you overrich star.

"Like you, I must *go under*—go down, as is said by man, to whom I want to descend.

"So bless me then, you quiet eye that can look even upon an all-too-great happiness without envy!

"Bless the cup that wants to overflow, that the water may flow from it golden and carry everywhere the reflection of your delight.

"Behold, this cup wants to become empty again, and Zarathustra wants to become man again."

Thus Zarathustra began to go under.

2

Zarathustra descended alone from the mountains, encountering no one. But when he came into the forest, all at once there stood before him an old man who had left his holy cottage to look for roots in the woods. And thus spoke the old man to Zarathustra:

"No stranger to me is this wanderer: many years ago he passed this way. Zarathustra he was called, but he has changed. At that time you carried your ashes to the mountains; would you now carry your fire into the valleys? Do you not fear to be punished as an arsonist?

"Yes, I recognize Zarathustra. His eyes are pure, and around his mouth there hides no disgust. Does he not walk like a dancer?

"Zarathustra has changed, Zarathustra has become a child, Zarathustra is an awakened one; what do you now want among the sleepers? You lived in your solitude as in the sea, and the sea carried you. Alas, would you now climb ashore? Alas, would you again drag your own body?"

Zarathustra answered: "I love man."

"Why," asked the saint, "did I go into the forest and the desert? Was it not because I loved man all-too-much? Now I love God; man I love not. Man is for me too imperfect a thing. Love of man would kill me."

Zarathustra answered: "Did I speak of love? I bring men a gift."

"Give them nothing!" said the saint. "Rather, take part of their load and help them to bear it—that will be best for them, if only it does you good! And if you want to give them something, give no more than alms, and let them beg for that!"

"No," answered Zarathustra. "I give no alms. For that I am not poor enough."

The saint laughed at Zarathustra and spoke thus: "Then see to it that they accept your treasures. They are suspicious of hermits and do not believe that we come with gifts. Our steps sound too lonely through the streets. And what if at night, in their beds, they hear a man walk by long before the sun has risen—they probably ask themselves, Where is the thief going?

"Do not go to man. Stay in the forest! Go rather even to the animals! Why do you not want to be as I am—a bear among bears, a bird among birds?"

"And what is the saint doing in the forest?" asked Zarathustra.

The saint answered: "I make songs and sing them; and when I make songs, I laugh, cry, and hum: thus I praise God. With singing, crying, laughing, and humming, I praise the god who is my god. But what do you bring us as a gift?"

When Zarathustra had heard these words he bade the saint farewell and said: "What could I have to give you? But let me go quickly lest I take something from you!" And thus they separated, the old one and the man, laughing as two boys laugh.

But when Zarathustra was alone he spoke thus to his heart: "Could it be possible? This old saint in the forest has not yet heard anything of this, that *God is dead!*"

3

When Zarathustra came into the next town, which lies on the edge of the forest, he found many people gathered together in the market place; for it had been promised that there would be a tightrope walker. And Zarathustra spoke thus to the people:

"*I teach you the overman.* Man is something that shall be overcome. What have you done to overcome him?

"All beings so far have created something beyond themselves; and do you want to be the ebb of this great flood and even go back to the beasts rather than overcome man? What is the ape to man? A laughingstock or a painful embarrassment. And man shall be just that for the overman: a laughingstock or a painful embarrassment. You have made your way from worm to man, and much in you is still worm. Once you were apes, and even now, too, man is more ape than any ape.

"Whoever is the wisest among you is also a mere conflict and cross between plant and ghost. But do I bid you become ghosts or plants?

"Behold, I teach you the overman. The overman is the meaning of the earth. Let your will say: the overman *shall be* the meaning of the earth! I beseech you, my brothers, *remain faithful to the earth,* and do not believe those who speak to you of otherworldly hopes! Poison-mixers are they, whether they know it or not. Despisers of life are they, decaying and poisoned themselves, of whom the earth is weary: so let them go.

"Once the sin against God was the greatest sin; but God died, and these sinners died with him. To sin against the earth is now the most dreadful thing, and to esteem the entrails of the unknowable higher than the meaning of the earth.

"Once the soul looked contemptuously upon the body, and then this contempt was the highest: she wanted the body meager, ghastly, and starved. Thus she hoped to escape it and the earth. Oh, this soul herself was still meager, ghastly, and starved: and cruelty was the lust of this soul. But you, too, my brothers, tell me: what does your body proclaim of your soul? Is not your soul poverty and filth and wretched contentment?

"Verily, a polluted stream is man. One must be a sea to be able to receive a polluted stream without becoming unclean. Behold, I teach you the overman: he is this sea; in him your great contempt can go under.

"What is the greatest experience you can have? It is the hour of the great contempt. The hour in which your happiness, too, arouses your disgust, and even your reason and your virtue.

"The hour when you say, 'What matters my happiness? It is poverty and filth and wretched contentment. But my happiness ought to justify existence itself.'

"The hour when you say, 'What matters my reason? Does it crave knowledge as the lion his food? It is poverty and filth and wretched contentment.'

"The hour when you say, 'What matters my virtue? As yet it has not made me rage. How weary I am of my good and my evil! All that is poverty and filth and wretched contentment.'

"The hour when you say, 'What matters my justice? I do not see that I am flames and fuel. But the just are flames and fuel.'

"The hour when you say, 'What matters my pity? Is not pity the cross on which he is nailed who loves man? But my pity is no crucifixion.'

"Have you yet spoken thus? Have you yet cried thus? Oh, that I might have heard you cry thus!

"Not your sin but your thrift cries to heaven; your meanness even in your sin cries to heaven.

"Where is the lightning to lick you with its tongue? Where is the frenzy with which you should be inoculated?

"Behold, I teach you the overman: he is this lightning, he is this frenzy."

When Zarathustra had spoken thus, one of the people cried: "Now we have heard enough about the tightrope walker; now let us see him too!" And all the people laughed at Zarathustra. But the tightrope walker, believing that the word concerned him, began his performance.

4

Zarathustra, however, beheld the people and was amazed. Then he spoke thus:

"Man is a rope, tied between beast and overman—a rope over an abyss. A dangerous across, a dangerous on-the-way, a dangerous looking-back, a dangerous shuddering and stopping.

"What is great in man is that he is a bridge and not an end: what can be loved in man is that he is an *overture* and a *going under*.

"I love those who do not know how to live, except by going under, for they are those who cross over.

"I love the great despisers because they are the great reverers and arrows of longing for the other shore.

"I love those who do not first seek behind the stars for a reason to go under and be a sacrifice, but who sacrifice themselves for the earth, that the earth may some day become the overman's.

"I love him who lives to know, and who wants to know so that the overman may live some day. And thus he wants to go under.

"I love him who works and invents to build a house for the overman and to prepare earth, animal, and plant for him: for thus he wants to go under.

"I love him who loves his virtue, for virtue is the will to go under and an arrow of longing.

"I love him who does not hold back one drop of spirit for himself, but wants to be entirely the spirit of his virtue: thus he strides over the bridge as spirit.

"I love him who makes his virtue his addiction and his catastrophe: for his virtue's sake he wants to live on and to live no longer.

"I love him who does not want to have too many virtues. One virtue is more virtue than two, because it is more of a noose on which his catastrophe may hang.

"I love him whose soul squanders itself, who wants no thanks and returns none: for he always gives away and does not want to preserve himself.

"I love him who is abashed when the dice fall to make his fortune, and asks, 'Am I then a crooked gambler?' For he wants to perish.

"I love him who casts golden words before his deeds and always does even more than he promises: for he wants to go under.

"I love him who justifies future and redeems past generations: for he wants to perish of the present.

"I love him who chastens his god because he loves his god: for he must perish of the wrath of his god.

"I love him whose soul is deep, even in being wounded, and who can perish of a small experience: thus he goes gladly over the bridge.

"I love him whose soul is overfull so that he forgets himself, and all things are in him: thus all things spell his going under.

"I love him who has a free spirit and a free heart: thus his head is only the entrails of his heart, but his heart drives him to go under.

"I love all those who are as heavy drops, falling one by one out of the dark cloud that hangs over men: they herald the advent of lightning, and, as heralds, they perish.

"Behold, I am a herald of the lightning and a heavy drop from the cloud; but this lightning is called *overman*."

5

When Zarathustra had spoken these words he beheld the people again and was silent. "There they stand," he said to his heart; "there they laugh. They do not understand me; I am not the mouth for these ears. Must one smash their ears before they learn to listen with their eyes? Must one clatter like kettledrums and preachers of repentance? Or do they believe only the stammerer?

"They have something of which they are proud. What do they call that which makes them proud? Education they call it; it distinguishes them from goatherds. That is why they do not like to hear the word 'contempt' applied to them. Let me then address their pride. Let me speak to them of what is most contemptible: but that is the *last man*."

And thus spoke Zarathustra to the people: "The time has come for man to set himself a goal. The time has come for man to plant the seed of his highest hope. His soil is still rich enough. But one day this soil will be poor and domesticated, and no tall tree will be able to grow in it. Alas, the time is coming when man will no longer shoot the arrow of his longing beyond man, and the string of his bow will have forgotten how to whir!

"I say unto you: one must still have chaos in oneself to be able to give birth to a dancing star. I say unto you: you still have chaos in yourselves.

"Alas, the time is coming when man will no longer give birth to a star. Alas, the time of the most despicable man is coming, he that is no longer able to despise himself. Behold, I show you the *last man*.

" 'What is love? What is creation? What is longing? What is a star?' thus asks the last man, and he blinks.

"The earth has become small, and on it hops the last man, who makes everything small. His race is as ineradicable as the flea-beetle; the last man lives longest.

" 'We have invented happiness,' say the last men, and they blink. They have left the regions where it was hard to live, for one needs warmth. One still loves one's neighbor and rubs against him, for one needs warmth.

"Becoming sick and harboring suspicion are sinful to them: one proceeds carefully. A fool, whoever still stumbles over stones or human beings! A little poison now and then: that makes for agreeable dreams. And much poison in the end, for an agreeable death.

"One still works, for work is a form of entertainment. But one is careful lest the entertainment be too harrowing. One no longer becomes poor or rich: both require too much exertion. Who still wants to rule? Who obey? Both require too much exertion.

"No shepherd and one herd! Everybody wants the same, everybody is the same: whoever feels different goes voluntarily into a madhouse.

" 'Formerly, all the world was mad,' say the most refined, and they blink.

"One is clever and knows everything that has ever happened: so there is no end of derision. One still quarrels, but one is soon reconciled—else it might spoil the digestion.

"One has one's little pleasure for the day and one's little pleasure for the night: but one has a regard for health.

" 'We have invented happiness,' say the last men, and they blink."

And here ended Zarathustra's first speech, which is also called "the Prologue"; for at this point he was interrupted by the clamor and delight of the crowd. "Give us this last man, O Zarathustra," they shouted. "Turn us into these last men! Then we shall make you a gift of the overman!" And all the people jubilated and clucked with their tongues.

But Zarathustra became sad and said to his heart: "They do not understand me: I am not the mouth for these ears. I seem to have lived too long in the mountains; I listened too much to brooks and trees: now I talk to them as to goatherds. My soul is unmoved and bright as the mountains in the morning. But they think I am cold and I jeer and make dreadful jests. And now they look at me and laugh: and as they laugh they even hate me. There is ice in their laughter."

6

Then something happened that made every mouth dumb and every eye rigid. For meanwhile the tightrope walker had begun his performance: he had stepped out of a small door and was walking over the rope, stretched between two towers and suspended over the market place and the people. When he had reached the exact middle of his course the small door opened once more and a fellow in motley clothes, looking like a jester, jumped out and followed the first one with quick steps. "Forward, lamefoot!" he shouted in an awe-inspiring voice. "Forward, lazybones, smuggler, pale-face, or I shall tickle you with my heel! What are you doing here between towers? The tower is where you belong. You ought to be locked up; you block the way for one better than yourself." And with every word he came closer and closer; but when he was but one step behind, the dreadful thing happened which made every mouth dumb and every eye rigid: he uttered a devilish cry and jumped over the man who stood in his way. This man, however, seeing his rival win, lost his head and the rope, tossed away his pole, and plunged into the depth even faster, a whirlpool of arms and legs. The market place became as the sea when a tempest pierces it: the people rushed apart and over one another, especially at the place where the body must hit the ground.

Zarathustra, however, did not move; and it was right next to him that the body fell, badly maimed and disfigured, but not yet dead. After a while the shattered man recovered consciousness and saw Zarathustra kneeling beside him. "What are you doing here?" he asked at last. "I have long known that the devil would trip me. Now he will drag me to hell. Would you prevent him?"

"By my honor, friend," answered Zarathustra, "all that of which you speak does not exist: there is no devil and no hell. Your soul will be dead even before your body: fear nothing further."

The man looked up suspiciously. "If you speak the truth," he said, "I lose nothing when I lose my life. I am not much more than a beast that has been taught to dance by blows and a few meager morsels."

"By no means," said Zarathustra. "You have made danger your vocation; there is nothing contemptible in that. Now you perish of your vocation: for that I will bury you with my own hands."

When Zarathustra had said this, the dying man answered no more; but he moved his hand as if he sought Zarathustra's hand in thanks.

7

Meanwhile the evening came, and the market place hid in darkness. Then the people scattered, for even curiosity and terror grow weary. But Zarathustra sat on the ground near the dead man, and he was lost in thought, forgetting the time. At last night came, and a cold wind blew over the lonely one.

Then Zarathustra rose and said to his heart: "Verily, it is a beautiful catch of fish that Zarathustra has brought in today! Not a man has he caught but a corpse. Human existence is uncanny and still without meaning: a jester can become man's fatality. I will teach men the meaning of their existence—the overman, the lightning out of the dark cloud of man. But I am still far from them, and my sense does not speak to their senses. To men I am still the mean between a fool and a corpse.

"Dark is the night, dark are Zarathustra's ways. Come, cold, stiff companion! I shall carry you where I may bury you with my own hands."

*   *   *   *   *

9

For a long time Zarathustra slept, and not only dawn passed over his face but the morning too. At last, however, his eyes opened: amazed, Zarathustra looked into the woods and the silence; amazed, he looked into himself. Then he rose quickly, like a seafarer who suddenly sees land, and jubilated, for he saw a new truth. And thus he spoke to his heart:

"An insight has come to me: companions I need, living ones—not dead companions and corpses whom I carry with myself wherever I want to. Living companions I need, who follow me because they want to follow themselves—wherever I want.

"An insight has come to me: let Zarathustra speak not to the people but to companions. Zarathustra shall not become the shepherd and dog of a herd.

"To lure many away from the herd, for that I have come. The people and the herd shall be angry with me: Zarathustra wants to be called a robber by the shepherds.

"Shepherds, I say; but they call themselves the good and the just. Shepherds, I say; but they call themselves believers in the true faith.

"Behold the good and the just! Whom do they hate most? The man who breaks their tables of values, the breaker, the lawbreaker; yet he is the creator.

"Behold the believers of all faiths! Whom do they hate most? The man who breaks their tables of values, the breaker, the lawbreaker; yet he is the creator.

"Companions, the creator seeks, not corpses, not herds and believers. Fellow creators, the creator seeks—those who write new values on new tablets. Companions, the creator seeks, and fellow harvesters; for everything about him is ripe for the harvest. But he lacks a hundred sickles: so he plucks ears and is annoyed. Companions, the creator seeks, and such as know how to whet their sickles. Destroyers they will be called, and despisers of good and evil. But they are the harvesters and those who celebrate. Fellow creators, Zarathustra seeks, fellow harvesters and fellow celebrants: what are herds and shepherds and corpses to him?

"And you, my first companion, farewell! I buried you well in your hollow tree; I have hidden you well from the wolves. But I part from you; the time is up. Between dawn and dawn a new truth has come to me. No shepherd shall I be, nor gravedigger. Never again shall I speak to the people: for the last time have I spoken to the dead.

"I shall join the creators, the harvesters, the celebrants: I shall show them the rainbow and all the steps to the overman. To the hermits I shall sing my song, to the lonesome and the twosome; and whoever still has ears for the unheard-of—his heart shall become heavy with my happiness.

"To my goal I will go—on my own way; over those who hesitate and lag behind I shall leap. Thus let my going be their going under."

10

This is what Zarathustra had told his heart when the sun stood high at noon; then he looked into the air, questioning, for overhead he heard the sharp call of a bird. And behold! An eagle soared through the sky in wide circles, and on him there hung a serpent, not like prey but like a friend: for she kept herself wound around his neck.

"These are my animals," said Zarathustra and was happy in his heart. "The proudest animal under the sun and the wisest animal under the sun—they have gone out on a search. They want to determine whether Zarathustra is still alive. Verily, do I still live? I found life more dangerous among men than among animals; on dangerous paths walks Zarathustra. May my animals lead me!"

When Zarathustra had said this he recalled the words of the saint in the forest, sighed, and spoke thus to his heart: "That I might be wiser! That I might be wise through and through like my serpent! But there I ask the impossible: so I ask my pride that it always go along with my wisdom. And when my wisdom leaves me one day—alas, it loves to fly away—let my pride then fly with my folly."

Thus Zarathustra began to go under.

Zarathustra's Speeches

ON THE THREE METAMORPHOSES

Of three metamorphoses of the spirit I tell you: how the spirit becomes a camel; and the camel, a lion; and the lion, finally, a child.

There is much that is difficult for the spirit, the strong reverent spirit that would bear much: but the difficult and the most difficult are what its strength demands.

What is difficult? asks the spirit that would bear much, and kneels down like a camel wanting to be well loaded. What is most difficult, O heroes, asks the spirit that would bear much, that I may take it upon myself and exult in my strength? Is it not humbling oneself to wound one's haughtiness? Letting one's folly shine to mock one's wisdom?

Or is it this: parting from our cause when it triumphs? Climbing high mountains to tempt the tempter?

Or is it this: feeding on the acorns and grass of knowledge and, for the sake of the truth, suffering hunger in one's soul?

Or is it this: being sick and sending home the comforters and making friends with the deaf, who never hear what you want?

Or is it this: stepping into filthy waters when they are the waters of truth, and not repulsing cold frogs and hot toads?

Or is it this: loving those who despise us and offering a hand to the ghost that would frighten us?

All these most difficult things the spirit that would bear much takes upon itself: like the camel that, burdened, speeds into the desert, thus the spirit speeds into its desert.

In the loneliest desert, however, the second metamorphosis occurs: here the spirit becomes a lion who would conquer his freedom and be master in his own desert. Here he seeks out his last master: he wants to fight him and his last god; for ultimate victory he wants to fight with the great dragon.

Who is the great dragon whom the spirit will no longer call lord and god? "Thou shalt" is the name of the great dragon. But the spirit of the lion says, "I will." "Thou shalt" lies in his way, sparkling like gold, an animal covered with scales; and on every scale shines a golden "thou shalt."

Values, thousands of years old, shine on these scales; and thus speaks the mightiest of all dragons: "All value of all things shines on me. All value has long been created, and I am all created value. Verily, there shall be no more 'I will.' " Thus speaks the dragon.

My brothers, why is there a need in the spirit for the lion? Why is not the beast of burden, which renounces and is reverent, enough?

To create new values—that even the lion cannot do; but the creation of freedom for oneself for new creation—that is within the power of the lion. The creation of freedom for oneself and a sacred "No" even to duty—for that, my brothers, the lion is needed. To assume the right to new values— that is the most terrifying assumption for a reverent spirit that would bear much. Verily, to him it is preying, and a matter for a beast of prey. He once loved "thou shalt" as most sacred: now he must find illusion and caprice even in the most sacred, that freedom from his love may become his prey: the lion is needed for such prey.

But say, my brothers, what can the child do that even the lion could not do? Why must the preying lion still become a child? The child is inno- cence and forgetting, a new beginning, a game, a self-propelled wheel, a first movement, a sacred "Yes." For the game of creation, my brothers, a sacred "Yes" is needed: the spirit now wills his own will, and he who had been lost to the world now conquers his own world.

Of three metamorphoses of the spirit I have told you: how the spirit became a camel; and the camel, a lion; and the lion, finally, a child.

Thus spoke Zarathustra. And at that time he sojourned in the town that is called The Motley Cow.

ON THE TEACHERS OF VIRTUE

A sage was praised to Zarathustra for knowing how to speak well of sleep and of virtue: he was said to be honored and rewarded highly for this, and all the youths were said to be sitting at his feet. To him Zarathustra went, and he sat at his feet with all the youths. And thus spoke the sage:

"Honor sleep and be bashful before it—that first of all. And avoid all who sleep badly and stay awake at night. Even the thief is bashful before sleep: he always steals silently through the night. Shameless, however, is the watchman of the night; shamelessly he carries his horn.

"Sleeping is no mean art: for its sake one must stay awake all day. Ten times a day you must overcome yourself: that makes you good and tired and is opium for the soul. Ten times you must reconcile yourself again with yourself; for, overcoming is bitterness, and the unreconciled sleep badly. Ten truths a day you must find; else you will still be seeking truth by night, and your soul will remain hungry. Ten times a day you must laugh and be cheerful; else you will be disturbed at night by your stomach, this father of gloom.

"Few know it, but one must have all the virtues to sleep well. Shall I bear false witness? Shall I commit adultery? Shall I covet my neighbor's maid? All that would go ill with good sleep.

"And even if one has all the virtues, there is one further thing one must know: to send even the virtues to sleep at the right time. Lest they quarrel with each other, the fair little women, about you, child of misfortune. Peace with God and the neighbor: that is what good sleep demands. And peace even with the neighbor's devil—else he will haunt you at night.

"Honor the magistrates and obey them—even the crooked magistrates. Good sleep demands it. Is it my fault that power likes to walk on crooked legs?

"I shall call him the best shepherd who leads his sheep to the greenest pasture: that goes well with good sleep.

"I do not want many honors, or great jewels: that inflames the spleen. But one sleeps badly without a good name and a little jewel.

"A little company is more welcome to me than evil company: but they must go and come at the right time. That goes well with good sleep.

"Much, too, do I like the poor in spirit: they promote sleep. Blessed are they, especially if one always tells them that they are right.

"Thus passes the day of the virtuous. And when night comes I guard well against calling sleep. For sleep, who is the master of the virtues, does not want to be called. Instead, I think about what I have done and thought during the day. Chewing the cud, I ask myself, patient as a cow, Well, what were your ten overcomings? and what were your ten reconciliations and the ten truths and the ten laughters with which your heart edified itself? Weighing such matters and rocked by forty thoughts, I am suddenly overcome by sleep, the uncalled, the master of the virtues. Sleep knocks at my eyes: they become heavy. Sleep touches my mouth: it stays open. Verily, on soft soles he comes to me, the dearest of thieves, and steals my thoughts: stupid I stand, like this chair here. But not for long do I stand like this: soon I lie."

When Zarathustra heard the sage speak thus he laughed in his heart, for an insight had come to him. And thus he spoke to his heart:

"This sage with his forty thoughts is a fool; but I believe that he knows well how to sleep. Happy is he that even lives near this sage! Such sleep is contagious—contagious even through a thick wall. There is magic even in his chair; and it is not in vain that the youths sit before this preacher of virtue. His wisdom is: to wake in order to sleep well. And verily, if life had no sense and I had to choose nonsense, then I too should consider this the most sensible nonsense.

"Now I understand clearly what was once sought above all when teachers of virtue were sought. Good sleep was sought, and opiate virtues for it. For all these much praised sages who were teachers of virtue, wisdom was the sleep without dreams: they knew no better meaning of life.

"Today too there may still be a few like this preacher of virtue, and not all so honest; but their time is up. And not for long will they stand like this: soon they will lie.

"Blessed are the sleepy ones: for they shall soon drop off."

Thus spoke Zarathustra.

ON THE AFTERWORLDLY

At one time Zarathustra too cast his delusion beyond man, like all the afterworldly. The work of a suffering and tortured god, the world then seemed to me. A dream the world then seemed to me, and the fiction of a god: colored smoke before the eyes of a dissatisfied deity. Good and evil and joy and pain and I and you—colored smoke this seemed to me before creative eyes. The creator wanted to look away from himself; so he created the world.

Drunken joy it is for the sufferer to look away from his suffering and to lose himself. Drunken joy and loss of self the world once seemed to me. This world, eternally imperfect, the image of an eternal contradiction, an imperfect image—a drunken joy for its imperfect creator: thus the world once appeared to me.

Thus I too once cast my delusion beyond man, like all the afterworldly. Beyond man indeed?

Alas, my brothers, this god whom I created was man-made and madness, like all gods! Man he was, and only a poor specimen of man and ego: out of my own ashes and fire this ghost came to me, and, verily, it did not come to me from beyond. What happened, my brothers? I overcame myself, the sufferer; I carried my own ashes to the mountains; I invented a brighter flame for myself. And behold, then this ghost *fled* from me. Now it would be suffering for me and agony for the recovered to believe in such ghosts: now it would be suffering for me and humiliation. Thus I speak to the afterworldly.

It was suffering and incapacity that created all afterworlds—this and that brief madness of bliss which is experienced only by those who suffer most deeply.

Weariness that wants to reach the ultimate with one leap, with one fatal leap, a poor ignorant weariness that does not want to want any more: this created all gods and afterworlds.

Believe me, my brothers: it was the body that despaired of the body and touched the ultimate walls with the fingers of a deluded spirit. Believe me, my brothers: it was the body that despaired of the earth and heard the belly of being speak to it. It wanted to crash through these ultimate walls with its head, and not only with its head—over there to "that world." But "that world" is well concealed from humans—that dehumanized inhuman world which is a heavenly nothing; and the belly of being does not speak to humans at all, except as a human.

Verily, all being is hard to prove and hard to induce to speak. Tell me, my brothers, is not the strangest of all things proved most nearly?

Indeed, this ego and the ego's contradiction and confusion still speak most honestly of its being—this creating, willing, valuing ego, which is the measure and value of things. And this most honest being, the ego, speaks of the body and still wants the body, even when it poetizes and raves and flutters with broken wings. It learns to speak ever more honestly, this ego: and the more it learns, the more words and honors it finds for body and earth.

A new pride my ego taught me, and this I teach men: no longer to bury one's head in the sand of heavenly things, but to bear it freely, an earthly head, which creates a meaning for the earth.

A new will I teach men: to *will* this way which man has walked blindly, and to affirm it, and no longer to sneak away from it like the sick and decaying.

It was the sick and decaying who despised body and earth and invented the heavenly realm and the redemptive drops of blood: but they took even these sweet and gloomy poisons from body and earth. They wanted to escape their own misery, and the stars were too far for them. So they sighed: "Would that there were heavenly ways to sneak into another state of being and happiness!" Thus they invented their sneaky ruses and bloody potions. Ungrateful, these people deemed themselves transported from their bodies and this earth. But to whom did they owe the convulsions and raptures of their transport? To their bodies and this earth.

Zarathustra is gentle with the sick. Verily, he is not angry with their kinds of comfort and ingratitude. May they become convalescents, men of overcoming, and create a higher body for themselves! Nor is Zarathustra angry with the convalescent who eyes his delusion tenderly and, at midnight, sneaks around the grave of his god: but even so his tears still betray sickness and a sick body to me.

Many sick people have always been among the poetizers and God-cravers; furiously they hate the lover of knowledge and that youngest among the virtues, which is called "honesty." They always look backward toward dark ages; then, indeed, delusion and faith were another matter: the rage of reason was godlikeness, and doubt was sin.

I know these godlike men all too well: they want one to have faith in them, and doubt to be sin. All too well I also know what it is in which they have mo⸱⸱ faith. Verily, it is not in afterworlds and redemptive drops of blood, but in the body, that they too have most faith; and their body is to them their thing-in-itself. But a sick thing it is to them, and gladly would they shed their skins. Therefore they listen to the preachers of death and themselves preach afterworlds.

Listen rather, my brothers, to the voice of the healthy body: that is a more honest and purer voice. More honestly and purely speaks the healthy body that is perfect and perpendicular: and it speaks of the meaning of the earth.

Thus spoke Zarathustra.

ON THE DESPISERS OF THE BODY

I want to speak to the despisers of the body. I would not have them learn and teach differently, but merely say farewell to their own bodies—and thus become silent.

"Body am I, and soul"—thus speaks the child. And why should one not speak like children?

But the awakened and knowing say: body am I entirely, and nothing else; and soul is only a word for something about the body.

The body is a great reason, a plurality with one sense, a war and a peace, a herd and a shepherd. An instrument of your body is also your little reason, my brother, which you call "spirit"—a little instrument and toy of your great reason.

"I," you say, and are proud of the word. But greater is that in which you do not wish to have faith—your body and its great reason: that does not say "I," but does "I."

What the sense feels, what the spirit knows, never has its end in itself. But sense and spirit would persuade you that they are the end of all things: that is how vain they are. Instruments and toys are sense and spirit: behind them still lies the self. The self also seeks with the eyes of the senses; it also listens with the ears of the spirit. Always the self listens and seeks: it compares, overpowers, conquers, destroys. It controls, and it is in control of the ego too.

Behind your thoughts and feelings, my brother, there stands a mighty ruler, an unknown sage—whose name is self. In your body he dwells; he is your body.

There is more reason in your body than in your best wisdom. And who knows why your body needs precisely your best wisdom?

Your self laughs at your ego and at its bold leaps. "What are these leaps and flights of thought to me?" it says to itself. "A detour to my end. I am the leading strings of the ego and the prompter of its concepts."

The self says to the ego, "Feel pain here!" Then the ego suffers and thinks how it might suffer no more—and that is why it is *made* to think.

The self says to the ego, "Feel pleasure here!" Then the ego is pleased and thinks how it might often be pleased again—and that is why it is *made* to think.

I want to speak to the despisers of the body. It is their respect that begets their contempt. What is it that created respect and contempt and worth and will? The creative self created respect and contempt; it created pleasure and pain. The creative body created the spirit as a hand for its will.

Even in your folly and contempt, you despisers of the body, you serve your self. I say unto you: your self itself wants to die and turns away from life. It is no longer capable of what it would do above all else: to create beyond itself. That is what it would do above all else, that is its fervent wish.

But now it is too late for it to do this: so your self wants to go under, O despisers of the body. Your self wants to go under, and that is why you have become despisers of the body! For you are no longer able to create beyond yourselves.

And that is why you are angry with life and the earth. An unconscious envy speaks out of the squint-eyed glance of your contempt.

I shall not go your way, O despisers of the body! You are no bridge to the overman!

Thus spoke Zarathustra.

ON ENJOYING AND SUFFERING THE PASSIONS

My brother, if you have a virtue and she is your virtue, then you have her in common with nobody. To be sure, you want to call her by name and pet her; you want to pull her ear and have fun with her. And behold, now you have her name in common with the people and have become one of the people and herd with your virtue.

You would do better to say, "Inexpressible and nameless is that which gives my soul agony and sweetness and is even the hunger of my entrails."

May your virtue be too exalted for the familiarity of names: and if you must speak of her, then do not be ashamed to stammer of her. Then speak and stammer, "This is *my* good; this I love; it pleases me wholly; thus alone do *I* want the good. I do not want it as divine law; I do not want it as human statute and need: it shall not be a signpost for me to overearths and paradises. It is an earthly virtue that I love: there is little prudence in it, and least of all the reason of all men. But this bird built its nest with me: therefore I love and caress it; now it dwells with me, sitting on its golden eggs." Thus you shall stammer and praise your virtue.

Once you suffered passions and called them evil. But now you have only your virtues left: they grew out of your passions. You commended your highest goal to the heart of these passions: then they become your virtues and passions you enjoyed.

And whether you came from the tribe of the choleric or of the voluptuous or of the fanatic or of the vengeful, in the end all your passions became virtues and all your devils, angels. Once you had wild dogs in your cellar, but in the end they turned into birds and lovely singers. Out of your poisons you brewed your balsam. You milked your cow, melancholy; now you drink the sweet milk of her udder.

And nothing evil grows out of you henceforth, unless it be the evil that grows out of the fight among your virtues. My brother, if you are fortunate you have only one virtue and no more: then you will pass over the bridge more easily. It is a distinction to have many virtues, but a hard lot; and many have gone into the desert and taken their lives because they had wearied of being the battle and battlefield of virtues.

My brother, are war and battle evil? But this evil is necessary; necessary are the envy and mistrust and calumny among your virtues. Behold how each of your virtues covets what is highest: each wants your whole spirit that it might become *her* herald; each wants your whole strength in wrath, hatred, and love. Each virtue is jealous of the others, and jealousy is a terrible thing. Virtues too can perish of jealousy. Surrounded by the flame of jealousy, one will in the end, like the scorpion, turn one's poisonous sting against oneself. Alas, my brother, have you never yet seen a virtue deny and stab herself?

Man is something that must be overcome; and therefore you shall love your virtues, for you will perish of them.

Thus spoke Zarathustra.

*   *   *   *   *

THE WILL TO POWER:
Notebooks of 1884–1886

Introduction

Along with the remarkable number of books Nietzsche published and readied for publication in the half-dozen years before his collapse, he continued to write a great deal in the notebooks he kept. Some of this material found its way into the books he completed during these last years; but much of it did not. Some of it also was included in the volume compiled and published after his death under the title *The Will to Power*. This material is of considerable interest, both for the further light his notes shed on things he has to say in his books, and because they in some cases have to do with matters he had hardly begun to address in the books he completed before his productive life abruptly ended.

The following set of notes from the first half of this period (1884–1886) was written in the years when Nietzsche completed the fourth part of *Thus Spoke Zarathustra* and returned to a more prosaic kind of philosophical writing. His next book was *Beyond Good and Evil*, his "Prelude to a Philosophy of the Future." This work appeared in 1886, the year when he also wrote a series of stock-taking retrospective prefaces to many of his earlier books.[1] His notebooks of 1884–1886 were thus the philosophical workshop from which this first set of his post-*Zarathustra* writings emerged; and these notes provide indications of some of the things he was thinking about as he undertook to write them. Some of these reflections received refinement and elaboration in *Beyond Good and Evil*. Others provide more extended discussions of some matters that are touched on only briefly and tentatively there.

A striking instance of the latter is the famous sketch of his conception of the world, culminating in his characterization of it in terms of the "will to power" in the long note placed by the compilers of *The Will to Power* at its end.[2] This note dates from the period under consideration, as do a number of others in which he elaborates further on his interpretation of the world and life along these lines. They thus are usefully recalled when one comes upon his references to it on a number of occasions in *Beyond Good and Evil*. He subsequently devoted a good deal more attention to it, in his notebooks of 1888 in particular, as shall be seen. These notes make

---

[1] These prefaces are to be found in Part VIII of this volume.

[2] *The Will to Power*, ed. Walter Kaufmann, trans. Walter Kaufmann and R. J. Hollingdale (New York: Random House, 1967), section 1067.

clear, however, that he was already experimenting seriously with this interpretation in this period, having first given expression to it in the Second Part of *Thus Spoke Zarathustra*.[3]

Others of these notes contain preliminary versions of some of the ideas he subsequently developed further (both in his published writings and in the notebooks of his last few years) concerning truth and knowledge, morality, and value. And several of them show that he had already begun to reflect during this period on a problem with which he became increasingly concerned in the years that followed, with which he wrestled even as his thinking on these other topics developed: the problem of "nihilism." (Later notes on this problem will be found in the first section of Part VI of this volume, which contains selections from his notebooks of 1886–1888.)

It must be stressed that the following selections from the notebooks of 1884–1886 represent only a fraction of the notes from this period to be found in *The Will to Power* and a far smaller fraction of the contents of these notebooks themselves. It also should be kept in mind that they are only notes Nietzsche wrote to himself, in the workshop of his notebooks, rather than reflections he intended for publication as they stand. I have not kept them in the order in which they were placed by the compilers of *The Will to Power*, who utterly disregarded their chronology. Rather, I have presented them in an order roughly reflecting the sequence of the notebooks in which they were written. By way of footnotes, however, I have indicated both the section numbers that were given to them in *The Will to Power*[4] and their locations in the relevant volumes of the critical edition of Nietzsche's writings.[5]

[3]*Thus Spoke Zarathustra*, Second Part, Chapter 12, "On Self-Overcoming."
[4]*The Will to Power*, see note 2. In German: *Der Wille zur Macht. Nietzsche's Werke* (Leipzig: Alfred Kroner Verlag), vols. 15 (1911) and 16 (1922). The same section numbers are used in all editions.
[5]*Nietzsche Werke: Kritische Gesamtausgabe*, eds. Giorgio Colli and Mazzino Montinari (Berlin and New York: Walter de Gruyter), vols. VII:2 (1973), VII:3 (1974), VIII:1 (1974).

The Will to Power:
Notebooks of 1884–1886
(*Selections*)

1884

Our presuppositions: no God; no purpose; finite force. We want to *guard* ourselves against following and endorsing the mode of thought of the lowly.[1]

* * * * *

(1) We want to hold fast to our senses and to belief in them—and think them through to the end! The non-sensuousness of previous philosophy as man's greatest nonsense.

(2) the world at hand, which everything earthly and living has been building, so that it appears as it does (durable and *slowly* changing), we want to build *further*—but not criticize it away as false!

(3) our valuations build at it, they emphasize and underscore. What does it matter if whole religions say: "It is all bad and false and evil!" This condemnation of the whole process can only be a judgment of misfits!

(4) to be sure, the misfits could be those who suffer most and are the most sensitive? The contented could be of little value?

(5) one must understand the artistic fundamental phenomenon that is called life—the *building* spirit, that builds under the most unfavorable circumstances: in the slowest manner—the *proof* for all of its combinations must first be given anew: *it preserves itself.*[2]

* * * * *

[1] *The Will to Power* [WP], ed. Walter Kaufmann, trans. Walter Kaufmann and R. J. Hollingdale (New York: Random House, 1967), 595; and *Nietzsche Werke: Kritische Gesamtausgabe* [KGW], eds. Giorgio Colli and Mazzino Montinari (Berlin and New York: Walter de Gruyter), vol. VII 25:299.
[2] WP 1046/KGW VII 25:438.

The best-believed *a priori* "truths" are for me—*assumptions for the time being,* e.g., the law of causality is a very well acquired habit of belief, so ingrained that *not* to believe in it would destroy the race. But are they therefore truths? What an inference! As though it were a proof of truth that man remains in existence![3]

*   *   *   *   *

The entire knowledge-apparatus is an apparatus for abstraction and simplification, directed not toward knowledge, but rather toward *getting control* of things: "end" and "means" are as remote from its nature as are "concepts." With "end" and "means" one gets control of a process (—one *invents* a process that is grasped!); with concepts, of the "things" that constitute the process.[4]

*   *   *   *   *

What the philosophers *lack:* (a) historical sense, (b) knowledge of physiology, (c) a goal in the future. To undertake a critique, without any irony and moral condemnation.[5]

*   *   *   *   *

If only we *could foresee* the most favorable conditions, under which beings of the highest value arise! It is a thousand times too complicated, and the probability of failure is *very great:* thus it is not encouraging to strive for them!—Skepticism.

On the other hand: we can increase courage, insight, hardness, independence, the feeling of responsibility, refine the sensitivity of the scales, and anticipate that fortunate accidents will come to our aid.[6]

*   *   *   *   *

Insight: all value-determination has to do with a particular perspective: the *preservation* of the individual, of a community, a race, a state, a church, a faith, a culture. Owing to the *forgetting* that there is only perspectival valuation, contradictory valuations and *consequently contradictory drives* of all sorts swarm in a single person. This is the *expression of the sickness of*

[3]WP 497/KGW VII 26:12.
[4]WP 503/KGW VII 26:61.
[5]WP 408/KGW VII 26:100.
[6]WP 907/KGW VII 26:117.

man, as opposed to the animal, in which all instincts to be found satisfy quite definite tasks.

This contradictory creature, however, has in its nature a great method of *knowledge:* one feels many pros and cons—one raises oneself *to justice*—to comprehension *beyond valuations of good and evil.*

The wisest human being would be the richest in *contradictions*, who has a similar taste for all kinds of human beings: and with it all, great moments of *grand-scale harmony*—a rare happenstance even in us!—a kind of planetary movement—[7]

* * * * *

To what extent our intellect also is a consequence of conditions of existence—we would not have it if we did not need it, and would not have it *as it is* if we did not need it as it is, if we could also live otherwise.[8]

* * * * *

Science—the transformation of nature into concepts for the purpose of the mastery of nature—that belongs under the rubric of "means."

But the purpose and will of man must likewise *grow*, the intention with regard to the whole.[9]

* * * * *

The philosophers are prejudiced *against* appearance, change, pain, death, the bodily, the senses, fate and unfreedom, the purposeless, everything human, even more the animal, more still the material; guided by instinctive value-determinations, in which earlier (more dangerous) cultural conditions are reflected.

They believe in absolute knowledge; knowledge for its own sake; the connection of virtue and happiness, desire and pain; the comprehensibility of human actions; good and evil. False opposites. The seductions of language.[10]

* * * * *

I want to talk no one into philosophy; it is necessary, it is perhaps also desirable, that the philosopher is a *rare* plant. Nothing is more contrary to

---

[7]WP 259/KGW VII 26:119.
[8]WP 498/KGW VII 26:137.
[9]WP 610/KGW VII 26:170.
[10]WP 407/KGW VII 26:300. Some parts of this note are omitted in WP 407.

me than the teacherly praise of philosophy, as in Seneca or especially Cicero. Philosophy has little to do with virtue. If I may say so, the scientific type also is something fundamentally different from the philosopher. —What I desire is that the genuine concept of the philosopher not be entirely extinguished in Germany. There are so many half-creatures of all kinds in Germany, who would gladly conceal their wretchedness under so noble a name.[11]

*   *   *   *   *

I teach: that there are higher and lower human beings, and that under certain conditions a single one can justify whole millennia—i.e., a full rich great whole human being in relation to countless incomplete human fragments.[12]

*   *   *   *   *

Man, in contrast to the animal, has extensively cultivated an abundance of *contrary* drives and impulses: owing to this syntheses he is master of the earth. —Morals are the expression of locally limited *rank-orders* in this multifarious world of drives: in order that man should not perish from their *contradictions*. Thus: one drive as master, its opposite drive weakened, refined, as an impulse that provides the stimulus for the activity of the dominant drive.

The highest human being would have the greatest multiplicity of drives, and also in the relatively greatest strength, that can still be endured. In point of fact: where the human plant shows itself strong, one finds instincts striving powerfully *against* each other (e.g., Shakespeare), but restrained.[13]

Early to Mid-1885

Philosophers (1) have always had a wonderful capacity for contradictions in terms. (2) They have trusted concepts as unconditionally as they have mistrusted the senses: they have not considered that concepts and words are our inheritance from times when what went on in the head was very murky and crude.

What dawns on philosophers last of all: they must no longer allow concepts simply to be given to them, nor simply purify and polish them, but rather above all must *make* them, *create* them, present them and make

[11]WP 420/KGW VII 26:452.
[12]WP 997/KGW VII 27:16.
[13]WP 986/KGW VII 27:59.

them convincing. Previously one has on the whole trusted one's concepts, as though they were a wonderful dowry from some sort of wonderland: but they are ultimately the legacy of our furthest, stupidest as well as cleverest ancestors. This *piety* toward that which is found in ourselves perhaps is part of the *moral* element in knowledge. What is needed first and foremost is absolute skepticism toward all inherited concepts (such as one philosopher *perhaps* once had—Plato: naturally, he *taught* the *opposite*—).[14]

*   *   *   *   *

The (At)tempter

There are many kinds of eyes. Even the Sphinx has eyes: and consequently there are many kinds of "truths," and consequently there is no truth.[15]

*   *   *   *   *

The victorious concept "force," with which our physicists have created God and the world, still requires an elaboration: an inner nature must be ascribed to it, which I designate as "will to power," i.e., as an insatiable craving for the manifestation of power; or for the use and exercise of power, as creative drive, etc. Physicists cannot eliminate "action at a distance" from their principles; likewise a repelling (or attracting) force. There is no alternative: one must conceive all movements, all "appearances," all "laws" only as symptoms of an inner event and make use of the analogy of man for that purpose. In the animal it is possible to derive all of its drives from the will to power; likewise, all functions of organic life from this one source.[16]

*   *   *   *   *

For a Plan. Introduction

1. The organic functions translated back into the fundamental will, the will to power—as having branched off from it.
2. Thinking, feeling, wanting in everything living—what is a pleasure other than: a stimulation of the feeling of power by an impediment (even stronger by rhythmic obstacles and resistances)—so that it thereby increases. Thus pain is involved in all pleasure. —If the pleasure is to become very great, the pains must last very long and the tension of the bow must be tremendous.

[14]WP 409/KGW VII 34:195.
[15]WP 540/KGW VII 34:230. In WP 540 the heading *Der Versucher* (which may mean either "attempter" or "tempter"—or both) is deleted.
[16]WP 619/KGW VII 36:31.

3. The will to power specializing itself as will to nourishment, property, tools, servants—obeying and ruling: the body.—The stronger will directs the weaker. There is no other kind of causality whatsoever than that of will upon will. It is certainly nothing mechanistic.

4. The spiritual functions. Will to formation, assimilation, etc.

Appendix. The great misunderstandings of the philosophers.[17]

* * * * *

On the whole I side more with the artists than with any philosophers previously: they have not lost the scent of the great trail that life leaves, they love the things of "this world"—they have loved their senses. To strive for desensualization: that seems to me to be a misunderstanding or a sickness or a cure, where it is not mere hypocrisy or self-deception. I wish for myself, and for all those who live—who are *permitted* to live— without the anxieties of a puritanical conscience, an ever greater spiritualization and multiplication of the senses; yes, we would be thankful to the senses for their subtlety, abundance and power, and in return offer them the best we have of spirit. What do the priestly and metaphysical slanders of the senses matter to us? We have nothing more to do with these slanders; it is a sign of having turned out well when, like Goethe, one clings with ever greater pleasure and affection to "the things of the world":—for in this manner one holds fast to the great conception of man, that man becomes the *transfigurer of existence* when he learns to transfigure himself.—But what are you saying? one may object to me. Are there not the most vexing pessimists among artists precisely today? For example, what do you think of Richard Wagner? Is he no pessimist?—I scratch my ear: (you are right, I forgot something for a moment.)[18]

* * * * *

"Truth": in my way of thinking this does not necessarily designate an opposite of error, but rather in the most fundamental cases only a placement of various errors in relation to each other: thus one might be older, deeper than another, perhaps even ineradicable in so far as an organic creature of our kind could not live without it; while other errors do not tyrannize over us as conditions of life in this way, and compared with such "tyrants" can be eliminated and "refuted." An assumption that is "irrefutable"—why should it thereby already be *true?* This proposition

---

[17]WP 658/KGW VII 35:15. In WP 658 the heading and last line are deleted.
[18]WP 820/KGW VII 37:12. In WP 820 the last part of this note, beginning with "But what are you saying?" is deleted.

will perhaps shock the logicians, who suppose *their* limits to be the limits of things—but I have long ago declared war on this logicians' optimism.[19]

* * * * *

And do you know what "the world" is to me? Shall I show it to you in my mirror? This world: a monster of energy, without beginning, without end; a fixed and firm quantity of energy that becomes neither larger nor smaller, that is not consumed but rather only transformed; as a whole of unchanging size, a household without expenditures and losses, but likewise without increase, without income, enclosed by "nothingness" as by a boundary; not something dissipating or squandering or infinitely extending but rather as a definite force set in a definite space—and not a space that might be "empty" anywhere, but rather as force throughout; as a play of forces and waves of force, at once one and "many," at once increasing here and diminishing there; a sea of forces raging and surging within itself, eternally changing, eternally running back again, with tremendous years of recurrence, with an ebb and flow of its forms; out of the simplest surging into the most complex, out of the stillest, stiffest, coldest into the hottest, wildest, most self-contradictory, and then homewardly returning to the simple again out of this fullness; out of the play of contradictions back to the pleasure of concord, affirming itself as that which must eternally return, as a becoming that knows no satiety, no disgust, no weariness—: This my *Dionysian* world of the eternally self-creating and eternally self-destroying, this mystery-world of the twofold ecstacy; this my beyond good and evil, without goal, unless the happiness of the circle is a goal; without will, unless a ring has goodwill toward itself—do you want a *name* for this world? A *solution* for all its mysteries? A *light* too for you, you best hidden, strongest, most daunt-less, most midnightly ones?—*This world is the will to power—and nothing besides!* And you yourselves are also this will to power—and nothing besides![20]

* * * * *

Fall 1885 to Fall 1886

Physiologists should think twice before positing the drive for preserva-tion as the cardinal drive of an organic creature: something living wants above all to *give vent* to its force: "preservation" is only one of the

---

[19]WP 535/KGW VII 38:4.
[20]WP 1067/KGW VII 38:12.

consequences thereof. —Beware of *superficial* teleological principles! And the entire concept of a "drive for preservation" is among them.[21]

*   *   *   *   *

The question of the origin of our evaluations and lists of what is good by no means coincides with their critique, as is so often believed; although, to be sure, the insight into some shameful origin brings with it a felt lessening of value of that which has arisen in that manner and sets the stage for a critical attitude and stance toward it.

What are our evaluations and moral goods-lists themselves worth? *What is the outcome of their dominance?* For whom? In relation to what?—Answer: for life. But *what is life?* Here a new, more definite conception of the concept "life" is needed. My formula for it is: life is will to power.

What is the meaning of evaluation itself? Does it refer back or down to another metaphysical world? As Kant still believed (coming as he did before the great historical movement). In short: Where did it "originate"? Or has it not "originated" at all? Answer: moral evaluation is a *construal*, a kind of interpreting. The construal itself is a *symptom* of particular physiological conditions, likewise of a particular spiritual level of dominant judgments. Who *construes?*—our affects.[22]

*   *   *   *   *

Toward a Preface to *Daybreak*

An attempt to try to think about morality without coming under its spell, mistrustful against being outwitted by its beautiful gestures and glances. A world that we are able to revere, that is fitting for our worshipful drives—that is constantly *proved*—through the guidance of one and all—: this the Christian idea, from which we all descend.

Through a growth of astuteness, mistrustfulness, scientificness (also through a more elevated instinct of truthfulness, therefore again under Christian influences), *this* interpretation has become *impermissible* to us any longer. . . .

My attempt to understand moral judgments as symptoms and sign-languages, which betray processes of physiological flourishing or failure, likewise the consciousness of conditions of preservation and growth: a mode of

---

[21]WP 650/KGW VIII 2:63.

[22]WP 254/KGW VIII 2:189, 190. The words rendered here as "construal" and "construes" (*Auslegung* and *auslegt*) can also be translated as "interpretation" and "interprets"; but since Nietzsche himself also uses the term *Interpretation* in the passage, as well as *Auslegung*, the use of a different English term for the latter seems appropriate.

interpretation of the same worth as astrology. Prejudices prompted by instincts (of races, communities, of various stages like growth or withering, etc.).

Applied to the specific Christian-European morality: our moral judgments are signs of decline, of no belief in life, a preparation for pessimism.

What does it mean that we have interpreted a *contradiction* into existence?—Decisive importance: behind all other evaluations these moral evaluations stand in command. Supposing they collapse—by what do we measure then? And what value then do knowledge, etc., etc. have?

My main proposition: There are no moral phenomena but rather only a moral(-istic) interpretation of these phenomena. This interpretation itself is of extramoral origin.[23]

*   *   *   *   *

That the value of the world lies in our interpretation (—that perhaps somewhere interpretations other than merely human ones are possible—); that previous interpretations are perspectival valuations, which have enabled us to preserve ourselves in life, that is, in will to power, for the growth of power; that every *elevation of man* involves the overcoming of narrower interpretations; that every attained strengthening and extension of power brings about new perspectives and means believing in new horizons—this runs through my writings. The world that *is of any concern to us* is false, i.e., is no matter of fact, but rather is a fabrication and approximation on the basis of a meager sum of observations; it is "in flux," as something becoming, as an ever newly shifting falsehood, which never approaches the truth: for—there is no "truth."[24]

*   *   *   *   *

The "meaninglessness of what happens"[25]: the belief in this is the consequence of an insight into the falsity of previous interpretations, a generalization of discouragement and weakness—not a *necessary* belief.

The presumptiousness of man: when one does not see meaning, to *deny* it![26]

*   *   *   *   *

[23]WP 258/KGW VIII 2:165. In WP 258 the heading and first two paragraphs are deleted, and the order of the last two paragraphs is reversed.
[24]WP 616/KGW VIII 2:108.
[25]*"Sinnlosigkeit des Geschehens."* Here and elsewhere in my translations of these notes I have rendered *Geschehen* as "what happens," rather than as "events" (as Kaufmann does), because the former is less philosophically problematical than the latter. The latter rendering wrongly suggests that Nietzsche accepts the view that what goes on in the world—what happens—does so in the form of discrete and definite "events."
[26]WP 599/KGW VIII 2:109.

Nihilism stands at the door: from whence comes this strangest and most sinister of all guests?

1. Starting point: it is an *error* to point to "social distress" or "psychological degeneration" or indeed to corruption as the *cause* of nihilism. These permit of a great many different construals. Nihilism lurks in an entirely specific interpretation, the Christian-moral. It is the most decent and compassionate of times. Need—need of the soul, of the body, of the intellect—is in itself incapable of giving rise to nihilism, i.e., the radical denial of value, meaning, desirability.

2. The demise of Christianity—from its morality (which is irreplaceable)—which turns against the Christian God (the sense of truthfulness, highly developed through Christianity, is nauseated by the falsehood and mendacity of all Christian interpretations of the world and history. Reaction from "God is the truth" to the fanatical belief "All is false." Buddhism of the *deed*. . .)

3. Skepticism in morals is what is decisive. The downfall of the moral world-interpretation which no longer has any sanction after it has attempted to flee into a beyond: ends in nihilism, "everything has no meaning" (the untenability of one world-interpretation—to which incredible energy has been devoted—awakens the suspicion that *all* world-interpretations are false). Buddhistic tendency, longing for nothingness. (Indian Buddhism does *not* have a fundamentally moral development behind it, therefore its nihilism contains morality that has not been overcome; existence as punishment, combined with existence as error, error thus as punishment—a moral evaluation.) The philosophical attempt to overcome the "moral God" (Hegel, pantheism). Overcoming of popular ideals: The sage. The saint. The poet. Antagonism of "true" and "beautiful" and "good."—

4. Against "meaninglessness" on the one hand, against moral value judgments on the other: to what extent all previous science and philosophy stand under moral judgments? and whether this won't earn one the hostility of science in the bargain? or the anti-scientific attitude? Critique of Spinoza. Christian value judgments linger on everywhere in the socialistic and positivistic systems. A *critique of Christian morality* is lacking.

5. The nihilistic consequences of contemporary natural science (together with its attempt to slip away into some beyond). From its pursuit eventually *follows* a self-disintegration, a turning against *itself*, an anti-scientificality.—Since Copernicus man has been rolling from the center into X.

6. The nihilistic consequences of political and economic ways of thinking, in which all "principles" are close to belonging to play-acting: the breath of mediocrity, wretchedness, dishonesty, etc. Nationalism, anar-

chism, etc. Punishment. The *redeeming* class and man are lacking, the justifiers—

7. The nihilistic consequences of history and the "*practical* historians," i.e., the romantics. The position of art: absolute *un*-originality of its position in the modern world. Its darkening. Goethe's purported Olympianness.

8. Art and the preparation of nihilism. Romantic (Wagner's *Nibelungen* ending).[27]

* * * * *

Conclusion

To what extent this self-destruction of morality is still a part of its own force. We Europeans have the blood in us of those who have died for their faith; we have looked upon morality seriously and fearfully, and there is nothing that we have not in one way or another sacrificed for it. On the other hand: our spiritual refinement has essentially been achieved through conscience-vivisection. We do not yet know the "whither" to which we are driven, now that we have in this way uprooted ourselves from our old ground. But this ground itself has provided us with the force that now drives us with the distance, into adventure, thrusting us out into the boundless, unexplored, undiscovered—we have no choice, we must be conquerors, since we have no country any longer where we are at home, where we would like to "conserve." No, you know better, my friends! The hidden Yes in you is stronger than all No's and Maybe's, by which you along with your time are sickened and addicted; and if you must go to sea, you emigrants, a *faith* thus compels you to do so. . . .[28]

---

[27]WP 1/KGW VIII 2:127.

[28]WP 405/KGW VIII 2:207. In WP 405 the next-to-last sentence and the portion of the last sentence after "than all No's" are omitted, and the following is added from elsewhere: "Our *strength* itself no longer has patience for the old marshy ground: we risk the distance, we risk *ourselves* in it: the world is still rich and undiscovered, and even perishing is better than living half-way and poisoned. Our strength itself compels us to take to the sea, and there, where all suns preciously have set: we *know* of a new world. . . ."

IV

Toward a Philosophy of the Future

(1886–1887)

Excerpts from

Beyond Good and Evil:
Prelude to a Philosophy of the Future
(Parts One to Three, Six, and Seven)

Joyful Wisdom (or The Gay Science)
(Book Five)

NEW PHILOSOPHERS AND TASKS

Introduction

"Prelude to a Philosophy of the Future": this subtitle indicates the way in which Nietzsche conceived of the task he undertook after *Thus Spoke Zarathustra*, under the banner of his next book's main title: *Beyond Good and Evil (Jenseits von Gut und Böse)*. Several years later (in *Ecce Homo*), he looked back on it, from the perspective of his conclusion toward the end of his active life that what was most needful was a "revaluation of all values," and saw it as the beginning of that critical reassessment: "After the Yes-saying part of my task has been solved, the time had come for the No-saying, *No-doing* part: the revaluation of our values so far, the great war. . . ." So he went on to say of *Beyond Good and Evil:* "This book . . . is in all essentials a *critique of modernity*, not excluding the modern sciences, modern arts, and even modern politics. . . ."[1]

That it certainly is. But it is more as well—as Nietzsche observed in adding that it also provides "pointers to a contrary type that is as little modern as possible—a noble, Yes-saying type."[2] In that respect it is not only a critical clearing of the ground to prepare the way for "a philosophy of the future" (analogous to Kant's *Prolegomena to Any Future Metaphysics*, which title Nietzsche's subtitle obviously echoes[3]). It also provides an indication of the sort of constructive undertaking this new approach to philosophy involves. His "philosophy of the future" would hold little interest and promise if it were to consist merely in an endless series of critical, "deconstructive" looks at past and present ways of thinking and living. To contribute positively to the enhancement of human understanding and human life, it must further find ways of getting on with the twin tasks of developing superior interpretations of ourselves and our world and of addressing problems of value and evaluation.

In *Beyond Good and Evil*, Nietzsche took his first steps in both of these directions after having arrived at the fundamentally "Yes-saying" position to which he had given expression in *Thus Spoke Zarathustra*. Many of his reflections are indeed critical; but they are conjoined with attempts to suggest constructive lines of thought alternative to and more promising

---

[1]*Ecce Homo*, Part III ("Why I Write Such Good Books"), "Beyond Good and Evil."
[2]*Ibid.*
[3]This seldom-noticed parallel to which Nietzsche's subtitle alludes is of no little interest and importance; for in his *Prolegomena*, Kant too attempts both to criticize the metaphysical endeavors of his predecessors and to suggest that and how future philosophical inquiry must differently proceed.

than the interpretations and evaluations that are subjected to criticism. In the works he completed during the last year of his active life (1888) his "revaluative" concerns came to predominate; but before them, and to some extent even in them, he continued to address himself to "reinterpretive" concerns as well—with respect to our human nature and possibilities in particular.

Indeed, the next "book" Nietzsche wrote and published after *Beyond Good and Evil* is devoted largely to concerns of this sort. It was the Fifth Book of *Die fröhliche Wissenschaft* (variously translated both as *The Gay Science* and as *Joyful Wisdom*), written in 1886 and published in the second edition of this work that came out in the next year. In it Nietzsche turned again to many of the matters with which he had dealt in its initial four-part version,[4] published just before *Thus Spoke Zarathustra*. He had already resumed his consideration of some of them in *Beyond Good and Evil*. This next "book" is usefully read together with the latter, which it closely followed; for it shows how Nietzsche went on with the constructive project of a "philosophy of the future" he sought to launch a year earlier. Excerpts from it are therefore included in the present section of this volume, following those from related parts of *Beyond Good and Evil*.[5]

The Fifth Book of *Joyful Wisdom* (or *The Gay Science*) is perhaps the best place to look among his later writings to find the mature Nietzsche as "philosopher of the future" at work. In it he takes up many important philosophical issues and shows—briefly, but as clearly as he ever does—how he proposes to deal with them, and what he thinks with respect to them. The fact that he chose to publish these reflections as an expansion of *Die fröhliche Wissenschaft*, under that title, indicates that he still found the title an apt characterization of his kind of philosophical thinking. It is "joyful" rather than pessimistic in its fundamentally affirmative stance with respect to life and the world, and "*wissenschaftlich*" in its manner of dealing with philosophical issues. While this term is usually translated as "scientific," it does not mean "scientific" in our narrower sense, in which the natural sciences are taken to be paradigmatic and decisive. Rather, it has a broader and more general meaning both in German and for Nietzsche. It conveys the idea of a kind of thinking that is devoted to the attainment of knowledge *(Wissen)*, guided by experience, and creative but also rigorous and disciplined in the analyses and interpretations undertaken. It is well exemplified in the two works from which the following excerpts are taken.

---

[4]See the excerpts from it presented in Part II of this volume.
[5]Excerpts from several other parts of *Beyond Good and Evil*, in which Nietzsche deals with morality and points to the alternative to prevailing forms of morality he envisions, are included in the following part of this volume, together with excerpts from *On the Genealogy of Morals*—his next complete book—in which he explores these matters further, and with which they therefore are appropriately read.

Beyond Good and Evil:
Prelude to a Philosophy
of the Future (1886)
(Excerpts)

PREFACE

Supposing that Truth is a woman—well, now, is there not some foundation for suspecting that all philosophers, insofar as they were dogmatists, have not known how to handle women? That the gruesome earnestness, the left-handed obtrusiveness, with which they have usually approached Truth have been unskilled and unseemly methods for prejudicing a woman (of all people!) in their favor? One thing is certain: she has not been so prejudiced. Today, every sort of dogmatism occupies a dismayed and discouraged position—if, indeed, it has maintained any position at all. For there are scoffers who maintain that dogma has collapsed, even worse, that it is laboring to draw its last breath. Seriously speaking, there are good grounds for hoping that all philosophic dogmatizing, however solemn, however final and ultimate it has pretended to be, may after all have been merely a noble child's-play and mere beginning. And perhaps the time is very near when we shall again and again comprehend *how* flimsy the cornerstone has been upon which the dogmatists have hitherto built their sublime and absolute philosophical edifices. Perhaps it was only some popular superstition of time immemorial (for example the soul-superstition which, in the guise of subject- and ego-superstition, has not ceased doing mischief even today); perhaps it was some play upon words, some seduction on the part of grammar, or some reckless generalization of very narrow, very personal, very human-all-too-human facts. The philosophy of the dogmatists, we hope, was only a promise held out over the millenniums, similar to astrology in still earlier times—astrology in whose service perhaps more labor, more money, more sharp-wittedness and patience have been spent than on any real science so far. To astrology and its "ultra-mundane" claims in Asia and Egypt we owe the grand style in architecture. It seems that in order to inscribe themselves upon the heart of humanity with everlasting claims, all great things must first sweep the earth disguised as enormous and fearsome grotesques. Dogmatic philosophy has been such a grotesque—witness the Vedanta doctrine in Asia and Platonism in Europe. Let us not be ungrateful to it, although it must surely be confessed that the worst, the most tiresome, and the most dangerous of all errors hitherto has been a dogmatist error: namely Plato's invention of Pure Spirit and of the Good in Itself. But now that it has been surmounted, now that Europe, rid of this nightmare, can again draw breath freely and at least enjoy a healthier sleep, now *we, whose task it is to stay awake,* we are the heirs of all the power gathered by the fight against this error. To be sure, it meant turning the truth upside down, denying *perspectivity* (the basic condition of all life), to speak of Spirit and of the Good as Plato had spoken of them. Indeed, like a physician one might ask, "How did such a disease attack that finest product of antiquity, Plato? Did that wicked Socrates really corrupt him after all? Was Socrates after all the corrupter of youth and deserving of his hemlock?" But the fight against Plato, or—to speak plainer and for "the people"—the fight against millenniums of Christian-ecclesiastical pressure (for Christianity is Platonism for "the people"), this fight created in Europe a magnificent tension of spirit, such as had not existed anywhere before. With such a tight-strung bow one can now aim at the remotest targets. European man, to be sure, feels this tension as a state of necessitation, and two attempts in grand style have been made to discharge the bow: once through Jesuitism and the second time through democratic enlightenment. This last attempt, in fact, aided by freedom of the press and the prevalence of newspaper-reading, might bring it to pass that Spirit will no longer so easily feel itself "necessary"! (The Germans invented gunpowder—all credit to them! But they made up for it by inventing the printing press.) We, however, who are neither Jesuits nor democrats nor even very German, we *good Europeans* and free, *very* free thinkers—we have it still, all the necessitation of spirit and all the tension of its bow! And perhaps also the arrow, the task, and (who knows?) the *target.* . . .

Sils-Maria, Upper Engadine. June, 1885

First Part
About Philosophers' Prejudices

1

The will to truth! That will which is yet to seduce us into many a venture, that famous truthfulness of which all philosophers up to this time have spoken reverently—think what questions this will to truth has posed for us! What strange, wicked, questionable questions! It has been a long story—and yet it seems hardly to have started. No wonder if just for once we become suspicious, and, losing our patience, impatiently turn around! Let us learn to ask this Sphinx some questions ourselves, for a change. Just *who* is it anyway who has been asking these questions? Just *what* is it in us that wants "to approach truth"? Indeed, we tarried a long time before the question of the cause of this will. And in the end we stopped altogether before the even more basic question. We asked "What is the value of this will?" Supposing we want truth: *why not rather* untruth? Uncertainty? Even Ignorance? The problem of the value of truth confronted us—or were we the ones who confronted the problem? Which of us is Oedipus? Which of us the Sphinx? It is a rendezvous of questions and question marks. It may be unbelievable, but it seems to us in the end as though the problem had never yet been posed—as though it were being seen, fixed, above all *risked,* for the first time. For there is a risk in posing it—perhaps no greater risk could be found.

2

How is it possible for anything to come out of its opposite? Truth, for example, out of error? Or the will to truth out of the will to deception? Or a selfless act out of self-interest? Or the pure sunny contemplation of a wise man out of covetousness? This sort of origin is impossible. Who dreams of it is a fool or worse; the things of highest value must have some other, *indigenous* origin; they cannot be derived from this ephemeral, seductive, deceptive, inferior world, this labyrinth of delusion and greed! Their basis must lie in the womb of Being, in the Eternal, in the hidden God, in the "Thing In Itself"—here, and nowhere else!—This type of judgment is the typical prejudice by which the metaphysicians of all time can be recognized. This type of valuation stands back of all their logical methods; this is the "faith" that enables them to struggle for what they call "knowing"—a something which at last they solemnly christen "truth." The basic faith of all metaphysicians is *faith in the antithetical nature of values.* It has never occurred to the most cautious of them, even though they had taken the vow to "doubt everything," to pause in doubt at the very threshold where doubt would have been most necessary. But we may indeed doubt: first, whether antitheses exist at all, and second, whether those popular valuations and value-antitheses upon which the metaphysicians have placed their stamp of approval are not perhaps merely superficial valuations, merely provisional perspectives—and perspectives from a tight corner at that, possibly from below, a "worm's eye view" so to speak. Admitting all the value accorded to the true, the truthful, the selfless, it is nonetheless possible that a higher value should be ascribed to appearance, to the will to deception, to self-interest, to greed—a higher value with respect to all life. Furthermore, it is quite possible that the very value of those good and honored things consists, in fact, in their insidious relatedness to these wicked, seemingly opposite things—it could be that they are inextricably bound up, entwined, perhaps even similar in their very nature. Perhaps! But who is willing to be troubled by such a perilous Perhaps? We must wait for a new species of philosopher to arrive, who will have some other, opposite tastes and inclinations than the previous ones. Philosophers of the Perilous Perhaps, in every sense! And seriously, I can see such new philosophers coming up over the horizon.

3

After keeping an eye on and reading between the lines of the philosophers for a long time, I find that I must tell myself the following: the largest part of conscious thinking must be considered an instinctual activity, even in the case of philosophical thinking. We must simply re-learn, as we have had to re-learn about heredity and "inborn" qualities. As little as the act of birth is of consequence in the whole process and progress of heredity, so little is consciousness in any decisive sense opposed to instinct. Most of the conscious thinking of a philosopher is secretly guided by his instincts and forced along certain lines. Even behind logic and its apparent sovereignty of development stand value judgments, or, to speak more plainly, physiological demands for preserving a certain type of life. Such as for example, that the definite is worth more than the indefinite, that appearance is less valuable than "the truth." Such valuations, all their regulative importance notwithstanding, can for *us* be only foreground-valuations, a definite type of ridiculous simplicity, possibly necessary for the preservation of the creature we happen to be. Assuming, to be sure, that man does not happen to be "the measure of all things." . . .

4

The falseness of a given judgment does not constitute an objection against it, so far as we are concerned. It is perhaps in this respect that our new language sounds strangest. The real question is how far a judgment furthers and maintains life, preserves a given type, possibly cultivates and trains a given type. We are, in fact, fundamentally inclined to maintain that the falsest judgments (to which belong the synthetic *a priori* judgments) are the most indispensable to us, that man cannot live without accepting the logical fictions as valid, without measuring reality against the purely invented world of the absolute, the immutable, without constantly falsifying the world by means of numeration. That getting along without false judgments would amount to getting along without life, negating life. To admit untruth as a necessary condition of life: this implies, to be sure, a perilous resistance against customary value-feelings. A philosophy that risks it nonetheless, if it did nothing else, would by this alone have taken its stand beyond good and evil.

5

What tempts us to look at all philosophers half suspiciously and half mockingly is not so much that we recognize again and again how innocent they are, how often and how easily they make mistakes and lose their way, in short their childishness and childlike-ness—but rather that they are not sufficiently candid, though they make a great virtuous noisy to-do as soon as the problem of truthfulness is even remotely touched upon. Every one of them pretends that he has discovered and reached his opinions through the self-development of cold, pure, divinely untroubled dialectic (in distinction to the mystics of every rank who, more honest and fatuous, talk about "inspiration"), whereas, at bottom, a pre-conceived dogma, a notion, an "institution," or mostly a heart's desire, made abstract and refined, is defended by them with arguments sought after the fact. They are all of them lawyers (though wanting to be called anything but that), and for the most part quite sly defenders of their prejudices which they christen "truths"—*very* far removed they are from the courageous conscience which admits precisely this; very remote from the courageous good taste which makes sure that others understand—perhaps to warn an enemy or a friend, perhaps from sheer high spirits and self-mockery. The spectacle of old Kant's Tartuffery, as stiff as it is respectable, luring us onto the dialectical crooked paths which lead (or better, mislead) to his "categorical imperative"—this spectacle makes us, used to diversions as we are, smile. For we find no small entertainment in keeping our eye on the delicate tricks of ancient moralists and morality-preachers. Or consider that hocus-pocus of mathematical form with which Spinoza masked and armor-plated as though in bronze his philosophy (or let us translate the word properly: "the love of *his own* wisdom")! He used it to intimidate at the very start the courageous attacker who might dare cast eyes on this invincible virgin and Pallas Athene—how much insecurity and vulnerability this masquerade of a sick recluse betrays!

6

Gradually I have come to realize what every great philosophy up to now has been: the personal confession of its originator, a type of involuntary and unaware memoir; also that the moral (or amoral) intentions of each philosophy constitute the protoplasm from which each entire plant has grown. Indeed, one will do well (and wisely), if one wishes to explain to himself how on earth the more remote metaphysical assertions of a philosopher ever arose, to ask each time: What sort of morality is this (is *he*) aiming at? Thus I do not believe that a "desire for comprehension" is the father of philosophy, but rather that a quite different desire has here as elsewhere used comprehension (together with miscomprehension) as tools to serve its own ends. Anyone who looks at the basic desires of man with a view to finding out how well they have played their part in precisely this field as inspirational genii (or demons or hobgoblins) will note that they have all philosophized at one time or another. Each individual desire wants badly to represent itself as *the* final aim of existence and as rightful master of all the others. For each desire is autocratic and *as such* it attempts to philosophize. In the case of scholars, to be sure, the specifically "scientific" men, it may be different— "better" if you wish. They may really have something like a "desire for comprehension," some small independent clockwork mechanism which, when properly wound, works bravely on *without* involving the remaining desires of the scholars. The real "interests," therefore, of the scholars lie in quite another field—in their family, perhaps, or their livelihood, or in politics. It makes almost no difference, in fact, whether the little machine is employed in one place or another to serve science, and whether the "promising" young worker makes of himself a philologist or a mushroom-fancier or a chemist—his becoming this or that does not *characterize* him. Conversely, there is nothing impersonal whatever in the philosopher. And particularly his morality testifies decidedly and decisively as to *who he is*—that is, what order of rank the innermost desires of his nature occupy.

*   *   *   *   *

8

In every philosophy there comes the point where the philosopher's "conviction" enters the scene—or, in the words of an ancient mystery,

> *adventavit asinus*
> *pulcher et fortissimus.*[1]

*   *   *   *   *

[1]"Entered now the ass / Beautiful and most strong" (trans.).

10

The eagerness and artfulness (I should perhaps better say shrewdness) with which everyone in Europe today attacks the problems of "the real and the apparent world" gives us to think and to listen. Anyone who hears only a "will to truth" in the background surely does not enjoy the keenest hearing. In individual and rare cases there may really be involved such a will to truth—some extravagant and adventurous bravery, some metaphysician's ambition to deal with a lost cause. There may be a few who really prefer a handful of "certainty" to a whole wagonload of beautiful possibilities; there may even be some puritanical fanaticists of conscience who would prefer a certain nothing to an uncertain something—for a deathbed! But this is nihilism and the token of a despairing soul, weary unto death, however brave the gestures of such a virtue may look. But the stronger, livelier thinkers who are still thirsty for life seem to feel otherwise. By taking sides *against* appearance, by pronouncing the word "perspective" with arrogance, by valuing the authenticity of their own bodies as highly as they value the evidence of their eyes which tells them that "the earth stands still," by thus letting their surest possession slip from their hands with apparent good humor (for what do we believe in more firmly nowadays than our own bodies?)—by doing all this—who knows?—perhaps they really want to re-conquer old ground, something that we used to possess with *greater certainty,* a something or other of the old domain of our former faith, perhaps the "immortal soul," perhaps the "ancient God." In short, they would discover ideas upon which to build better, i.e. stronger and more serene lives than one can build on "modern ideas." [. . .]

11

It seems to me that everyone nowadays tries to divert attention from Kant's actual influence on German philosophy and wisely to gloss over the value which Kant himself ascribed to himself. Above everything else, Kant was proud of his table of categories. With this tablet in his hands, he proclaimed that "it is the most difficult task that ever could have been undertaken in the service of metaphysics." Let us understand rightly his "could have been"! He was proud of having *discovered* a new faculty in man—the faculty of making synthetic *a priori* judgments. Agreed that he deceived himself, nonetheless the development and rapid efflorescence of German philosophy depends on this pride. It is the ambition and rivalry of all the younger philosophers to discover something even more proud, if possible—and in any case to discover "new faculties"! But let us take thought: the time for it has come. How are synthetic *a priori* judgments *possible*, Kant asked himself. And what was actually his answer? *By virtue of a virtue*—but unfortunately not in five words but so complicatedly, respectably, with such a show of German profundity and sinuosity, that one failed to hear the funny German simple-mindedness inherent in such an answer. [. . .] "By virtue of a virtue," he had said, or at least meant. But is that—an answer? An explanation? Isn't it merely begging the question? How does opium induce sleep? "By virtue of a virtue"—the *virtus dormitiva*, says that physician in Molière:

> *quia est in eo virtus dormitiva,*
> *cujas est natura sensus assoupire*[2]

But this kind of answer belongs to comedy. It is finally time to replace the Kantian question, "How are synthetic *a priori* judgments possible?" with another question: "Why is it *necessary* to believe in such judgments?" It is time for us to comprehend that such judgments must be *believed* true (false as they may actually be!) in order to preserve creatures such as we are. Or, to say it more plainly, rudely, and forthrightly: Synthetic *a priori* judgments should not "be possible" at all; we have no right to them; coming from us they are all false judgments. Only it must not be forgotten that faith in their truth is necessary; necessary as a provisional faith, an "eyewitness faith," that has its place in the perspectivity-optics of life. [. . .]

12

About materialistic atomism: it belongs among the best refuted things that exist. Perhaps no one among the scholars of Europe today is still so unscholarly as to attach serious significance to it (other than employing it as a handy abbreviation of means of expression), thanks mainly to the Dalmatian, Boscovich, who, together with the Pole Copernicus, has turned out to be the greatest and most successful opponent of "eyewitness" evidence. Whereas Copernicus persuaded us to believe, contrary to the evidence of all our senses, that the earth is *not* standing still, Boscovich taught us to disavow our belief in the last thing which remained "fast" on earth—namely our faith in "substance," in "matter," in the final residue of the universe, the little clod of atom. It was the greatest triumph over the senses that has ever been achieved on earth. But we must go further and declare war even on the "need for atomism," which still leads a dangerous after-life in fields where no one suspects its existence. We must next declare relentless war onto death, as we did with that better

---

[2]"Because there is in it a soporific virtue / The nature of which is to numb the senses" (trans.).

known "need for metaphysics," on that other and more fateful atomism which Christianity has best and longest taught: *psychic atomism*. With this expression let me designate the belief that the soul is something inde-structible, eternal, non-divisible; that it is a monad, an *atomon*. *This* faith ought to be eradicated from science. Between ourselves, it will by no means be necessary to get rid of the "soul" itself in this process, and thereby do without one of the oldest and most honorable hypotheses. This often happens to unskilled naturalists: as soon as they touch the "soul," they lose it. But we want the way open to new formulations and refinements of the soul-hypothesis. Concepts like "mortal soul" and "the psyche as a manifold of subjectivity" and "the psyche as social structure of the impulses and the emotions" want henceforth to be admitted to scientific legitimacy. By putting an end to the superstitions hitherto al-most tropically rampant around the ideas of soul, the *new* psychologist has pushed himself out, as it were, into new barrenness and new suspicions. It may be that the older psychologists had a jollier and more comfortable time—but in the end the new psychologist has sentenced himself to new inventions—and who knows?—perhaps new discoveries!

13

The physiologists should take heed before they assume self-preservation as the cardinal drive of an organic being. Above all, a living thing wants to *discharge* its energy: life as such is will to power. Self-preservation is only one of its indirect and most frequent *consequences*. In short, here as elsewhere, beware of superfluous teleological principles, such as the instinct for self-preservation. (We owe it to Spinoza's inconsistency.) This is the first demand of methodology, which must in its essence be economy of principles.

14

Today it is dawning on perhaps five or six minds that physics, too, is only an interpretation of the universe, an arrangement of it (to suit us, if I may be so bold!), rather than a clarification. Insofar as it builds on faith in sense-evidence, however, it is and shall long be taken for more—namely for a clarification. Physics has our eyes and fingers in its favor; it has eye-witness evidence and handiness on its side. This has an enchanting, per-suasive, and *convincing* effect on any era with basically plebeian tastes; why, it follows instinctively the canon of truth of forever-popular sensualism. What is clear? What is "clarified"? Only that which can be seen and touched—to this extent must each problem be pursued. Conversely, the magic of Platonic thinking, a *distinguished* type of thinking, lay precisely in *resisting* obvious sense-evidence. This was the thinking of men who perhaps enjoyed stronger and more demanding senses than our contemporaries. But they knew how to find a greater triumph in remaining master of these senses, and they accomplished their aim by casting pale, cold, gray concept-nets over the motley sense-turmoil, the "pandemic" as Plato put it. There was an *enjoyment* in this kind of world-conquest and world-interpretation in the manner of Plato, quite different from that which the physicists of today offer us. And not only the physicists but the Darwinists and anti-teleologists among the physiological workers, with their principle of the "least possible effort" and the greatest possible stupidity. "Where there is nothing for man to see and grasp, man has no business to look"! That, to be sure, is an imperative quite different from the Platonic one. Yet, for a rough, industrious race of machinists and engineers of the future, who have nothing but rough work to do, it may just be the correct imperative.

15

In order to work in the field of physiology with a clear conscience, one must insist that the sense organs are *not* phenomena in the idealist's sense—for if they were, they could not be causes! Thus we need sensualism at least as a regulative hypothesis if not as a heuristic principle. What? Others even say that the external world is the creation of our sense organs? But then our body, which is a part of the external world, would be the creation of our sense organs! But then our sense organs would be the creation of—our sense organs! This seems to me to be a thoroughgoing *reductio ad absurdum*, assuming that the concept *causa sui* is something thoroughly absurd. It follows, does it, that the external world is *not* the creation of our sense organs? . . .

16

Even today there are still harmless self-observers who believe in "immediate certainties," such as, for example, "I think" or, in the formulation of Schopenhauer's superstition, "I will." They believe that cognition here gets hold of its object, naked and pure, as "thing in itself," and that there is no falsification, either by the subject or by the object. But I shall repeat a hundred times that "immediate certainty" as well as "absolute knowledge" and "thing in itself" are all contradictions in terms. Let us finally free ourselves of the seduction inherent in our vocabulary! Let the people believe that cognition has to do with simple recognition; the philosopher must say to himself something like this: when I analyze the process which is expressed in the sentence "I think," then I get a series of bold assertions whose proof would be difficult, perhaps impossible. For example, that it is *I* who do the thinking; that, more generally, there is a something which performs thinking; that thinking is an activity and an effect of a creature which is thought of as its cause; that there exists an "I"; finally, that it is already determined what is to be designated with the word "think," in other words, that I *know* what thinking is. For if I hadn't already decided what it was, how should I be able to distinguish what is happening now from what happens when I "will" or "feel"? Enough—the "I think" assumes that I *compare* my present condition with other conditions that I know in myself, in order to determine what it is. Because of this referral to other knowledge, "I think" for me at least cannot have "immediate certainty."—In place of that "immediate certainty," in which we shall have to let the people believe in certain given cases, the philosopher, as we see, gets his hands on a series of metaphysical questions. They are real intellectual questions of conscience: "Where do I get the concept 'thinking'? Why do I believe in cause and effect? What justifies me in speaking of an 'I,' further, an 'I' which is a cause, further, an 'I' which is a thought-cause?" Whoever dares make an immediate answer to such metaphysical questions, basing his certainty on a sort of *intuition* of cognition (like the man who says "I think and know that this at least is true, real, certain")—will get a smile and two question marks from a philosopher nowadays. "My dear sir," the philosopher will most likely give him to understand, "it is in truth unlikely that you are not in error—but why must we have truth at all cost, anyway?"—

17

So far as the superstitiousness of logicians is concerned, I do not tire of emphasizing again and again one little briefly stated fact which these superstitious ones do not like to admit it. It is simply this: A thought comes when "it" will and not when "I" will. It is thus a *falsification* of the evidence to say that the subject "I" conditions the predicate "think." *It* is thought, to be sure, but that this "it" should be that old famous "I" is, to put it mildly, only a supposition, an assertion. Above all it is not an "immediate certainty." In the end even "it is thought" says too much. Even this "it" contains an *interpretation* of the process and does not belong to the process itself. Our conclusion is here formulated out of our grammatical custom: "Thinking is an activity; every activity presumes something which is active, hence. . . ." According to this same approximate scheme, our older "atomism" was looking for the "force" that has an effect, for that little clod of matter that it inhabits, from which it acts; in short, the atom. More rigorous minds finally learned to get along without such "earthly remains," and perhaps in logic too we will some day become accustomed to getting along without that little "it" (into which the good old honest "I" has evaporated).

18

It is surely not the smallest charm of a theory that it is refutable: this precisely attracts the subtler minds. It seems that the theory of "freedom of the will," a hundred times refuted, owes its permanence to just this charm. Someone always comes along who feels strong enough to refute it once more.

19

Philosophers are in the habit of speaking of "will" as though it were the best-known thing in the world. Schopenhauer in fact gave us to understand that will alone is really known to us, completely known, known without deduction or addition. But it seems to me once again that Schopenhauer in this case too did only what philosophers are always doing: he took over and exaggerated a *popular judgment*. Willing seems to me to be, above all, something *complicated*, something that is a unity in word only. The popular judgment lies just in this word "only," and it has become master of the forever incautious philosophers. Let us be more cautious, then; let us be "unphilosophical"; let us say: in every willing there is first of all a multiplicity of feelings: the feeling of a condition to get *away* from, the feeling of a condition to get *to;* then the feeling of this "away" and "to"; furthermore, an accompanying muscular feeling which, from a sort of habit, begins a game of its own as soon as we "will"—even without our moving our "arms and legs." In the first place, then, feeling— many kinds of feeling—is to be recognized as an ingredient in willing. Secondly, there is thinking: in every act of the will there is a thought which gives commands—and we must not imagine that we can separate this thought out of "willing" and still have something like will left! Thirdly, the will is not merely a complex of feeling and thinking but above all it is a passion—the passion of commanding. What is called "freedom of the will" is essentially a passionate superiority toward a someone who must obey. "I am free; 'he' must obey"—the consciousness of this is the very willing; likewise that tension of alertness, that straight-forward look which fixes on one thing exclusively, that absolute valuation which means "just now this, and nothing else, is necessary," that inner certainty that there will be obedience—all this and whatever else is part of the condition of one who is in command. A man who *wills* is giving a command to something in himself that obeys, or which he believes will obey. But now let us note the oddest thing about the will, this manifold something for which the people have only one word: because we, in a given case, are simultaneously the commanders *and* the obeyers and, as obeyers, know the feelings of forcing, crowding, pressing, resisting, and moving which begin immediately after the act of the will: because, on the other hand, we are in the habit of glossing over this duality with the help of the synthetic concept "I"—for these reasons a whole chain of erroneous conclusions, and consequently false valuations of the will, has weighted down our notion of willing, so much so that the willer believes in good faith that willing *suffices* to produce action. Because in the majority of cases there was a willing only where the effect of the command, the obedience, i.e. the action, was an *expected* one, the *appearance* translated itself into the feeling that there had been a *necessary effect*. In short, the willer believes, with a considerable degree of certainty, that will and action are somehow one. He credits the success, the execution of the willing, to the will itself, therewith luxuriating in an increase of the feeling of power which all success produces. "Freedom of the will" is the word for that manifold pleasurable condition of the willer who is in command and at the same time considers himself as one with the executor of the command—as such enjoying the triumph over the resistance, but possessed of the judgment that it is his will itself that is overcoming the resistance. In this fashion the willer adds the pleasurable feelings of the executing, successful instruments, the subservient "lower wills" or "lower souls" (for our body is nothing but a social structure of many souls) to his pleasurable feeling as Commander. *L'effet c'est moi*[3]—the same thing happens here that happens in any well constructed and happy community: the ruling class identifies itself with the success of the community. In all willing, then, there is commanding and obeying on the basis, as we have seen, of a social structure of many "souls." This is why a philosopher should consider himself justified in including willing within the general sphere of morality— morality understood as the doctrine of the rank-relations that produce the phenomenon we call "life."—

20

The various philosophical concepts do not evolve at random or autonomously but in reference and relationship to one another; although they seem to occur suddenly and arbitrarily in the history of thought, they belong to a system exactly like all the members of the fauna of a continent. This is revealed by the fact that the most diverse philosophers again and again fill in a basic scheme of *possible* philosophies. Invisibly compelled,

---

[3]"I am the effect"—a play on Louis XIV's *L'etat c'est moi*, "I am the state."

they revolve again and again in the same orbit. No matter how independent of each other they feel with their critical or systematic will—something or other in them leads them; something or other keeps them running, one after another, in a definite sequence. They share an inborn systematization and relation of concepts. Their thinking is in fact not so much a discovering as a recognizing, remembering, a return and a homecoming to a remote, ancient, commonly stocked household of the soul out of which the concepts grew. Seen in this light, philosophizing is a sort of atavism of the highest order. The odd family resemblance between all Indic, Greek, and German philosophizing is simple enough to explain. For especially where the languages are related it cannot possibly be avoided that, thanks to a common philosophy of grammar (by this I mean thanks to the unconscious domination and leadership of similar grammatical functions), everything lies prepared for a similar development and sequence of the various philosophical systems. For the same reason, the road seems closed to certain other possibilities of world-interpretation. Philosophers belonging to the Ural-Altaic linguistic group (containing languages in which the concept of "subject" is least developed) most probably "view the world" quite differently and will be found on paths other than those travelled by speakers of Indo-European or by Moslems. The compulsion exerted by certain grammatical functions is in the end the compulsion of *physiological* value judgments and of the conditions that determine race. —This much by way of rejecting Locke's superficiality on the subject of the origin of ideas.

21

The *causa sui*[4] is the best self-contradiction hitherto thought up; it is a sort of logical rape and perversion. But man's extravagant pride has managed to tie itself up deeply and dreadfully with just this nonsense. The demand for "freedom of the will," in that metaphysical superlative sense in which it still rules the minds of the half-learned, the demand to assume the total and final responsibility for one's own actions, thereby relieving God, world, ancestors, accident, and society; this demand is nothing less than to be the *causa sui* oneself, to pull oneself by one's own bootstraps into existence out of the bog of non-existence—a feat dreamed up with a recklessness exceeding that of Baron Munchhausen! But supposing someone recognizes the peasant-like simplicity of our famous "freedom of the will" and deletes it from his thinking. I would now beg him to carry his "enlightenment" one step farther and to delete also contrary of that "free will" monstrosity. I mean the "non-free will," which amounts to a misuse

[4]"Cause of oneself."

of cause and effect. One should not mistakenly *objectivize* "cause" and "effect" in the manner of the natural scientists (and whoever else nowadays naturalizes in his thinking), in accordance with the ruling mechanistic oafishness that pushes and pulls the cause until it becomes "effective." One should make use of "cause" and "effect" only as pure *concepts*, i.e. as conventional fictions for the purpose of designation and mutual understanding, *not* for explanation. In "being-as-such" there are no "causal connections" or "necessities" or "psychological lack of freedom"; effect there does *not* follow upon a cause; there *is* no "law" which rules phenomena. It is *we*, we alone, who have dreamed up the causes, the one-thing-after-anothers, the one-thing-reciprocating-anothers, the relativity, the constraint, the numbers, the laws, the freedom, the "reason why," the purpose. And when we mix up this world of symbols with the world of things as though the symbols existed "in themselves," then we are merely doing once more what we have always done: we are creating myths. The "non-free will" is a piece of mythology; in real life there is only *strong* will and *weak* will. It is almost always a symptom of what the man lacks when a thinker feels something of constraint, necessity, having-to-obey, pressure, and lack of freedom in all his "causal connections" and "psychological necessities." It is revealing to feel these things: the personality betrays itself. On the whole, if I have observed correctly, there are two diametrically opposed factions which have picked the "non-freedom" of the will for their problem — but both sides reveal a profoundly *personal* bias. The ones want to avoid giving up at any cost their "responsibility," their faith in *themselves*, their personal right to *their* merit. (These are the vain races!) The others, conversely, do not want to be responsible for anything; they do not want to be guilty of anything; they demand, from an inner self-contempt, to *get rid of the burden* of themselves in some direction or other. When this latter type writes books, nowadays, they usually interest themselves in criminals: a sort of socialistic compassion is their favorite disguise. And they are right: the fatalism of the weak of will is astonishingly beautified by its claim to be *"la religion de la souffrance humaine."*[5] Herein lies its type of "good taste."

22

One will forgive, I hope, an old philologist who cannot desist from the malice of pointing his finger at poor interpretation. But really, that "conformity of nature unto law" of which you physicists talk so proudly as if . . . , that lawfulness is the result only of your *explication de texte*,[6] of your

[5]"The religion of human suffering."
[6]"Interpretation of the text."

bad philology! It is not a fact, not a "text" at all, but only a naive, humanitarian arrangement and misinterpretation that you use for truckling to the democratic instincts of the modern soul. "Everywhere equality before the law—and nature is no better off than we are"—surely a fine *arrière-pensée*[7] in which are disguised first, a vulgar hostility to everything privileged and autocratic, and second, a very subtle atheism. "*Ni dieu, ni maitre*"[8]—you, too, want that, and therefore "Long live natural law"! Am I right? But, as I have said, this is explication, not text, and someone might come along who, with opposite intention and interpretive skill, might read out of the same nature and the same phenomena quite another thing: a tyrannical, inconsiderate, relentless enforcement of claims to power. There may arise an interpreter who might so focus your eyes on the unexceptionality and unconditionality of all "will to power" that almost every word that you now know, including the word "tyranny" would finally become useless and sound like a weakening and palliative metaphor—as something too human. And yet he might end by asserting about this world exactly what you assert, namely that it runs a "necessary" and "calculable" course—but *not* because it is ruled by laws but because laws are absolutely lacking, because at each moment each power is ultimately self-consistent. Let us admit that this, too, would be only an interpretation—and you will be eager enough to make this objection! Well, all the better!

23

All psychology hitherto has become stuck in moral prejudices and fears: none has ventured into the depths. To consider psychology as the morphology and evolutionary doctrine of the will to power—as I consider it—this no one has touched upon even in thought (insofar as it is allowable to recognize in what has been written the symptoms of what has been kept dark). The force of moral prejudices has penetrated deeply into the most spiritual, the seemingly coldest and most open-minded world, and, as one may imagine, with harmful, obstructionist, blinding, and distorting results. A proper physio-psychology must battle with unconscious resistances in the heart of the investigator; his "heart" sides against it. Even a doctrine of the reciprocally limiting interaction of the "good" and "wicked" impulses causes, as being a subtle form of immorality, some distress and aversion in a still strong and hearty conscience. Even worse is a doctrine that all the good impulses are derived from the wicked ones. But imagine someone who takes the very passions—hatred, envy, greed,

---

[7]"Ulterior motivation."
[8]"Neither God nor master."

domineering—to be the passions upon which life is conditioned, as things which must be present in the total household of life. Takes them to be necessary in order to preserve the very nature of life, to be further developed if life is to be further developed! Such a man suffers from the inclination of his judgment as though from seasickness! But even this hypothesis is by no means the most painful or the strangest in this enormous, almost totally unknown domain of dangerous insights. Indeed, there are a hundred good reasons for staying away from it if one—can! On the other hand, if our ship has once taken us there—very well, let us go ahead, grit our teeth, open our eyes, grip the rudder and—ride out morality! Perhaps we will crush and destroy our own remaining morality, but what do *we* matter! Never yet has a *deeper* world of insight been opened to bold travellers and adventurers. And the psychologist who can make this sort of "sacrifice" (it is not the *sacrifizio dell' intelletto*[9]—on the contrary!) will at least be in a position to demand that psychology be acknowledged once more as the mistress of the sciences, for whose service and preparation the other sciences exist. For psychology is now again the road to the basic problems.

Second Part
The Free Thinker

24

O sancta simplicitas![10] How strangely simplified and falsified does man live! One does not cease to wonder, once one has eyes to see this wonder! How bright and free and easy and simple we have made everything around us! How well we knew to give our senses a free ticket to everything superficial! How we have given our thinking a divine yen for exuberant jumps and faulty conclusions! How from the very beginning we have managed to preserve our ignorance in order to enjoy a scarcely comprehensible freedom, impetuosity, carelessness, heartiness, and gaiety of life, in short—life! And science up to now was allowed to rise only on this firm, granite rock of ignorance; the will to know on the foundation of a much more forceful will, namely the will to not-know, to un-certainty, to un-truth! Not as its opposite—no, as its refinement! Let *language*, here as elsewhere, retain its awkwardness and continue to talk about antitheses

[9]"Sacrifice of the intellect."
[10]"Oh holy simplicity!"

where there are only degrees and diverse subtle levels; let the inveterate Tartuffery of morality which has become our invincible flesh and blood twist even the words of us knowing ones around in our mouths: nevertheless! Here and there we comprehend (and can laugh about it) that the very best of science wants to hold us fast to this *over-simplified*, thoroughly artificial, made-over and falsified world. Why? Because science loves error, involuntarily-willingly; because science, alive, loves—life!

*   *   *   *   *

32

For the longest period in human history (we call it the prehistoric period), the value or worthlessness of an action was inferred from its consequences. The action itself or the origin of the action was considered in the same light in which China even today considers the excellence or disgrace of a child—something which is a reflected quality of the parents. It was the reflecting force of success or failure which caused man to think well or ill of an action. Let us call this period of mankind the *pre-moral* period. The imperative "know thyself" was still unknown to it. In the last ten millenniums, on the other hand, we have progressed step by step in several large areas of the world to the point where we let not the consequences but the origins of an action determine its value. This, on the whole, was a momentous occurrence, a considerable refinement of our view and our criteria. It was the unconscious influence of the rule of aristocratic values, of belief in "descent"—tokens of a period which we may designate as *moral*, in the more narrow sense. It constitutes the first experiment in self-knowledge. Origin instead of consequences: what a reversal of perspective! A reversal surely arrived at only after long struggle and wavering! To be sure, it produced the rule of a new fateful superstition, a peculiar narrowness of interpretation. The origin of an action was interpreted to rest, in a very definite sense, on an *intent*. Everyone united in the one faith that the value of an action lay in the value of its intent. Intent as the sole origin and pre-history of an action: this is the prejudice that has dictated our moral praise, censure, judgments, and philosophy on earth till the most recent times.—But haven't we really arrived at the necessity today of once more resolving that there has been another reversal and basic shift of values, thanks to further self-recognition and self-deepening of man? Aren't we standing on the threshold of a period which, provisionally, we ought to label negatively as the *amoral* period? At least among us immoralists today there is arising a suspicion that the decisive value of an action is precisely in what is *not* intentional in it; that all its intentionality, everything that can be seen, known, made conscious in it belongs only to its surface, its skin which, like any skin, reveals something but *conceals* even more! In short, we believe that intent is only a symbol and symptom, requiring interpretation; furthermore that it is a symbol which signifies too much and consequently means little if nothing by itself; that morality in the old sense, i.e. morality of intent, was a preju- dice, a premature, perhaps a preliminary thing; something in the order of astrology or alchemy, but in any event something which must be sur- passed. The surpassing of morality, the self-surpassing of morality in a certain sense: this may be taken to be the name for that long secret labor which is in store for the subtlest, most candid, also most malicious con- sciences of today. They are the living touchstones of the soul!

* * * * *

34

No matter from what philosophic point of vantage one looks today, from any position at all, the *fallaciousness* of the world in which we think we live is the firmest and most certain sight that meets our eye. We find reason upon reason for this, and they would lure us to surmise a deceptive principle in "the nature of things." But whoever makes our thinking, i.e. "mind," responsible for the world's falseness (an honorable loophole through which every conscious or unconscious *advocatus dei*[11] slips), who- ever takes this world together with its space, time, form and motion, to be falsely *inferred*, such a man would have good reason to learn to distrust all thinking altogether. [. . . The philosopher] is the creature who has here- tofore been most easily fooled. Today he has the *duty* to be mistrustful, to squint most maliciously from every abyss of suspicion. —Forgive the jest of this gloomy caricature and turn of thought. But I myself have had to re-learn long ago; I have had to re-evaluate deceiving and being deceived; and I hold in readiness at least a couple of jabs in the ribs for the blind rage of philosophers who struggle against being deceived. *Why not?* It is no more than a moral prejudice that truth is worth more than semblance; in fact it is the worst-proved supposition that exists. Why don't we admit at least this much: there could be no life except on the basis of perspectival valuations and semblances. And if, with the virtuous enthusiasm and ineptitude of many philosophers, you wanted to get rid of the "world of semblance" altogether (assuming *you* could do this), well, there would be nothing left of your "truth," either. Whatever forces us, furthermore, to assume at all that there is an essential difference between "true" and "false"? Is it not sufficient to assume levels of semblance, lighter and

---

[11]"Advocate of God"—a play on *advocatus diaboli*, "devil's advocate."

darker shadows and tones of semblance as it were, different "values" in the painters' sense of the term? Why couldn't the world *which matters to us* be a fiction? And if someone asks, "But doesn't an originator go with a fiction?", couldn't he be answered roundly with "Why?" Couldn't this "go with" go with the fiction? Aren't we going to be allowed to be a little ironical about the subject, as much as about the predicate and the object? Isn't the philosopher allowed to raise himself above faith in grammar? All due respect to our schoolmarms, but isn't it time for philosophy to renounce the faith of schoolmarms?—

*   *   *   *   *

36

Let us assume that nothing is "given" as real except our world of desires and passions, that we cannot step down or step up to any kind of "reality" except the reality of our drives—for thinking is nothing but the interrelation and interaction of our drives. Would we not be allowed to experiment with the question whether these "givens" are not *sufficient* for understanding the so-called mechanistic (or material) world? I mean not as an illusion, "a semblance," an "idea" (in Berkeley's or Schopenhauer's sense), but as equal in reality-stature to our passions? To understand it as a more primitive form of the world of passions in which everything, still contained in a powerful unison, later branches off and develops (also, as is fair enough, weakens and is refined) in the organic processes? As a sort of primitive life in which all the organic functions, together with self-regulation, assimilation, nutrition, secretion and metabolism, are still synthetically bound up with one another? To understand the material world as a *preform* of life? In the end this experimental question is not merely allowed; it is demanded by the conscience of *methodology*. Not to assume several types of causality until the experiment of getting along with a single one has been followed to its utmost conclusion (to the point of absurdity, if I may be permitted to say so): this is the morality of methodology which one may not escape today. It follows "from its definition" as a mathematician would say. In the end, the question is whether we really acknowledge the will as *effective;* whether we believe in the causality of the will. If we do (and basically our faith in the causality of the will amounts to our belief in causality itself), we *must* experiment with taking will-causality as our only hypothesis. Will, of course, can only act on will, not on matter (on "nerves," for example). Enough said: we must risk the hypothesis that everywhere we recognize "effects" there is an effect of will upon will; that all mechanical happenings, insofar as they are activated by some energy, are will-power, will-effects.—Assuming, finally, that we succeeded in explaining our entire

instinctual life as the development and ramification of one basic form of
will (of the will to power, as I hold); assuming that one could trace back
all the organic functions to this will to power, including the solution of the
problem of generation and nutrition (they are one problem)—if this were
done, we should be justified in defining *all* effective energy unequivocally
as *will to power*. The world seen from within, the world designated and
defined according to its "intelligible character"—this world would be *will
to power* and nothing else.[12]

*   *   *   *   *

39

No one very easily takes a doctrine as true merely because it makes one
happy or virtuous. No one, that is, but the lovely "idealists," who yearn
over the good, the true, and the beautiful and let every kind of colorful,
clumsy, and good-natured desirability swim at random in their pool. Happiness and virtue are not arguments. But we like to forget—even sensible
thinkers do—that things making for unhappiness or for evil are not counter-
arguments, either. Something might be true, even though it is harmful and
dangerous in the greatest degree; it might in fact belong to the basic
make-up of things that one should perish from its full recognition. Then
the strength of a given thinker would be measured by the amount of "the
truth" that he could stand. Or, to say it more plainly, to what degree he
would *need* to have it adulterated, shrouded, sweetened, dulled, and falsified. But there can be no doubt that for the discovery of certain *parts* of
the truth, evil and unhappy men are better suited and have a greater probability of obtaining success—not to speak of those evil ones who are happy
(a species of man which the moralists keep dark). Perhaps hardness and
guile are better qualifications for the development of a strong independent
thinker and philosopher than that gentle, delicate, yielding good nature
and skill for taking things lightly that we value in an intellectual.

*   *   *   *   *

42

A new species of philosopher is coming up over the horizon. I risk
baptizing them with a name that is not devoid of peril. As I read them (as

[12]This is the first appearance of this interpretation in Nietzsche's published writings after
its initial announcement in *Thus Spoke Zarathustra*.

they allow themselves to be read—for it is characteristic of their type that they wish to remain riddles in some sense), these philosophers of the future have a right (perhaps also a wrong!) to be called: *Experimenters.*[13] This name itself is only an experiment, and, if you will, a temptation.

43

Will they be new friends of "truth," these coming philosophers? Most probably, for all philosophers thus far have loved their truths. But surely they will not be dogmatists. It must run counter to their pride and their taste that their truth should be a truth for everyman, this having been the secret wish and ultimate motive of all dogmatic striving. "My judgment is *my* judgment, to which hardly anyone else has a right," is what the philosopher of the future will say. One must get rid of the bad taste of wishing to agree with many others. "Good" is no longer good in the mouth of my neighbor. And how could there be a "common good"! The expression contradicts itself: what can be common cannot have much value. In the end it must be as it always was: great things remain for the great; abysses for the deep; delicacies and tremors for the subtle; and, all in all, all things rare for the rare!—

44

After all this need I say especially that they shall be free, *very* free thinkers, these philosophers of the future? It is certain, however, that they will not be merely free thinkers but something more, something superior, greater, and thoroughly different, something that does not want to be misjudged or mistaken for something else. But, as I am saying this, I feel the *obligation* (almost as much toward them as toward ourselves, who are their heralds and fore-runners, we free thinkers) to blow away from all of us an old stupid prejudice and misunderstanding which for too long a time has made the concept "free thinker" opaque, like a fog. In all the countries of Europe and in America there is something nowadays which abuses this concept. There is a very narrow, imprisoned, enchained sort of thinker who wants approximately the opposite of our intentions and instincts, not to mention that in reference to the *new* philosophers coming up this sort would have to be a closed window and a bolted door. They belong, to make it short and sad, among the *levellers*, these falsely named "free thinkers." They are glib-tongued and scribble-mad slaves of democratic taste and its "modern ideas"; all of them are men without solitude,

---

[13]The German word for attempt, tempt, and experiment is *versuchen*. Nietzsche here explicitly and elsewhere implicitly puns on it (trans.).

without solitude of their own; rough and ready boys to whom we cannot deny courage or respectable conduct but of whom we must say that they are unfree and absurdly superficial, especially in their basic inclination to see the cause for *all* human misery and failure in the structure of society as it has been up to now. This about turns the truth upside down. What they would like to strive for with all their power is the universal green pasture-happiness of the herd: security, lack of danger, comfort and alleviation of life for everyone. Their most frequently repeated songs and doctrines are "equal rights" and "compassion for all that suffers." Suffering is taken by them to be something that must be *abolished*. We opposed thinkers, who have opened our eyes and our consciences to the question, "How and where has the plant 'man' flourished most strongly so far?", we imagine that it has happened every time under the opposite conditions: that the peril of man's position had to grow to enormity; that his power of invention and dissembling (his "mind") had to develop subtlety and boldness under long pressure and compulsion; that his life-will had to be stepped up to an unconditional power-will. We imagine that hardness, violence, slavery, peril in the street and in the heart, concealment, Stoicism, temptation, and deviltry of every sort, everything evil, frightful, tyrannical, brutal, and snake-like in man, serves as well for the advancement of the species "man" as their opposite. In fact we are not even saying enough when we say this much. At any rate, with our speech and our silence, we have arrived at the *other* end of all modern ideologies and herd-desires. Perhaps we are their antipodes. No wonder that we "free thinkers" are not exactly the most communicative of thinkers. No wonder that we do not want to reveal in every particular what a mind can be made free *from*, and *to* what it might feel driven. As for the dangerous formula "beyond good and evil" which at least keeps us from being mistaken for someone else, we *are* something different from *"libres-penseurs," "liberi pensatori,"* "free thinkers," and whatever else these good proponents of "modern ideas" like to be called. At home, or at least a guest, in many lands of the spirit; escaped many times from the stuffy pleasant corners into which preference and prejudice, youth, origin, accidental meetings with men and books, or even the weariness of our wanderings have seemed to pin us down; full of malice against the bait of dependence that lies hidden in honors or money or offices or sensuous enthusiasms; grateful even for distress and vicissitudinous disease because it always frees us from some kind of a rule and its "prejudice"; grateful to God, the devil, the sheep and the worm in us; curious to a fault; investigative to the point of cruelty; with impetuous fingers for the impalpable; with teeth and stomachs for the indigestible; ready for any trade demanding sharp-wittedness and sharp wits; ready for any venture thanks to an excess of "free will"; with fore-souls and back-souls whose ultimate intentions are not easily fathomed; with foregrounds and backgrounds that no foot can explore to the end; concealed beneath cloaks of light; conquerors, though we may look like inheritors and wastrels; arrangers and collectors from early till late; misers of our wealth and our full stuffed drawers; economical in learning and forgetting; inventive of schemes; occasionally proud of tables of categories; occasionally pedantic; occasionally night owls of work in the midst of daylight; scarecrows, even, when necessary—and today it is necessary insofar as we are the born, sworn, jealous friends of *solitude*, our own deepest midnight and mid-day solitude: this is the type of man we are, we free thinkers! And perhaps *you* too, you coming *new* philosophers, perhaps you too belong to this type.

*   *   *   *   *

Third Part
Religion

53

Why atheism today? The "Father" in God is thoroughly refuted, likewise the "judge" and the "rewarder." Also his "free will"—he does not hear us, and even if he heard us he could not help. The worst of it is that he seems to be incapable of communicating clearly. Is he unclear?—This is what I have found out from many questions and conversations as to the cause of the decline of European theism. It seems to me that the religious instinct is growing powerfully but is rejecting theistic gratification with deep distrust.

54

What, basically, is all modern philosophy doing? Since Descartes (and more in spite of him than proceeding from his premises), all philosophers are assaulting the old concept of soul, under the pretence of criticizing our subject and predicate concept. This means an assault on the basic premise of Christian doctrine. Modern philosophy, being epistemological skepticism, is secretly or openly anti-Christian, though by no means anti-religious. (But that is said for subtle ears only.) We used to believe in the "soul" as we believed in grammar and the grammatical subject; we used to say that "I" was the condition, "think" the predicate that conditioned, and thinking an activity for which a subject *had to be* thought of as its cause. But then we tried, with admirable persistence and guile, to see whether the reverse might not perhaps be true. "Think" was now the condition, "I" the thing conditioned, hence "I" only a synthesis which was *created* by thinking. Kant basically wanted to prove that the subject could not be proved by the subject—nor the object either. The possibility of an *illusory existence* of the individual subject (the "soul") may not have been a thought foreign to him. It is the same thought which has already existed as an immense power on earth, in the form of Vedanta philosophy.

*　*　*　*　*

61

The philosopher, as we free thinkers understand him, the man with the most extensive responsibility, whose conscience must do for the total development of mankind, this philosopher will use religions for his educational and training purposes, just as he uses the political and economic institutions of his time.[. . .] To ordinary people, finally, to the great majority who exist to serve the general welfare (and who *should* exist only for this), religion gives an invaluable contentedness with their situation and their type, manifold peace of heart, an ennobling of their obedience, one more joy and grief to share with their peers, and something that transfigures and beautifies them, something that justifies the every-day quality of their life, their inferiority, and the whole half-animal poverty of their soul.[. . .] Perhaps nothing in Christianity and Buddhism is so worthy of respect as their skill in teaching even the lowest that they can be included in a higher illusionary order of things through piety. This enables the religion to keep them satisfied to remain in the real order in which they find it difficult enough to live—but precisely this difficulty is necessary!

62

Finally, to be sure, we must draw up the wicked counter-evidence that these religions present and so bring to light their uncanny dangerousness. One must always pay dearly and frightfully when religions do *not* operate as a cultivating and educating force in the hands of philosophers, but rule sovereign and cut-off; when they want to be ultimate ends in themselves instead of means among other means. Mankind, like any other animal species, produces an excess of abortive, diseased, degenerate, defective, and necessarily suffering specimens; the successful specimens, in men as well, are always the exception. And considering that man is *the not yet stabilized* animal, they are the rare exception. Even worse, the higher the type of which an individual is a specimen, the greater the improbability of his *turning out well*. The forces of chance, the law of nonsense in the total economy of mankind, shows up most horrifyingly in its destructive effect on the superior individuals whose proper life conditions are subtle, manifold, and difficult to calculate. Now what is the conduct of the two above mentioned great religions toward the *excess* of defective specimens? They seek to maintain, to retain for life, what can possibly be retained; they principally side with the defectives, being religions *for sufferers;* they confirm the rights of all those who suffer from life as though it were a disease; they would like to render invalid and impossible any other sentiment besides theirs. No matter how justly and carefully we evaluate this protective and preservative care (which in addition to all the others applies to the highest type of man who also belongs to the greatest sufferers), it nonetheless remains that in the total reckoning the present, *sovereign* religions are among the main causes that have held mankind as a type down to a lower level. They preserved too much of what *should have perished*. We have an *inestimable* debt of gratitude to them; who is there so rich in gratitude that he would not grow poor when he thinks of all that the "spiritual men" of Christendom, for example, have done for Europe! And yet—if they gave consolation to the suffering, courage to the oppressed and despairing, a staff and a support to the dependent; if they lured the inwardly ravaged and savage away from society and into monasteries and psychic reformatories—what else must they not have done to work thus, principally, with a clear conscience, on the preservation of the diseased and the suffering, indeed and in truth, on the *deterioration of the European race!* To turn upside down all valuations—*that* is what they had to do! To shatter the strong, to infect great hopes, to cast suspicion on the enjoyment of beauty, to break down everything autonomous, manly, victorious, dominating, all the instincts natural to the highest and best turned-out type of mankind, and bend it over into uncertainty, distress of conscience, and self-destruction—to reverse every bit of love for the earth and things earthly and control of the earth into hatred of things earthly and of the earth: *this* was the self-assumed task of the church.[. . .] Men who were not superior and rigorous enough to work *on mankind* in the way artists must work, men who were not strong and farsighted enough, who did not have enough sublime self-control to *allow* the preliminary law of thousandfold failures and mortalities to operate, men who were not distinguished enough to see the abysmally different orders of rank and the distances between ranks in man—*such* men have heretofore administered the fate of Europe with their "equality before God," until they have managed to cultivate a wizened, almost ludicrous type, a herd-animal, a creature compounded of good will, sickliness, and mediocrity: the European of today. . . .

*   *   *   *   *

Sixth Part
We Intellectuals

205

The dangers to the development of a philosopher are truly so manifold today, that one may well doubt if such fruit can still ripen. The extent and height of the sciences has grown to be enormous; hence also the probability that a philosopher will grow fatigued while he is still learning, and will permit himself to be attached somewhere and become specialized. This means, of course, that he will never reach his own potential height, hence that he will never get an overall view, a view of the whole, a view *from the top down*. Or else he will get to the top too late; he will get there when his best time and power are over, or so injured, coarsened, and deteriorated, that his view, his total value judgment, signifies little. Precisely the subtlety of his intellectual conscience may make him hesitate and tarry on the way; he fears the temptation to become a dilettante, or else a millepede or a milleantenna; he knows all too well that someone who has lost reverence for himself no longer commands, even so far as cognition is concerned. He no longer *leads*, not, at least, unless he becomes a great actor, a philosophic Cagliostro or Pied Piper, i.e. a seducer. In the end it becomes a question of taste, even if it were not a question of conscience. Add to this, to double the philosopher's difficulties, that he demands of himself a judgment, a Yes and No, not as to some science, but as to life and life's worth. But he dislikes learning to believe that he has the right or, worse yet, the duty to make such a judgment; only from his most extensive, perhaps most disturbing and destructive experiences can he search out his way to that right, that belief. Often he will search hesitantly, doubtfully, and increasingly silently. The masses have mistaken and misrecognized the philosopher for a long time in fact; sometimes they took him for a scientific man and an ideal intellectual; sometimes for a religiously-elevated, "demoralized," "unworldly" enthusiast—a divine alcoholic, as it were. If by any chance one hears praise today for someone who lives "wisely" or "philosophically," it amounts to hardly more than "shrewdly and passively." Wisdom to the rabble is a sort of escape, a trick for withdrawing successfully from an outrageous game. But for *us*, my friends, the philosopher lives "unphilosophically" and "unwisely" and above all un-shrewdly. He feels the burden and duty to take up the hundreds of experiments and temptations of life; he constantly risks *himself*; he plays the outrageous game. . . .

*　*　*　*　*

210

If we admit, then, that in the image of the philosophers of the future some trait leads us to wonder whether they must not perhaps be skeptics in the last suggested sense, still it would be only something in them which could be so characterized, *not* they themselves. With equal justice they might allow themselves to be called critics; and surely they will be experimenters. By the name with which I ventured to christen them, I expressly emphasized their experimentation and their delight in experimentation. Did I do this because, as critics in body and soul, they will love to make use of experimentation in a new, perhaps wider, perhaps more dangerous sense? In their passion for new insight, must they go farther in bold and painful experiments than the emasculate and morbid taste of a democratic century can approve?—Of one thing there is no doubt: these future philosophers will be least able to dispense with the serious and not unobjectionable qualities that distinguish the critic from the skeptic. I mean a sureness as to standards of value, a conscious employment of a single method, a wary courage, an ability to stand alone and be responsible for themselves. In fact, among themselves they will admit to a certain pleasure in saying "no," in dissecting, and in a certain circumspect cruelty which knows how to handle the knife surely and delicately, even when the heart is bleeding. They will be *harder* (and perhaps not always only toward themselves) than humane people might wish; they will not go in for truth in order to be "pleased" or "elevated" or "inspired." On the contrary, they will have little faith that "truth" of all things should carry along such delights for the feelings. [. . .] Critical discipline, and every habit that leads to purity and rigor in matters of the spirit, will be demanded not only from themselves by these philosophers of the future. They may in fact wear them as a sort of jewel, for all to see. But they do not wish to be called critics on this account. It seems to them no small indignity to philosophy when it is decreed, as happens so readily today, "Philosophy itself is criticism and critical science—and nothing else besides." Let this evaluation of philosophy enjoy the applause of all the Positivists of France and Germany (it might even have flattered the heart and taste of Kant—let us remember the titles of his principal works!), our new philosophers will nonetheless say: Critics are instruments of the philosopher, and being instruments, are precisely for that reason far from being philosophers themselves! Even the great Chinaman of Koenigsberg[14] was only a great critic. —

[14] I.e., Kant.

211

I insist that we finally stop mistaking the workers in philosophy, and the scientific people generally, for philosophers, that this is the very point at which we must sternly give "to each his own," which means not too much to the former and not far too little to the latter. It may be necessary to the education of a genuine philosopher that he should have stood once on all the steps on which his servants, the scientific workers in philosophy, have now stopped—*must* have stopped; he himself must perhaps have been a critic and a skeptic and a dogmatist and a historian, not to mention poet, collector, traveller, riddle-reader, moralist, seer, "free thinker," and almost everything else, in order to run the entire circumference of human values and value-feelings, in order to be *able* to gaze with many eyes and many consciences from the heights to any distance, from the depths to any height, from the corners to any open spaces. But all these are only prerequisites for his task. The task itself is something else: it demands that he *create values*. Those philosophical workers in the noble tradition of Kant and Hegel have to determine and formalize some large reservoir of value-judgments, that is *former value-creations*, which have come to the fore and for a certain length of time are called "truth." They may lie in the realm of logic or of politics (morality) or of esthetics. The role of the researchers is to make everything that has heretofore happened and been evaluated into a visible, thinkable, comprehensible and handy pattern; to abbreviate everything that is long, to abbreviate time itself; to *overpower* the entire past. It is an enormous and wonderful task in whose service any subtle pride and any tough will may surely take satisfaction. *But the real philosophers are commanders and legislators.* They say, "It *shall* be thus!" They determine the "whither" and the "to what end" of mankind—having the preliminary work of all the workers in philosophy, the overpowerers of the past, at their disposal. But they grope with creative hands toward the future—everything that is and was becomes their means, their instrument, their hammer. Their "knowing" is *creating*. Their creating is legislative. Their will to truth is—*will to power.* Are there such philosophers today? Were there ever such philosophers? *Must* there not be such philosophers? . . .

212

It seems to me more and more that the philosopher, being *necessarily* a man of tomorrow and the day after tomorrow, has at all times stood, and has *had* to stand, in opposition to his today. His enemy each time was the ideal of the day. All these extraordinary furtherers of mankind (who are called philosophers but who rarely feel like lovers of wisdom, more like disagreeable fools and dangerous question marks), have hitherto found their task, their hard, unwanted, peremptory task—but ultimately also the greatness of their task—in being the bad conscience of their time. By putting the vivisectionist's knife to the *virtues of their time*, they revealed their own secret: they knew a *new* magnitude of man, a new un-worn path to his magnification. At all times they showed how much hypocrisy, indolence, letting oneself go and letting oneself fall, how many lies, were hidden under the most respected type of their current morality, how much virtue was out-lived. At all times they said, "We must go away, out there, where *you* today are least at home!" Faced with a world of "modern ideas" which would like to lock everyone into a corner and "specialty" of his own, a philosopher (if there could be philosophers today) would be forced to see the greatness of man, the very concept of "greatness," in all man's magnitude and multiplicity, in his "oneness in the many." He would determine human worth and rank by the amount and variety that an individual could carry within himself, by the *distance* his responsibility could span. The current taste and the current virtues weaken and adulterate the will today; nothing is as timely as weakness of will. Hence the philosopher must include strength of will, hardness, and ability to make far-reaching decisions in his ideal of human greatness. [. . .] Today, when in Europe the herd-animal alone is honored and alone doles out the honors, when "equality of rights" could all too easily turn into equality of wrong-doings—by which I mean the joint war on everything rare, strange, privileged; on superior men, superior souls, superior duties, superior responsibilities, on creative fullness of powers and the ability to rule—today the concept of greatness must embrace the spirit who is distinguished, who wants to be himself, who can be different, who can stand alone, and who must live by his own resources. A philosopher reveals something of his own ideal when he legislates that "The greatest shall be the one most capable of solitude, the most hidden, the most deviative, the man beyond good and evil, the master of his virtues, the one whose will can overflow. *Greatness* shall consist in being as many-faceted as one is whole, as wide as one is full." To ask the question once more: is greatness today—possible?

*   *   *   *   *

Seventh Part
Our Virtues

225

Whether it is hedonism, pessimism, utilitarianism, or eudemonism—all these ways of thinking which measure the value of things according to *pleasure* and *pain*, i.e. according to subsidiary circumstances and secondary considerations, are superficial ways of thinking. They are naïvetés upon which anyone who is conscious of *formative* powers and of an artist's conscience will look with scorn and not without some compassion. Compassion for *you!* That is, to be sure, not the compassion you have in mind. It is not compassion with "social distress," with "society" and its sick and maimed, with those who are vice-laden and broken from their very beginnings, as they lie strewn on the ground around us; even less is it compassion with grumbling, oppressed, revolutionary slave strata who seek domination and call it "freedom." *Our* compassion is a superior, more farsighted compassion. We see how *mankind* is depreciating, how *you* are depreciating mankind. There are moments in which we look with indescribable anxiety at *your* compassion, when we defend ourselves against what you call compassion, when we find your earnestness more dangerous than any wantonness. You want, if possible (and there is no more insane "if possible") to *do away with suffering.* And we—it seems that *we* want it worse and more than it ever was! Well-being as you think of it is no aim; to us it seems more like an *end*—a finish! A condition which makes men ridiculous and contemptible, which creates the *desire* that man might perish. The discipline of suffering, of suffering in the *great* sense: don't you know that all the heightening of man's powers has been created by only this discipline? That tension of the soul in misfortune which trains it to strength, its shudders at the sight of great perdition, its inventiveness and courageousness in enduring, maintaining itself in, interpreting, and utilizing, misfortune—whatever was given to the soul by way of depth, mystery, mask, mind, guile, and greatness: was it not given through suffering, through the discipline of great suffering? In man there is united both *creature* and *creator;* in man there is material, fragment, excess, clay, filth, nonsense, and chaos. But in man there is also creator, image-maker, hammer-hardness, spectator-divinity, and day of rest: do you understand this antithesis? And do you understand that *your* compassion is spent on the "creature" in man, on that which must be formed, broken, forged, torn, burnt, brought to white heat, purified, on all that which must necessarily suffer and *ought* to suffer! And our compassion—don't you comprehend on whom our *opposite* compassion is spent, when it defends itself against your compassion, as though against the worst coddling and weakness? Compassion, in other words, against compassion!—But, as I said before, there are problems higher than any pleasure and pain problems, including that of the pain of compassion; any philosophy which seeks to culminate here is a naïveté.

*   *   *   *   *

227

Candor[15]: granted that this is the virtue from which we free thinkers cannot escape. Well, let us work on this virtue in all malice and all love. Let us not weary of "perfecting" *our* virtue, the only one left to us. Let its glow some day rest on this aging culture and its dull gloomy earnestness, like a golden, blue, mocking after-glow. But if our candor, nonetheless, grows tired one day, and sighs and stretches its limbs and finds us too hard and would like to have something better, easier, more tender, something like a pleasant vice, then let us remain *hard*, we last Stoics! Let us send to our candor's aid whatever devilment we possess: our nausea at grossness and lack of definition, our *nitimur in vetitum,*[16] our adventurous courage, our quick-witted and fastidious inquisitiveness, our subtlest, most disguised, most spiritual will to power and world-overcoming, that roams and flutters desirously about all the fields of the future. Let us come to the aid of our "god" with all our "devils"! Most probably we shall be misunderstood and not recognized for what we are, but what does it matter! They will say that "their candor is their very devilishness, and nothing but that"—what does it matter!

*   *   *   *   *

230

[. . .] The command-giving something which is called "mind" by the people wants to be master in itself and all around itself and to feel that it is master. It has the will to make simplicity out of multiplicity; it is a will that ties things up, tames them—a domineering and really dominant will. Its needs and capabilities are the same as those which the physiologists assign to everything that lives and grows and reproduces. The power of mind to absorb foreign elements reveals itself in its strong tendency to make the new like the old, to simplify the manifold, to overlook or reject the totally contradictory; mind also arbitrarily underlines, emphasizes, falsifies—in order to suit its own purposes—certain features and charac-

[15]*Redlichkeit,* which might better be translated as "honesty."
[16]"We strive for the forbidden."

teristics of things foreign to itself, i.e. every bit of "outside world" that comes into its ken. Its purpose is the incorporation of new "experiences," the adding of new material to old, its *growth* in other words, or more strictly defined, the *feeling* of its growth, the feeling of its increased power. A servant of this same will is an apparently opposite drive of the mind: a suddenly erupting decision to be ignorant, to be arbitrarily shut off, a closing of windows, an inward "no" to this or that, a refusal to be approached, a sort of defense against much that might be known, a satisfaction at being in the dark, at being enclosed within a limiting horizon, a "yes" and a benediction upon ignorance—all according to the present needs of its appropriating power, its "digestive power, metaphorically speaking. [. . .] Counter to *this* will to illusion, to simplification, to the mask, to the cloak, in short this will to surfaces (for every surface is a cloak) operates that sublime impulse of the man of insight, that spirit which takes and *wants* to take things deeply, complicatedly, and thoroughly. This is the cruelty characteristic of the intellectual conscience and taste. Every courageous thinker will acknowledge it in himself, provided that he has trained and sharpened his eyes for it long enough, as is proper, and is accustomed to rigorous discipline and to rigorous words as well. He will say "There is something cruel about the tendency of my mind," regardless of the virtuous and amiable people who will try to dissuade him! Indeed, it would sound prettier if they talked about us or whispered after us or admired us in terms of "excessive candor," let us say, instead of cruelty. We free, *very* free thinkers—perhaps that will be our posthumous reputation! Meanwhile—and a long while it will be—we should be the least inclined to ornament ourselves with such moralistic word-spangles and bangles. Our entire work ruins us for that sort of taste and its cheerful lushness. They are beautiful, glittering, jingling, festive words: candor, love for truth, love for wisdom, self-sacrifice for insight, heroism of the truthful! Something about them swells one's pride. But we anchorites and marmots, we have convinced ourselves long ago, in all the secrecy of our anchorite's conscience, that this worthy word-pomp too belongs to the old lying bangles, to all the deceptive junk and gold dust of unconscious human vanity; that even beneath such flattering colors and cosmetics the frightful basic text *homo natura*,[17] must be recognized for what it is. For to retranslate man back into nature, to master the many vain enthusiastic glosses which have been scribbled and painted over the everlasting text, *homo natura*, so that man might henceforth stand before man as he stands today before that *other* nature, hardened under the discipline of science, with unafraid Oedipus eyes and stopped up Ulysses ears, deaf to the lures of the old metaphysical bird catchers who have been fluting in at him all too long that "you are more! You are superior! You are

[17]"Natural man."

of another origin!''—this may be a strange, mad task, but who could deny that it is a *task!* Why did we choose it, this mad task? Or, to ask it with different words, ''Why insight, anyway?'' Everyone will ask us this. And we, pressed for an answer, having asked the same question of ourselves hundreds of times, we have found and shall find no better answer. . . .

*   *   *   *   *

Joyful Wisdom (or The Gay Science) Book Five (1887)
(Excerpts)

We Fearless Ones

343

What our Cheerfulness Signifies. —The most important of more recent events—that "God is dead," that the belief in the Christian God has become unworthy of belief—already begins to cast its first shadows over Europe. To the few at least whose eye, whose *suspecting* glance, is strong enough and subtle enough for this drama, some sun seems to have set, some old, profound confidence seems to have changed into doubt: our old world must seem to them daily more darksome, distrustful, strange and "old." In the main, however, one may say that the event itself is far too great, too remote, too much beyond most people's power of apprehension, for one to suppose that so much as the report of it could have *reached* them; not to speak of many who already knew *what* had taken place, and what must all collapse now that this belief had been undermined,—because so much was built upon it, so much rested on it, and had become one with it: for example, our entire European morality. This lengthy, vast and uninterrupted process of crumbling, destruction, ruin and overthrow which is now imminent: who has realised it sufficiently to-day to have to stand up as the teacher and herald of such a tremendous logic of terror, as the prophet of a period of gloom and eclipse, the like of which has probably never taken place on earth before? . . . Even we, the born riddle-readers, who wait as it were on the mountains posted 'twixt to-day and to-morrow, and engirded by their contradiction, we, the firstlings and premature children of the coming century, into whose sight especially the shadows which must forthwith envelop Europe *should* already have come—how is it that even we, without genuine sympathy for this period of gloom, contemplate its advent without any *personal* solicitude or fear? Are we still, perhaps, too much under the *immediate effects* of the event— and are these effects, especially as regards *ourselves*, perhaps the reverse of what was to be expected—not at all sad and depressing, but rather like a new and indescribable variety of light, happiness, relief, enlivenment, encouragement, and dawning day? . . . In fact, we philosophers and "free spirits" feel ourselves irradiated as by a new dawn by the report that the "old God is dead"; our hearts overflow with gratitude, astonishment, presentiment and expectation. At last the horizon seems open once more, granting even that it is not bright; our ships can at last put out to sea in face of every danger; every hazard is again permitted to the discerner; the sea, *our* sea, again lies open before us; perhaps never before did such an "open sea" exist. —

344

To what Extent even We are still Pious. It is said with good reason that convictions have no civic rights in the domain of science: it is only when a conviction voluntarily condescends to the modesty of an hypothesis, a preliminary standpoint for experiment, or a regulative fiction, that its access to the realm of knowledge, and a certain value therein, can be conceded, — always, however, with the restriction that it must remain under police supervision, under the police of our distrust. — Regarded more accurately, however, does not this imply that only when a conviction *ceases* to be a conviction can it obtain admission into science? Does not the discipline of the scientific spirit just commence when one no longer harbours any conviction? . . . It is probably so: only, it remains to be asked whether, *in order that this discipline may commence*, it is not necessary that there should already be a conviction, and in fact one so imperative and absolute, that it makes a sacrifice of all other convictions. One sees that science also rests on a belief: there is no science at all "without premises." The question whether *truth* is necessary, must not merely be affirmed beforehand, but must be affirmed to such an extent that the principle, belief, or conviction finds expression, that "there is *nothing more necessary* than truth, and in comparison with it everything else has only secondary value."—This absolute will to truth: what is it? Is it the will *not to allow ourselves to be deceived?* Is it the will *not to deceive?* For the will to truth could also be interpreted in this fashion, provided one included under the generalisation, "I will not deceive," the special case, "I will not deceive myself." But why not deceive? Why not allow oneself to be deceived? — Let it be noted that the reasons for the former eventuality belong to a category quite different from those for the latter: one does not want to be deceived oneself, under the supposition that it is injurious, dangerous, or fatal to be deceived, — in this sense science would be a prolonged process of caution, foresight and utility; against which, however, one might reasonably make objections. What? is not-wishing-to-be-deceived really less injurious, less dangerous, less fatal? What do you know of the character of existence in all its phases to be able to decide whether the greater advantage is on the side of absolute distrust, or of absolute trustfulness? In case, however, of both being necessary, much trusting *and* much distrusting, whence then should science derive the absolute belief, the conviction on which it rests, that truth is more important than anything else, even than every other conviction? This conviction could not have arisen if truth *and* untruth had both continually proved themselves to be useful: as is the case. Thus—the belief in science, which now undeniably exists, cannot have had its origin in such a utilitarian calculation, but rather *in spite of* the fact of the inutility and dangerousness of the "Will to truth," of "truth at all costs," being continually demonstrated. "At all costs": alas, we understand that sufficiently well, after having sacrificed and slaughtered one belief after another at this altar!—Consequently, "Will to truth" does *not* imply, "I will not allow myself to be deceived," but—there is no other alternative—"I will not deceive, not even myself": *and thus we have reached the realm of morality.* For, let one just ask oneself fairly: "Why wilt thou not deceive?" especially if it should seem—and it does seem—as if life were laid out with a view to appearance, I mean, with a view to error, deceit, dissimulation, delusion, self-delusion; and when on the other hand it is a matter of fact that the great type of life has always manifested itself on the side of the most unscrupulous πολύτροποι.[1] Such an intention might perhaps, to express it mildly, be a piece of Quixotism, a little enthusiastic craziness; it might also, however, be something worse, namely, a destructive principle, hostile to life. . . . "Will to Truth,"—that might be a concealed Will to Death.—Thus the question, Why is there science? leads back to the moral problem: *What in general is the purpose of morality,* if life, nature, and history are "non-moral"? There is no doubt that the conscientious man in the daring and extreme sense in which he is presupposed by the belief in science, *affirms thereby a world other than* that of life, nature, and history; and in so far as he affirms this "other world," what? must he not just thereby—deny its counterpart, this world, *our* world? . . . But what I have in view will now be understood, namely, that it is always a *metaphysical belief* on which our belief in science rests,— and that even we knowing ones of to-day, the godless and anti-metaphysical, still take *our* fire from the conflagration kindled by a belief a millennium old, the Christian belief, which was also the belief of Plato, that God is truth, that the truth is divine. . . . But what if this itself always becomes more untrustworthy, what if nothing any longer proves itself divine, except it be error, blindness, and falsehood;—what if God himself turns out to be our most persistent lie?—

---

[1]*Polytropoi*, a Greek term literally meaning "many-turned [ones]." It has the sense of "men of the world," i.e., those who have "been around" and are wise to the ways of the world. So, for example, Odysseus is referred to as "*polytropos*" at the beginning of the *Odyssey* and is a paradigm case of such a person (as Nietzsche well knew).

345

[. . .] It is obvious that up to the present morality has not been a problem at all; it has rather been the very ground on which people have met after all distrust, dissension and contradiction, the hallowed place of peace, where thinkers could obtain rest even from themselves, could recover breath and revive. I see no one who has ventured to *criticise* the estimates of moral worth. I miss in this connection even the attempts of scientific curiosity, and the fastidious, groping imagination of psychologists and historians, which easily anticipates a problem and catches it on the wing, without rightly knowing what it catches. With difficulty I have discovered some scanty data for the purpose of furnishing a *history of the origin* of these feelings and estimates of value (which is something different from a criticism of them, and also something different from a history of ethical systems). In an individual case I have done everything to encourage the inclination and talent for this kind of history—in vain, as it would seem to me at present. There is little to be learned from those historians of morality (especially Englishmen): they themselves are usually, quite unsuspiciously, under the influence of a definite morality, and act unwittingly as its armour-bearers and followers— perhaps still repeating sincerely the popular superstition of Christian Europe, that the characteristic of moral action consists in abnegation, self-denial, self-sacrifice, or in fellow-feeling and fellow-suffering. The usual error in their premises is their insistence on a certain *consensus* among human beings, at least among civilised human beings, with regard to certain propositions of morality, from thence they conclude that these propositions are absolutely binding even upon you and me; or reversely, they come to the conclusion that *no* morality is binding, after the truth has dawned upon them that among different peoples moral valuations are *necessarily* different: both of which conclusions are equally childish follies. The error of the more subtle amongst them is that they discover and criticise the probably foolish opinions of a people about its own morality, or the opinions of mankind about human morality generally (they treat accordingly of its origin, its religious sanctions, the superstition of free will, and such matters), and they think that just by so doing they have criticised the morality itself. But the worth of a precept, "Thou shalt," is fundamentally different from and independent of such opinions about it, and must be distinguished from the weeds of error with which it has perhaps been overgrown: just as the worth of a medicine to a sick person is altogether independent of the question whether he has a scientific opinion about medicine, or merely thinks about it as an old wife would do. A morality could even have grown *out of* an error: but with this knowledge the problem of its worth would not even be touched. —Thus, no one hitherto has tested the *value* of that most celebrated of all medicines, called morality: for which purpose it is first of all necessary for one—*to call it in question*. Well, that is just our work. —

346

Our Note of Interrogation.[2]—But you don't understand it? As a matter of fact, an effort will be necessary in order to understand us. We seek for words; we seek perhaps also for ears. Who are we after all? If we wanted simply to call ourselves in older phraseology, atheists, unbelievers, or even immoralists, we should still be far from thinking ourselves designated thereby: we are all three in too late a phase for people generally to conceive, for *you*, my inquisitive friends, to be able to conceive, what is our state of mind under the circumstances. No! we have no longer the bitterness and passion of him who has broken loose, who has to make for himself a belief, a goal, and even a martyrdom out of his unbelief! We have become saturated with the conviction (and have grown cold and hard in it) that things are not at all divinely ordered in this world, nor even according to human standards do they go on rationally, mercifully, or justly: we know the fact that the world in which we live is ungodly, immoral, and "inhuman,"—we have far too long interpreted it to ourselves falsely and mendaciously, according to the wish and will of our veneration, that is to say, according to our *need*. For man is a venerating animal! But he is also a distrustful animal: and that the world is *not* worth what we believed it to be worth is about the surest thing our distrust has at last managed to grasp. So much distrust, so much philosophy! We take good care not to say that the world is of *less* value: it seems to us at present absolutely ridiculous when man claims to devise values *to surpass* the values of the actual world,—it is precisely from that point that we have retraced our steps; as from an extravagant error of human conceit and irrationality, which for a long period has not been recognised as such. This error had its last expression in modern Pessimism; an older and stronger manifestation in the teaching of Buddha; but Christianity also contains it, more dubiously, to be sure, and more ambiguously, but none the less seductive on that account. The whole attitude of "man *versus* the world," man as world-denying principle, man as the standard of the value of things, as judge of the world, who in the end puts existence itself on his scales and finds it too light—the monstrous impertinence of this attitude has dawned upon us as such, and has disgusted us,—we now laugh when we find, "Man *and* World" placed beside one another, separated by the sublime presumption of the little word "and"! But how is it? Have we not in our very laughing just made a further step in despising mankind? And consequently also in Pessimism, in despising the existence cognisable *by us?* Have we not just thereby awakened suspicion that there is an opposition between the world in which we have hitherto been at home with our venerations—for the sake of which we perhaps *endure* life—and another

[2]I.e., *"Our Question Mark."*

world *which we ourselves are:* an inexorable, radical, most profound suspicion concerning ourselves, which is continually getting us Europeans
more annoyingly into its power, and could easily face the coming generation with the terrible alternative: Either do away with your venerations,
or—*with yourselves!*" The latter would be Nihilism—but would not the
former also be Nihilism? This is *our* note of interrogation.

347

Believers and their Need of Belief. —How much *faith* a person requires in
order to flourish, how much "fixed opinion" he requires which he does
not wish to have shaken, because he *holds* himself thereby—is a measure
of his power (or more plainly speaking, of his weakness). Most people in
old Europe, as it seems to me, still need Christianity at present, and on
that account it still finds belief. For such is man: a theological dogma
might be refuted to him a thousand times,—provided, however, that he
had need of it, he would again and again accept it as "true,"—according
to the famous "proof of power" of which the Bible speaks. Some have still
need of metaphysics; but also the impatient *longing for certainty* which at
present discharges itself in scientific, positivist fashion among large numbers of the people, the longing by all means to get at something stable
(while on account of the warmth of the longing the establishing of the
certainty is more leisurely and negligently undertaken):—even this is still
the longing for a hold, a support; in short, the *instinct of weakness*, which,
while not actually creating religions, metaphysics, and convictions of all
kinds, nevertheless—preserves them. [. . .] When a man arrives at the
fundamental conviction that he *requires* to be commanded, he becomes "a
believer." Reversely, one could imagine a delight and a power of self-
determining, and a *freedom* of will, whereby a spirit could bid farewell to
every belief, to every wish for certainty, accustomed as it would be to
support itself on slender cords and possibilities, and to dance even on the
verge of abysses. Such a spirit would be the *free spirit par excellence.*

*   *   *   *   *

349

The Origin of the Learned once more. —To seek self-preservation merely, is
the expression of a state of distress, or of limitation of the true, fundamental instinct of life, which aims at the *extension of power*, and with this
in view often enough calls in question self-preservation and sacrifices it.

It should be taken as symptomatic when individual philosophers, as for example, the consumptive Spinoza, have seen and have been obliged to see the principal feature of life precisely in the so-called self-preservative instinct: — they have just been men in states of distress. That our modern natural sciences have entangled themselves so much with Spinoza's dogma (finally and most grossly in Darwinism, with its inconceivably one-sided doctrine of the "struggle for existence" —), is probably owing to the origin of most of the inquirers into nature: they belong in this respect to the people, their forefathers have been poor and humble persons, who knew too well by immediate experience the difficulty of making a living. Over the whole of English Darwinism there hovers something of the suffocating air of over-crowded England, something of the odour of humble people in need and in straits. But as an investigator of nature, a person ought to emerge from his paltry human nook: and in nature the state of distress does not *prevail*, but superfluity, even prodigality to the extent of folly. The struggle for existence is only an *exception*, a temporary restriction of the will to live; the struggle, be it great or small, turns everywhere on predominance, on increase and expansion, on power, in conformity to the will to power, which is just the will to live.

*　*　*　*　*

354

The "Genius of the Species." — The problem of consciousness (or more correctly: of becoming conscious of oneself) meets us only when we begin to perceive in what measure we could dispense with it: and it is at the beginning of this perception that we are now placed by physiology and zoology (which have thus required two centuries to overtake the hint thrown out in advance by Leibnitz). For we could in fact think, feel, will, and recollect, we could likewise "act" in every sense of the term, and nevertheless nothing of it all need necessarily "come into consciousness" (as one says metaphorically). The whole of life would be possible without its seeing itself as it were in a mirror: as in fact even at present the far greater part of our life still goes on without this mirroring, — and even our thinking, feeling, volitional life as well, however painful this statement may sound to an older philosopher. *What* then is *the purpose* of consciousness generally, when it is in the main *superfluous?* — Now it seems to me, if you will hear my answer and its perhaps extravagant supposition, that the subtlety and strength of consciousness are always in proportion to the *capacity for communication* of a man (or an animal), the capacity for communication in its turn being in proportion to the *necessity for communication:* the latter not to be understood as if precisely the individual himself who is master in the art of communicating and making known his necessities would at the same time have to be most dependent upon others for his necessities. It seems to me, however, to be so in relation to whole races and successions of generations: where necessity and need have long compelled men to communicate with their fellows and understand one another rapidly and subtly, a surplus of the power and art of communication is at last acquired, as if it were a fortune which had gradually accumulated, and now waited for an heir to squander it prodigally (the so-called artists are these heirs, in like manner the orators, preachers, and authors: all of them men who come at the end of a long succession, "late-born" always, in the best sense of the word, and as has been said, *squanderers* by their very nature). Granted that this observation is correct, I may proceed further to the conjecture that *consciousness generally has only been developed under the pressure of the necessity for communication,* —that from the first it has been necessary and useful only between man and man (especially between those commanding and those obeying), and has only developed in proportion to its utility. Consciousness is properly only a connecting network between man and man,—it is only as such that it has had to develop; the recluse and wild-beast species of men would not have needed it. The very fact that our actions, thoughts, feelings and motions come within the range of our consciousness—at least a part of them—is the result of a terrible, prolonged "must" ruling man's destiny: as the most endangered animal he *needed* help and protection; he needed his fellows, he was obliged to express his distress, he had to know how to make himself understood—and for all this he needed "consciousness" first of all: he had to "know" himself what he lacked, to "know" how he felt, and to "know" what he thought. For, to repeat it once more, man, like every living creature, thinks unceasingly, but does not know it; the thinking which is becoming *conscious of itself* is only the smallest part thereof, we may say, the most superficial part, the worst part:—for this conscious thinking alone *is done in words, that is to say, in the symbols for communication,* by means of which the origin of consciousness is revealed. In short, the development of speech and the development of consciousness (not of reason, but of reason becoming self-conscious) go hand in hand. Let it be further accepted that it is not only speech that serves as a bridge between man and man, but also the looks, the pressure and the gestures; our becoming conscious of our sense impressions, our power of being able to fix them, and as it were to locate them outside of ourselves, has increased in proportion as the necessity has increased for communicating them to *others* by means of signs. The sign-inventing man is at the same time the man who is always more acutely self-conscious; it is only as a social animal that man has learned to become conscious of himself,—he is doing so still, and doing so more and more.—As is obvious, my idea is that consciousness does not properly belong to the individual existence of man, but rather to the social and gregarious nature in him; that, as follows there-from, it is only in relation to communal and gregarious utility that it is finely developed; and that consequently each of us, in spite of the best intention of *understanding* himself as individually as possible, and of "knowing himself," will always just call into consciousness the non-individual in him, namely, his "averageness";—that our thought itself is continuously as it were *outvoted* by the character of consciousness—by the imperious "genius of the species" therein—and is translated back into the perspective of the herd. Fundamentally our actions are in an incomparable manner altogether personal, unique and absolutely individual—there is no doubt about it; but as soon as we translate them into consciousness, they *do not appear so any longer.* . . . This is the proper phenomenalism and perspectivism as I understand it: the nature of *animal consciousness* involves the notion that the world of which we can become conscious is only a superficial and symbolic world, a generalised and vulgarised world;—that everything which becomes conscious *becomes* just thereby shallow, meagre, relatively stupid,—a generalisation, a symbol, a characteristic of the herd; that with the evolving of consciousness there is always combined a great, radical perversion, falsification, superficialisation, and generalisation. Fi-nally, the growing consciousness is a danger, and whoever lives among the most conscious Europeans knows even that it is a disease. As may be conjectured, it is not the antithesis of subject and object with which I am here concerned: I leave that distinction to the epistemologists who have remained entangled in the toils of grammar (popular metaphysics). It is still less the antithesis of "thing in itself" and phenomenon, for we do not "know" enough to be entitled even *to make such a distinction.* Indeed, we have not any organ at all for *knowing*, or for "truth": we "know" (or believe, or fancy) just as much as may be *of use* in the interest of the human herd, the species; and even what is here called "usefulness" is ultimately only a belief, a fancy, and perhaps precisely the most fatal stupidity by which we shall one day be ruined.

355

The Origin of our Conception of "Knowledge."—I take this explanation from the street. I heard one of the people saying that "he knew me," so I asked myself: What do the people really understand by knowledge? what do they want when they seek "knowledge"? Nothing more than that what is strange is to be traced back to something *known.* And we philosophers—have we really understood *anything more* by knowledge? The known, that is to say, what we are accustomed to so that we no longer marvel at it, the commonplace, any kind of rule to which we are habitu-ated, all and everything in which we know ourselves to be at home:—

what? is our need of knowing not just this need of the known? the will to discover in everything strange, unusual, or questionable, something which no longer disquiets us? Is it not possible that it should be the *instinct of fear* which enjoins upon us to know? Is it not possible that the rejoicing of the discerner should be just his rejoicing in the regained feeling of security? . . . One philosopher imagined the world "known" when he had traced it back to the "idea": alas, was it not because the idea was so known, so familiar to him? because he had so much less fear of the "idea"—Oh, this moderation of the discerners! let us but look at their principles, and at their solutions of the riddle of the world in this con-nection! When they again find aught in things, among things, or behind things that is unfortunately very well known to us, for example, our multiplication table, or our logic, or our willing and desiring, how happy they immediately are! For "what is known is understood": they are unan-imous as to that. Even the most circumspect among them think that the known is at least *more easily understood* than the strange; that for example, it is methodically ordered to proceed outward from the "inner world," from "the facts of consciousness," because it is the world which is *better known to us!* Error of errors! The known is the accustomed, and the accustomed is the most difficult of all to "understand," that is to say, to perceive as a problem, to perceive as strange, distant, "outside of us." . . . The great certainty of the natural sciences in comparison with psychology and the criticism of the elements of consciousness—*unnatural* sciences, as one might almost be entitled to call them—rests precisely on the fact that they take *what is strange* as their object: while it is almost like something contradictory and absurd *to wish* to take generally what is not strange as an object. . . .

*   *   *   *

357

The old Problem: "What is German?"—Let us count up apart the real acquisitions of philosophical thought for which we have to thank German intellects: are they in any allowable sense to be counted also to the credit of the whole race? [. . .] Did our philosophers perhaps even go counter to the *need* of the "German soul"? In short, were the German philosophers really philosophical *Germans?*—I call to mind three cases. Firstly, *Leibnitz's* incomparable insight—with which he obtained the advantage not only over Descartes, but over all who had philosophised up to his time, — that consciousness is only an accident of mental representation, and *not* its necessary and essential attribute; that consequently what we call consciousness only constitutes a state of our spiritual and psychical world (perhaps a morbid state), and is *far from being that world itself:*—is there anything German in this thought, the profundity of which has not as yet been exhausted? Is there reason to think that a person of the Latin race would not readily have stumbled on this reversal of the apparent?—for it is a reversal. Let us call to mind secondly, the immense note of interrogation which *Kant* wrote after the notion of causality. Not that he at all doubted its legitimacy, like Hume: on the contrary, he began cautiously to define the domain within which this notion has significance generally (we have not even yet got finished with the marking out of these limits). Let us take thirdly, the astonishing hit of *Hegel*, who stuck at no logical usage or fastidiousness when he ventured to teach that the conceptions of kinds develop *out of one another:* with which theory the thinkers in Europe were prepared for the last great scientific movement, for Darwinism—for without Hegel there would have been no Darwin. Is there anything German in this Hegelian innovation which first introduced the decisive conception of evolution into science?—Yes, without doubt we feel that there is something of ourselves "discovered" and divined in all three cases; we are thankful for it, and at the same time surprised; each of these three principles is a thoughtful piece of German self-confession, self-understanding, and self-knowledge. We feel with Leibnitz that "our inner world is far richer, ampler, and more concealed"; as Germans we are doubtful, like Kant, about the ultimate validity of scientific knowledge of nature, and in general about whatever *can* be known *causaliter:* the *knowable* as such now appears to us of *less* worth. We Germans should still have been Hegelians, even though there had never been a Hegel, inasmuch as we (in contradistinction to all Latin peoples) instinctively attribute to becoming, to evolution, a profounder significance and higher value than to that which "is"—we hardly believe at all in the validity of the concept "being." This is all the more the case because we are not inclined to concede to our human logic that it is logic in itself, that it is the only kind of logic (we should rather like, on the contrary, to convince ourselves that it is only a special case, and perhaps one of the strangest and most stupid).—A fourth question would be whether also *Schopenhauer* with his Pessimism, that is to say, the problem of *the worth of existence*, had to be a German. I think not. The event *after* which this problem was to be expected with certainty, so that an astronomer of the soul could have calculated the day and the hour for it—namely, the decay of the belief in the Christian God, the victory of scientific atheism,—is a universal European event, in which all races are to have their share of service and honour. On the contrary, it has to be ascribed precisely to the Germans—those with whom Schopenhauer was contemporary,—that they delayed this victory of atheism longest, and endangered it most. Hegel especially was its retarder *par excellence*, in virtue of the grandiose attempt which he made to persuade us at the very last of the divinity of existence, with the help of our sixth sense, "the historical sense." As philosopher, Schopenhauer was the *first* avowed and inflexible atheist we Germans have had: his hostility to Hegel had here its motive. The non-divinity of existence was regarded by him as something understood, palpable, indisputable; he always lost his philosophical composure and got into a passion when he saw anyone hesitate and beat about the bush here. It is at this point that his thorough uprightness of character comes in: unconditional, honest atheism is precisely the *preliminary condition* for his raising the problem, as a final and hardwon victory of the European conscience, as the most prolific act of two thousand years' discipline to truth, which in the end no longer tolerates the *lie* of the belief in a God. . . . One sees what has really gained the victory over the Christian God—, Christian morality itself, the conception of veracity, taken ever more strictly, the confessional subtlety of the Christian conscience, translated and sublimated to the scientific conscience, to intellectual purity at any price. To look upon nature as if it were a proof of the goodness and care of a God; to interpret history in honour of a divine reason, as a constant testimony to a moral order in the world and a moral final purpose; to explain personal experiences as pious men have long enough explained them, as if everything were a dispensation or intimation of Providence, something planned and sent on behalf of the salvation of the soul: all that is now *past*, it has conscience *against* it, it is regarded by all the more acute consciences as disreputable and dishonourable, as mendaciousness, femininism, weakness, and cowardice,—by virtue of this severity, if by anything, we are *good* Europeans, the heirs of Europe's longest and bravest self-conquest. When we thus reject the Christian interpretation, and condemn its "significance" as a forgery, we are immediately confronted in a striking manner with the *Schopenhauerian* question: *Has existence then a significance at all?*—the question which will require a couple of centuries even to be completely heard in all its profundity. Schopenhauer's own answer to this question was—if I may be forgiven for saying so—a premature, juvenile reply, a mere compromise, a stoppage and sticking in the very same Christian-ascetic moral perspectives, *the belief in which had been renounced* along with the belief in God. . . . But he *raised* the question—as a good European, as we have said, and *not* as a German.

*   *   *   *   *

<h2 align="center">360</h2>

Two Kinds of Causes which are Confounded.—It seems to me one of my most essential steps and advances that I have learned to distinguish the cause of an action generally from the cause of an action in a particular manner, say, in this direction, with this aim. The first kind of cause is a quantum of stored-up force, which waits to be used in some manner, for some purpose; the second kind of cause, on the contrary, is something quite unimportant in comparison with the first, an insignificant hazard for the most part, in conformity with which the quantum of force in question "discharges" itself in some unique and definite manner: the lucifer-match in relation to the barrel of gunpowder. Among those insignificant hazards and lucifer-matches I count all the so-called "aims," and similarly the still more so-called "occupations" of people: they are relatively optional, arbitrary, and almost indifferent in relation to the immense quantum of force which presses on, as we have said, to be used up in any way whatever. One generally looks at the matter in a different manner: one is accustomed to see the *impelling* force precisely in the aim (object, calling, &c.), according to a primeval error,—but it is only the *directing* force; the steersman and the steam have thereby been confounded. And yet it is not even always a steersman, the directing force. . . . Is the "aim," the "purpose," not often enough only an extenuating pretext, an additional self-blinding of conceit, which does not wish it to be said that the ship *follows* the stream into which it has accidentally run? That it "wishes" to go that way, *because* it *must* go that way? That it has a direction, sure enough, but—not a steersman? We still require a criticism of the conception of "purpose."

*   *   *   *   *

367

How one has to Distinguish first of all in Works of Art.—Everything that is thought, versified, painted and composed, yea, even built and moulded, belongs either to monologic art, or to art before witnesses. Under the latter there is also to be included the apparently monologic art which involves the belief in God, the whole lyric of prayer; because for a pious man there is no solitude,—we, the godless, have been the first to devise this invention. I know of no profounder distinction in all the perspective of the artist than this: Whether he looks at his growing work of art (at "himself—") with the eye of the witness; or whether he "has forgotten the world," as is the essential thing in all monologic art,—it rests *on forgetting*, it is the music of forgetting.

*   *   *   *   *

370

What is Romanticism?—It will be remembered perhaps, at least among my friends, that at first I assailed the modern world with some gross errors and exaggerations, but at any rate with *hope* in my heart. I recognised—who knows from what personal experiences?—the philosophical pessimism of the nineteenth century as the symptom of a higher power of thought, a more daring courage and a more triumphant *plenitude* of life than had been characteristic of the eighteenth century, the age of Hume, Kant, Condillac, and the sensualists: so that the tragic view of things seemed to me the peculiar *luxury* of our culture, its most precious, noble, and dangerous mode of prodigality; but nevertheless, in view of its overflowing wealth, a *justifiable* luxury. In the same way I interpreted for myself German music as the expression of a Dionysian power in the German soul: I thought I heard in it the earthquake by means of which a primeval force that had been imprisoned for ages was finally finding vent—indifferent as to whether all that usually calls itself culture was thereby made to totter. It is obvious that I then misunderstood what constitutes the veritable character both of philosophical pessimism and of German music,—namely, their *Romanticism*. What is Romanticism? Every art and every philosophy may be regarded as a healing and helping appliance in the service of growing, struggling life: they always presuppose suffering and sufferers. But there are two kinds of sufferers: on the one hand those that suffer from *overflowing vitality*, who need Dionysian art, and require a tragic view and insight into life; and on the other hand those who suffer from *reduced vitality*, who seek repose, quietness, calm seas, and deliverance from themselves through art or knowledge, or else intoxication, spasm, bewilderment and madness. All Romanticism in art and knowledge responds to the twofold craving of the *latter;* to them Schopenhauer as well as Wagner responded (and responds),—to name those most celebrated and decided romanticists, who were then *misunderstood* by me (*not* however to their disadvantage, as may be reasonably conceded to me). The being richest in overflowing vitality, the Dionysian God and man, may not only allow himself the spectacle of the horrible and questionable, but even the fearful deed itself, and all the luxury of destruction, disorganisation and negation. With him evil, senselessness and ugliness seem as it were licensed, in consequence of the overflowing plenitude of procreative, fructifying power, which can convert every desert into a luxuriant orchard. Conversely, the greatest sufferer, the man poorest in vitality, would have most need of mildness, peace and kindliness in thought and action: he would need, if possible, a God who is specially the God of the sick, a "Saviour"; similarly he would have need of logic, the abstract intelligibility of existence—for logic soothes and gives confidence;—in short he would need a certain warm, fear-dispelling narrowness and imprisonment within optimistic horizons. In this manner I gradually began to understand Epicurus, the opposite of a Dionysian pessimist;—in a similar manner also the "Christian," who in fact is only a type of Epicurean, and like him essentially a romanticist:—and my vision has always become keener in tracing that most difficult and insidious of all forms of *retrospective inference*, in which most mistakes have been made—the inference from the work to its author from the deed to its doer, from the ideal to him who *needs* it, from every mode of thinking and valuing to the imperative *want* behind it.—In regard to all aesthetic values I now avail myself of this radical distinction: I ask in every single case, "Has hunger or superfluity become creative here?" At the outset another distinction might seem to recommend itself more—it is far more conspicuous,— namely, to have in view whether the desire for rigidity, for perpetuation, for *being* is the cause of the creating, or the desire for destruction, for change, for the new, for the future—for *becoming*. But when looked at more carefully, both these kinds of desire prove themselves ambiguous, and are explicable precisely according to the before-mentioned, and, as it seems to me, rightly preferred scheme. The desire for *destruction*, change and becoming, may be the expression of overflowing power, pregnant with futurity (my *terminus* for this is of course the word "Dionysian"); but it may also be the hatred of the ill-constituted, destitute and unfortunate, which destroys, and *must* destroy, because the enduring, yea, all that endures, in fact all being, excites and provokes it. To understand this emotion we have but to look closely at our anarchists. The will to *perpetuation* requires equally a double interpretation. It may on the one hand proceed from gratitude and love:—art of this origin will always be an art of apotheosis, perhaps dithyrambic, as with Rubens, mocking divinely, as with Hafiz, or clear and kind-hearted as with Goethe, and spreading a Homeric brightness and glory over everything (in this case I speak of *Apollonian* art). It may also, however, be the tyrannical will of a sorely-suffering, struggling or tortured being, who would like to stamp his most personal, individual and narrow characteristics, the very idiosyncrasy of his suffering, as an obligatory law and constraint on others; who, as it were, takes revenge on all things, in that he imprints, enforces and brands *his* image, the image of *his* torture, upon them. The latter is *romantic pessimism* in its most extreme form, whether it be as Schopenhauerian will-philosophy, or as Wagnerian music:—romantic pessimism, the last *great* event in the destiny of our civilisation. (That there *may be* quite a different kind of pessimism, a classical pessimism—this presentiment and vision belongs to me, as something inseparable from me, as my *proprium* and *ipsissimum*[3]; only that the word "classical" is repugnant to my ears, it has become far too worn, too indefinite and indistinguishable. I call that pessimism of the future,—for it is coming! I see it coming!—*Dionysian* pessimism.)

*　*　*　*　*

[3]My own and innermost self.

372

Why we are not Idealists.—Formerly philosophers were afraid of the senses: have we, perhaps, been far too forgetful of this fear? We are at present all of us sensualists, we representatives of the present and of the future in philosophy,—*not* according to theory, however, but in *praxis*, in practice. . . . Those former philosophers, on the contrary, thought that the senses lured them out of *their* world, the cold realm of "ideas," to a dangerous southern island, where they were afraid that their philosopher-virtues would melt away like snow in the sun. "Wax in the ears," was then almost a condition of philosophising; a genuine philosopher no longer listened to life, in so far as life is music, he *denied* the music of life—it is an old philosophical superstition that all music is Sirens' music.—Now we should be inclined at the present day to judge precisely in the opposite manner (which in itself might be just as false), and to regard *ideas*, with their cold, anæmic appearance, and not even in spite of this appearance, as worse seducers than the senses. They have always lived on the "blood" of the philosopher, they always consumed his senses, and indeed, if you will believe me, his "heart" as well. Those old philosophers were heart-less: philosophising was always a species of vampirism. At the sight of such figures even as Spinoza, do you not feel a profoundly enigmatical and disquieting sort of impression? Do you not see the drama which is here performed, the constantly *increasing pallor*—, the spiritualisation always more ideally displayed? Do you not imagine some long-concealed blood-sucker in the background, which makes its beginning with the senses, and in the end retains or leaves behind nothing but bones and their rattling?—I mean categories, formulæ, and *words* (for you will pardon me in saying that what *remains* of Spinoza, *amor intellectualis dei*,[4] is rattling and nothing more! What is *amor*, what is *deus*, when they have lost every drop of blood? . . .) *In summa:* all philosophical idealism has hitherto been something like a disease, where it has not been, as in the case of Plato, the prudence of superabundant and dangerous healthfulness, the fear of *over-powerful* senses. [. . .]

373

"Science" as Prejudice.—It follows from the laws of class distinction that the learned, in so far as they belong to the intellectual middle-class, are

---

[4]Intellectual love of God.

debarred from getting even a sight of the really *great* problems and notes of interrogation. Besides, their courage, and similarly their outlook, does not reach so far,—and above all their need which makes them investigators, their innate anticipation and desire that things should be constituted *in such and such a way*, their fears and hopes, are too soon quieted and set at rest. [. . .] It is just the same with the belief with which at present so many materialistic natural-scientists are content, the belief in a world which is supposed to have its equivalent and measure in human thinking and human valuations, a "world of truth" at which we might be able ultimately to arrive with the help of our insignificant, four-cornered human reason! What? do we actually wish to have existence debased in that fashion to a ready-reckoner exercise and calculation for stay-at-home mathematicians? We should not, above all, seek to divest existence of its *ambiguous* character: *good* taste forbids it, gentlemen, the taste of reverence for everything that goes beyond your horizon! That a world-interpretation is alone right by which *you* maintain your position, by which investigation and work can go on scientifically in *your* sense (you really mean *mechanically?*), an interpretation which acknowledges numbering, calculating, weighing, seeing and handling, and nothing more—such an idea is a piece of grossness and naïveté, provided it is not lunacy and idiocy. Would the reverse not be quite probable, that the most superficial and external characters of existence—its most apparent quality, its outside, its embodiment—should let themselves be apprehended first? perhaps alone allow themselves to be apprehended? A "scientific" interpretation of the world as you understand it might consequently still be one of the *stupidest*, that is to say, the most destitute of significance, of all possible world-interpretations:—I say this in confidence to my friends the Mechanicians, who to-day like to hobnob with philosophers, and absolutely believe that mechanics is the teaching of the first and last laws upon which, as upon a ground-floor, all existence must be built. But an essentially mechanical world would be an essentially *meaningless* world! Supposing we valued the *worth* of a music with reference to how much it could be counted, calculated, or formulated—how absurd such a "scientific" estimate of music would be! What would one have apprehended, understood, or discerned in it! Nothing, absolutely nothing of what is really "music" in it! . . .

374

Our new "Infinite."—How far the perspective character of existence extends, or whether it has any other character at all, whether an existence without explanation, without "sense" does not just become "nonsense," whether, on the other hand, all existence is not essentially an *explaining* existence—these questions, as is right and proper, cannot be determined even by the most diligent and severely conscientious analysis and self-examination of the intellect, because in this analysis the human intellect cannot avoid seeing itself in its perspective forms, and *only* in them. We cannot see round our corner: it is hopeless curiosity to want to know what other modes of intellect and perspective there *might* be: for example, whether any kind of being could perceive time backwards, or alternately forwards and backwards (by which another direction of life and another conception of cause and effect would be given). But I think that we are to-day at least far from the ludicrous immodesty of decreeing from our nook that there *can* only be legitimate perspectives from that nook. The world, on the contrary, has once more become "infinite" to us: in so far we cannot dismiss the possibility that it *contains infinite interpretations*. Once more the great horror seizes us—but who would desire forthwith to deify once more *this* monster of an unknown world in the old fashion? And perhaps worship *the* unknown thing as *the* "unknown person" in future? Ah! there are too many *ungodly* possibilities of interpretation comprised in this unknown, too much devilment, stupidity and folly of interpretation,—our own human, all too human interpretation itself, which we know. . . .

*   *   *   *   *

380

"The Wanderer" Speaks.—In order for once to get a glimpse of our European morality from a distance, in order to compare it with other earlier or future moralities, one must do as the traveller who wants to know the height of the towers of a city: for that purpose he *leaves* the city. "Thoughts concerning moral prejudices," if they are not to be prejudices concerning prejudices, presuppose a position *outside of* morality, some sort of world beyond good and evil, to which one must ascend, climb, or fly—and in the given case at any rate, a position beyond *our* good and evil, an emancipation from all "Europe," understood as a sum of inviolable valuations which have become part and parcel of our flesh and blood. That one does *want* to get outside, or aloft, is perhaps a sort of madness, a peculiar, unreasonable "thou must"—for even we thinkers have our idiosyncrasies of "unfree will"—: the question is whether one *can* really get there. That may depend on manifold conditions: in the main it is a question of how light or how heavy we are, the problem of our "specific gravity." One must be *very light* in order to impel one's will to knowledge to such a distance, and as it were beyond one's age, in order to create eyes for oneself for the survey of millenniums, and a pure heaven in these eyes

besides! One must have freed oneself from many things by which we Europeans of to-day are oppressed, hindered, held down, and made heavy. The man of such a "Beyond," who wants to get even in sight of the highest standards of worth of his age, must first of all "surmount" this age in himself—it is the test of his power—and consequently not only his age, but also his past aversion and opposition *to* his age, his suffering *caused by* his age, his unseasonableness, his Romanticism. . . .

381

The Question of Intelligibility.—One not only wants to be understood when one writes, but also—quite as certainly—*not* to be understood. It is by no means an objection to a book when someone finds it unintelligible: perhaps this might just have been the intention of its author,—perhaps he did not *want* to be understood by "anyone." A distinguished intellect and taste, when it wants to communicate its thoughts, always selects its hearers; by selecting them, it at the same time closes its barriers against "the others." It is there that all the more refined laws of style have their origin: they at the same time keep off, they create distance, they prevent "access" (intelligibility, as we have said,)—while they open the ears of those who are acoustically related to them. And to say it between ourselves and with reference to my own case,—I do not desire that either my ignorance, or the vivacity of my temperament, should prevent me being understood by *you*, my friends: I certainly do not desire that my vivacity should have that effect, however much it may impel me to arrive quickly at an object, in order to arrive at it at all. For I think it is best to do with profound problems as with a cold bath—quickly in, quickly out. That one does not thereby get into the depths, that one does not get deep enough *down*—is a superstition of the hydrophobic, the enemies of cold water; they speak without experience. Oh! the great cold makes one quick!—And let me ask by the way: Is it a fact that a thing has been misunderstood and unrecognised when it has only been touched upon in passing, glanced at, flashed at? Must one absolutely sit upon it in the first place? Must one have brooded on it as on an egg? *Diu noctuque incubando,*[5] as Newton said of himself? At least there are truths of a peculiar shyness and ticklishness which one can only get hold of suddenly, and in no other way,—which one must either *take by surprise,* or leave alone. . . . Finally, my brevity has still another value: on those questions which pre-occupy me, I must say a great deal briefly, in order that it may be heard yet more briefly. For as immoralist, one has to take care lest one ruins innocence, I mean the asses and old maids of both sexes, who get nothing from life but their innocence;

---

[5]By incubating day and night.

moreover my writings are meant to fill them with enthusiasm, to elevate them, to encourage them in virtue. I should be at a loss to know of anything more amusing than to see enthusiastic old asses and maids moved by the sweet feelings of virtue: and "that have I seen"—spake Zarathustra. So much with respect to brevity; the matter stands worse as regards my ignorance, of which I make no secret to myself. There are hours in which I am ashamed of it; to be sure there are likewise hours in which I am ashamed of this shame. Perhaps we philosophers, all of us, are badly placed at present with regard to knowledge: science is growing, the most learned of us are on the point of discovering that we know too little. But it would be worse still if it were otherwise,—if we knew too much; our duty is and remains first of all, not to get into confusion about ourselves. We *are* different from the learned; although it cannot be denied that amongst other things we are also learned. We have different needs, a different growth, a different digestion: we need more, we need also less. There is no formula as to how much an intellect needs for its nourishment; if, however, its taste be in the direction of independence, rapid coming and going, travelling, and perhaps adventure for which only the swiftest are qualified, it prefers rather to live free on poor fare, than to be unfree and plethoric. Not fat, but the greatest suppleness and power is what a good dancer wishes from his nourishment,—and I know not what the spirit of a philosopher would like better than to be a good dancer. For the dance is his ideal, and also his art, in the end likewise his sole piety, his "divine service." [. . .]

382

Great Healthiness. —We, the new, the nameless, the hard-to-understand, we firstlings of a yet untried future—we require for a new end also a new means, namely, a new healthiness, stronger, sharper, tougher, bolder and merrier than any healthiness hitherto. He whose soul longs to experience the whole range of hitherto recognised values and desirabilities, and to circumnavigate all the coasts of this ideal "Mediterranean Sea," who, from the adventures of his most personal experience, wants to know how it feels to be a conqueror and discoverer of the ideal—as likewise how it is with the artist, the saint, the legislator, the sage, the scholar, the devotee, the prophet, and the godly Nonconformist of the old style:—requires one thing above all for that purpose, *great healthiness*—such healthiness as one not only possesses, but also constantly acquires and must acquire, because one continually sacrifices it again, and must sacrifice it! And now, after having been long on the way in this fashion, we Argonauts of the ideal, who are more courageous perhaps than prudent, and often enough shipwrecked and brought to grief, nevertheless, as said above, healthier than people would like to admit, dangerously healthy, always healthy again,—it would seem, as if in recompense for it all, that we have a still undiscovered country before us, the boundaries of which no one has yet seen, a beyond to all countries and corners of the ideal known hitherto, a world so over-rich in the beautiful, the strange, the questionable, the frightful, and the divine, that our curiosity as well as our thirst for possession thereof, have got out of hand—alas! that nothing will now any longer satisfy us! How could we still be content with *the man of the present day* after such peeps, and with such a craving in our conscience and consciousness? What a pity; but it is unavoidable that we should look on the worthiest aims and hopes of the man of the present day with ill-concealed amusement, and perhaps should no longer look at them. Another ideal runs on before us, a strange, tempting ideal, full of danger, to which we should not like to persuade any one, because we do not so readily acknowledge any one's *right thereto:* the ideal of a spirit who plays naïvely (that is to say involuntarily and from overflowing abundance and power) with everything that has hitherto been called holy, good, inviolable, divine; to whom the loftiest conception which the people have reasonably made their measure of value, would already imply danger, ruin, abasement, or at least relaxation, blindness, or temporary self-forgetfulness; the ideal of a humanly superhuman welfare and benevolence, which may often enough appear *inhuman,* for example, when put by the side of all past seriousness on earth, and in comparison with all past solemnities in bearing, word, tone, look, morality and pursuit, as their truest involuntary parody,—but with which, nevertheless, perhaps *the great seriousness* only commences, the proper interrogation mark is set up, the fate of the soul changes, the hour-hand moves, and tragedy *begins.* . . .

*   *   *   *   *

V
Morality Reconsidered
(1886–1887)

Excerpts from

Beyond Good and Evil:
Prelude to a Philosophy of the Future
(Parts Five and Nine)

On the Genealogy of Morals

THE PROBLEM OF MORALITY

Introduction

Nietzsche gave the title *Beyond Good and Evil* to his "Prelude to a Philosophy of the Future." As this title suggests, overcoming the influence of the morality of "good and evil" came to be as central to his philosophical enterprise as overcoming the legacy of otherworldly religious and metaphysical ways of thinking. He had long been concerned with what he called "the problem of morality"[1] and now saw that it was not an isolated problem. It gradually became clear to him that moralities not only reflect underlying needs, interests, and conditions but also influence the ways in which many other (seemingly unrelated) matters are interpreted and assessed. He further became convinced both that the particular kind of morality prevalent in the modern world is only one possible kind of morality, and that its influence is profoundly detrimental—to the enhancement of human life and to the advancement of philosophy as well. The general point underscored by the title of this work is that the ways of thinking associated with this morality must be transcended if either of them is to flourish.

The following excerpts from *Beyond Good and Evil* and from Nietzsche's next book,[2] *On the Genealogy of Morals (Zur Genealogie der Moral)*, show how he sought to come to terms with this morality—what he took it to be, how and why it originated, what interests it serves, and why he took objection to it. They also provide some indication of his ideas about alternatives to it that have been and are humanly possible. His views on these matters are easily misunderstood and are highly provocative in any event. Even so, however, he will have succeeded in at least a part of his intention if his discussions have the effect of prompting serious reflection about "the problem of morality," which all too often is not realized to be any problem at all.

Nietzsche's analysis and critique of the kind of morality he took to be triumphant in the modern world is a central instance of a larger project that he came to call the "revaluation of all values." It was above all with the "value of moral values" that he was concerned—and more specifically,

---

[1]At least as early as *Daybreak*, as he observes in his 1886 preface to that work. This entire preface (included with his other prefaces of 1886–1888 in the final section of this volume) is of considerable interest in connection with his discussions of morality in *Beyond Good and Evil* and *On the Genealogy of Morals*, between which it was written.

[2]That is, his next *entire* book. The "Fifth Book" of *The Gay Science* (or *Joyful Wisdom*) (along with a series of prefaces to his earlier books, which he reissued in 1886) came first.

with their "value for life." As he realized, however, the assessment of their value is not a simple matter. These "moral values" must be identified, distinguished from other modes of valuation, examined with respect to their origins and functions, and considered in relation to their benefits and disadvantages for different types of human beings under differing conditions, before any final conclusions can be reached.

In writing *On the Genealogy of Morals*, Nietzsche expanded on some of the ideas he had advanced a year or so earlier in the part of *Beyond Good and Evil* with which this section begins. The following excerpts from these two works thus are usefully read together. It is important to observe, however, that there is more to his thinking about morality than is to be found in the *Genealogy of Morals*. The perspectives on morality explored in its three essays enabled him to develop some of these ideas in important and illuminating ways; but they are narrower than the scope of his discussion in *Beyond Good and Evil* (and elsewhere[3]) in others. These three essays deal chiefly with only one of the kinds of questions about morality needing to be asked—How is the "*genealogy* of morals" to be understood, and what light does this shed on the nature of the kind of morality that has come to prevail? They contribute to Nietzsche's project of "revaluation," but do not suffice to complete it[4]; and they stop well short of the larger and more important task to which this entire project is only preliminary, of considering what sorts of morality would be most appropriate for different types of human beings in various circumstances.

Nietzsche also has little to say in the *Genealogy of Morals* about the kind of "higher morality" he envisions in the last part of *Beyond Good and Evil*. As his remarks there show, it differs importantly from *both* of the moralities he discusses in the *Genealogy*. It would be "beyond" the "slave-morality" of "good and evil" but would by no means amount merely to a reversion to the barbarian sort of "master-morality" over which this "slave-morality" is held to have triumphed.[5] Nietzsche sought to change the very way in which we think about morality, as well as to break the grip of the prevailing form of morality on us—although that certainly was his immediate objective here. It was for the sake of restoring morality—as *moralities*, attuned to human differences—to the "service of life" that he sought to expose and dethrone *that* morality.

It should also be observed that, in *On the Genealogy of Morals* as well as *Beyond Good and Evil*, Nietzsche deals with a good many important philo-

---

[3]See, e.g., the preceding excerpts from *Human, All Too Human* and *Daybreak*, and the subsequent excerpts from *Twilight of the Idols*.

[4]See the Preface to the *Genealogy*, in Part VIII of this volume.

[5]For this reason one would do well to reread the selections from the Ninth Book of *Beyond Good and Evil* after reading the selections from the *Genealogy*, and also to consider Nietzsche's reflections relating to this topic in the notes from his notebooks of these years, some of which are included in this volume.

sophical topics in addition to morality; and what he has to say about them is of great interest and significance. Along with the "genealogy of morals," he is also concerned with the related "genealogies" of ourselves as "knowers," and more fundamentally of our human nature as it has developed in the course of human events. So, for example, he has a good deal to say about the conditions contributing to the emergence of the various characteristics that are commonly taken for granted as aspects of our humanity—including personal identity, self-consciousness, conscience, agency, and responsibility for our actions. The account he offers serves both to subvert and to supplant the notion that each of us is endowed with a substantial self (the prototype of which is the idea of the God-given soul), transcending everything deriving from both nature and nurture. *On the Genealogy of Morals* thus is a further contribution to Nietzsche's reinterpretation of ourselves as well as of morality; and the selections from it can and should be read with an eye to what they show of his thinking with respect to both of these concerns.

Beyond Good and Evil:
Prelude to a Philosophy
of the Future (1886)
(Excerpts)

Fifth Part
Contributions to the Natural History of Morality

186

Moral sensibility in Europe today is just as subtle, ancient, manifold, sensitive, and refined as the "science of morality" that goes with it is young, raw, clumsy, and inept. This is a fascinating opposition which occasionally takes on color and flesh in the person of some moralist. The very expression, "science of morality," is much too arrogant and in bad taste for that which is designated by it. (Good taste being usually a pre-taste for more modest words.) One ought rigorously to admit *what* it is that will be necessary for a long time to come, *what* alone is justified now— namely the collection of the material, the conceptual formalization and arrangement of an enormous field of delicate value-feelings and value-differences which are living, growing, generating others, and perishing, and—possibly—some experiments to illustrate the more recurrent and frequent forms of this living crystallization. All this to prepare a *typology* of morality. Hitherto, to be sure, we have not been so modest. All the philosophers, with a stiff, ludicrous earnestness, demanded something much higher, more pretentious, more solemn of themselves, as soon as they dealt with morality as a science. What they wanted was to *establish the derivation* of morality, and each philosopher thought he had done so; morality itself he took to be "given." How far from their brash pride lay the apparently insignificant task of description. It was left to collect dust and mold, when the subtlest hands and senses would hardly be subtle enough for it. Precisely because the moral philosophers knew the facts of morality only roughly, arbitrarily abstracted or randomly abbreviated (as the morality of their environment, for example, or their profession, or their church, or the spirit of their time, or their climate and continent), precisely because they were poorly informed and not very inquisitive about other peoples, epochs, and times—for these reasons they never even saw the real problems of morality. For the real problems only appear when one compares *many* moralities. All "science of morality" thus far lacked (peculiar as it may sound) the problem of morality itself; it lacked the suspicion that there was something problematical in morality. What the philosophers claimed for themselves and called "derivation of morality" was, seen in the proper light, only a learned form of good *faith* in the prevailing morality, only another means for expressing it—in other words only another piece of evidence of a given morality. Ultimately it was a sort of denial that this given morality *could* be looked upon as problematical. In any event, it was the converse of a testing, an analysis, a doubt, a vivisection of just this faith of theirs.

187

Aside from asking the value of certain assertions such as "There is a categorical imperative in us," one may also ask what such an assertion tells of the asserter. There are moralities which are supposed to justify their originator in the eyes of other men; those which are supposed to quiet him and resign him to himself; those with which the originator wants to crucify and humiliate himself; those with the help of which he wants revenge; those with which to hide himself or transfigure himself or put altitude and distance between himself and other men. One morality helps its originator forget something; another morality helps him or something about him to be forgotten. Some moralists want to exercise their power and creative caprice on mankind; others, Kant perhaps among them, want us to understand something like "What must be respected in me is my capacity for obedience and—*you shall not* be any better off than I am!" In short, moralities too are but a *symbolic language of the passions.*

*   *   *   *

199

Since at all times, as long as there have been human beings, there have been human herds (clan unions, communities, tribes, nations, states, churches) and very many who obeyed compared with very few who were in command; since, therefore, obedience was the trait best and longest exercised and cultivated among men, one may be justified in assuming that on the average it has become an innate need, a kind of *formal conscience* that bids "thou shalt do something or other absolutely, and absolutely refrain from something or other," in other words, "thou shalt." This need seeks to satisfy itself and to fill its form with some content. Depending on how strong, impatient, and tense it is, it seizes upon things with little discrimination, like a gross appetite, and accepts whatever meets its ear, whatever any representative of authority (parents, teachers, laws, class prejudices, public opinion) declaims into it.

The strange limitation of human evolution, the factors that make for
hesitation, protractedness, retrogression, and circular paths, is due to the
fact that the herd-instinct of obedience is best inherited at the expense
of knowing how to command. Let us imagine this instinct taken to its
limits: in the end there would be none whatever who could command or
be independent; or else all those in command would in the end suffer
inwardly from a bad conscience and have to practice a self-deception
before they could command, namely pretend that they too are only
obeying. [. . .]

*   *   *   *   *

201

As long as the principle of utility that rules moral value judgments is
only utility for the herd, as long as the outlook is directed solely at the
preservation of the social community and immorality is sought exactly and
exclusively in whatever seems dangerous to the status quo—there can be
no "morality of neighborly love." Agreed that even then there is some
constant minor exercise of consideration, compassion, fairness, gentleness, and mutual helpfulness, agreed that even in this state of society all
the impulses are active that will later be honored as "virtues" and finally
coincide, practically speaking, with the very concept of morality—
nonetheless, in the period of which we speak, they do not yet belong in
the realm of moral values; they are still *amoral*. A compassionate deed
during the best period of Rome, for example, was labelled neither good
nor evil, neither moral nor immoral. If it was praised, a sort of reluctant
disdain was not at all incompatible with the praise—as soon as the deed
was compared to an act which served the furtherance of the whole, the *res
publica*.[1] Ultimately, love for one's neighbor is always something subsidiary, partly conventional and arbitrarily manifested, when compared with
fear of one's neighbor. After the social structure as a whole is stabilized and
secured against external dangers, it is the fear of one's neighbor that
creates new perspectives of moral valuations. Certain strong and dangerous drives, such as love for enterprise, foolhardiness, revenge, cunning,
rapacity, and love for domination, all of them traits that had just been not
only honored as being socially useful (under other names than these, as
seems fair enough), but actually cultivated and fostered (because they
were constantly needed to overcome the common danger imposed by the
common enemy)—now, with the outlet channels gone, are gradually
branded as immoral and given over to defamation. Now the antithetical
drives and inclinations come into their own so far as morality is concerned.
The herd-instinct draws its conclusions, step by step. How much or how

[1]Commonwealth (literally, "public entity").

little the common good is endangered, the dangers to the status quo that lie in a given opinion, or state, or passion, in a given will or talent—these now furnish the moral perspective. Here too fear is once again the mother of morality. Communal solidarity is annihilated by the highest and strongest drives that, when they break out passionately, whip the individual far past the average low level of the herd-conscience; society's belief in itself, its backbone as it were, breaks. Hence such drives will best be branded and defamed. A superior, independent intellect, a will to stand alone, even a superior rationality, are felt to be dangers; everything that lifts the individual above the herd and causes fear in his neighbor is from now on called *evil;* the fair-minded, unassuming disposition that adapts and equalizes, all mediocrity of desires comes to be called and honored by the name of morality. Finally, when conditions are very peaceful, all opportunity and necessity for cultivating one's feelings for rigor and hardness disappear; now any rigor, even in the operations of justice, begins to disturb men's conscience. Any superior and rigorous distinction and self-responsibility is felt to be almost insulting; it awakens mistrust; the "lambs" and even more the "sheep" gain respect. There is a point of pathological hollowness and overindulgence in the history of social groups where they even side with those who harm them, with their criminals— and they feel this way seriously and honestly. Punishment seems somehow unfair; at any rate it is certain that the idea of punishment, of having to punish, hurts the group. It creates fear in them. "Isn't it enough to render him *harmless?* Why punish on top of that? Punishment itself is frightful!" With this sentiment the morality of timidity, the herd-morality, draws its ultimate conclusion. If one could abolish danger, abolish the grounds for fear, one would have abolished this morality along with it; it would no longer be necessary; it would no longer consider *itself* necessary! Anyone who tests the conscience of today's European, will pull the same imperative out of a thousand moral folds and hiding places, the imperative of herd-timidity: "We desire that someday there shall be *nothing more to fear.*" Someday—the will and way to that someday is everywhere in Europe today called "progress."

202

Let us immediately say once again what we have said a hundred times already, for today's ears are not good-naturedly open to such truths—to any of *our* truths. We know very well how insulting it sounds when someone counts man among the animals, without further ado and without allegory; but they will almost consider us *guilty* for constantly talking about the man of "modern ideas" in terms of "herd" and "herd-instinct" and such. How can it be helped! We cannot do otherwise, for this precisely is the point of our new insight. We found that so far as all the major moral judgments are concerned, Europe is today of one mind (including the countries that are affected by European influence): Europe obviously *knows* today what Socrates thought he did not know and what that famous old serpent promised to teach—they "know" today what is good and what is evil. Now of course it sounds harsh and hard on the ears when we keep insisting that whatever believes it knows, whatever glorifies itself with its praise and blame, whatever approves of itself, is the instinct of the human herd-animal, the instinct which has broken out, is more and more preponderating, more and more dominating the other instincts, in accordance with the growing physiological approximation and resemblance of which it is the symptom. *Morality in Europe today is herd-animal morality,* that is—as we understand things—*one type* of human morality, beside which and before and after which many other moralities, above all, more superior moralities, are possible or *should* be possible. But against such a possibility and against such a "should" this morality defends itself with all its might; stubbornly and inexorably it says, "I myself am morality itself and nothing other than myself is morality!" With the aid of a religion, in fact, which agreed with and flattered the most sublime desires of herd-animals, we have come to the point where even in the political and social institutions an increasingly visible expression of this morality can be found: the *democratic* movement comes into the Christian inheritance. But that the democratic tempo is much too slow and sleepy for the impatient ones, the sick sufferers from the above mentioned instinct, is attested by the ever more raging howls, the ever more open baring of the teeth of the anarchist-dogs who are now flitting through the alleys of European culture. They are seemingly opposed to the peaceable and hard-working democrats, to the ideological revolutionaries, and even more to the bungling philosophasters and brotherhood-visionaries who call themselves Socialists and desire a "free society"—but in actuality the anarchists are of the same breed, of the same thorough and instinctive hostility against any social structure other than that of the *autonomous* herd [. . .]; they are one in their faith in the morality of *commonly felt* compassion as though this feeling constituted morality itself, as though it were the summit, the *attained* summit of mankind, the only hope of the future, the consolation of the living, the great deliverance from all the guilt of yore—they are all one in their faith in fellowship as that which will *deliver* them, their faith in the herd, in other words, in "themselves." [. . .]

203

We, who are of a different faith, for whom the democratic movement is not only a deteriorated form of political organization but a deterioration, that is to say, a depreciation of a human type, a mediocritizing and lowering of values—where must our hopes look? We have no other choice: we must seek *new philosophers*, spirits strong or original enough to give an impulse to opposing valuations, to transvalue and turn upside down the "eternal values"; we must seek heralds, men of the future, who will now tie the knot and start the pressure that shall force the will of millenniums to run *new* orbits. Men who will teach man that man's future is man's *will*, dependent on man's will; who will prepare great ventures and all-involving experiments of discipline and culture so that there will be an end to that gruesome rule of nonsense and accident that is called "history" (the nonsense of the "greatest number" is merely its last manifestation). For such tasks we shall some day require a new type of philosopher and commander, compared with whom any previous concealed, frightful, or well-intentioned spirits will seem pale and dwarfish. The image of such leaders is what hovers before *our* eyes. May I say it aloud, you free thinkers? The conditions one would have to partly create, partly utilize, for their development, the presumable paths and tests by which a soul could grow to such height and might, by which it could learn to feel the *compulsion* to such tasks, a transvaluation of values beneath whose new pressure and hammer a conscience is forged, a heart is transformed into bronze, so that it might bear the weight of such a responsibility; furthermore the necessity for such leaders, the horrifying danger that they might fail to appear, or turn out wrong or degenerate—all these are *our* essential cares and depressions. You free thinkers know it is so. These are the grave distant thoughts, the thunderclouds that pass over the skies of *our* lives. There are few pains as keen as to have seen, guessed and felt how some extraordinary man has degenerated and falls out of his orbit. But whoever has that rare eye for the universal danger, the danger that mankind itself might deteriorate; whoever like us has once recognized the monstrous randomness which hitherto has played its game with the future of man, a game in which no hand, not even a "finger of God" has ever taken part; whoever intuits the doom that lies hidden in the idiotic guilelessness and blind self-confidence of "modern ideas," even more of all Christian-European morality—such a man suffers an anxiety with which none other can be compared. For he comprehends with a glance what all *could be cultivated in mankind* if there were a favorable accumulation and heightening of powers and tasks; he knows with all the science of his conscience how unexhausted man still is for his greatest possibilities, and how often the type "mankind" has faced mysterious decisions and new paths; he knows even better through his most painful recollections that wretched things usually have caused some development of the highest potential rank to break apart, break off, sink back, become wretched. *The universal degeneration of mankind* down to what the Socialist bunglers and flatheads today call the "man of the future," down to their

ideal, the degeneration and depreciation of man until he is a perfect herd
animal (or, to use their words, "man in a free society"), this brutalization
of man until he is a dwarfed beast with equal rights and equal demands—
this is *possible*. There can be no doubt about it. Whoever has fully thought
out this possibility has one more nausea than the others—and also, perhaps, a new *task*. —

*   *   *   *   *

Ninth Part
What Does "Distinguished" Mean?[2]

257

Every heightening of the type "man" hitherto has been the work of an
aristocratic society—and thus it will always be; a society which believes in
a long ladder of rank order and value differences in men, which needs
slavery in some sense. Without the *pathos of distance* as it grows out of the
deep-seated differences of caste, out of the constant view, the downward
view, that the ruling caste gets of its subordinates and tools, out of its
equally constant exercise in obeying and commanding, in keeping apart
and keeping a distance—without this pathos of distance there could not
grow that other more mysterious pathos, that longing for ever greater
distances within the soul itself, the evolving of ever higher, rarer, more
spacious, more widely arched, more comprehensive states—in short: the
heightening of the type "man," the continued "self-mastery of man," to
take a moral formula in a supra-moral sense. To be sure, we must not yield
to humanitarian self-deception about the history of the origins of an aristocratic society (in other words, the presuppositions for the heightening of
the type "man"): the truth is hard. Let us tell ourselves without indulging
ourselves how every superior culture on earth got its *start!* Men whose
nature was still natural, barbarians in every frightful sense of the word,
men of prey, men still in possession of unbroken strength of will and

---

[2]Nietzsche's title of this Ninth Part is *"Was ist Vornehm?"* The translator rendered this as
"What Does 'Distinguish' Mean?" This has been changed to "What Does 'Distinguished'
Mean?" because *"vornehm"* is an adjective, as is "distinguished," whereas "distinguish" is
a verb and so is grammatically incorrect. The adjective *"vornehm"* may equally appropriately
be translated as "superior," "noble," or "refined"; and for Nietzsche it means all of these
things. No one of them adequately captures its meaning. Thus, a more grammatically
accurate and conceptually adequate translation of *"Was ist vornehm?"* would be: "What is
superior, noble, refined, and distinguished?"

power-drives—such men threw themselves upon weaker, better-behaved, more peaceable races, possibly those engaged in commerce or cattle-raising, or else upon old hollow cultures in which the last life powers were flickering away in flashing fireworks of intellect and corruption. The distinguished caste in the beginning was always the barbarian caste; their superiority lay not primarily in their physical but in their psychic power; they were more whole as human beings (which on every level also means "more whole as beasts").

*   *   *   *   *

259

To refrain from wounding, violating, and exploiting one another, to acknowledge another's will as equal to one's own: this can become proper behavior, in a certain coarse sense, between individuals when the conditions for making it possible obtain (namely the factual similarity of the individuals as to power and standards of value, and their co-existence in one greater body). But as soon as one wants to extend this principle, to make it the *basic principle of society*, it shows itself for what it is: the will to negate life, the principle of dissolution and decay. Here one must think radically to the very roots of things and ward off all weakness of sensibility. Life itself is essential assimilation, injury, violation of the foreign and the weaker, suppression, hardness, the forcing of one's own forms upon something else, ingestion and—at least in its mildest form—exploitation. But why should we always use such words which were coined from time immemorial to reveal a calumniatory intention? Even that body to which we referred, the body within which individuals may treat each other with equality (and it is so in any healthy aristocracy)—even this body itself, if it is alive and not dying off, must do to other bodies all the things from which its members refrain; it will have to be the will to power incarnate; it will have to want to grow, to branch out, to draw others into itself, to gain supremacy. And not because it is moral or immoral in any sense but because it is *alive*, and because life simply *is* will to power. But there is no point at which the common consciousness in Europe today is less willing to learn than just here; everywhere today, and even in the guise of science, there is grandiose talk about future social conditions where there is to be no more "exploitation." To my ears that sounds as though they promised to invent a kind of life that would refrain from all the organic functions. "Exploitation" is not a part of a vicious or imperfect or primitive society: it belongs to the *nature* of living things, it is a basic organic function, a consequence of the will to power which is the will to life. Admitted that this is a novelty as a theory—as a reality it is the *basic fact* underlying all history. Let us be honest with ourselves at least this far!

260

Wandering through the many fine and coarse moralities which have hitherto ruled on earth, as well as those which still rule, I found certain features regularly occurring together and bound up with one another. Finally they revealed two basic types to me, and a basic difference leaped to my eye. There is *master-morality* and *slave-morality:*[3] I add immediately that in all higher and mixed cultures there are also attempts at a mediation between these two, and even more frequently a mix-up of them and a mutual misunderstanding; at times in fact a relentless juxtaposition even within the psyche of a single individual. The moral value-differentiations arose either among a ruling type which was pleasantly conscious of its difference from the ruled—or else among the ruled, the slaves and dependents of all kinds. In the first case, when the rulers determine the concept "good," it is the elevated and proud conditions of the psyche which are felt to be what excels and determines the order of rank. The distinguished human being divorces himself from the being in whom the opposite of such elevated and proud conditions is expressed. He despises them. One may note immediately that in the first type of morality the antithesis "good vs. bad" means "distinguished vs. despicable"; the antithesis "good vs. evil" has a different origin. What is despised is the coward, the timid man, and the petty man, he who thinks in terms of narrow utility; likewise the suspicious man with his cowed look, the one who humiliates himself, the dog-type who lets himself be mistreated, the begging flatterer, and above all the liar: it is the basic faith of all aristocrats that the common people are liars. "We truthful ones" the nobles called themselves in ancient Greece. It is obvious that the moral value-characteristics are at first applied to *people* and only later, in a transferred sense, to *acts*. This is why it is a sad mistake when moral historians begin with questions like "Why was the compassionate act praised?" The distinguished type of human being feels *himself* as value-determining; he does not need to be ratified: he judges that "which is harmful to me is harmful as such"; he knows that *he* is the something which gives honor to objects; he *creates values*. This type honors everything he knows about himself; his morality is self-glorification. In the foreground is the feeling of fullness, of power that would flow forth, the bliss of high tension, the consciousness of riches which would like to give and lavish. The distinguished man, too, helps the unhappy, but not—at least not mainly—from compassion, but more from an internal pressure that has been built up by an excess of power. The distinguished man honors himself in the mighty, including those who have power over themselves; those who know when

[3]This is where Nietzsche first introduces this famous contrast, which he discusses at greater length in the first essay of *On the Genealogy of Morals* (excerpts from which follow).

to talk and when to keep silent; those who take delight in being rigorous and hard with themselves and who have respect for anything rigorous and hard. "Wotan placed a hard heart in my breast," says an old Scandinavian saga: this is the proper poetic expression for the soul of a proud Viking. Such a type of man is proud *not* to have been made for compassion; hence the hero of the saga adds a warning: "Whoever has not a hard heart when young will never get it at all." Distinguished and courageous men with such thoughts are at the opposite end from that morality which sees the characteristic function of morality in pity or in doing for others or *désintéressement*. Belief in oneself, pride in oneself, basic hostility and irony against "selflessness" is as sure a part of distinguished morality as an easy disdain and cautious attitude toward the fellow-feelings and the "warm heart." It is the powerful men who *understand* how to accord honor: that is their art, the domain of their invention. Profound respect for old age and for origins: their whole law stands on this twofold respect. Faith in and prepossession for one's ancestors and prejudice against the future ones is typical of the morality of the powerful. Contrariwise, when men of "modern ideas" believe almost instinctively in "progress" and in "the future" and have less and less respect for the old, that alone reveals clearly enough the undistinguished origin of their "ideas." But the point at which the morality of rulers is most foreign to current taste and most painstakingly strict in principle is this: one has duties only toward one's equals; toward beings of a lower rank, toward everything foreign to one, one may act as one sees fit, "as one's heart dictates"—in any event, "beyond good and evil." The ability and the duty to sustain enduring gratitude and enduring vengefulness—both only toward one's equals; subtlety in requital and retaliation; a subtly refined concept of friendship; a certain need to have enemies (as outlets for the passions: envy, quarrelsomeness and wantonness—basically, in order to be capable of being a good *friend*): all these are typical marks of the distinguished type of morality which, as I have indicated, is not the morality of "modern ideas" and hence is difficult today to empathize with, and equally difficult to dig out and uncover.—The situation is different with the second type of morality, the slave morality. Assuming that the violated ones, the oppressed, the suffering, the unfree, those who are uncertain and tired of themselves—assuming that they moralize: What will they have in common in their moral evaluations? Probably a pessimistic suspiciousness against the whole situation of mankind will appear; perhaps a judgment against mankind together with its position. The eye of the slave looks unfavorably upon the virtues of the powerful; he *subtly* mistrusts all the "good" that the others honor—he would like to persuade himself that even their happiness is not real. Conversely, those qualities are emphasized and illuminated which serve to make existence easier for the sufferers: here compassion, the complaisant helping hand, the warm heart, patience, diligence, humility and friendliness are honored, for these are the useful qualities and almost the only means for enduring the pressure of existence. Slave-morality is essentially a utility-morality. Here is the cornerstone for the origin of that famous antithesis "good vs. evil." Power and dangerousness, a certain frightfulness, subtlety and strength which do not permit of despisal, are felt to belong to evil. Hence according to slave morality, the "evil" man inspires fear; according to master morality, the "good" man does and wants to, where as the "bad" man is felt to be despicable. The antithesis reaches its sharpest point when ultimately the "good" man within a slave morality becomes the logical target of a breath of disdain—however slight and well-meaning, because he is the *undangerous* element in his morality: good natured, easily deceived, perhaps a little stupid, *un bonhomme.*[4] Whenever slave morality preponderates, language shows a tendency to reconcile the meanings of "good" and "dumb." A final basic distinction is that the longing for *freedom*, the instinct for happiness and the subtleties of the freedom-feelings belong as necessarily to slave morality as skill and enthusiasm for reverence, for devotion, is the regular symptom of an aristocratic manner of thinking and evaluating.

*   *   *   *   *

287

What is distinguished?[5] What can the word "distinguished" still mean to us today? What reveals, how does one recognize, the distinguished human being beneath today's sky heavily overcast by the beginnings of a plebeian rule that makes everything opaque and leaden? It is not his actions by which he can be proved: actions are always ambiguous, always unfathomable; neither is it his "works." Among artists and scholars there are many to be found today who reveal through their works a drive, a deep desire, for distinction. But precisely the need *for* distinction is fundamentally different from the needs of the distinguished soul. It is in fact the most persuasive and dangerous mark of what they lack. It is not works but "faith" that here decides, that determines the order or rank—to reactivate an old religious formula in a new and deeper sense. There is some kind of basic certainty about itself which a distinguished soul possesses, something which cannot be sought nor found nor perhaps lost. *The distinguished soul has reverence for itself.* —

*   *   *   *   *

[4]"A good (nice) person."
[5]"*Was ist vornehm?*" See note 2.

On the Genealogy of Morals (1887)
(Excerpts)

First Essay
"Good and Evil," "Good and Bad"

1

These English psychologists, whom one has also to thank for the only attempts hitherto to arrive at a history of the origin of morality—they themselves are no easy riddle; I confess that, as living riddles, they even possess one essential advantage over their books—*they are interesting!* These English psychologists—what do they really want? One always discovers them voluntarily or involuntarily at the same task, namely at dragging the *partie honteuse*[1] of our inner world into the foreground and seeking the truly effective and directing agent, that which has been decisive in its evolution, in just that place where the intellectual pride of man would least *desire* to find it. [. . .]

But I am told they are simply old, cold, and tedious frogs, creeping around men and into men as if in their own proper element, that is, in a *swamp*. I rebel at that idea; more, I do not believe it; and if one may be allowed to hope where one does not know, then I hope from my heart they may be the reverse of this—that these investigators and microscopists of the soul may be fundamentally brave, proud, and magnanimous animals, who know how to keep their hearts as well as their sufferings in bounds and have trained themselves to sacrifice all desirability to truth, *every* truth, even plain, harsh, ugly, repellent, unchristian, immoral truth.—For such truths do exist.—

2

All respect then for the good spirits that may rule in these historians of morality! But it is, unhappily, certain that the *historical spirit* itself is lacking in them, that precisely all the good spirits of history itself have left them in the lurch! As is the hallowed custom with philosophers, the

---

[1]Shameful past.

thinking of all of them is *by nature* unhistorical; there is no doubt about that. The way they have bungled their moral genealogy comes to light at the very beginning, where the task is to investigate the origin of the concept and judgment "good." "Originally"—so they decree—"one approved unegoistic actions and called them good from the point of view of those to whom they were done, that is to say, those to whom they were *useful;* later one *forgot* how this approval originated and, simply because unegoistic actions were always *habitually* praised as good, one also felt them to be good—as if they were something good in themselves." One sees straightaway that this primary derivation already contains all the typical traits of the idiosyncrasy of the English psychologists—we have "utility," "forgetting," "habit," and finally "error," all as the basis of an evaluation of which the higher man has hitherto been proud as though it were a kind of prerogative of man as such. This pride *has* to be humbled, this evaluation disvalued: has that end been achieved?

Now it is plain to me, first of all, that in this theory the source of the concept "good" has been sought and established in the wrong place: the judgment "good" did *not* originate with those to whom "goodness" was shown! Rather it was "the good" themselves, that is to say, the noble, powerful, high-stationed and high-minded, who felt and established themselves and their actions as good, that is, of the first rank, in contra-distinction to all the low, low-minded, common and plebeian. It was out of this *pathos of distance* that they first seized the right to create values and to coin names for values: what had they to do with utility! The viewpoint of utility is as remote and inappropriate as it possibly could be in face of such a burning eruption of the highest rank-ordering, rank-defining value judgments: for here feeling has attained the antithesis of that low degree of warmth which any calculating prudence, any calculus of utility, presupposes—and not for once only, not for an exceptional hour, but for good. The pathos of nobility and distance, as aforesaid, the protracted and domineering fundamental total feeling on the part of a higher ruling order in relation to a lower order, to a "below"—*that* is the origin of the antith-esis "good" and "bad." (The lordly right of giving names extends so far that one should allow oneself to conceive the origin of language itself as an expression of power on the part of the rulers: they say "this *is* this and this," they seal every thing and event with a sound and, as it were, take possession of it.) It follows from this origin that the word "good" was definitely *not* linked from the first and by necessity to "unegoistic" ac-tions, as the superstition of these genealogists of morality would have it. Rather it was only when aristocratic value judgments *declined* that the whole antithesis "egoistic" "unegoistic" obtruded itself more and more on the human conscience—it is, to speak in my own language, the *herd instinct* that through this antithesis at last gets its word (and its *words*) in.

And even then it was a long time before that instinct attained such dominion that moral evaluation was actually stuck and halted at this antithesis (as, for example, is the case in contemporary Europe: the prejudice that takes "moral," "unegoistic," "*désintéressé*"[2] as concepts of equivalent value already rules today with the force of a "fixed idea" and brain-sickness).

* * * * *

10

The slave revolt in morality begins when *ressentiment*[3] itself becomes creative and gives birth to values: the *ressentiment* of natures that are denied the true reaction, that of deeds, and compensate themselves with an imaginary revenge. While every noble morality develops from a triumphant affirmation of itself, slave morality from the outset says No to what is "outside," what is "different," what is "not itself"; and *this* No is its creative deed. This inversion of the value-positing eye—this *need* to direct one's view outward instead of back to oneself—is of the essence of *ressentiment:* in order to exist, slave morality always first needs a hostile external world; it needs, physiologically speaking, external stimuli in order to act at all—its action is fundamentally reaction.

The reverse is the case with the noble mode of valuation: it acts and grows spontaneously, it seeks its opposite only so as to affirm itself more gratefully and triumphantly—its negative concept "low," "common," "bad" is only a subsequently-invented pale, contrasting image in relation to its positive basic concept—filled with life and passion through and through—"we noble ones, we good, beautiful, happy ones!"

While the noble man lives in trust and openness with himself, [. . .] the man of *ressentiment* is neither upright nor naïve nor honest and straightforward with himself. His soul *squints;* his spirit loves hiding places, secret paths and back doors, everything covert entices him as *his* world, *his* security, *his* refreshment; he understands how to keep silent, how not to forget, how to wait, how to be provisionally self-deprecating and humble. A race of such men of *ressentiment* is bound to become eventually *cleverer* than any noble race; it will also honor cleverness to a far greater degree: namely, as a condition of existence of the first importance; while with noble men cleverness can easily acquire a subtle flavor of luxury and

---

[2]"Disinterested."

[3]"Resentment" is the usual translation of this French term; but Nietzsche's use of the term is usually retained to call attention to the special meaning it has for him that is spelled out in the following discussion.

subtlety—for here it is far less essential than the perfect functioning of the regulating *unconscious* instincts or even than a certain imprudence, perhaps a bold recklessness whether in the face of danger or of the enemy, or that enthusiastic impulsiveness in anger, love, reverence, gratitude, and revenge by which noble souls have at all times recognized one another. *Ressentiment* itself, if it should appear in the noble man, consummates and exhausts itself in an immediate reaction, and therefore does not *poison:* on the other hand, it fails to appear at all on countless occasions on which it inevitably appears in the weak and impotent.

To be incapable of taking one's enemies, one's accidents, even one's misdeeds seriously for very long—that is the sign of strong, full natures in whom there is an excess of the power to form, to mold, to recuperate and to forget. [. . .] In contrast to this, picture "the enemy" as the man of *ressentiment* conceives him—and here precisely is his deed, his creation: he has conceived "the evil enemy," *"the Evil One,"* and this in fact is his basic concept, from which he then evolves, as an afterthought and pendant, a "good one"—himself!

11

This, then, is quite the contrary of what the noble man does, who conceives the basic concept "good" in advance and spontaneously out of himself and only then creates for himself an idea of "bad"! This "bad" of noble origin and that "evil" out of the cauldron of unsatisfied hatred—the former an after-production, a side issue, a contrasting shade, the latter on the contrary the original thing, the beginning, the distinctive *deed* in the conception of a slave morality—how different these words "bad" and "evil" are, although they are both apparently the opposite of the same concept "good." But it is *not* the same concept "good": one should ask rather precisely *who* is "evil" in the sense of the morality of *ressentiment*. The answer, in all strictness, is: *precisely* the "good man" of the other morality, precisely the noble, powerful man, the ruler, but dyed in another color, interpreted in another fashion, seen in another way by the venomous eye of *ressentiment*.

Here there is one thing we shall be the last to deny: he who knows these "good men" only as enemies knows only *evil enemies*, and the same men who are held so sternly in check *inter pares*[4] by custom, respect, usage, gratitude, and even more by mutual suspicion and jealousy, and who on the other hand in their relations with one another show themselves so resourceful in consideration, self-control, delicacy, loyalty, pride, and friendship—once they go outside, where the strange, the *stranger* is

---

[4]Among equals.

found, they are not much better than uncaged beasts of prey. There they savor a freedom from all social constraints, they compensate themselves in the wilderness for the tension engendered by protracted confinement and enclosure within the peace of society, they go *back* to the innocent conscience of the beast of prey, as triumphant monsters who perhaps emerge from a disgusting procession of murder, arson, rape, and torture, exhilarated and undisturbed of soul, as if it were no more than a students' prank, convinced they have provided the poets with a lot more material for song and praise. One cannot fail to see at the bottom of all these noble races the beast of prey, the splendid *blond beast* prowling about avidly in search of spoil and victory; this hidden core needs to erupt from time to time, the animal has to get out again and go back to the wilderness: the Roman, Arabian, Germanic, Japanese nobility, the Homeric heroes, the Scandinavian Vikings—they all shared this need. [. . .]

Supposing that what is at any rate believed to be the "truth" really is true, and the *meaning of all culture* is the reduction of the beast of prey "man" to a tame and civilized animal, a *domestic animal*, then one would undoubtedly have to regard all those instincts of reaction and *ressentiment* through whose aid the noble races and their ideals were finally confounded and overthrown as the actual *instruments of culture;* which is not to say that the *bearers* of these instincts themselves represent culture. Rather is the reverse not merely probable—no! today it is *palpable!* These bearers of the oppressive instincts that thirst for reprisal, the descendants of every kind of European and non-European slavery, and especially of the entire pre-Aryan populace—they represent the *regression* of mankind! These "instruments of culture" are a disgrace to man and rather an accusation and counterargument against "culture" in general! One may be quite justified in continuing to fear the blond beast at the core of all noble races and in being on one's guard against it: but who would not a hundred times sooner fear where one can also admire than *not* fear but be permanently condemned to the repellent sight of the ill-constituted, dwarfed, atrophied, and poisoned? And is that not *our* fate? What today constitutes *our* antipathy to "man"?—for we *suffer* from man, beyond doubt.

Not fear; rather that we no longer have anything left to fear in man; that the maggot "man" is swarming in the foreground; that the "tame man," the hopelessly mediocre and insipid man, has already learned to feel himself as the goal and zenith, as the meaning of history, as "higher man"—that he has indeed a certain right to feel thus, insofar as he feels himself elevated above the surfeit of ill-constituted, sickly, weary and exhausted people of which Europe is beginning to stink today, as something at least relatively well-constituted, at least still capable of living, at least affirming life.

*   *   *   *   *

13

But let us return: the problem of the *other* origin of the "good," of the good as conceived by the man of *ressentiment*, demands its solution.

That lambs dislike great birds of prey does not seem strange: only it gives no ground for reproaching these birds of prey for bearing off little lambs. And if the lambs say among themselves: "these birds of prey are evil; and whoever is least like a bird of prey, but rather its opposite, a lamb—would he not be good?" there is no reason to find fault with this institution of an ideal, except perhaps that the birds of prey might view it a little ironically and say: "*we* don't dislike them at all, these good little lambs; we even love them: nothing is more tasty than a tender lamb."

To demand of strength that it should *not* express itself as strength, that it should *not* be a desire to overcome, a desire to throw down, a desire to become master, a thirst for enemies and resistances and triumphs, is just as absurd as to demand of weakness that it should express itself as strength. A quantum of force is equivalent to a quantum of drive, will, effect—more, it is nothing other than precisely this very driving, willing, effecting, and only owing to the seduction of language (and of the fundamental errors of reason that are petrified in it) which conceives and misconceives all effects as conditioned by something that causes effects, by a "subject," can it appear otherwise. For just as the popular mind separates the lightning from its flash and takes the latter for an *action*, for the operation of a subject called lightning, so popular morality also separates strength from expressions of strength, as if there were a neutral substratum behind the strong man, which was *free* to express strength or not to do so. But there is no such substratum; there is no "being" behind doing, effecting, becoming; "the doer" is merely a fiction added to the deed—the deed is everything. The popular mind in fact doubles the deed; when it sees the lightning flash, it is the deed of a deed: it posits the same event first as cause and then a second time as its effect. Scientists do no better when they say "force moves," "force causes," and the like—all its coolness, its freedom from emotion notwithstanding, our entire science still lies under the misleading influence of language and has not disposed of that little changeling, the "subject" (the atom, for example, is such a changeling, as is the Kantian "thing-in-itself"); no wonder if the submerged, darkly glowering emotions of vengefulness and hatred exploit this belief for their own ends and in fact maintain no belief more ardently than the belief that *the strong man is free* to be weak and the bird of prey to be a lamb—for thus they gain the right to make the bird of prey *accountable* for being a bird of prey. [. . .]

*   *   *   *   *

16

Let us conclude. The two *opposing* values "good and bad," "good and evil" have been engaged in a fearful struggle on earth for thousands of years; and though the latter value has certainly been on top for a long time, there are still places where the struggle is as yet undecided. One might even say that it has risen ever higher and thus become more and more profound and spiritual: so that today there is perhaps no more decisive mark of a *"higher nature,"* a more spiritual nature, than that of being divided in this sense and a genuine battleground of these opposed values. [. . .]

17

[. . .] Must the ancient fire not some day flare up much more terribly, after much longer preparation? More: must one not desire it with all one's might? even will it? even promote it?

Whoever begins at this point, like my readers, to reflect and pursue his train of thought will not soon come to the end of it—reason enough for me to come to an end, assuming it has long since been abundantly clear what my *aim* is, what the aim of that dangerous slogan is that is inscribed at the head of my last book *Beyond Good and Evil.* —At least this does *not* mean "Beyond Good and Bad."——

Note[5]   I take the opportunity provided by this treatise to express publicly and formally a desire I have previously voiced only in occasional conversation with scholars; namely, that some philosophical faculty might advance *historical* studies *of morality* through a series of academic prize-essays—perhaps this present book will serve to provide a powerful impetus in this direction. In case this idea should be implemented, I suggest the following question: it deserves the attention of philologists and historians as well as that of professional philosophers:

"What light does linguistics, and especially the study of etymology, throw on the history of the evolution of moral concepts?"

[5]This note is Nietzsche's.

On the other hand, it is equally necessary to engage the interest of physiologists and doctors in these problems (of the *value* of existing evaluations); it may be left to academic philosophers to act as advocates and mediators in this matter too, after they have on the whole succeeded in the past in transforming the originally so reserved and mistrustful relations between philosophy, physiology, and medicine into the most amicable and fruitful exchange. Indeed, every table of values, every "thou shalt" known to history or ethnology, requires first a *physiological* investigation and interpretation, rather than a psychological one; and every one of them needs a critique on the part of medical science. The question: what is the *value* of this or that table of values and "morals"? should be viewed from the most divers perspectives; for the problem "value for *what?*" cannot be examined too subtly. Something, for example, that possessed obvious value in relation to the longest possible survival of a race (or to the enhancement of its power of adaptation to a particular climate or to the preservation of the greatest number) would by no means possess the same value if it were a question, for instance, of producing a stronger type. The well-being of the majority and the well-being of the few are opposite viewpoints of value: to consider the former *a priori* of higher value may be left to the naïveté of English biologists. —*All* the sciences have from now on to prepare the way for the future task of the philosophers: this task understood as the solution of the *problem of value*, the determination of the *order of rank among values*.

Second Essay
"Guilt," "Bad Conscience," and the Like

1

To breed an animal *with the right to make promises*—is not this the paradoxical task that nature has set itself in the case of man? is it not the real problem regarding man?

That this problem has been solved to a large extent must seem all the more remarkable to anyone who appreciates the strength of the opposing force, that of *forgetfulness*. Forgetting is no mere *vis inertiae*[6] as the superficial imagine; it is rather an active and in the strictest sense positive faculty of repression, that is responsible for the fact that what we experience and absorb enters our consciousness as little while we are digesting

---

[6]Force of inertia.

it (one might call the process "inpsychation") as does the thousandfold process involved in physical nourishment—so-called "incorporation." To close the doors and windows of consciousness for a time; to remain undisturbed by the noise and struggle of our underworld of utility organs working with and against one another; a little quietness, a little *tabula rasa*[7] of the consciousness, to make room for new things, above all for the nobler functions and functionaries, for regulation, foresight, premeditation (for our organism is an oligarchy)—that is the purpose of active forgetfulness, which is like a doorkeeper, a preserver of psychic order, repose, and etiquette: so that it will be immediately obvious how there could be no happiness, no cheerfulness, no hope, no pride, no *present*, without forgetfulness. The man in whom this apparatus of repression is damaged and ceases to function properly may be compared (and more than merely compared) with a dyspeptic—he cannot "have done" with anything.

Now this animal which needs to be forgetful, in which forgetting represents a force, a form of *robust* health, has bred in itself an opposing faculty, a memory, with the aid of which forgetfulness is abrogated in certain cases—namely in those cases where promises are made. This involves no mere passive inability to rid oneself of an impression, no mere indigestion through a once-pledged word with which one cannot "have done," but an active *desire* not to rid oneself, a desire for the continuance of something desired once, a real *memory of the will:* so that between the original "I will," "I shall do this" and the actual discharge of the will, its *act*, a world of strange new things, circumstances, even acts of will may be interposed without breaking this long chain of will. But how many things this presupposes! To ordain the future in advance in this way, man must first have learned to distinguish necessary events from chance ones, to think causally, to see and anticipate distant eventualities as if they belonged to the present, to decide with certainty what is the goal and what the means to it, and in general be able to calculate and compute. Man himself must first of all have become *calculable, regular, necessary,* even in his own image of himself, if he is to be able to stand security for *his own future*, which is what one who promises does!

2

This precisely is the long story of how *responsibility* originated. The task of breeding an animal with the right to make promises evidently embraces and presupposes as a preparatory task that one first *makes* men to a certain

---

[7]Blank slate, i.e., something that may be written upon but that begins without anything already inscribed upon it.

degree necessary, uniform, like among like, regular, and consequently calculable. The tremendous labor of that which I have called "morality of mores" (*Dawn*, sections 9, 14, 16)[8]—the labor performed by man upon himself during the greater part of the existence of the human race, his entire *prehistoric* labor, finds in this its meaning, its great justification, notwithstanding the severity, tyranny, stupidity, and idiocy involved in it: with the aid of the morality of mores and the social straitjacket, man was actually *made* calculable.

If we place ourselves at the end of this tremendous process, where the tree at last brings forth fruit, where society and the morality of custom at last reveal *what* they have simply been the means to: then we discover that the ripest fruit is the *sovereign individual,* like only to himself, liberated again from morality of custom, autonomous and supramoral (for "autonomous" and "moral" are mutually exclusive), in short, the man who has his own independent, protracted will and the *right to make promises*—and in him a proud consciousness, quivering in every muscle, of *what* has at length been achieved and become flesh in him, a consciousness of his own power and freedom, a sensation of mankind come to completion. This emancipated individual, with the actual *right* to make promises, this master of a *free* will, this sovereign man—how should he not be aware of his superiority over all those who lack the right to make promises and stand as their own guarantors, of how much trust, how much fear, how much reverence he arouses—he *"deserves"* all three—and of how this mastery over himself also necessarily gives him mastery over circumstances, over nature, and over all more short-willed and unreliable creatures? The "free" man, the possessor of a protracted and unbreakable will, also possesses his *measure of value:* looking out upon others from himself, he honors or he despises; and just as he is bound to honor his peers, the strong and reliable (those with the *right* to make promises)—that is, all those who promise like sovereigns, reluctantly, rarely, slowly, who are chary of trusting, whose trust is a mark of *distinction,* who give their word as something that can be relied on because they know themselves strong enough to maintain it in the face of accidents, even "in the face of fate"—he is bound to reserve a kick for the feeble windbags who promise without the right to do so, and a rod for the liar who breaks his word even at the moment he utters it. The proud awareness of the extraordinary privilege of *responsibility,* the consciousness of this rare freedom, this power over oneself and over fate, has in his case penetrated to the profoundest depths and become instinct, the dominating instinct. What will he call this dominating

---

[8]*Dawn* and *Daybreak* are alternative translations of the title of this work *(Morganröthe).* The first and most important of the sections to which Nietzsche here refers the reader is included in the excerpts from *Daybreak* found earlier in this volume.

instinct, supposing he feels the need to give it a name? The answer is beyond doubt: this sovereign man calls it his *conscience.*

3

His conscience?—It is easy to guess that the concept of "conscience" that we here encounter in its highest, almost astonishing, manifestation, has a long history and variety of forms behind it. To possess the right to stand security for oneself and to do so with pride, thus to possess also the *right to affirm oneself*—this, as has been said, is a ripe fruit, but also a *late* fruit: how long must this fruit have hung on the tree, unripe and sour! And for a much longer time nothing whatever was to be seen of any such fruit: no one could have promised its appearance, although everything in the tree was preparing for and growing toward it!

"How can one create a memory for the human animal? How can one impress something upon this partly obtuse, partly flighty mind, attuned only to the passing moment, in such a way that it will stay there?"

One can well believe that the answers and methods for solving this primeval problem were not precisely gentle; perhaps indeed there was nothing more fearful and uncanny in the whole prehistory of man than his *mnemotechnics.* "If something is to stay in the memory it must be burned in: only that which never ceases to *hurt* stays in the memory"—this is a main clause of the oldest (unhappily also the most enduring) psychology on earth. One might even say that wherever on earth solemnity, seriousness, mystery, and gloomy coloring still distinguish the life of man and a people, something of the terror that formerly attended all promises, pledges, and vows on earth is *still effective:* the past, the longest, deepest and sternest past, breathes upon us and rises up in us whenever we become "serious." Man could never do without blood, torture, and sacrifices when he felt the need to create a memory for himself; the most dreadful sacrifices and pledges (sacrifices of the first-born among them), the most repulsive mutilations (castration, for example), the cruelest rites of all the religious cults (and all religions are at the deepest level systems of cruelties)—all this has its origin in the instinct that realized that pain is the most powerful aid to mnemonics.

In a certain sense, the whole of asceticism belongs here: a few ideas are to be rendered inextinguishable, ever-present, unforgettable, "fixed," with the aim of hypnotising the entire nervous and intellectual system with these "fixed ideas"—and ascetic procedures and modes of life are means of freeing these ideas from the competition of all other ideas, so as to make them "unforgettable." The worse man's memory has been, the more fearful has been the appearance of his customs; the severity of the penal code provides an especially significant measure of the degree of effort needed to overcome forgetfulness and to impose a few primitive demands of social existence as *present realities* upon these slaves of momentary affect and desire. [. . .] With the aid of such images and procedures one finally remembers five or six "I will not's," in regard to which one had given one's *promise* so as to participate in the advantages of society—and it was indeed with the aid of this kind of memory that one at last came "to reason"! Ah, reason, seriousness, mastery over the affects, the whole somber thing called reflection, all these prerogatives and showpieces of man: how dearly they have been bought! how much blood and cruelty lie at the bottom of all "good things"!

4

But how did that other "somber thing," the consciousness of guilt, the "bad conscience," come into the world?—And at this point we return to the genealogists of morals. To say it again—or haven't I said it yet?—they are worthless. A brief span of experience that is merely one's own, merely modern; no knowledge or will to knowledge of the past; even less of historical instinct, of that "second sight" needed here above all—and yet they undertake history of morality: it stands to reason that their results stay at a more than respectful distance from the truth. Have these genealogists of morals had even the remotest suspicion that, for example, the major moral concept *Schuld* [guilt] has its origin in the very material concept *Schulden* [debts]? Or that punishment, as requital, evolved quite independently of any presupposition concerning freedom or nonfreedom of the will?—to such an extent, indeed, that a *high* degree of humanity had to be attained before the animal "man" began even to make the much more primitive distinctions between "intentional," "negligent," "accidental," "accountable," and their opposites and to take them into account when determining punishments. The idea, now so obvious, apparently so natural, even unavoidable, that had to serve as the explanation of how the sense of justice ever appeared on earth—"the criminal deserves punishment *because* he could have acted differently"—is in fact an extremely late and subtle form of human judgment and inference: whoever transposes it to the beginning is guilty of a crude misunderstanding of the psychology of more primitive mankind. Throughout the greater part of human history punishment was *not* imposed *because* one held the wrongdoer responsible for his deed, thus *not* on the presupposition that only the guilty one should be punished: rather, as parents still punish their children, from anger at some harm or injury, vented on the one who caused it—but this anger is held in check and modified by the idea that every injury has its *equivalent* and can actually be paid back, even if only through the *pain* of the culprit. And whence did this primeval, deeply rooted, perhaps by now ineradicable idea draw its power—this idea of an equivalence between injury and pain? I have already divulged it: in the contractual relationship between *creditor* and *debtor*, which is as old as the idea of "legal subjects" and in turn points back to the fundamental forms of buying, selling, barter, trade, and traffic.

*   *   *   *

6

It was in *this* sphere then, the sphere of legal obligations, that the moral conceptual world of "guilt," "conscience," "duty," "sacredness of duty" had its origin: its beginnings were, like the beginnings of everything great on earth, soaked in blood thoroughly and for a long time. And might one not add that, fundamentally, this world has never since lost a certain odor of blood and torture? (Not even in good old Kant: the categorical imperative smells of cruelty.) It was here, too, that that uncanny intertwining of the ideas "guilt and suffering" was first effected—and by now they may well be inseparable. To ask it again: to what extent can suffering balance debts or guilt? To the extent that to *make* suffer was in the highest degree pleasurable, to the extent that the injured party exchanged for the loss he had sustained, including the displeasure caused by the loss, an extraordinary counterbalancing pleasure: that of *making* suffer—a genuine *festival*, something which, as aforesaid, was prized the more highly the more violently it contrasted with the rank and social standing of the creditor. This is offered only as a conjecture; for the depths of such subterranean things are difficult to fathom, besides being painful; and whoever clumsily interposes the concept of "revenge" does not enhance his insight into the matter but further veils and darkens it (—for revenge merely leads us back to the same problem: "how can making suffer constitute a compensation?").

It seems to me that the delicacy and even more the tartuffery of tame domestic animals (which is to say modern men, which is to say us) resists a really vivid comprehension of the degree to which *cruelty* constituted the great festival pleasure of more primitive men and was indeed an ingredient of almost every one of their pleasures; and how naïvely, how innocently their thirst for cruelty manifested itself, how, as a matter of principle, they posited "disinterested malice" (or, in Spinoza's words, *sympathia malevolens*) as a *normal* quality of man—and thus as something to which the conscience cordially *says Yes!* A more profound eye might perceive enough of this oldest and most fundamental festival pleasure of man even in our time; in *Beyond Good and Evil*, section 229 (and earlier in *The Dawn*, sections 18, 77, 113) I pointed cautiously to the ever-increasing spiritualization and "deification" of cruelty which permeates the entire history of higher culture (and in a significant sense actually constitutes it). [. . .] To see others suffer does one good, to make others suffer even more: this is a hard saying but an ancient, mighty, human, all-too-human principle to which even the apes might subscribe; for it has been said that in devising bizarre cruelties they anticipate man and are, as it were, his "prelude." Without cruelty there is no festival: thus the longest and most ancient part of human history teaches—and in punishment there is so much that is *festive!*—

7

With this idea, by the way, I am by no means concerned to furnish our pessimists with more grist for their discordant and creaking mills of life-satiety. On the contrary, let me declare expressly that in the days when mankind was not yet ashamed of its cruelty, life on earth was more cheerful than it is now that pessimists exist. The darkening of the sky above mankind has deepened in step with the increase in man's feeling of shame *at man*. The weary pessimistic glance, mistrust of the riddle of life, the icy No of disgust with life—these do not characterize the most *evil* epochs of the human race: rather do they first step into the light of day as the swamp weeds they are when the swamp to which they belong comes into being—I mean the morbid softening and moralization through which the animal "man" finally learns to be ashamed of all his instincts. [. . .]

Today, when suffering is always brought forward as the principal argument *against* existence, as the worst question mark, one does well to recall the ages in which the opposite opinion prevailed because men were unwilling to refrain from *making* suffer and saw in it an enchantment of the first order, a genuine seduction *to* life. [. . .]

What really arouses indignation against suffering is not suffering as such but the senselessness of suffering: but neither for the Christian, who has interpreted a whole mysterious machinery of salvation into suffering, nor for the naïve man of more ancient times, who understood all suffering in relation to the spectator of it or the causer of it, was there any such thing as *senseless* suffering. So as to abolish hidden, undetected, unwitnessed suffering from the world and honestly to deny it, one was in the past virtually compelled to invent gods and genii of all the heights and depths, in short something that roams even in secret, hidden places, sees even in the dark, and will not easily let an interesting painful spectacle pass unnoticed. For it was with the aid of such inventions that life then knew how to work the trick which it has always known how to work, that of justifying itself, of justifying its "evil." [. . .]

*   *   *   *   *

12

Yet a word on the origin and the purpose of punishment—two problems that are separate, or ought to be separate: unfortunately, they are usually confounded. How have previous genealogists of morals set about solving these problems? Naïvely, as has always been their way: they seek out some "purpose" in punishment, for example, revenge or deterrence, then guilelessly place this purpose at the beginning as *causa fiendi*[9] of punishment, and—have done. The "purpose of law," however, is absolutely the last thing to employ in the history of the origin of law: on the contrary, there is for historiography of any kind no more important proposition than the one it took such effort to establish but which really *ought to be* established now: the cause of the origin of a thing and its eventual utility, its actual employment and place in a system of purposes, lie worlds apart; whatever exists, having somehow come into being, is again and again reinterpreted to new ends, taken over, transformed, and redirected by some power superior to it; all events in the organic world are a subduing, a *becoming master*, and all subduing and becoming master involves a fresh interpretation, an adaptation through which any previous "meaning" and "purpose" are necessarily obscured or even obliterated. However well one has understood the *utility* of any physiological organ (or of a legal institution, a social custom, a political usage, a form in art or in a religious cult), this means nothing regarding its origin: however uncomfortable and disagreeable this may sound to older ears—for one had always believed that to understand the demonstrable purpose, the utility of a thing, a form, or an institution, was also to understand the reason why it originated—the eye being made for seeing, the hand being made for grasping.

Thus one also imagined that punishment was devised for punishing. But purposes and utilities are only *signs* that a will to power has become master of something less powerful and imposed upon it the character of a function; and the entire history of a "thing," an organ, a custom can in this way be a continuous sign-chain of ever new interpretations and adaptations whose causes do not even have to be related to one another but, on the contrary, in some cases succeed and alternate with one another in a purely chance fashion. The "evolution" of a thing, a custom, an organ is thus by no means its *progressus*[10] toward a goal, even less a logical *progressus* by the shortest route and with the smallest expenditure of force— but a succession of more or less profound, more or less mutually independent processes of subduing, plus the resistances they encounter, the attempts at transformation for the purpose of defense and reaction, and

[9]The cause of the origin.
[10]Progression.

the results of successful counteractions. The form is fluid, but the "meaning" is even more so. [. . .]

I emphasize this major point of historical method all the more because it is in fundamental opposition to the now prevalent instinct and taste which would rather be reconciled even to the absolute fortuitousness, even the mechanistic senselessness of all events than to the theory that in all events a *will to power* is operating. [. . .] Under the influence of the above-mentioned idiosyncrasy, one places instead "adaptation" in the foreground, that is to say, an activity of the second rank, a mere reactivity; indeed, life itself has been defined as a more and more efficient inner adaptation to external conditions (Herbert Spencer). Thus the essence of life, its *will to power*, is ignored; one overlooks the essential priority of the spontaneous, aggressive, expansive, form-giving forces that give new interpretations and directions, although "adaptation" follows only after this; the dominant role of the highest functionaries within the organism itself in which the will to life appears active and form-giving is denied. [. . .]

*   *   *   *   *

16

At this point I can no longer avoid giving a first, provisional statement of my own hypothesis concerning the origin of the "bad conscience": it may sound rather strange and needs to be pondered, lived with, and slept on for a long time. I regard the bad conscience as the serious illness that man was bound to contract under the stress of the most fundamental change he ever experienced—that change which occurred when he found himself finally enclosed within the walls of society and of peace. The situation that faced sea animals when they were compelled to become land animals or perish was the same as that which faced these semi-animals, well adapted to the wilderness, to war, to prowling, to adventure: suddenly all their instincts were disvalued and "suspended." From now on they had to walk on their feet and "bear themselves" whereas hitherto they had been borne by the water: a dreadful heaviness lay upon them. They felt unable to cope with the simplest undertakings; in this new world they no longer possessed their former guides, their regulating, unconscious and infallible drives: they were reduced to thinking, inferring, reckoning, co-ordinating cause and effect, these unfortunate creatures; they were reduced to their "consciousness," their weakest and most fallible organ! I believe there has never been such a feeling of misery on earth, such a leaden discomfort—and at the same time the old instincts had not suddenly ceased to make their usual demands! Only it was hardly or rarely possible to humor them: as a rule they had to seek new and, as it were, subterranean gratifications.

All instincts that do not discharge themselves outwardly *turn inward*— this is what I call the *internalization* of man: thus it was that man first developed what was later called his "soul." The entire inner world, originally as thin as if it were stretched between two membranes, expanded and extended itself, acquired depth, breadth, and height, in the same measure as outward discharge was *inhibited*. Those fearful bulwarks with which the political organization protected itself against the old instincts of freedom—punishments belong among these bulwarks—brought about that all those instincts of wild, free, prowling man turned backward *against man himself*. Hostility, cruelty, joy in persecuting, in attacking, in change, in destruction—all this turned against the possessors of such instincts: *that* is the origin of the "bad conscience."

The man who, from lack of external enemies and resistances and forcibly confined to the oppressive narrowness and punctiliousness of custom, impatiently lacerated, persecuted, gnawed at, assaulted, and maltreated himself; this animal that rubbed itself raw against the bars of its cage as one tried to "tame" it; this deprived creature, racked with homesickness for the wild, who had to turn himself into an adventure, a torture chamber, an uncertain and dangerous wilderness—this fool, this yearning and desperate prisoner became the inventor of the "bad conscience." But thus began the gravest and uncanniest illness, from which humanity has not yet recovered, man's suffering *of man*, *of himself*—the result of a forcible sundering from his animal past, as it were a leap and plunge into new surroundings and conditions of existence, a declaration of war against the old instincts upon which his strength, joy, and terribleness had rested hitherto.

Let us add at once that, on the other hand, the existence on earth of an animal soul turned against itself, taking sides against itself, was something so new, profound, unheard of, enigmatic, contradictory, *and pregnant with a future* that the aspect of the earth was essentially altered. Indeed, divine spectators were needed to do justice to the spectacle that thus began and the end of which is not yet in sight—a spectacle too subtle, too marvelous, too paradoxical to be played senselessly unobserved on some ludicrous planet! From now on, man is *included* among the most unexpected and exciting lucky throws in the dice game of Heraclitus' "great child," be he called Zeus or chance; he gives rise to an interest, a tension, a hope, almost a certainty, as if with him something were announcing and preparing itself, as if man were not a goal but only a way, an episode, a bridge, a great promise. —

17

Among the presuppositions of this hypothesis concerning the origin of the bad conscience is, first, that the change referred to was not a gradual or voluntary one and did not represent an organic adaptation to new conditions but a break, a leap, a compulsion, an ineluctable disaster which precluded all struggle and even all *ressentiment*. Secondly, however, that the welding of a hitherto unchecked and shapeless populace into a firm form was not only instituted by an act of violence but also carried to its conclusion by nothing but acts of violence—that the oldest "state" thus appeared as a fearful tyranny, as an oppressive and remorseless machine, and went on working until this raw material of people and semi-animals was at last not only thoroughly kneaded and pliant but also *formed*.

I employed the word "state": it is obvious what is meant—some pack of blond beasts of prey, a conqueror and master race which, organized for war and with the ability to organize, unhesitatingly lays its terrible claws upon a populace perhaps tremendously superior in numbers but still formless and nomad. That is after all how the "state" began on earth: I think that sentimentalism which would have it begin with a "contract" has been disposed of. He who can command, he who is by nature "master," he who is violent in act and bearing—what has he to do with contracts! One does not reckon with such natures; they come like fate, without reason, consideration, or pretext; they appear as lightning appears, too terrible, too sudden, too convincing, too "different" even to be hated. Their work is an instinctive creation and imposition of forms; they are the most involuntary, unconscious artists there are—wherever they appear something new soon arises, a ruling structure that *lives*, in which parts and functions are delimited and coordinated, in which nothing whatever finds a place that has not first been assigned a "meaning" in relation to the whole. They do not know what guilt, responsibility, or consideration are, these born organizers; they exemplify that terrible artists' egoism that has the look of bronze and knows itself justified to all eternity in its "work," like a mother in her child. It is not in *them* that the "bad conscience" developed, that goes without saying— but it would not have developed *without them*, this ugly growth, it would be lacking if a tremendous quantity of freedom had not been expelled from the world, or at least from the visible world, and made as it were *latent* under their hammer blows and artists' violence. This *instinct for freedom* forcibly made latent—we have seen it already—this instinct for freedom pushed back and repressed, incarcerated within and finally able to discharge and vent itself only on itself: that, and that alone, is what the *bad conscience* is in its beginnings.

18

One should guard against thinking lightly of this phenomenon merely on account of its initial painfulness and ugliness. For fundamentally it is the same active force that is at work on a grander scale in those artists of violence and organizers who build states, and that here, internally, on a smaller and pettier scale, directed backward, in the "labyrinth of the breast," to use Goethe's expression, creates for itself a bad conscience and builds negative ideals—namely, the *instinct for freedom* (in my language: the will to power); only here the material upon which the form-giving and ravishing nature of this force vents itself is man himself, his whole ancient animal self—and *not*, as in that greater and more obvious phenomenon, some *other* man, *other* men. This secret self-ravishment, this artists' cruelty, this delight in imposing a form upon oneself as a hard, recalcitrant, suffering material and in burning a will, a critique, a contradiction, a contempt, a No into it, this uncanny, dreadfully joyous labor of a soul voluntarily at odds with itself that makes itself suffer out of joy in making suffer—eventually this entire *active* "bad conscience"—you will have guessed it—as the womb of all ideal and imaginative phenomena, also brought to light an abundance of strange new beauty and affirmation, and perhaps beauty itself. —

*   *   *   *   *

24

I end up with three question marks; that seems plain. "What are you really doing, erecting an ideal or knocking one down?" I may perhaps be asked.

But have you ever asked yourselves sufficiently how much the erection of *every* ideal on earth has cost? How much reality has had to be misunderstood and slandered, how many lies have had to be sanctified, how many consciences disturbed, how much "God" sacrificed every time? If a temple is to be erected *a temple must be destroyed:* that is the law—let anyone who can show me a case in which it is not fulfilled!

We modern men are the heirs of the conscience-vivisection and self-torture of millennia: this is what we have practiced longest, it is our distinctive art perhaps, and in any case our subtlety in which we have acquired a refined taste. Man has all too long had an "evil eye" for his natural inclinations, so that they have finally become inseparable from his "bad conscience." An attempt at the reverse would *in itself* be possible—but who is strong enough for it?—that is, to wed the bad conscience to all the *unnatural* inclinations, all those aspirations to the beyond, to that which runs counter to sense, instinct, nature, animal, in short all ideals hitherto, which are one and all hostile to life and ideals that slander the world. To whom should one turn today with *such* hopes and demands?

One would have precisely the *good* men against one; and, of course, the comfortable, the reconciled, the vain, the sentimental, the weary.

What gives greater offense, what separates one more fundamentally, than to reveal something of the severity and respect with which one treats oneself? And on the other hand—how accommodating, how friendly all the world is toward us as soon as we act as all the world does and "let ourselves go" like all the world!

The attainment of this goal would require a *different* kind of spirit from that likely to appear in this present age: spirits strengthened by war and victory, for whom conquest, adventure, danger, and even pain have become needs; it would require habituation to the keen air of the heights, to winter journeys, to ice and mountains in every sense; it would require even a kind of sublime wickedness, an ultimate, supremely self-confident mischievousness in knowledge that goes with great health; it would require, in brief and alas, precisely this *great health!*

Is this even possible today?—But some day, in a stronger age than this decaying, self-doubting present, he must yet come to us, the *redeeming* man of great love and contempt, the creative spirit whose compelling strength will not let him rest in any aloofness or any beyond, whose isolation is misunderstood by the people as if it were flight *from* reality— while it is only his absorption, immersion, penetration *into* reality, so that, when he one day emerges again into the light, he may bring home the *redemption* of this reality: its redemption from the curse that the hitherto reigning ideal has laid upon it. This man of the future, who will redeem us not only from the hitherto reigning ideal but also from that which was bound to grow out of it, the great nausea, the will to nothingness, nihilism; this bell-stroke of noon and of the great decision that liberates the will again and restores its goal to the earth and his hope to man; this Antichrist[11] and antinihilist; this victor over God and nothingness—*he must come one day.*—

---

[11]*Antichrist.* This German term may mean either "Antichrist" or "anti-Christian"; and of the two, the latter more accurately expresses Nietzsche's meaning, as Nietzsche's discussion of Christianity (which he frequently contrasts to his view of Christ's teachings and significance) in the subsequent work he entitled *Der Antichrist* and elsewhere clearly shows.

Third Essay
What Is the Meaning of Ascetic Ideals?

Unconcerned, mocking, violent—thus wisdom wants *us:* she is a
woman and always loves only a warrior.

Thus Spoke Zarathustra

1

What is the meaning of ascetic ideals?—In the case of artists they mean
nothing or too many things; in the case of philosophers and scholars
something like a sense and instinct for the most favorable preconditions of
higher spirituality; in the case of women at best one *more* seductive charm,
a touch of *morbidezza*[12] in fair flesh, the angelic look of a plump pretty
animal; in the case of the physiologically deformed and deranged (the
majority of mortals) an attempt to see themselves as "too good" for this
world, a saintly form of debauch, their chief weapon in the struggle
against slow pain and boredom; in the case of priests the distinctive
priestly faith, their best instrument of power, also the "supreme" license
for power; in the case of saints, finally [. . .] their repose in nothingness
("God"), their form of madness. *That* the ascetic ideal has meant so many
things to man, however, is an expression of the basic fact of the human
will, its *horror vacui:*[13] *it needs a goal*—and it will rather will *nothingness* than
not will.

*   *   *   *   *

11

Only now that we behold the *ascetic priest* do we seriously come to grips
with our problem: what is the meaning of the ascetic ideal?—only now
does it become "serious": we are now face to face with the actual *representative* of seriousness. [. . .]

The idea at issue here is the *valuation* the ascetic priest places on our
life: he juxtaposes it (along with what pertains to it: "nature," "world,"
the whole sphere of becoming and transitoriness) with a quite different
mode of existence which it opposes and excludes, *unless* it turn against
itself, *deny itself:* in that case, the case of the ascetic life, life counts as a
bridge to that other mode of existence. The ascetic treats life as a wrong
road on which one must finally walk back to the point where it begins, or

[12]Morbidity.
[13]Abhorrence of a vacuum.

as a mistake that is put right by deeds—that we *ought* to put right: for he *demands* that one go along with him; where he can he compels acceptance of *his* evaluation of existence.

What does this mean? So monstrous a mode of valuation stands inscribed in the history of mankind not as an exception and curiosity, but as one of the most widespread and enduring of all phenomena. [. . .] For an ascetic life is a self-contradiction: here rules a *ressentiment* without equal, that of an insatiable instinct and power-will that wants to become master not over something in life but over life itself, over its most profound, powerful, and basic conditions; here an attempt is made to employ force to block up the wells of force; here physiological well-being itself is viewed askance, and especially the outward expression of this well-being, beauty and joy; while pleasure is felt and *sought* in ill-constitutedness, decay, pain, mischance, ugliness, voluntary deprivation, self-mortification, self-flagellation, self-sacrifice. All this is in the highest degree paradoxical: we stand before a discord that *wants* to be discordant, that *enjoys* itself in this suffering and even grows more self-confident and triumphant the more its own presupposition, its physiological capacity for life, *decreases*. "Triumph in the ultimate agony": the ascetic ideal has always fought under this hyperbolic sign; in this enigma of seduction, in this image of torment and delight, it recognized its brightest light, its salvation, its ultimate victory. *Crux, nux, lux*[14]—for the ascetic ideal these three are one. —

12

Suppose such an incarnate will to contradiction and antinaturalness is induced to *philosophize:* upon what will it vent its innermost contrariness? Upon what is felt most certainly to be real and actual: it will look for error precisely where the instinct of life most unconditionally posits truth. It will, for example, like the ascetics of the Vedanta philosophy, downgrade physicality to an illusion; likewise pain, multiplicity, the entire conceptual antithesis "subject" and "object"—errors, nothing but errors! To renounce belief in one's ego, to deny one's own "reality"—what a triumph! not merely over the senses, over appearance, but a much higher kind of triumph, a violation and cruelty against *reason*—a voluptuous pleasure that reaches its height when the ascetic self-contempt and self-mockery of reason declares: "*there is* a realm of truth and being, but reason is *excluded* from it!"

(Incidentally, even in the Kantian concept of the "intelligible character of things" something remains of this lascivious ascetic discord that loves

---

[14]Cross, nut, light. ("Nut" here is meant in the sense of something to be cracked, as in "a tough nut to crack.")

to turn reason against reason: for "intelligible character" signifies in Kant that things are so constituted that the intellect comprehends just enough of them to know that for the intellect they are—*utterly incomprehensible.*)

But precisely because we seek knowledge, let us not be ungrateful to such resolute reversals of accustomed perspectives and valuations with which the spirit has, with apparent mischievousness and futility, raged against itself for so long: to see differently in this way for once, to *want* to see differently, is no small discipline and preparation of the intellect for its future "objectivity"—the latter understood not as "contemplation without interest" (which is a nonsensical absurdity), but as the ability *to control* one's Pro and Con and to dispose of them, so that one knows how to employ a *variety* of perspectives and affective interpretations in the service of knowledge.

Henceforth, my dear philosophers, let us be on guard against the dangerous old conceptual fiction that posited a "pure, will-less, painless, timeless knowing subject"; let us guard against the snares of such contradictory concepts as "pure reason," "absolute spirituality," "knowledge in itself": these always demand that we should think of an eye that is completely unthinkable, an eye turned in no particular direction, in which the active and interpreting forces, through which alone seeing becomes seeing *something*, are supposed to be lacking; these always demand of the eye an absurdity and a nonsense. There is *only* a perspective seeing, *only* a perspective "knowing"; and the *more* affects we allow to speak about one thing, the *more* eyes, different eyes, we can use to observe one thing, the more complete will our "concept" of this thing, our "objectivity," be. But to eliminate the will altogether, to suspend each and every affect, supposing we were capable of this—what would that mean but to *castrate* the intellect?—

13

But let us return to our problem. It will be immediately obvious that such a self-contradiction as the ascetic appears to represent, "life *against* life," is, physiologically considered and not merely psychologically, a simple absurdity. It can only be *apparent;* it must be a kind of provisional formulation, an interpretation and psychological misunderstanding of something whose real nature could not for a long time be understood or described *as it really was*—a mere word inserted into an old *gap* in human knowledge. Let us replace it with a brief formulation of the facts of the matter: *the ascetic ideal springs from the protective instinct of a degenerating life* which tries by all means to sustain itself and to fight for its existence; it indicates a partial physiological obstruction and exhaustion against which the deepest instincts of life, which have remained intact, continually struggle with new expedients and devices. The ascetic ideal is such an expedient; the case is therefore the opposite of what those who reverence this ideal believe: life wrestles in it and through it with death and *against* death; the ascetic ideal is an artifice for the *preservation* of life.

That this ideal acquired such power and ruled over men as imperiously as we find it in history, especially wherever the civilization and taming of man has been carried through, expresses a great fact: the *sickliness* of the type of man we have had hitherto, or at least of the tamed man, and the physiological struggle of man against death (more precisely: against disgust with life, against exhaustion, against the desire for the "end"). The ascetic priest is the incarnate desire to be different, to be in a different place, and indeed this desire at its greatest extreme, its distinctive fervor and passion; but precisely this power of his desire is the chain that holds him captive so that he becomes a tool for the creation of more favorable conditions for being here and being man—it is precisely this *power* that enables him to persuade to existence the whole herd of the ill-constituted, disgruntled, underprivileged, unfortunate, and all who suffer of themselves, by instinctively going before them as their shepherd. You will see my point: this ascetic priest, this apparent enemy of life, this *denier*—precisely he is among the greatest *conserving* and yes-creating forces of life.

Where does it come from, this sickliness? For man is more sick, uncertain, changeable, indeterminate than any other animal, there is no doubt of that—he is *the* sick animal: how has that come about? Certainly he has also dared more, done more new things, braved more and challenged fate more than all the other animals put together: he, the great experimenter with himself, discontented and insatiable, wrestling with animals, nature, and gods for ultimate dominion—he, still unvanquished, eternally directed toward the future, whose own restless energies never leave him in peace, so that his future digs like a spur into the flesh of every present—how should such a courageous and richly endowed animal not also be the most imperiled, the most chronically and profoundly sick of all sick animals?

Man has often had enough; there are actual epidemics of having had enough (as around 1348, at the time of the dance of death); but even this nausea, this weariness, this disgust with himself—all this bursts from him with such violence that it at once becomes a new fetter. The No he says to life brings to light, as if by magic, an abundance of tender Yeses; even when he *wounds* himself, this master of destruction, of self-destruction— the very wound itself afterward compels him *to live*. —

*   *   *   *   *

25

No! Don't come to me with science when I ask for the natural antagonist of the ascetic ideal, when I demand: "where is the opposing will expressing the *opposing ideal?*" Science is not nearly self-reliant enough to be that; it first requires in every respect an ideal of value, a value-creating power, in the *service* of which it could *believe* in itself—it never creates values. Its relation to the ascetic ideal is by no means essentially antagonistic; it might even be said to represent the driving force in the latter's inner development. It opposes and fights, on closer inspection, not the ideal itself but only its exteriors, its guise and masquerade, its temporary dogmatic hardening and stiffening, and by denying what is exoteric in this ideal, it liberates what life is in it. This pair, science and the ascetic ideal, both rest on the same foundation—I have already indicated it: on the same overestimation of truth (more exactly: on the same belief that truth is inestimable and cannot be criticized). Therefore they are *necessarily* allies, so that if they are to be fought they can only be fought and called in question together. A depreciation of the ascetic ideal unavoidably involves a depreciation of science: one must keep one's eyes and ears open to this fact!

(*Art*—to say it in advance, for I shall some day return to this subject at greater length—art, in which precisely the *lie* is sanctified and the *will to deception* has a good conscience, is much more fundamentally opposed to the ascetic ideal than is science: this was instinctively sensed by Plato, the greatest enemy of art Europe has yet produced. Plato versus Homer: that is the complete, the genuine antagonism—there the sincerest advocate of the "beyond," the great slanderer of life; here the instinctive deifier, the *golden* nature. To place himself in the service of the ascetic ideal is therefore the most distinctive *corruption* of an artist that is at all possible; unhappily, also one of the most common forms of corruption, for nothing is more easily corrupted than an artist.)

*   *   *   *   *

27

Enough! Enough! Let us leave these curiosities and complexities of the most modern spirit, which provoke as much laughter as chagrin: *our* problem, the problem of the *meaning* of the ascetic ideal, can dispense with them: what has this problem to do with yesterday or today! I shall probe these things more thoroughly and severely in another connection (under the title "On the History of European Nihilism"; it will be contained in a work in progress: *The Will to Power: Attempt at a Revaluation of All Values*[15]). All I have been concerned to indicate here is this: in the most spiritual sphere, too, the ascetic ideal has at present only *one* kind of real enemy capable of *harming* it: the comedians of this ideal—for they arouse mistrust of it. Everywhere else that the spirit is strong, mighty, and at work without counterfeit today, it does without ideals of any kind—the popular expression for this abstinence is "atheism"—*except for its will to truth*. But this will, this *remnant* of an ideal, is, if you will believe me, this ideal itself in its strictest, most spiritual formulation, esoteric through and through, with all external additions abolished, and thus not so much its remnant as its *kernel*. Unconditional honest atheism (and *its* is the only air we breathe, we more spiritual men of this age!) is therefore *not* the antithesis of that ideal, as it appears to be; it is rather only one of the latest phases of its evolution, one of its terminal forms and inner consequences—it is the awe-inspiring *catastrophe* of two thousand years of training in truthfulness that finally forbids itself the *lie involved in belief in God.* [. . .]

In this way Christianity *as a dogma* was destroyed by its own morality; in the same way Christianity as *morality* must now perish, too: we stand on the threshold of *this* event. After Christian truthfulness has drawn one inference after another, it must end by drawing its *most striking inference*, its inference *against* itself; this will happen, however, when it poses the question *"what is the meaning of all will to truth?"*

And here I again touch on my problem, on our problem, my *unknown* friends (for as yet I *know* of no friend): what meaning would *our* whole being possess if it were not this, that in us the will to truth becomes conscious of itself as a *problem?*

As the will to truth thus gains self-consciousness—there can be no doubt of that—morality will gradually *perish* now: this is the great spectacle in a hundred acts reserved for the next two centuries in Europe—the most terrible, most questionable, and perhaps also the most hopeful of all spectacles. —

28

Apart from the ascetic ideal, man, the human *animal*, had no meaning so far. His existence on earth contained no goal; "why man at all?"—was a question without an answer; the *will* for man and earth was lacking; behind every great human destiny there sounded as a refrain a yet greater

---

[15]Although this is the title that was given to a collection of notes from Nietzsche's notebooks of 1883–1888 gathered together and published after his death, he never published or completed the "work in progress" to which he here refers—although he did use the title *Revaluation of All Values* as the main title of *The Antichrist*, with the latter being designated as its "First Book" (i.e., first part).

"in vain!" *This* is precisely what the ascetic ideal means: that something was *lacking*, that man was surrounded by a fearful *void*—he did not know how to justify, to account for, to affirm himself; he *suffered* from the problem of his meaning. He also suffered otherwise, he was in the main a sickly animal: but his problem was *not* suffering itself, but that there was no answer to the crying question, "*why* do I suffer?"

Man, the bravest of animals and the one most accustomed to suffering, does *not* repudiate suffering as such; he *desires* it, he even seeks it out, provided he is shown a *meaning* for it, a *purpose* of suffering. The meaninglessness of suffering, *not* suffering itself, was the curse that lay over mankind so far—*and the ascetic ideal offered man meaning!* It was the only meaning offered so far; any meaning is better than none at all; the ascetic ideal was in every sense the *"faute de mieux"*[16] *par excellence* so far. In it, suffering was *interpreted;* the tremendous void seemed to have been filled; the door was closed to any kind of suicidal nihilism. This interpretation— there is no doubt of it—brought fresh suffering with it, deeper, more inward, more poisonous, more life-destructive suffering: it placed all suffering under the perspective of *guilt.*

But all this notwithstanding—man was *saved* thereby, he possessed a meaning, he was henceforth no longer like a leaf in the wind, a plaything of nonsense—the "sense-less"—he could now *will* something; no matter at first to what end, why, with what he willed: *the will itself was saved.*

We can no longer conceal from ourselves *what* is expressed by all that willing which has taken its direction from the ascetic ideal: this hatred of the human, and even more of the animal, and more still of the material, this horror of the senses, of reason itself, this fear of happiness and beauty, this longing to get away from all appearance, change, becoming, death, wishing, from longing itself—all this means—let us dare to grasp it—*a will to nothingness*, an aversion to life, a rebellion against the most fundamental presuppositions of life; but it is and remains a *will!* . . . And, to repeat in conclusion what I said at the beginning: man would rather will *nothingness* than *not* will. —

---

[16]"Fault of mine," i.e., "my guilt."

VI

Notes from a Philosopher's Workshop

(1886–1888)

Selections from

The Will to Power:
Notebooks of 1886–1888

on

Nihilism
Reason and Knowledge
The World and Life
Values, Moralities, Religions

PHILOSOPHICAL EXPERIMENTS

Introduction

Following Nietzsche's completion of the Fifth Book of *Joyful Wisdom* (or *The Gay Science*) in mid-1886, and while writing *On the Genealogy of Morals*, he continued to reflect on many issues in addition to morality, involving reinterpretation as well as revaluation. At this time he was planning and gathering material for a much more comprehensive work.[1] In view of the shortness of the time that remained to him and the difficulties posed by his deteriorating condition, it is not surprising that it was never completed. As his end drew near, he abandoned the larger project in favor of one last series of critiques—of ways of thinking that still persisted among his contemporaries (*Twilight of the Idols*), of the artistic culture represented and promoted by Wagner (*The Case of Wagner*), and of Christianity (*The Antichrist*). Each of these critiques was a contribution to what he came to regard as the most pressing task on his agenda: the "revaluation of all values."[2]

Before concentrating his efforts on them in the last half of 1888, however, Nietzsche devoted considerable attention to the broader range of issues with which he intended to deal in the larger work he envisioned, in his notebooks of the preceding two years (mid-1886 to mid-1888). His reflections on them are of considerable interest, despite the fact that the work into which some version of them might have been incorporated never materialized under his own authorship. (The following selections from them did in fact appear in the volume *The Will to Power* that was assembled and published in his name after his death; but their inclusion in it and its publication were the decisions of its compilers rather than his own.) These notes provide indications of how Nietzsche was attempting to deal further with many of the matters he had only touched on in his first post-*Zarathustra* works,[3] in which he had just arrived at his conception of a "philosophy of the future" and sought to inaugurate it. They therefore shed considerable light on the character of his mature philosophical thinking, suggesting what some of his later concerns and interests were and what further ideas he was trying out with respect to them.

---

[1]Cf. *On the Genealogy of Morals*, trans. Walter Kaufmann and R. J. Hollingdale (New York: Vintage, 1967), III:27, where he writes: "I shall probe these things more thoroughly and severely in another connection (under the title "On the History of European Nihilism"; it will be contained in a work in progress: *The Will to Power: Attempt at a Revaluation of All Values*)."

[2]This was the main title of *The Antichrist*, which he designated as the "First Book" of a projected four, each of which was to deal with a different part of this "revaluation."

[3]I.e., *Beyond Good and Evil* and the Fifth Book of *Joyful Wisdom* (or *The Gay Science*).

This sampling of Nietzsche's philosophical experiments from his note-books written in this period, between mid-1886 and mid-1888, are grouped by general topic. Within these groupings, they are for the most part ar-ranged in accordance with the chronology of the notebooks and the order in which the notes appear in them. (As in the case of the previous set of notes, the numbering they were given in *The Will to Power* and their location in the relevant volumes of the critical edition of Nietzsche's writings[4] are indicated in the footnotes.) The notes in the first group have to do with the problem of nihilism. As has been seen, Nietzsche had discerned and articulated this problem somewhat earlier, but had not previously discussed it in detail. There is no comparable discussion of it in any of the writings he completed—although it is clear that he was expecting to deal with it in a future book, presumably along the lines he develops here.[5]

There also is no discussion in Nietzsche's completed writings compa-rable to the material in the group of notes in which he elaborates on his interpretation of the world in terms of the "will to power." References to this interpretation are found both in his published writings from *Thus Spoke Zarathustra* on and in his notebooks from the mid-1880s.[6] It was only in his relatively late notebooks (primarily from the first part of 1888), however, that he began to try to work it out and apply it. It is not clear why he abandoned this effort; but his realization that he was incapable of carrying it through, together with his conviction that the "revaluation of values" had greater urgency, would certainly provide an explanation. In any event, this group of notes indicates the lines along which he was thinking as he sought to flesh out this interpretation.

The other groups of notes from this period presented here pertain to topics on which Nietzsche had been reflecting previously both in his notebooks and in his published writings. He also later dealt with some of them in works he subsequently completed. These notes too are nonethe-less of considerable interest for the further insights they afford into his thinking on these topics in the last years of his active life.

Once again, readers should bear in mind the cautions expressed in the introduction to the previous set of notes. These cautions apply equally here. In this case, however, we are dealing with later reflections and experiments, to which somewhat more weight presumably may be given—and they are closer to being Nietzsche's last words on these topics. The preoccupations of the final months of 1888 precluded further atten-tion to some of them. His collapse in January of 1889 brought an end to his thinking about all of them—when he was only forty-four.

---

[4]See the footnotes to the first set of selections from Nietzsche's notebooks (Part III of this volume) for their bibliographical citations. The volumes of the critical condition in which the present set of notes are found are VIII:1 (1974), VIII:2 (1970), and VIII:3 (1972).

[5]See note 1.

[6]Several such notes are included in the first set of selections from Nietzsche's notebooks.

The Will to Power:
Notebooks of 1886–1888
(Selections)

Nihilism

Fall 1886–Fall 1887

Critique of previous *pessimism*

Resistance to the eudaimonistic point of view as the final reduction of the question: what *meaning* does it have? Reduction of gloom. —*Our* pessimism: the world does not have the value that we believed—our faith itself has so intensified our drive for knowledge that today we *must* say this. At first it thereby is taken as worth less: it is so *experienced at first*—only in this sense are we pessimists, namely, with a will to face up to this revaluation unreservedly, and no longer to tell ourselves stories, lies, in the old way. . . . Precisely thereby we find the passion that perhaps will impel us to seek *new values*. In sum: the world could be worth much more than we believed. —We must get beyond the *naivete of our ideals*, and see that while we perhaps had in mind to give it the loftiest interpretation, we may not once have given our human existence even a moderately fair value.

> what has been *deified?* The value instincts within the *community* (that which conduces to its continuation);
> what has been *slandered?* That which sets the higher human beings apart from the lower, the gap-producing drives.[1]

* * * * *

> To *impress* the character of being upon becoming—that is the highest *will to power.*
> Twofold falsification, arising from the senses and from the spirit, in order to preserve a world of beings, of what persists, of equivalences, etc.

[1]*The Will to Power* [WP], ed. Walter Kaufmann, trans. Walter Kaufmann and R. J. Hollingdale (New York: Random House, 1967), 32; and *Nietzsche Werke: Kritische Gesamtausgabe* [KGW], eds. Giorgio Colli and Mazzino Montinari (Berlin and New York: Walter de Gruyter), vol. VIII 6:25.

That *everything recurs is the closest approximation of a world of becoming to being:* culmination of the reflection.

From the values accorded to that which has "being" derive the condemnations of and dissatisfactions with that which becomes: after such a world of being was first invented.

The metamorphosis of beings (body, God, ideas, laws of nature, formulas, etc.)

"Beings" as appearance; reversal of values; appearance was the *value-conferring—*

Knowledge in itself in becoming [is] impossible; so how is knowledge possible? As error about oneself, as will to power, as will to deception.

Becoming as inventing, wanting, self-denial, self-overcoming: no subject, but rather a deed, a positing, creative, no "cause and effect."

Art as will to the overcoming of becoming, as "eternalization," but shortsighted, depending on the perspective: as it were, repeating the tendency of the whole on a small scale.

What *all life* shows, as scaled-down formula for the overall tendency to be observed: therefore, a new specification of the concept "life," as will to power.

Instead of "cause and effect" the struggle of becomers with each other, often with absorption of the opponent; no constant number of becomers.

Uselessness of old ideals for the interpretation of all that happens, once one recognizes their animal origin and utility; all moreover contrary to life.

Uselessness of mechanistic theory—it gives the impression of *meaninglessness.*

The entire *idealism* of previous humanity is on the verge of turning into *nihilism*—into the belief in absolute *value*-lessness, that is, *meaning*-lessness. . . .

The destruction of ideals, the new desert, the new arts needed to endure it, we *amphibians.*

Presupposition: bravery, patience, no "going back," no hurry to go forward

NB. Zarathustra, constantly adopting a parodic stance toward all previous values, out of abundance.[2]

* * * * *

[2]WP 617/KGW VIII 7:54.

European Nihilism[3]

(1) What *advantage* did the Christian moral-hypothesis offer?
  (a) It ascribed an absolute *value* to man, in contrast to his smallness and fortuitousness in the flow of becoming and passing away.
  (b) It served the advocates of God, insofar as it granted the character of *perfection* to the world despite suffering and evil— "freedom" included—evil seemed full of *meaning.*
  (c) It posited a *knowledge* with respect to absolute values on the part of man and gave him therewith *adequate cognition* precisely for what is most important.

It prevented man from despising himself as man, from taking sides against life, from despairing about knowing: it was a *means of preservation;*—in sum, morality was the great *antidote* against practical and theoretical nihilism.[4]

(2) But among the forces that morality cultivated was *truthfulness: this* finally turned itself against morality, discovered its *teleology,* its *interested* point of view—and the *insight* into this long-ingrained mendacity that one despairs of getting rid of now serves precisely as a stimulant. To nihilism. We now find needs in ourselves, planted during the long moral-interpretation, which appear to us as needs for untruth; on the other hand, it seems that they are those on which the value depends by means of which we can endure to live. This antagonism—that which we know, we do *not* esteem, and that which we would like to lie to ourselves about, we are no longer *permitted* to esteem—results in a process of dissolution.[5]

(3) Actually we no longer are so much in need of an antidote against the *first* nihilism: life in our Europe is no longer so very uncertain, chancy, absurd. Such a tremendous *heightening* of the *value* of man, of the value of evils, etc., is now not so needful, we can bear a significant *reduction* of this value, we can allow much absurdity and chance to be removed: the attained *power* of man now permits a curtailment of the means of cultivation, of which the moral interpretation was the strongest. "God" is much too extreme a hypothesis.[6]

(4) But extreme positions are not replaced by moderate ones, but rather again by extremes—of the opposite kind. And so the belief in the absolute immorality of nature, in aim- and meaninglessness, is the

[3]KGW VIII 5:71. This long note was divided by the compilers of WP into four different sections: WP 4, 5, 114, and 55. They are restored here to their original form in Nietzsche's notebook.
[4]WP 4/KGW VIII 5:71.
[5]WP 5/KGW VIII 5:71.
[6]WP 114/KGW VIII 5:71.

psychologically necessary *effect*, if the belief in God and an essential moral order is not held any longer. Nihilism now appears, *not* because the aversion to existence is greater than previously, but rather because one has become generally mistrustful of a "meaning" in evil and, indeed, in existence. *One* interpretation has collapsed, but because it was taken to be *the* interpretation, it seems as if there were no meaning at all in existence, as if all were *pointless*.

(5) That this "Pointless!" is the character of our present-day nihilism remains to be shown. Mistrust toward our earlier valuations grows into the question: "Aren't all 'values' lures with which the comedy continues, but without coming any closer to a solution?" *Duration*, regarded as "pointless," without goal or purpose, is the most *paralyzing* thought, especially if one grasps that one is being fooled and yet is powerless to keep oneself from being fooled.

(6) Let us think this thought in its most awful form: existence, just as it is, without meaning and goal, but unavoidably recurring, without a finale in nothingness: "the eternal return."

That is the extremest form of nihilism: nothingness (the "meaningless") eternally!

European form of Buddhism: the energy of knowledge and strength *forces* one to such a belief. It is the *most scientific* of all possible hypotheses. We deny final goals: if existence had one, it would have had to have been reached. [. . .]

(10) [. . .] There is nothing in life that has value, other than the degree of power—given precisely that life itself is will to power. Morality protected those who have turned out badly from nihilism, in that it assigned to *each* an infinite value, a metaphysical value, and placed them in an order that did not accord with worldly power and ranking: it taught resignation, meekness, etc. Supposing that the belief in this morality perishes, then the badly turned out would no longer have their comfort—and would perish.

(11) This perishing manifests itself as *doing oneself in*, or as an instinctive selecting of that which *must destroy*. *Symptoms* of this self-destruction of the badly-turned-out: self-vivisection, intoxication, romanticism, above all the instinctive compulsion to actions by which one makes *mortal enemies* of the powerful (—like raising one's own hangman oneself), the *will to destruction* as the will of a still deeper instinct, the instinct of self-destruction, the *will to nothingness*.

(12) Nihilism, as a symptom of the badly turned out no longer having any comfort left: of their destroying in order to be destroyed, of their no

longer having any reason to "resign themselves" now that they are cut loose from morality—of their having placed themselves on the ground of the opposing principle, and also *wanting power* themselves, by which they *compel* the powerful to become their hangmen. This is the European form of Buddhism, a *doing-no*, after all existence has lost its "meaning."

(13) "Distress" has not grown especially greater: on the contrary! "God, morality, resignation" were remedies on frightfully deep levels of misery: *active nihilism* makes its appearance under relatively much more favorable conditions. For morality to be experienced as overcome already presupposes a considerable degree of spiritual culture—and this in turn presupposes a relatively comfortable life. A certain spiritual weariness, brought through the long conflict of philosophical opinions to a hopeless scepticism *toward* philosophy, likewise characterizes the by no means miserable situation of these nihilists. One might think of the situation in which the Buddha appeared. The teaching of the eternal recurrence would have *scholarly* presuppositions (as Buddha's teaching did, e.g., the concept of causality, etc.). [. . .]

(15) Who will show themselves to be the *strongest* in this situation? The most moderate, those who have no *need* of extreme articles of faith, those who not only can tolerate but enjoy a good bit of chance and nonsense, those who are able to think of man with a significant reduction of his value without thereby becoming small and weak: the richer in health, who can take most misfortunes in stride and therefore are not so fearful of them— human beings who are *confident of their power,* and who represent the *attained* strength of humanity with conscious pride.

(16) How would such a person think of the eternal return?[7]

*   *   *   *   *

1. Nihilism a *normal* condition.[8]
   Nihilism: the goal is lacking; there is no answer to the question "Why?" What does nihilism mean?—*that the highest values devalue themselves.*[9]

---

[7]WP 55/KGW VIII 5:71. WP 55 consists of all of this note from the section numbered 4 on (with the section numbers deleted). Some portions of this material have been omitted here.
[8]KGW VIII 9:35. Like the previous one, this long note was divided by the compilers of WP into four different sections: WP 2, 13, 22, and 23. This note is restored here to its original form.
[9]WP 2/KGW VIII 9:35. WP 13, 22, and 23 were carved out of the remainder of KGW VIII 9:35.

It is *ambiguous:*

A. Nihilism as sign of *increased power of the spirit: as active nihilism.*

It can be a sign of *strength:* the energy of the spirit can have grown so great that *previous* goals ("convictions," articles of faith) are insufficient.

—a belief in general expresses the pressure of *conditions of existence,* a subjugation under the authority of relations under which a creature *flourishes, grows, attains power.* . . .

On the other hand, a sign of *insufficient* strength now to go on productively to *posit* a goal, a why, a faith.

Its *maximum* of relative strength is attained as the violent strength of *destruction: as active nihilism.* Its opposite would be the tired nihilism that no longer *asserts itself:* Buddhism, its most famous form: as *passive* nihilism.

Nihilism represents a pathological transitional condition (what is pathological is the tremendous generalization, the inference *to no meaning at all*): whether because the productive forces are not yet strong enough, or because decadence still lingers on and has not yet discovered this remedy.

B. Nihilism as *decline and decrease of the power of the spirit: passive nihilism:*

as a sign of weakness: the strength of the spirit can be tired, exhausted, so that the previous goals and values are insufficient and no longer inspire belief—

That the synthesis of values and goals (on which every strong culture depends) dissolves, so that the various values war with each other: disintegration.

That everything that delights, heals, soothes, anesthetizes comes to the foreground, in various *disguises,* religious, or moral or political or aesthetic etc.

2. Presupposition of this hypothesis.

That there is no truth; that there is no absolute constitution of things, no "thing in itself."

—*This is itself a nihilism,* and *indeed the most extreme.* It takes the value of things to consist precisely in that this value corresponds and has corresponded to *no* reality, but rather is only a symptom of strength on the part of the *value-determiner,* a simplification for the purpose of life.[10]

*   *   *   *   *

What is a *belief?* How does it arise? Every belief is a *taking-to-be-true.* The most extreme form of nihilism would be: that *every* belief, every

---

[10]WP 13, 22, 23/KGW VIII 9:35.

taking-to-be-true, is necessarily false: *because there is absolutely no true world.* Thus: a *perspectival appearance,* whose origin lies in us (insofar as we continually *have need* of a narrower, abbreviated, simplified world).

—that it is the *measure of strength* how far we are able to acknowledge *appearance* and the necessity of lies—without perishing.

To that extent *nihilism,* as the *denial of a truthful world,* of being, *could be a divine way of thinking;* —[11]

* * * * *

On the Genesis of the Nihilist

It is only late that one comes to have the courage for what one really *knows.* That I have previously been fundamentally a nihilist is something I have recognized only recently: the energy, the nonchalance with which I have gone ahead as a nihilist deceived me about this basic fact. If one is moving toward a goal, it seems impossible that our most basic assumption is "goal-lessness as such."[12]

* * * * *

Toward a Plan[13]

Radical nihilism is the conviction of the absolute untenability of existence as far as the highest values one acknowledges are concerned, together with the *insight* that we do not have the slightest right to posit a beyond or an in-itself of things that is "divine" or the embodiment of morality.

This insight is a consequence of highly developed "truthfulness": thereby itself a consequence of the belief in morality.[14]

This is the antinomy: to the extent that we believe in morality, we *condemn* existence.

The logic of pessimism carried all the way to *nihilism: what is at work there?*—Concept of *valuelessness, meaninglessness:* to what extent moral valuations lurk behind all other high values.

—Result: *moral valuations are condemnations, negations, morality is the denial of the will to existence . . .*

Problem: *but what is morality?*[15]

---

[11]WP 15/KGW VIII 9:41.
[12]WP 25/KGW VIII 9:123.
[13]KGW VIII 10:192. This note was divided by the compilers of WP into two sections: WP 3 and 11.
[14]WP 3/KGW VIII 10:192.
[15]WP 11/KGW VIII 10:192.

Late 1887–1888

Critique of Nihilism

(1) Nihilism as a psychological condition will have to arrive *first* when we have sought a "meaning" in all that happens that is not there: so that the seeker finally becomes dismayed. Nihilism in this instance is the realization of the long *waste* of strength, the torment of the "pointless," the insecurity, the lack of opportunity somehow to recover and in some way to regain one's composure—being ashamed of oneself, as if one had *deceived* oneself for all too long. . . . This sought-for *meaning* might have been: the "fulfillment" of an ethically supreme principle in all that happens, the ethical world-order; or the increase of love and harmony in the interactions of creatures; or the approach of a general condition of happiness; or even the movement toward a general condition of nothingness—a goal is still a meaning. The common denominator of all of these notions is that something or other is to be attained through the process: and now one comprehends that in all this becoming *nothing* is achieved, *nothing* is attained. . . . Thus: disappointment concerning a supposed *goal* of *becoming* as cause of nihilism: whether it is with reference to a quite specific goal or is generalized, the insight into the untenability of all previous goal-hypotheses that apply to the entire "development" (—man *no longer* collaborator of becoming, let alone its centerpoint).

Nihilism as a psychological condition arrives *second* when one has postulated a *totality*, a *systematization*, even an *organization* in all that happens and beneath all that happens: so that the soul that craves to admire and revere can revel in the totalizing conception of a supreme form of domination and control (—if it is the soul of a logician, mere complete consistency and derivability suffice for reconciliation with everything . . .); a kind of unity, some form of "monism": such a belief is enough to give one a deep feeling of belonging and dependence in relation to a whole that infinitely transcends him, a mode of the divinity. . . . "The general well-being requires the devotion of the individual." . . . But now one sees that there *is* no such thing! At bottom man has lost the belief in his own value if no infinitely valuable whole is working through him: i.e., he has conceived of such a whole *in order to be able to believe in his own value.*

Nihilism as a psychological condition has a *third* and *last* form. Assuming these two *insights*,—that in becoming nothing is to be attained, and that there is no great unity at work beneath all becoming in which the individual may completely immerse himself as in a substance of the highest value—the *subterfuge* remains to condemn this entire world of becoming as deception and to discover a world lying beyond it as the *true* world. But as soon as one finds out that this world is constructed merely out of psychological needs, and that one has no right whatsoever to it, the last form of nihilism arises, which involves *disbelief in a metaphysical world*— which rules out belief in a *true* world. From this standpoint one affirms the reality of becoming as the *only* reality, rules out every sort of sneak-path to afterworlds and false divinities—but *finds unendurable this world that one refuses to deny.* . . .

What at bottom has happened? The feeling of *valuelessness* was reached when one comprehended that it is not permitted to interpret the general character of existence either with the concept "purpose" or with the concept "unity" or with the concept "truth." Existence achieves and attains nothing, any overarching unity in the multiplicity of happening is lacking; the character of existence is not "true," it is *false,* . . . one simply no longer has any way to persuade oneself of a true world. . . .

In short: the categories "purpose," "unity," "being," with which we have attributed value to the world, are *withdrawn* by us again—and now the world *looks valueless.* . . .

(2) Suppose we have recognized to what extent the world may no longer be *interpreted* with these three categories, and that after having this insight the world begins to seem valueless for us: we then must ask, Where did our faith in these three categories come from?—let us see whether it might not be possible to terminate our faith in *them.* If we *devalue* these three categories, then the demonstration of their inapplicability to the universe is no longer any reason *to devalue the universe.*

Upshot: the faith in the categories of reason is the cause of nihilism—we have measured the value of the world by categories *that have to do with a purely fictitious world.*

Final upshot: all values with which we up to now have sought to make the world estimable for ourselves, and which finally have *devalued* it as they have turned out not to apply—all these values are, psychologically considered, results of specific perspectives of utility for the maintenance and extension of human forms of domination: and only falsely *projected* into the nature of things. It is always the *hyperbolic naivete* of man to take himself as the meaning and value-standard of things. . . .[16]

*   *   *   *   *

The highest values, in whose service human beings are supposed to live, especially if they are very burdensome and impose a high cost: for the purpose of amplification, as if they were commandments of God, these *social values* were erected over humanity, as "reality," as "true" world, as hope and *future* world. Now, when the unsavory origins of these

[16]WP 12/KGW VIII 11:99.

values have become clear, it seems to us that everything has therewith been devalued and has become "meaningless" . . . but that is only a *transitional condition.*[17]

* * * * *

The time is coming when we will have to *pay* for having been *Christians* for two thousand years: we are losing the *importance* that has enabled us to live—we don't know for a while what to do. We plunge abruptly into the *opposed* valuations, with the same degree of energy with which we have been Christians—with which we have gone in for Christian nonsensical exaggeration—

(1) The "immortal soul"; the eternal value of the "person"
(2) Salvation, judgment, evaluation in the "beyond"
(3) Moral value as the highest value, the "salvation of the soul" as cardinal interest
(4) "sin," "earthly," "flesh," "pleasures"—stigmatized as "world"

Now everything is false through and through, mere "words," jumbled, weak or overheated. [. . .][18]

* * * * *

Preface

(1) Great things require that one either remain silent or speak with greatness about them: with greatness, that means cynically and with innocence.

(2) What I relate is the history of the next two centuries. I describe what is coming, what no longer can come otherwise: *the advent of nihilism.* This history can now already be told; for necessity itself is here at work. This future already speaks in a hundred signs, this destiny everywhere announces itself; for this music of the future all ears are already perked. Our entire European culture has long been moving, with a tortured tension that has grown from decade to decade, as if toward a catastrophe: restlessly, violently, plunging: like a river that wants to reach its end, that reflects no longer, that is afraid to reflect about it.

(3) He who speaks here, in contrast, has previously done nothing but *reflect:* as a philosopher and hermit by instinct, who has found his advan-

---

[17]WP 7/KGW VIII 11:100.
[18]WP 30/KGW VIII 11:148. In WP 30, the four numbered points were deleted by the compilers. The note continues at some length after the last sentence here.

tage in being apart and outside, in patience, in delay, in hanging back; as a daring and experimenting spirit that has already gotten lost in every labyrinth of the future; as a prophetic bird of a spirit that *looks back* when it relates what is to come; as the first consummate nihilist of Europe, who however has already lived nihilism itself through to the end in himself— who has left it behind himself, beneath himself, outside himself. . . .

(4) For one should not misconstrue the meaning of the title with which this gospel of the future wants to be named. *"The Will to Power: Attempt at a Revaluation of All Values"*—with this formula a *countermovement* is brought to expression, with respect to principle and task: a movement that in some future time will replace this consummate nihilism, but that *presupposes* it, logically and psychologically, and that in any event can only come *after it* and *out of it.* For why is the advent of nihilism *necessary?* Because it is our previous values themselves that draw out their final consequence in it; because nihilism is the logical outcome of our great values and ideas thought through to the end—because we must first experience nihilism, in order to get to the bottom of what the *value* of these "values" really is. . . . We have need, sometime, of *new values.* . . .[19]

Reason and Knowledge

1886–1888

Fundamental solution:

We have faith in reason: but this is the philosophy of gray *concepts;* language is built on the most naive prejudices.

Now we read disharmonies and problems into things, because we *think only* in linguistic form—and along with it believe in the "eternal truth" of reason (e.g. subject, predicate, etc.).

We cease to think if we are unwilling to do so under linguistic constraint, we hardly even reach the doubt that sees a boundary as a boundary here.

Rational thought is an interpretation in accordance with a scheme that we are unable to let go of.[20]

* * * * *

[19]WP Preface/KGW VIII 11:411.
[20]WP 552/KGW VIII 5:22.

Against positivism, which stops at phenomena—"there are only facts"—
I would say: No, there precisely are no facts, only interpretations. We
are unable to ascertain any fact "in itself": perhaps it is nonsense to
want to do any such thing. "It is all subjective," you say; but that is already
interpretation, the "subject" is nothing given, but rather something ficti-
tiously added, stuck in underneath.—Is it even necessary to posit an interpreter behind the interpretation? That is already invention, hypothesis.

To the extent that the word "knowledge" has meaning, the world is
knowable: but it can be *construed* otherwise; it has no meaning behind it,
but rather countless meanings. "Perspectivism."

It is our needs *that interpret the world:* our drives and their for and
against. Every drive is a kind of lust to dominate; each has its perspective,
which it would like to impose as a norm on all other drives.[21]

*   *   *   *   *

Psychological Derivation of Our Faith in Reason

The concept "reality being" is borrowed from our "subject"-feeling.

"Subject": interpreted out of ourselves, so that the ego is taken as
subject, as cause of all doings, as *doer.*

The logical-metaphysical postulates, the belief in substance, accident,
attribute etc. gets its convincing force from the habit of regarding all our
doings as consequences of our will:—so that the ego, as substance, does
not dissolve in the multiplicity of change.—*But there is no will.*

We have no categories at all that allow us to distinguish a "world in itself"
from a world as appearance. All our *categories of reason* are of sensual origin:
read off of the empirical world. "The soul," "the ego"—here too the history of these concepts shows the oldest distinction ("breath," "life")—

If there is nothing material, there is nothing immaterial either. The
concept no longer *contains* anything . . .

No subject-"atoms." The sphere of a subject continually *growing* or
diminishing—the center of the system continually *shifting*—; in cases in which
it is unable to organize the appropriated mass, it breaks in two. On the other
hand it can turn a weaker subject into its functionary without destroying it,
and to a certain extent constitute a new unity together with it. No "substance"; rather, something that intrinsically strives for strengthening, and that
only indirectly wants to "preserve" itself (it wants to *surpass* itself—)[22]

*   *   *   *   *

[21]WP 481/KGW VIII 7:60.
[22]WP 488/KGW VIII 9:98.

On "Logical Apparentness"

The concepts "individual" and "species" [are] equally false and merely apparent. "Species" only expresses the fact that a multitude of similar creatures come along at the same time and that the tempo of further growth and self-alteration has slowed down for a long time: so that the actual small continuations and increases are not very noticeable (—a developmental phase in which the self-developing is not visible, so that an equilibrium *seems* to have been reached, and the false idea is made possible that *here a goal has been attained*—and that the development has a given goal . . .)

The *form* is taken to be something enduring and therefore valuable; but the form is merely invented by us; and however often "the same form is attained," that does not mean that it is *the same* form—*rather it is always something new that appears*—and it is only we who compare them, who reckon the new, insofar as it is similar to the old, together in the unity of "form." As if a *type* is supposedly attained, and so to speak is intended by and inherent in the formative process.

Form, species, law, idea, purpose—the same error is made here in all of them, of wrongly attributing a false reality to a fiction: as if what happens has something obedient about it—an artificial distinction in what happens is then drawn between *what* does the doing and *that toward which* this doing is directed (but the *what* and the *toward which* are only laid down by us in obedience to our metaphysical-logical dogmatism; no "matter of fact")

One should not understand this *compulsion* to fashion concepts, species, forms, purposes, laws—"a world of identical cases"—as if we were in a position to ascertain the *true* world by means of them; but rather, as the compulsion to arrange for ourselves a world in which *our existence* is facilitated—with them we create a world that is calculable, simplified, comprehensible, etc. for us.

This same compulsion is to be found in the *sense-activities* that support the understanding—the simplifying, coarsening, emphasizing, and elaborating, on which all "re-cognition," all being-able-to-make-oneself-understandable depends. Our *needs* have made our senses so precise that the "same world of appearance" always recurs and thereby has acquired the semblance of *reality*.

Our subjective compulsion to have faith in logic only shows that, long before logic itself came to consciousness, we did nothing less than *insert its postulates into what happens:* now we discover them in what happens—we no longer can do otherwise—and suppose that this compulsion establishes something about "truth." It is we who have created "the thing," "the identical thing," subject, attribute, doing, object, substance, form, after we have long pursued *making* the identical, *making* the coarse and simple.

The world *appears* logical to us, because *we* first logicized it.[23]

*   *   *   *   *

On Theory of Knowledge: entirely empirical

There is neither "spirit" nor reason nor thought nor consciousness nor soul nor will nor truth: all fictions that are useless. We have to do not with "subject and object" but rather a particular animal species that can flourish only through a certain relative *accuracy,* above all *regularity* of its perceptions (so that it can capitalize on its experience). . . .

Knowledge works as a *tool* of power. Thus it is obvious that it grows with every increase of power. . . .

Meaning of "knowledge": here, as in the cases of "good" or "beautiful," the concept is to be taken in a strict and narrow anthropocentric and biological sense. In order for a particular species to preserve itself—and grow in its power—it must register enough of the calculable and constant in its conception of reality to be able to construct a scheme of behavior on it. *The utility of preservation,* not some abstract-theoretical need not to be deceived, stands as the motive behind the development of the organs of knowledge. . . . They develop in such a way that their observations suffice to preserve us. In other words: the *extent* of the desire for knowledge depends upon the extent of the growth of the *will to power* of a species: a species grasps a certain amount of reality *in order to become master over it, in order to make use of it.*[24]

*   *   *   *   *

Will to Power as Knowledge

Not "to know," but rather to schematize, to impose as much regularity and form on chaos as will be sufficient for our practical needs.

In the formation of reason, logic, the categories, it was need that was decisive: the need not to "know" but rather to subsume, to schematize, for the purpose of comprehensibility, of calculation. . . .

Adjustment, filling out to make similar, equal—the development of reason is the same process that every sense-impression undergoes!

There was no pre-existing "Idea" at work here: but rather usefulness, that it is only when we see things as made coarse and equal that they become calculable and manageable for us. . . .

[23]WP 521/KGW VIII 9:144.
[24]WP 480/KGW VIII 14:122.

Finality in reason is an effect, not a cause: with any other kind of reason, to which there are constant impulses, life goes badly—it is poorly arranged—too unequal—

The categories are "truths" only in the sense that they are conditions of life for us: as Euclidean space is such a conditioned "truth." (Candidly speaking: since no one will seriously maintain the necessity of the existence of human beings exactly as they are, reason as well as Euclidean space is a mere idiosyncrasy of a particular animal species and one among many others. . . .)

The subjective compulsion to be unable to contradict here is a biological compulsion: the instinct for the utility of inferring as we infer is implanted in our bodies, we almost *are* this instinct. . . . But what naivete to draw from that a proof that we therewith possess a "truth as such." . . .

Not being able to contradict is proof of an inability, not a "truth."[25]

The World and Life

1888

Will to Power   Philosophy

Power quanta. *Critique of Mechanism*[26]

Let us here put aside the two popular concepts "necessity" and "law": the first inserts a false compulsion into the world, the second a false freedom. "Things" do not conduct themselves regulatedly, in accordance with a *rule;* there are no things (—that is a fiction of ours); they conduct themselves just as little under a compulsion of necessity. Here there is no obeying; for *that something is as it is*, as strong or as weak, is not the consequence of obedience or of a rule or of a compelling. . . .

The degree of resistance and the degree of superior power—in all that happens that is what is decisive: if, for our ordinary purposes of calculation, we know how to express that in formulas of "laws," all the better for us! But we have not inserted any "morality" into the world by imagining it to be obedient.

There are no laws: every power draws its ultimate consequence in every moment. Calculability depends precisely on the fact that there is no middle term.

[25]WP 515/KGW VIII 14:152.
[26]KGW VIII 14:79. This long note was divided by the compilers of WP into two notes: WP 634 and 635. They also deleted the words "Will to Power," "Philosophy," and "Power Quanta" from the heading.

A power-quantum is characterized by the effect that it produces and that it resists. The adiaphorous state is lacking, conceivable in principle though it may be. It is essentially a will to violate and to defend itself against violation. Not self-preservation: every atom affects the whole of reality—it is thought away if one thinks away this radiation of power-will. That is why I call it a quantum of "will to power": the characteristic is thereby expressed that cannot *be* thought away from the mechanistic order without thinking it itself away.

A translation of this world of effect into a *visible* world—a world for the eye—is the concept "movement." Here it is always taken for granted that *something* is moved—thereby a thing that does the effecting is always supposed, whether it be now in the fiction of a clump-atom or even as its abstraction, the dynamic atom—i.e., we have not gotten rid of the habits to which the senses and language seduce us. Subject, object, a doer added to a doing, the doing and that which does it sundered: let us not forget that what is thereby indicated is mere semiotics and nothing real. Mechanics as a doctrine of *motion* is already a translation into the sense-language of man.[27]

We have need of unities in order to be able to calculate: it does not follow that there are such unities. We have derived the concept of unity from our "ego"-concept—our oldest article of faith. If we did not take ourselves to be unities, we never would have formed the concept "thing." Now, much later, we are honestly convinced that our conception of the ego-concept does not attest to any real unity. Thus in order to uphold the mechanistic theory of the world, we must always enter a caveat concerning the extent to which we rely on fictions in doing so: the concept of movement (taken from our sense language) and the concept of the atom = unity (deriving from our psychical "experience"): it has a *sense prejudice* and a *psychological prejudice* among its presuppositions.

The *mechanistic* world is imagined in the only way the eye and touch can picture such a world (as "moved").

> to enable it to be calculated—unities are invented
> in order to invent causal unities, "things" (atoms), whose effect
>   remains constant (—transference of the false subject-concept to
>   the atom-concept)
> concept of number
> concept of thing (concept of the subject)
> concept of activity (separation of being-a-cause and effect)
> movement (eye and touch)
> that all effect is *movement*
> that where there is movement, *something* is moved

[27]WP 634/KGW VIII 14:79.

Phenomenal therefore are: the mixing in of the concept of number, the concept of the subject, the concept of movement; our *eye*, our *psychology* are still involved.

If we eliminate these additions, then no things remain, but rather dynamic quanta, in a relation of tension to all other dynamic quanta: whose nature consists in their relation to all other quanta, in their "effect" on them—The will to power, not a being, not a becoming, but rather a *pathos*, is the most elemental fact, from which becoming and effecting first emerge. . . .

Mechanics formulates succession-phenomena semiotically, going beyond that, using sensuous and psychological means of expression; it does not touch upon the causal force. . . .[28]

*   *   *   *   *

Critique of the Concept "Cause"

Psychologically regarded: the concept "cause" is our feeling of power from so-called willing—our concept "effect," the superstition that the feeling of power is itself the power that impels. . . .

a condition that accompanies an event, and already is an effect of
    the event, is projected as its "sufficient basis"
the relation of tension in our feeling of power: pleasure as the
    feeling of power: of resistance overcome—are these illusions?
if we translate the concept "cause" back again into the only
    sphere known to us, from which we have taken it: we cannot
    conceive of any *change* in which there is not a will to power. We
    do not know how to explain a change except as the encroach-
    ment of power upon other power.
mechanics shows us only results, and then only in images (motion
    is a speech-image)
gravitation itself has no mechanistic cause, since it is the initial
    basis for mechanistic results
the will to accumulation of force as specific for the phenomena of
    life, for nourishment, reproduction, heredity
for society, state, custom, authority
should we not be permitted to assume this will as the moving
    cause in chemistry as well?
and in the cosmic order?

[28]WP 635/KGW VIII 14:79.

not merely conservation of energy, but rather maximal economy of
use: so that the *will-to-become-stronger of every force-center* is the
only reality—not self-preservation, but rather appropriation, willing to become master, more, stronger.

that science is possible—that is supposed to *prove* to us a principle
of causality?

"from like causes, like effects"

"a permanent law of things"

"an immutable order"

just because something is calculable, is it therefore necessary?

if something happens thus and not otherwise, that involves no
"principle," no "law," no "order"

Power-quanta, whose nature consists in the exercise of power on
all other power-quanta

In the belief in cause and effect the main thing is always forgotten: the *happening* itself.

one has inserted a doer, one has again hypothesized the done[29]

Can we assume a *striving for power* without a sensation of pleasure
and displeasure, i.e., without a feeling of the increase and decrease of power?

is mechanism only a sign language for the *internal* factual world of
struggling and conquering will-quanta?

all presuppositions of mechanism, matter, atom, pressure and impact, gravity are not "facts in themselves," but rather interpretations with the aid of *psychical* fictions.

life as the form of being best known to us is specifically a will to
the accumulation of force

all processes of life have their impetus here

nothing wants to preserve itself, all is to be added and accumulated

Life as a special case: hypothesis from it to the total character of
existence.

strives for a *maximal feeling of power*

is essentially a striving for an increase of power

striving is nothing other than striving for power

that which is most basic and innermost remains this will:
mechanics is a mere semiotics of the results.[30]

*   *   *   *   *

[29]WP 689/KGW VIII 14:81. The compilers of WP combined this note and the following
one into WP 689.
[30]WP 689/KGW VIII 14:82.

Will to power psychologically

Unitary Conception of Psychology

We are used to considering the development of an incredible abundance of forms to be consistent with an origin from a unity.

So that the will to power is the primitive affect-form, and that all other affects are only its developments;

So that it is importantly enlightening to replace individual "happiness," as that for which everything living supposedly strives, with power: "it strives for power, for an increase in power"—pleasure is only a symptom of the feeling of attained power, a consciousness of a difference—

—it does not strive for pleasure; rather, pleasure occurs when that for which it strives is attained: pleasure accompanies, pleasure does not impel. . . .

So that all driving force is will to power, and that there is no other physical, dynamic or psychical force. [. . .][31]

*   *   *   *   *

Physicists believe in a "true world" in their way: a firm atom-systematization in necessary motion, the same for all creatures—so that for them the "apparent world" is reduced to the aspect of universal and universally necessary being accessible to each creature after its own fashion (accessible and at the same time adjusted—made "subjective"). But they are thereby mistaken: the atom that they posit is derived in accordance with the logic of the perspectivism of consciousness—and is thereby also itself a subjective fiction. This world-picture that they devise is throughout not essentially different from the subjective world-picture: it is merely constructed with more widely extended senses, but throughout with *our* senses. . . . And in the end they have left something out of the constellation without knowing it: precisely the necessary perspectivism, owing to which every power-center—and not only man—construes the entire rest of the world out of itself, i.e., measures, feels, forms in accordance with its power. . . . They have forgotten to include this perspective-*establishing* force in "true being." . . . Put in academic language: subjectivity. They think this was "developed," added subsequently—

But even the chemists require it: it is *specificity*, acting and reacting thus and so in particular ways, accordingly.

Perspectivism is only a complex form of specificity.

My idea is that every particular body thus strives to become master of all space and to extend its force (—its will to power:) and to push back whatever resists its extension. But it continually runs up against

[31]WP 688/KGW VIII 14:121. This note continues at some length.

similar efforts of other bodies and ends up coming to an arrangement ("unification") with those that are sufficiently related: *they then conspire together for power*. And the process goes on. . . .[32]

*   *   *   *   *

(1) The world exists; it is nothing that comes to be, nothing that passes away. Or rather: it comes to be, it passes away, but it has never begun to come to be and never ceases to pass away—it *maintains* itself in both. . . . It lives on itself: its excrements are its nourishment. . . .

(2) The hypothesis of a *created* world should not for a moment concern us. The concept "create" is today completely indefinable, inoperable; merely a word, rudimentary from superstitious times; with a word one explains nothing. The latest attempt to conceive of a world that *began* has recently been made with the aid of a logical procedure—for the most part, as is to be suspected, with an ulterior theological aim. [. . .]

(4) I have run into this thought in earlier thinkers; every time it was conditioned by other, ulterior considerations (—mostly theological, to the advantage of the *creator spiritus*). If the world as a whole could become rigid, dry, dead, *nothing*, or if it could reach a condition of equilibrium, or if it as a whole had some sort of goal that involved duration, immutability, some once-and-for-all-time (in short, metaphysically expressed: if becoming *could* wind up in being or in nothingness), this condition would have had to have been reached. But it has not been reached: from which it follows. . . . That is the only certainty that we can get our hands on, to serve as a corrective to a great many intrinsically possible world-hypotheses. If, e.g., mechanistic theory cannot avoid the consequence of a final condition, which Thompson has derived from it, mechanistic theory is thereby *refuted*.

(5) If the world *permits* of being thought of as a determinate quantity of force and as a determinate number of force-centers—and every other representation remains indeterminate and consequently *unusable*—then it follows from this that it has to pass through a calculable number of combinations, in the great dice-game of its existence. In an infinite time, every possible combination would have to be reached at some time or other; moreover, it would have to be reached infinitely many times. And since between every "combination" and its next "recurrence" all combinations that are in any way possible would have to come about, and each of these combinations conditions the entire sequence of combinations in the same series, then a circular course of absolutely identical series would thereby be demonstrated: the world as a circular course that has already repeated itself infinitely often and that plays its game *in infinitum*.

[32]WP 636/KGW VIII 14:186.

This conception is not simply a mechanistic one; for if it were, it would not necessitate an infinite recurrence of identical cases, but rather a final state. *Because* the world has not reached such a state, mechanistic theory must be considered an imperfect and only provisional hypothesis.[33]

Values, Moralities, Religions

1887

Toward a Plan[34]

In place of *moral values*, purely *naturalistic* values. Naturalization of morality.

In place of "sociology," a doctrine of the *forms of domination*.

In place of "theory of knowledge," a *perspective-doctrine of the affects* (to which a hierarchy of the affects belongs).

the *transfigured* affects: their *higher ordering*, their "spirituality."

In place of metaphysics and religion, *the doctrine of the eternal recurrence* (this as a means of breeding and selection).[35]

In place of "society," the *culture-complex* as *my* chief interest (both as a whole and with regard to its parts).[36]

*   *   *   *   *

To take into service everything terrible, singly, gradually, experimentally: this is what the task of culture requires; but until it is *strong* enough for this, it must oppose, moderate, conceal, even curse. . . .

—everywhere, where a culture *posits* something as *evil*, it gives expression to a relation of *fear*, thus a *weakness* . . .

Thesis: everything good is a former evil made serviceable.

Standard: the more terrible and the greater the passions are that an age, a people, an individual can permit themselves, because they are able to employ them *as means, the higher stands their culture* (—the realm of the evil grows ever *smaller* . . .)

—the more mediocre, weak, submissive and cowardly a person is, the more he will take to *be evil:* for him the realm of the evil is the most

[33]WP 1066/KGW VIII 14:188. This note is the main place in Nietzsche's writings where he attempts to construct and spell out an argument for the doctrine of "eternal recurrence" construed as a cosmological hypothesis applying to all events and sequences of events. A portion of the note that is not part of the argument he proposes has been omitted here (the section numbered 3 in the note manuscript).

[34]WP 462/KGW VIII 9:8, 10:28. The compilers of WP combined notes from two different notebooks to make this section and also substituted the heading "Fundamental Innovations" for this heading of the first note.

[35]KGW VIII 9:8. The compilers of WP omitted the remainder of this note.

[36]KGW VIII 10:28.

encompassing; the lowest person will see the realm of the evil (i.e., of that which is forbidden and dangerous to him) everywhere.[37]

*   *   *   *   *

In summa: mastery over the passions, *not* their weakening or eradication!

The greater the mastering strength of a will is, the more freedom may be allowed to the passions.

The "great man" is great owing to the freedom of scope of his desires and through the even greater power that knows how to take these magnificent monsters into service.

—the "good man" at every stage of civilization is at once the *undangerous and the useful* one: a kind of *mean;* the expression in the common mind of one *of whom one has nothing to fear and whom one nonetheless is not permitted to despise . . .*

Schooling: essentially the means of *ruining* the exception, by distraction, seduction, sickening, for the benefit of the rule.

That is harsh; but economically considered, perfectly reasonable. At least for a long time. —

Acculturating: essentially, the means of setting taste against the exception for the benefit of the mediocre.

A culture of the exception, of attempts, of danger, of nuance as the consequence of a great *wealth of energies: every* aristocratic culture tends that way.

It is only when a culture has an overflow of energies at its disposal that a hothouse of cultural surplus can arise on its foundation—[38]

*   *   *   *   *

Whose Will to Power Is Morality?

The *common* theme in the history of Europe since Socrates is the attempt to bring about the dominance of *moral values* over all other values: so that they are to be the leader and judge not only of life but also of (1) knowledge, (2) art, (3) political and social affairs.

"becoming better" as the sole task, everything else the *means* to it (or disturbance, restriction, danger: consequently to be combated unto annihilation . . .)

A similar movement in *China*. A similar movement in *India*.

What is signified by this *will to power on the part of moral powers*, which has been manifested on earth in such tremendous developments?

[37]WP 1025/KGW VIII 9:138.
[38]WP 933/KGW VIII 9:139.

Answer: *three powers are at work within it:* (1) the instinct of the *herd* against the strong and independent; (2) the instinct of the *suffering* and of those who have turned out badly against the fortunate; (3) the instinct of the *mediocre* against the exceptions. —*Tremendous advantage of this movement,* how much cruelty, falseness and narrow-mindedness have also assisted in it (for the history of the *struggle of morality with the fundamental instincts of life* is itself the greatest immorality that there has ever been on earth . . .)[39]

*   *   *   *   *

The affects are one and all *useful,* some directly, others indirectly; with respect to utility it is utterly impossible to specify a gradation of values—thus certainly, economically considered, the forces of nature are one and all good, i.e., useful, just as terrible and irrevocable consequences also follow from them. The most one can say is that the most powerful affects are the most valuable: insofar as there are no greater sources of energy.[40]

*   *   *   *   *

Points of view for *my* values: whether out of abundance or out of longing . . . ; whether one looks on or gets involved . . . or looks away, passes by . . . ; whether "spontaneously" out of pent up force or merely *reactively* stimulated, incited . . . ; whether *simply* out of paucity of elements *or* out of overwhelming mastery over many, so that they are pressed into service when they are needed . . . ; whether one is *problem* or *solution* [. . .][41]

*   *   *   *   *

Consider the *damage* that is done to all human institutions, whenever a divine and otherworldly *higher sphere* is posited that must first *sanction* these institutions. By then becoming accustomed to seeing their value in this sanction (e.g., in the case of marriage), one has *diminished their natural worth,* in some situations *denied* it. . . . To the extent that one has bestowed honor upon the anti-nature of a God, nature is unfavorably assessed. "Nature" becomes akin to "despicable," "bad" . . .

The fatefulness of a belief in the *reality of the highest moral qualities as God:* with it all actual values were denied and fundamentally construed as

[39]WP 274/KGW VIII 9:159.
[40]WP 931/KGW VIII 10:133.
[41]WP 1009/KGW VIII 10:145. This note continues at some length.

un-values. Thus *antinaturalness* ascended to the throne. With an inexorable logic one arrived at the absolute call for the *denial of nature.*[42]

*   *   *   *   *

"Morality for morality's sake"—an important stage in its denaturalization: it itself appears as the ultimate value. In this phase it permeates religion: e.g., in Judaism. And there likewise is a phase in which it *separates itself* again from religion, and in which no God is "moral" enough for it: then it gives preference to the impersonal ideal. . . . That is now the case.

"Art for art's sake"—that is the most dangerous principle: one thereby introduces a false opposition into things,—it leads to a slandering of reality ("idealization" into *ugliness*). When one separates an ideal from reality, one denigrates reality, one impoverishes it, one slanders it. "The beautiful for its own sake," "the true for its own sake," "the good for its own sake"—these are three forms of the *evil eye* for reality.

—*Art, knowledge, morality* are *means:* instead of recognizing in them the aim of enhancing life, one has related them to the *opposite of life,* to "God"—so to speak, as revelations of a higher world, which in them peeks through here and there. . . .

—"beautiful and ugly," "true and false," "good and evil"—these *distinctions* and *antagonisms* betray conditions of existence and advancement not of humanity in general, but rather of certain fixed and enduring complexes which separate themselves from their adversaries. The *war* that is thereby created is the essential thing about them: as a means of *separation* that *strengthens* the isolation. . . .[43]

*   *   *   *   *

We Hyperboreans

My conclusion is: that the *actual* human being represents a much higher value than the "wished-for" human being of any previous ideal; that all "wishfulnesses" with respect to man have been absurd and dangerous extravagances, with which a particular sort of human being sought to hang *its* conditions of preservation and growth over humanity as a law; that every "wishfulness" of such an origin that has been brought to dominance up to now has *diminished* the value of man, his strength, his certainty of a future; that the poverty and small-mindedness of man reveals itself most, even today, when he *wishes;* that the capacity of human beings to establish

---

[42]WP 245/KGW VIII 10:152.
[43]WP 298/KGW VIII 10:194.

values has up to now been too little developed to do justice to the actual and not merely "wishful" *value of man;* that "the ideal" up to now has been the truly world- and humanity-slandering force, the poison cloud over reality, the great *seduction to nothingness.* . . .[44]

*   *   *   *   *

1888

Which values have prevailed so far

1. Morality as the highest value, in all phases of philosophy (even among the skeptics).

Result: this world is worthless, there must be a "true world."

2. *What* really determined the highest value here? What really is morality? The instinct of decadence; it is the exhausted and disinherited that take their *revenge* in this way and play the *masters.* . . .

Historical proof: the philosophers [are] always decadents, always in the service of nihilistic religions.

3. The instinct of decadence, which steps forth as will to power. Introduction of its system of means: absolute unmorality of the means.

General view: the highest values so far are a special case of the will to power: morality itself is a special case of *unmorality.*

Purification of formerly depreciated values.

We have grasped *what* so far has determined the highest value and *why* it has become master over the opposing valuation: it was *stronger.* . . .

Let us now purify the *opposing valuation* of the infection and half-heartedness, of the *degeneration,* in which it is familiar to us all.

Theory of their *denaturing* and *restoration of nature: moraline-free.*[45] [. . .]

*   *   *   *   *

A Preface

I have the fortune, and the honor that goes along with it, after whole millennia of error and confusion, to have rediscovered the path that leads to a Yes and a No.

I teach No to all that makes weak—that exhausts.

I teach Yes to all that strengthens, that accumulates energy, that conduces to pride—

[44]WP 390/KGW VIII 11:118.

[45]WP 401/KGW VIII 14:137, 138. Portions of this material are omitted here. The term "moraline" is coined by Nietzsche on the model of words like caffeine and codeine, to indicate that morality is of a like nature in its effects.

Previously one has taught neither the one nor the other: one has taught virtue, becoming selfless, pity, even the negation of life. . . . These are all values of the exhausted.[46]

*   *   *   *   *

Christianity

One has previously always attacked Christianity in a false and not merely timid way. As long as one has not seen the morality of Christianity as a *capital crime against life*, its defenders have had the advantage. The question of the mere "truth" of Christianity, whether with respect to the existence of its God or to the historicity of the legend of its origin, not even to speak of Christian astronomy and natural science—is an entirely incidental matter, as long as the question of the value of Christian morality is not addressed. Is the morality of Christianity *worth* anything, or is it a shame and disgrace despite all the holiness of its arts of seduction? There are hiding places of all sorts for the problem of truth; and the most faithful are ultimately able to make use of the logic of the unbelievers in order to devise for themselves a right to affirm certain things as—irrefutable that is, as *beyond* the means of refutation (—this ploy today is called "Kantian criticism"—).[47]

*   *   *   *   *

One should never forgive Christianity for having destroyed such men as Pascal. One should never cease combating exactly this in Christianity, that it has the will to break precisely the strongest and noblest souls. One should never rest as long as this one thing is not completely destroyed: the ideal of man that was invented by Christianity. The entire absurd remainder of Christian fable, concept-cobwebs and theology do not matter to us; it could be a thousand times more absurd, and we would not lift a finger against it. But we do combat this ideal, which with its sickly beauty and feminine seductiveness, with its stealthy eloquence of slander, appeals to all the cowardices and vanities of wearied souls (for even the strongest have weary hours), as if all of that which might in such circumstances seem most useful and desirable—trust, guilelessness, modesty, patience, love of one's fellows, resignation, submission to God, a sort of unharnessing and dismissing of one's entire ego—were also intrinsically the most useful and desirable things; as if the paltry modest abortion of a soul—the virtuous average-animal and herd-sheep human being—not only were

---

[46]WP 54/KGW VIII 15:13. Portions of this note are omitted here.
[47]WP 251/KGW VIII 15:19.

superior to the stronger, more evil, more covetous, more defiant, more extravagant and therefore a hundred times more endangered kind of human being, but moreover provided the ideal, the goal, the standard, the highest desirability for humanity in general. The erection of *this* ideal was the most sinister temptation ever placed before man; for with it the more strongly constituted exceptions and fortunate cases among human beings, in whom the will to power and to growth of the entire type man takes a step forward, were threatened with going under. With its values, it cuts at the roots of the growth of these higher human beings—who for the sake of their higher demands and tasks willingly endure a more dangerous life (economically expressed: an increase in the cost to the entrepreneurs as well as in the improbability of success). What is it that we combat in Christianity? That it wants to break the strong, that it wants to discourage their courage, exploit their bad hours and weariness, invert their proud assurance into distress and bad conscience, that it knows how to poison and sicken the noble instincts to the point that their strength, their will to power turns backward, turns against itself—until the strong perish through orgies of self-contempt and self-torment: that horrible sort of perishing the most famous example of which is provided by Pascal.[48]

*   *   *   *   *

Countermovement: Religion

The two types: *Dionysus* and the *Crucified*

To bear in mind: the typical *religious* person—a decadence-type?

The great innovators are one and all pathological and epileptic . . . but aren't we then leaving out one type of religious person, the *pagan?* Isn't the pagan cult a form of thanksgiving and affirmation of life? Mustn't its highest representation be a justification and deification of life?

Type of a well-turned-out and ecstatic-overflowing spirit. . . . A type that takes into itself and *redeems* the contradictions and questionable aspects of existence?

It is here that I locate the *Dionysus* of the Greeks: the religious affirmation of life, life as a whole, not denied or divided; typical that the sex-act awakens profundity, mystery, reverence.

Dionysus versus the "Crucified": there you have the antithesis. It is *not* a difference with respect to martyrdom—the same thing has a different meaning. Life itself, its eternal fruitfulness and recurrence gave rise to torment, destruction, the will to annihilation. . . . In the other case suffering, the "Crucified as the innocent," was taken to be objection against life, as a formula for its condemnation.

[48]WP 252/KGW VIII 11:55.

One discerns: the problem is that of the meaning of life: whether a Christian meaning or a tragic meaning. . . . In the first case, it is supposed to be the way to a blessed state of being; ultimately, being is taken to be *blessed enough* to be able to justify a monstrous amount of suffering.

The tragic human being affirms even the harshest suffering: he is strong, full, deifying enough to do so.

The Christian denies even the happiest lot on earth; he is weak, poor, discontented enough to suffer of life in every form. . . .

"The God on the cross" is a curse on life, a sign to free oneself from it. Dionysus cut in pieces is a *promise* of life: it will ever again be born and come back from destruction.[49]

*   *   *   *   *

That nothing of that which formerly was taken to be true is true; that what was formerly rejected by us as unholy, forbidden, despicable, disastrous—all these flowers grow today along the lovely paths of truth.

This entire old morality no longer matters to us: there is not a concept in it that still deserves respect. We have outlived it—we are no longer crude and naive enough to have to allow ourselves to tell ourselves lies in this way. . . . More politely expressed: we are too virtuous for that. . . .

And if truth in the old sense was only "truth" because the old morality affirmed it, was allowed to affirm it: then it also follows that we have no more such truth left. . . . Our *criterion* of truth is by no means morality: we *refute* a supposition by showing that it is dependent on morality, that it is inspired by lofty feelings.[50]

*   *   *   *   *

How I recognize my kindred spirits: Philosophy, as I have so far understood and lived it, is the voluntary search even for the accursed and heinous sides of existence. From long experience, gained from such wanderings through ice and desert, I learned to see differently all that has previously philosophized: —the *hidden* history of philosophy, the psychology of its great names came to light for me. "How much truth does a spirit *endure,* how much truth does it *dare?*"—This became the real measure of value for me. Error is *cowardice,* . . . every achievement of knowledge *derives* from courage, from hardness against oneself, from cleanliness toward oneself. . . . Such an experimental philosophy as I live anticipates even the possibility of the most fundamental nihilism: but this is not to say that it must stop with a No, with a negation, with a will to say No. It wants far

[49]WP 1052/KGW VIII 14:89.
[50]WP 459/KGW VIII 15:77.

more to come through to the opposite—to a *Dionysian affirmation* of the world, as it is, without subtraction, exception or selection—it wants the eternal circulation—the same things, the same logic and unlogic of things knotted together. Highest condition that a philosopher can attain: to stand in a Dionysian manner to existence—; my formula for this is *amor fati*. . . .

It is a part of this to comprehend the previously repudiated sides of existence not only as *necessary* but also as desirable: and not only as desirable in relation to the previously affirmed sides (as something like their complements or preconditions) but rather for their own sake, as the more powerful, more fruitful, *truer* sides of existence, in which its will more clearly expresses itself. Along with this belongs the depreciation of the previously exclusively *affirmed* sides of existence; to comprehend where these valuations came from and how little they are binding upon a Dionysian value standard for existence: I extracted and comprehended *what* it is that really says Yes here (in one kind of case the instinct of the suffering, in another the instinct of the herd, and in a third the *instinct of the majority* in opposition to the exceptions—). I therewith surmised to what extent another stronger sort of human being necessarily would have to think of the enhancement and elevation of mean along different lines: *higher creatures*, beyond good and evil, beyond those values that cannot deny their origin in the sphere of suffering, of the herd and of the majority—I sought for the beginnings of this inverted formation of ideals in history (the concepts "pagan," "classical," "noble" newly discovered and presented—).[51]

[51]WP 1041/KGW VIII 16:32.

VII
Final Reckonings
(1888)

Excerpts from

The Case of Wagner

Twilight of the Idols

The Antichrist:
Attempt at a Critique of Christianity

THREE LAST POLEMICS

Introduction

The last year of Nietzsche's active life—1888—was an increasingly frenzied one. During the first part of the year, he still hoped to write a major work comprehensively reinterpreting life and the world as well as our own nature, providing a critique of nihilism, and extending to a "revaluation of all values" in the light of that reinterpretation. In the course of the year, however, his attention focused chiefly on the latter task. In an extraordinary final burst of productivity, he completed four books in quick succession, of which his autobiographical *Ecce Homo* was the last. Excerpts from the other three—*Twilight of the Idols*, *The Case of Wagner*, and *The Antichrist* (or *Antichristian*)—are presented in this section.

Like the *Genealogy* that immediately preceded them, these three penultimate books give expression to aspects of the reinterpretation of our human nature in which Nietzsche remained engaged; but they are primarily contributions to his "revaluation" project. As in the case of the *Genealogy*, each represents a final reckoning with one of his main preoccupations throughout his philosophical life. It is as though he realized that he had not yet dealt decisively enough with these stumbling blocks, and so decided that his most urgent task was to confront them in a way that would remove them if anything could. Otherwise they would continue to obstruct the enhancement of human life and understanding alike.

It is also as though Nietzsche sensed that his time was running out and that he had better try to finish this most important unfinished business while he still could. His escalating polemical rhetoric undoubtedly foreshadowed his impending loss of sanity. But it also reflected both his frustration that his previous more temperate critiques had had little discernible effect and his determination to use every means at his disposal to shatter these hollow but seductive and detrimental idols. It was time to take the gloves off.

Nietzsche's target in the *Genealogy* had been the type of morality that had come to be commonly accepted and taken for granted in the modern world. The targets that now again drew his fire were the kind of art and sensibility associated with the triumph of Wagner (in *The Case of Wagner*), the kind of religion Christianity had become (in *The Antichrist*), and the kind of philosophy that had long prevailed, together with a variety of other features of modern intellectual and cultural life (in *Twilight of the Idols*). He considered these kinds of morality, art, religion, and "life of the mind" to cry out for "revaluation," and indeed for the severest criticism.

297

They are commonly supposed to reflect and reveal the highest values, and so are widely and highly esteemed; but he regarded them as dangerous influences undermining the very possibility of any genuine enhancement of human life. Small wonder, then, that he attacked them so vehemently.

Nietzsche's attack on Wagner may be the hardest for many today to appreciate, because Wagner and his art no longer loom large even among most of those to whom "high culture" matters. But Nietzsche's concern here is with a much more general phenomenon. It is as widespread today as it was in his time, if not more so—and at the level of "*popular* culture" most of all (in the media of film, television, and music), which he might well have regarded as a kind of "Wagnerianism for the people." For what he took Wagner to epitomize was art turned into a kind of insidious narcotic, stimulating artificially at the price of addiction and working not in the service of life but to its detriment.

Nietzsche's attack on Christianity is found by many to be both easier to understand and harder to take. It may well be that he does Christianity an injustice by identifying it so sweepingly with certain of its forms and tendencies to the neglect of others that are not all so blatantly "hostile to life." And of course, if Christians are *not* mistaken in their basic articles of faith, then it is Nietzsche who is in the wrong. But if it is supposed (with Nietzsche) that these articles of faith are fictions, his attack cannot be lightly dismissed. The fundamental problem of concern to him here is the logic of making the locus of all value something apart from this life in this world—a logic that leads to the devaluation of this life, and ultimately to nihilism upon the collapse of faith. And for Nietzsche, even a "this-worldly" Christianity, conceived fundamentally as a "way of life" (the kind of Christianity he associates with Jesus himself) rather than as an "other-worldly" faith, would still be objectionable. For to him it would amount to little more than a Western form of Buddhism, spelling the stultification and decline of life rather than its enhancement through creative activity.

Nietzsche's targets in *Twilight of the Idols (Götzen-Dämmerung,* a pun on Wagner's opera title *Götterdämmerung,* "Twilight of the Gods") are numerous and diverse. These "idols" include many other things that have long been revered and include many of our basic assumptions and cherished ideas about ourselves and our world. Beginning with metaphysically minded philosophers and modern-day morality, Nietzsche went on to offer a wide range of further critiques, of which the following excerpts provide only a few examples. He also set out his own views on a number of philosophical issues one last time. In this respect, *Twilight of the Idols* recalls such earlier works as *The Gay Science* and *Beyond Good and Evil.* It is the last of his works in which Nietzsche the philosopher can be found dealing with many of these issues. As such, it is perhaps of the greatest philosophical interest among the final works he completed.

The Case of Wagner (1888)
(Excerpts)

5

To *the artist of decadence:* there we have the crucial words. And here my seriousness begins. I am far from looking on guilelessly while this decadent corrupts our health—and music as well. Is Wagner a human being at all? Isn't he rather a sickness? He makes sick whatever he touches—*he has made music sick—*

A typical decadent who has a sense of necessity in his corrupted taste, who claims it as a higher taste, who knows how to get his corruption accepted as law, as progress, as fulfillment.

And he is not resisted. His seductive force increases tremendously, smoke clouds of incense surround him, the misunderstandings about him parade as "gospel"—he hasn't by any means converted only the *poor in spirit.*

I feel the urge to open the windows a little. Air! More air!—[1]

That people in Germany should deceive themselves about Wagner does not surprise me. The opposite would surprise me. The Germans have constructed a Wagner for themselves whom they can revere: they have never been psychologists; their gratitude consists in misunderstanding. But that people in Paris, too, deceive themselves about Wagner, though there they are hardly anything anymore except psychologists! And in St. Petersburg, where they guess things that aren't guessed even in Paris! How closely related Wagner must be to the whole of European decadence to avoid being experienced by them as a decadent. He belongs to it: he is its protagonist, its greatest name.—One honors oneself when raising him to the clouds.

For that one does not resist him, this itself is a sign of decadence. The instincts are weakened. What one ought to shun is found attractive. One puts to one's lips what drives one yet faster into the abyss.

[1] *Luft! Mehr Luft!* Goethe's last words are said to have been: *Licht! Mehr Licht!* "Light! More light!" (trans.).

Is an example desired? One only need observe the regimen that those suffering from anemia or gout or diabetes prescribe for themselves. Definition of a vegetarian: one who requires a corroborant diet. To sense that what is harmful is harmful, to be *able* to forbid oneself something harmful, is a sign of youth and vitality. The exhausted are *attracted* by what is harmful: the vegetarian by vegetables. Sickness itself can be a stimulant to life: only one has to be healthy enough for this stimulant.

Wagner increases exhaustion: that is why he attracts the weak and exhausted. Oh, the rattlesnake-happiness of the old master when he always saw precisely "the little children" coming unto him!

I place this perspective at the outset: Wagner's art is sick. The problems he presents on the stage—all of them problems of hysterics—the convulsive nature of his affects, his overexcited sensibility, his taste that required ever stronger spices, his instability which he dressed up as principles, not least of all the choice of his heroes and heroines—consider them as physiological types (a pathological gallery)!—all of this taken together represents a profile of sickness that permits no further doubt. *Wagner est une névrose.*[2] Perhaps nothing is better known today, at least nothing has been better studied, than the Protean character of degeneration that here conceals itself in the chrysalis of art and artist. Our physicians and physiologists confront their most interesting case in Wagner, at least a very complete case. Precisely because nothing is more modern than this total sickness, this lateness and overexcitement of the nervous mechanism, Wagner is *the modern artist par excellence*, the Cagliostro of modernity. In his art all that the modern world requires most urgently is mixed in the most seductive manner: the three great *stimulantia* of the exhausted—the *brutal*, the *artificial*, and the *innocent* (idiotic).

Wagner represents a great corruption of music. He has guessed that it is a means to excite weary nerves—and with that he has made music sick. His inventiveness is not inconsiderable in the art of goading again those who are weariest, calling back into life those who are half dead. He is a master of hypnotic tricks, he manages to throw down the strongest like bulls. Wagner's *success*—his success with nerves and consequently women—has turned the whole world of ambitious musicians into disciples of his secret art. And not only the ambitious, the *clever*, too.— Only sick music makes money today; our big theaters subsist on Wagner.

* * * * *

7

Enough! Enough! My cheerful strokes, I fear, may have revealed sinister reality all too clearly—the picture of a decay of art, a decay of the

[2]"Wagner is a neurosis" (trans.).

artists as well. The latter, the decay of a character, could perhaps find preliminary expression in this formula: the musician now becomes an actor, his art develops more and more as a talent to *lie*. I shall have an opportunity (in a chapter of my main work, entitled "Toward a Physiology of Art"[3]) to show in more detail how this over-all change of art into histrionics is no less an expression of physiological degeneration (more precisely, a form of hystericism) than every single corruption and infirmity of the art inaugurated by Wagner: for example, the visual restlessness which requires one continually to change one's position. One doesn't understand a thing about Wagner as long as one finds in him merely an arbitrary play of nature, a whim, an accident. He was no "fragmentary," "hapless," or "contradictory" genius, as people have said. Wagner was something *perfect*, a typical decadent in whom there is no trace of "free will" and in whom every feature is necessary. If anything in Wagner is interesting it is the logic with which a physiological defect makes move upon move and takes step upon step as practice and procedure, as innovation in principles, as a crisis in taste.

For the present I merely dwell on the question of *style*. —What is the sign of every *literary decadence?* That life no longer dwells in the whole. The word becomes sovereign and leaps out of the sentence, the sentence reaches out and obscures the meaning of the page, the page gains life at the expense of the whole—the whole is no longer a whole. But this is the simile of every style of *decadence:* every time, the anarchy of atoms, disgregation of the will, "freedom of the individual," to use moral terms— expanded into a political theory, "*equal* rights for all." Life, *equal* vitality, the vibration and exuberance of life pushed back into the smallest forms; the rest, *poor* in life. Everywhere paralysis, arduousness, torpidity *or* hostility and chaos: both more and more obvious the higher one ascends in forms of organization. The whole no longer lives at all: it is composite, calculated, artificial, and artifact. —

* * * * *

POSTSCRIPT

The seriousness of the last words permits me to publish at this point a few sentences from an as yet unprinted essay. At least they should leave no room for doubt about my seriousness in this matter. This essay bears the title: *The Price We Are Paying for Wagner.*

---

[3]Nietzsche here refers to a book he was planning at this time to write (and for which he presumably was gathering notes on such topics as this one), which he elsewhere says he planned to call *The Will to Power: Attempt at a Revaluation of All Values* (cf. *On the Genealogy of Morals*, III: 27). He never completed it; but the collection of notes from his notebooks of this period published after his death under the title *The Will to Power* contains some of the material on this topic that he may have intended to use in the planned chapter to which he here refers.

One pays heavily for being one of Wagner's disciples. An obscure recognition of this fact is still encountered even today. Wagner's success, his
triumph, has not eradicated it. But formerly it was strong, it was terrible,
it was like a dark hatred—through almost three quarters of Wagner's life.
The resistance he encountered among us Germans cannot be esteemed
too highly or honored too much. He was resisted like a sickness—not with
reasons—one does not refute a sickness—but with inhibition, mistrust,
vexation, and disgust, with a gloomy seriousness, as if he represented
some great creeping danger. Our honored aestheticians have compromised
themselves when, coming from three schools of German philosophy, they
waged an absurd war against Wagner's principles with "if" and "for"—as
if he cared about principles, even his own!
    The Germans themselves had reason enough in their instincts to rule
out any "if" and "for." An instinct is weakened when it rationalizes itself:
for *by* rationalizing itself it weakens itself. If there are any signs that, in
spite of the total character of European decadence, the German character
still possesses some degree of health, some instinctive sense for what is
harmful and dangerous, this *dim* resistance to Wagner is the sign I should
like least to see underestimated. It does us honor, it even permits a hope:
France would not have that much health any more. The Germans, the
delayers par excellence in history, are today the most retarded civilized nation
in Europe: this has its advantages—by the same token they are relatively
the *youngest*. [. . .]
    One pays heavily for being one of Wagner's disciples. Let us take the
measure of this discipleship by considering its cultural effects. Whom did
his movement bring to the fore? What did it breed and multiply?—Above
all, the presumption of the layman, the art-idiot. That kind now organizes
associations, wants its "taste" to prevail, wants to play the judge even in
rebus musicis et musicantibus. Secondly: an ever growing indifference
against all severe, noble, conscientious training in the service of art; all
this is to be replaced by faith in genius or, to speak plainly, by impudent
dilettantism (—the formula for this is to be found in the *Meistersinger*).
Thirdly and worst of all: *theatrocracy*—the nonsense of a faith in the *pre-
cedence* of the theater, in the right of the theater to *lord it* over the arts, over
art.—[. . .]
    His last work is in this respect his greatest masterpiece. In the art of
seduction, *Parsifal* will always retain its rank—as *the stroke of genius* in
seduction. —I admire this work; I wish I had written it myself; failing that,
I understand it.—Wagner never had better inspirations than in the end.
Here the cunning in his alliance of beauty and sickness goes so far that,
as it were, it casts a shadow over Wagner's earlier art—which now seems
too bright, too healthy. Do you understand this? Health, brightness having the effect of a shadow? almost of an *objection?*—To such an extent have
we become *pure fools*. —Never was there a greater master in dim, hieratic

aromas—never was there a man equally expert in all *small* infinities, all that trembles and is effusive, all the feminisms from the *idioticon*[4] of happiness!—Drink, O my friends, the philters of this art! Nowhere will you find a more agreeable way of enervating your spirit, of forgetting your manhood under a rosebush.—Ah, this old magician! This Klingsor[5] of all Klingsors! How he thus wages war against *us!* us, the free spirits! How he indulges every cowardice of the modern soul with the tones of magic maidens!—Never before has there been such a *deadly hatred* of the search for knowledge!—One has to be a cynic in order not to be seduced here; one has to be able to bite in order not to worship here. Well then, you old seducer, the cynic warns you—*cave canem.*—[6]

* * * * *

---

[4]A dictionary confined to a particular dialect (trans.).
[5]Magician in *Parsifal* (trans.).
[6]Beware of the dog! Greek *kynikos* (cynical) means literally "doglike" (trans.).

Twilight of the Idols (1888)
(Excerpts)

THE PROBLEM OF SOCRATES

1

Concerning life, the wisest men of all ages have judged alike: *it is no good*. Always and everywhere one has heard the same sound from their mouths—a sound full of doubt, full of melancholy, full of weariness of life, full of resistance to life. Even Socrates said, as he died: "To live—that means to be sick a long time: I owe Asclepius the Savior a rooster." Even Socrates was tired of it. What does that evidence? What does it evince? Formerly one would have said (—oh, it has been said, and loud enough, and especially by our pessimists): "At least something of all this must be true! The consensus of the sages evidences the truth." Shall we still talk like that today? *May* we? "At least something must be *sick* here," *we* retort. These wisest men of all ages—they should first be scrutinized closely. Were they all perhaps shaky on their legs? late? tottery? decadents? Could it be that wisdom appears on earth as a raven, inspired by a little whiff of carrion?

2

This irreverent thought that the great sages are *types of decline* first occurred to me precisely in a case where it is most strongly opposed by both scholarly and unscholarly prejudice: I recognized Socrates and Plato to be symptoms of degeneration, tools of the Greek dissolution, pseudo-Greek, anti-Greek (*Birth of Tragedy*, 1872). The consensus of the sages—I comprehended this ever more clearly—proves least of all that they were right in what they agreed on: it shows rather that they themselves, these wisest men, agreed in some *physiological* respect, and hence adopted the same negative attitude to life—*had to* adopt it. Judgments, judgments of value, concerning life, for it or against it, can, in the end, never be true:

they have value only as symptoms, they are worthy of consideration only as symptoms; in themselves such judgments are stupidities. One must by all means stretch out one's fingers and make the attempt to grasp this amazing finesse, *that the value of life cannot be estimated.* Not by the living, for they are an interested party, even a bone of contention, and not judges; not by the dead, for a different reason. For a philosopher to see a problem in the value of life is thus an objection to him, a question mark concerning his wisdom, an un-wisdom. Indeed? All these great wise men—they were not only decadents but not wise at all?

*   *   *   *   *

11

I have given to understand how it was that Socrates fascinated: he seemed to be a physician, a savior. Is it necessary to go on to demonstrate the error in his faith in "rationality at any price"? It is a self-deception on the part of philosophers and moralists if they believe that they are extricating themselves from decadence when they merely wage war against it. Extrication lies beyond their strength: what they choose as a means, as salvation, is itself but another expression of decadence; they change its expression, but they do not get rid of decadence itself. Socrates was a misunderstanding; *the whole improvement-morality, including the Christian, was a misunderstanding.* The most blinding daylight; rationality at any price; life, bright, cold, cautious, conscious, without instinct, in opposition to the instincts—all this too was a mere disease, another disease, and by no means a return to "virtue," to "health," to happiness. To *have* to fight the instincts—that is the formula of decadence: as long as life is *ascending,* happiness equals instinct.

*   *   *   *   *

"REASON" IN PHILOSOPHY

1

You ask me which of the philosophers' traits are really idiosyncrasies? For example, their lack of historical sense, their hatred of the very idea of becoming, their Egypticism. They think that they show their *respect* for a subject when they de-historicize it, *sub specie aeterni*[1]—when they turn it into a mummy. All that philosophers have handled for thousands of years

[1]Under the aspect of eternity.

have been concept-mummies; nothing real escaped their grasp alive. When these honorable idolators of concepts worship something, they kill it and stuff it; they threaten the life of everything they worship. Death, change, old age, as well as procreation and growth, are to their minds objections—even refutations. Whatever has being does not become; whatever becomes does not have being. Now they all believe, desperately even, in what has being. But since they never grasp it, they seek for reasons why it is kept from them. "There must be mere appearance, there must be some deception which prevents us from perceiving that which has being: where is the deceiver?"

"We have found him," they cry ecstatically; "it is the senses! These senses, which are so immoral in other ways too, deceive us concerning the *true* world. Moral: let us free ourselves from the deception of the senses, from becoming, from history, from lies; history is nothing but faith in the senses, faith in lies. Moral: let us say No to all who have faith in the senses, to all the rest of mankind; they are all 'mob.' Let us be philosophers! Let us be mummies! Let us represent monotono-theism by adopting the expression of a gravedigger! And above all, away with the body, this wretched *idée fixe*[2] of the senses, disfigured by all the fallacies of logic, refuted, even impossible, although it is impudent enough to behave as if it were real!"

2

With the highest respect, I except the name of *Heraclitus*. When the rest of the philosophic folk rejected the testimony of the senses because they showed multiplicity and change, he rejected their testimony because they showed things as if they had permanence and unity. Heraclitus too did the senses an injustice. They lie neither in the way the Eleatics believed, nor as he believed—they do not lie at all. What we *make* of their testimony, that alone introduces lies; for example, the lie of unity, the lie of thinghood, of substance, of permanence. "Reason" is the cause of our falsification of the testimony of the senses. Insofar as the senses show becoming, passing away, and change, they do not lie. But Heraclitus will remain eternally right with his assertion that being is an empty fiction. The "apparent" world is the only one: the "true" world is merely added by a lie.

3

And what magnificent instruments of observation we possess in our senses! This nose, for example, of which no philosopher has yet spoken

[2]Fixed idea.

with reverence and gratitude, is actually the most delicate instrument so far at our disposal: it is able to detect minimal differences of motion which even a spectroscope cannot detect. Today we possess science precisely to the extent to which we have decided to *accept* the testimony of the senses—to the extent to which we sharpen them further, arm them, and have learned to think them through. The rest is miscarriage and not-yet-science—in other words, metaphysics, theology, psychology, epistemology—or formal science, a doctrine of signs, such as logic and that applied logic which is called mathematics. In them reality is not encountered at all, not even as a problem—no more than the question of the value of such a sign-convention as logic.

4

The other idiosyncrasy of the philosophers is no less dangerous; it consists in confusing the last and the first. They place that which comes at the end—unfortunately! for it ought not to come at all!—namely, the "highest concepts," which means the most general, the emptiest concepts, the last smoke of evaporating reality, in the beginning, *as* the beginning. This again is nothing but their way of showing reverence: the higher *may* not grow out of the lower, may not have grown at all. Moral: whatever is of the first rank must be *causa sui*.[3] Origin out of something else is considered an objection, a questioning of value. All the highest values are of the first rank; all the highest concepts, that which has being, the unconditional, the good, the true, the perfect—all these cannot have become and must therefore be *causa sui*. All these, moreover, cannot be unlike each other or in contradiction to each other. Thus they arrive at their stupendous concept, "God." That which is last, thinnest, and emptiest is put first, as *the* cause, as *ens realissimum*.[4] Why did mankind have to take seriously the brain afflictions of sick web-spinners? They have paid dearly for it!

5

At long last, let us contrast the very different manner in which we conceive the problem of error and appearance. (I say "we" for politeness' sake.) Formerly, alteration, change, any becoming at all, were taken as proof of mere appearance, as an indication that there must be something which led us astray. Today, conversely, precisely insofar as the prejudice of reason forces us to posit unity, identity, permanence, substance, cause,

---

[3]Cause of itself.
[4]The most real being.

thinghood, being, we see ourselves somehow caught in error, compelled into error. So certain are we, on the basis of rigorous examination, that this is where the error lies.

It is no different in this case than with the movement of the sun: there our eye is the constant advocate of error, here it is our language. In its origin language belongs in the age of the most rudimentary form of psychology. We enter a realm of crude fetishism when we summon before consciousness the basic presuppositions of the metaphysics of language, in plain talk, the presuppositions of reason. Everywhere it sees a doer and doing; it believes in will as *the* cause; it believes in the ego, in the ego as being, in the ego as substance, and it projects this faith in the ego-substance upon all things—only thereby does it first *create* the concept of "thing." Everywhere "being" is projected by thought, pushed underneath, as the cause; the concept of being follows, and is a derivative of, the concept of ego. In the beginning there is that great calamity of an error that the will is something which is effective, that will is a capacity. Today we know that it is only a word.

Very much later, in a world which was in a thousand ways more enlightened, philosophers, to their great surprise, became aware of the sureness, the subjective certainty, in our handling of the categories of reason: they concluded that these categories could not be derived from anything empirical—for everything empirical plainly contradicted them. Whence, then, were they derived?

And in India, as in Greece, the same mistake was made: "We must once have been at home in a higher world (instead of a very much lower one, which would have been the truth); we must have been divine, *for* we have reason!" Indeed, nothing has yet possessed a more naïve power of persuasion than the error concerning being, as it has been formulated by the Eleatics, for example. After all, every word we say and every sentence speak in its favor. Even the opponents of the Eleatics still succumbed to the seduction of their concept of being: Democritus, among others, when he invented his atom. "Reason" in language—oh, what an old deceptive female she is! I am afraid we are not rid of God because we still have faith in grammar.

6

It will be appreciated if I condense so essential and so new an insight into four theses. In that way I facilitate comprehension; in that way I provoke contradiction.

First proposition. The reasons for which "this" world has been characterized as "apparent" are the very reasons which indicate its reality; any other kind of reality is absolutely indemonstrable.

Second proposition. The criteria which have been bestowed on the "true being" of things are the criteria of not-being, of *naught;* the "true world" has been constructed out of contradiction to the actual world: indeed an apparent world, insofar as it is merely a moral-optical illusion.

Third proposition. To invent fables about a world "other" than this one has no meaning at all, unless an instinct of slander, detraction, and suspicion against life has gained the upper hand in us: in that case, we avenge ourselves against life with a phantasmagoria of "another," a "better" life.

Fourth proposition. Any distinction between a "true" and an "apparent" world—whether in the Christian manner or in the manner of Kant (in the end, an underhanded Christian)—is only a suggestion of decadence, a symptom of the *decline of life.* That the artist esteems appearance higher than reality is no objection to this proposition. For "appearance" in this case means reality *once more,* only by way of selection, reinforcement, and correction. The tragic artist is no pessimist: he is precisely the one who says Yes to everything questionable, even to the terrible—he is *Dionysian.*

HOW THE "TRUE WORLD" FINALLY BECAME A FABLE
The History of an Error

1. The true world—attainable for the sage, the pious, the virtuous man; he lives in it, *he is it.*

(The oldest form of the idea, relatively sensible, simple, and persuasive. A circumlocution for the sentence, "I, Plato, *am* the truth.")

2. The true world—unattainable for now, but promised for the sage, the pious, the virtuous man ("for the sinner who repents").

(Progress of the idea: it becomes more subtle, insidious, incomprehensible—*it becomes female,* it becomes Christian.)

3. The true world—unattainable, indemonstrable, unpromisable; but the very thought of it—a consolation, an obligation, an imperative.

(At bottom, the old sun, but seen through mist and skepticism. The idea has become elusive, pale, Nordic, Königsbergian.[5])

4. The true world—unattainable? At any rate, unattained. And being unattained, also *unknown.* Consequently, not consoling, redeeming, or obligating: how could something unknown obligate us?

(Gray morning. The first yawn of reason. The cockcrow of positivism.)

5. The "true" world—an idea which is no longer good for anything, not even obligating—an idea which has become useless and superfluous—*consequently,* a refuted idea: let us abolish it!

(Bright day; breakfast; return of *bon sens*[6] and cheerfulness; Plato's embarrassed blush; pandemonium of all free spirits.)

[5]I.e., Kantian.
[6]Good sense.

6. The true world—we have abolished. What world has remained? The apparent one perhaps? But no! *With the true world we have also abolished the apparent one.*

(Noon; moment of the briefest shadow; end of the longest error; high point of humanity; INCIPIT ZARATHUSTRA.[7])

MORALITY AS ANTI-NATURE

1

All passions have a phase when they are merely disastrous, when they drag down their victim with the weight of stupidity—and a later, very much later phase when they wed the spirit, when they "spiritualize" themselves. Formerly, in view of the element of stupidity in passion, war was declared on passion itself, its destruction was plotted; all the old moral monsters are agreed on this: *il faut tuer les passions.*[8] The most famous formula for this is to be found in the New Testament, in that Sermon on the Mount, where, incidentally, things are by no means looked at from a height. There it is said, for example, with particular reference to sexuality: "If thy eye offend thee, pluck it out." Fortunately, no Christian acts in accordance with this precept. *Destroying* the passions and cravings, merely as a preventive measure against their stupidity and the unpleasant consequences of this stupidity—today this itself strikes us as merely another acute form of stupidity. We no longer admire dentists who "pluck out" teeth so that they will not hurt any more.

To be fair, it should be admitted, however, that on the ground out of which Christianity grew, the concept of the *"spiritualization* of passion" could never have been formed. After all the first church, as is well known, fought *against* the "intelligent" in favor of the "poor in spirit." How could one expect from it an intelligent war against passion? The church fights passion with excision in every sense: its practice, its "cure," is *castratism.* It never asks: "How can one spiritualize, beautify, deify a craving?" It has at all times laid the stress of discipline on extirpation (of sensuality, of pride, of the lust to rule, of avarice, of vengefulness). But an attack on the roots of passion means an attack on the roots of life: the practice of the church is *hostile to life.*

*   *   *   *   *

[7]Zarathustra begins.
[8]"One must kill the passions."

4

I reduce a principle to a formula. Every naturalism in morality—that is, every healthy morality—is dominated by an instinct of life; some commandment of life is fulfilled by a determinate canon of "shalt" and "shalt not"; some inhibition and hostile element on the path of life is thus removed. *Anti-natural* morality—that is, almost every morality which has so far been taught, revered, and preached—turns, conversely, *against* the instincts of life: it is *condemnation* of these instincts, now secret, now outspoken and impudent. When it says, "God looks at the heart," it says No to both the lowest and the highest desires of life, and posits God as the *enemy of life*. The saint in whom God delights is the ideal eunuch. Life has come to an end where the "kingdom of God" begins.

5

Once one has comprehended the outrage of such a revolt against life as has become almost sacrosanct in Christian morality, one has, fortunately, also comprehended something else: the futility, apparentness, absurdity, and *mendaciousness* of such a revolt. A condemnation of life by the living remains in the end a mere symptom of a certain kind of life: the question whether it is justified or unjustified is not even raised thereby. One would require a position *outside* of life, and yet have to know it as well as one, as many, as all who have lived it, in order to be permitted even to touch the problem of the *value* of life: reasons enough to comprehend that this problem is for us an unapproachable problem. When we speak of values, we speak with the inspiration, with the way of looking at things, which is part of life: life itself forces us to posit values; life itself values through us when we posit values. From this it follows that even that anti-natural morality which conceives of God as the counter-concept and condemnation of life is only a value judgment of life—but of what life? of what kind of life? I have already given the answer: of declining, weakened, weary, condemned life. Morality, as it has so far been understood—as it has in the end been formulated once more by Schopenhauer, as "negation of the will to life"—is the very *instinct of decadence*, which makes an imperative of itself. It says: *"Perish!"* It is a condemnation pronounced by the condemned.

* * * * *

THE FOUR GREAT ERRORS

1

The error of confusing cause and effect. There is no more dangerous error than that of mistaking the effect for the cause: I call it the real corruption of reason. Yet this error belongs among the most ancient and recent habits of mankind: it is even hallowed among us and goes by the name of "religion" or "morality." Every single sentence which religion and morality formulate contains it; priests and legislators of moral codes are the originators of this corruption of reason. [. . .]

*   *   *   *   *

3

The error of a false causality. People have believed at all times that they knew what a cause is; but whence did we take our knowledge—or more precisely, our faith that we had such knowledge? From the realm of the famous "inner facts," of which not a single one has so far proved to be factual. We believed ourselves to be causal in the act of willing: we thought that here at least we caught causality in the act. Nor did one doubt that all the antecedents of an act, its causes, were to be sought in consciousness and would be found there once sought—as "motives": else one would not have been free and responsible for it. Finally, who would have denied that a thought is caused? that the ego causes the thought?

Of these three "inward facts" which seem to guarantee causality, the first and most persuasive is that of the will as cause. The conception of a consciousness ("spirit") as a cause, and later also that of the ego as cause (the "subject"), are only afterbirths: first the causality of the will was firmly accepted as given, as *empirical.*

Meanwhile we have thought better of it. Today we no longer believe a word of all this. The "inner world" is full of phantoms and will-o'-the-wisps: the will is one of them. The will no longer moves anything, hence does not explain anything either—it merely accompanies events; it can also be absent. The so-called *motive:* another error. Merely a surface phenomenon of consciousness, something alongside the deed that is more likely to cover up the antecedents of the deeds than to represent them. And as for the *ego!* That has become a fable, a fiction, a play on words: it has altogether ceased to think, feel, or will!

What follows from this? There are no mental causes at all. The whole of the allegedly empirical evidence for that has gone to the devil. That is what follows! And what a fine abuse we had perpetrated with this "empirical evidence"; we *created* the world on this basis as a world of causes, a world of will, a world of spirits. The most ancient and enduring psychology was at work here and did not do anything else: all that happened was considered a doing, all doing the effect of a will; the world became to it a multiplicity of doers; a doer (a "subject") was slipped under all that happened. It was out of himself that man projected his three "inner facts"—that in which he believed most firmly, the will, the spirit, the ego. He even took the concept of being from the concept of the ego; he posited "things" as "being," in his image, in accordance with his concept of the ego as a cause. Small wonder that later he always found in things only that *which he had put into them*. The thing itself, to say it once more, the concept of thing is a mere reflex of the faith in the ego as cause. And even your atom, my dear mechanists and physicists—how much error, how much rudimentary psychology is still residual in your atom! Not to mention the "thing-in-itself," the *horrendum pudendum*[9] of the metaphysicians! The error of the spirit as cause mistaken for reality! And made the very measure of reality! And called God!

4

The error of imaginary causes. To begin with dreams: *ex post facto*, a cause is slipped under a particular sensation (for example, one following a far-off cannon shot)—often a whole little novel in which the dreamer turns up as the protagonist. The sensation endures meanwhile in a kind of resonance: it waits, as it were, until the causal instinct permits it to step into the foreground—now no longer as a chance occurrence, but as "meaning." The cannon shot appears in a *causal* mode, in an apparent reversal of time. What is really later, the motivation, is experienced first—often with a hundred details which pass like lightning—and the shot *follows*. What has happened? The representations which were *produced* by a certain state have been misunderstood as its causes.

In fact, we do the same thing when awake. Most of our general feelings—every kind of inhibition, pressure, tension, and explosion in the play and counterplay of our organs, and particularly the state of the *nervus sympathicus*[10]—excite our causal instinct: we want to have a reason for feeling this way or that—for feeling bad or for feeling good. We are never satisfied merely to state the fact that we feel this way or that: we admit this fact only—become conscious of it only—when we have furnished some kind of motivation. Memory, which swings into action in such cases, unknown to us, brings up earlier states of the same kind, together with the causal

[9]Horrible shame.
[10]Sympathetic nervous system.

interpretations associated with them—not their real causes. The faith, to be sure, that such representations, such accompanying conscious processes, are the causes, is also brought forth by memory. Thus originates a habitual acceptance of a particular causal interpretation, which, as a matter of fact, inhibits any investigation into the real cause—even precludes it.

*   *   *   *   *

7

The error of free will. Today we no longer have any pity for the concept of "free will": we know only too well what it really is—the foulest of all theologians' artifices, aimed at making mankind "responsible" in their sense, that is, *dependent upon them.* Here I simply supply the psychology of all "making responsible."

Wherever responsibilities are sought, it is usually the instinct of wanting to judge and punish which is at work. Becoming has been deprived of its innocence when any being-such-and-such is traced back to will, to purposes, to acts of responsibility: the doctrine of the will has been invented essentially for the purpose of punishment, that is, because one wanted to impute guilt. The entire old psychology, the psychology of will, was conditioned by the fact that its originators, the priests at the head of ancient communities, wanted to create for themselves the right to punish—or wanted to create this right for God. Men were considered "free" so that they might be judged and punished—so that they might become *guilty:* consequently, every act had to be considered as willed, and the origin of every act had to be considered as lying within the consciousness (and thus the most fundamental counterfeit *in psychologicis*[11] was made the principle of psychology itself).

Today, as we have entered into the reverse movement and we immoralists are trying with all our strength to take the concept of guilt and the concept of punishment out of the world again, and to cleanse psychology, history, nature, and social institutions and sanctions of them, there is in our eyes no more radical opposition than that of the theologians, who continue with the concept of a "moral world-order" to infect the innocence of becoming by means of "punishment" and "guilt." Christianity is a metaphysics of the hangman.

8

What alone can be *our* doctrine? That no one *gives* man his qualities—neither God, nor society, nor his parents and ancestors, nor he himself.

---

[11]The most fundamental psychological counterfeit.

(The nonsense of the last idea was taught as "intelligible freedom" by Kant—perhaps by Plato already.) No one is responsible for man's being there at all, for his being such-and-such, or for his being in these circumstances or in this environment. The fatality of his essence is not to be disentangled from the fatality of all that has been and will be. Man is not the effect of some special purpose, of a will, and end; nor is he the object of an attempt to attain an "ideal of humanity" or an "ideal of happiness" or an "ideal of morality." It is absurd to wish to devolve one's essence on some end or other. We have invented the concept of "end": in reality there is no end.

One is necessary, one is a piece of fatefulness, one belongs to the whole, one is in the whole; there is nothing which could judge, measure, compare, or sentence our being, for that would mean judging, measuring, comparing, or sentencing the whole. But there is nothing besides the whole. That nobody is held responsible any longer, that the mode of being may not be traced back to a *causa prima*,[12] that the world does not form a unity either as a sensorium or as "spirit"—that alone is the great liberation; with this alone is the innocence of becoming restored. The concept of "God" was until now the greatest objection to existence. We deny God, we deny the responsibility in God: only thereby do we redeem the world.

THE "IMPROVERS" OF MANKIND

1

My demand upon the philosopher is known, that he take his stand *beyond* good and evil and leave the illusion of moral judgment *beneath* himself. This demand follows from an insight which I was the first to formulate: that *there are altogether no moral facts*. Moral judgments agree with religious ones in believing in realities which are no realities. Morality is merely an interpretation of certain phenomena—more precisely, a mis-interpretation. Moral judgments, like religious ones, belong to a stage of ignorance at which the very concept of the real and the distinction between what is real and imaginary, are still lacking; thus "truth," at this stage, designates all sorts of things which we today call "imaginings." Moral judgments are therefore never to be taken literally: so understood, they always contain mere absurdity. Semeiotically, however, they remain invaluable: they reveal, at least for those who know, the most valuable realities of cultures and inwardnesses which did not know enough to "understand" themselves. Morality is mere sign language, mere symptomatology: one must know what it is all about to be able to profit from it.

*　　*　　*　　*　　*

[12]First cause.

SKIRMISHES OF AN UNTIMELY MAN

36

Morality for physicians. The sick man is a parasite of society. In a certain state it is indecent to live longer. To go on vegetating in cowardly dependence on physicians and machinations, after the meaning of life, the right to life, has been lost, that ought to prompt a profound contempt in society. The physicians, in turn, would have to be the mediators of this contempt—not prescriptions, but every day a new dose of nausea with their patients. To create a new responsibility, that of the physician, for all cases in which the highest interest of life, of ascending life, demands the most inconsiderate pushing down and aside of degenerating life—for example, for the right of procreation, for the right to be born, for the right to live.

To die proudly when it is no longer possible to live proudly. Death freely chosen, death at the right time, brightly and cheerfully accomplished amid children and witnesses: then a real farewell is still possible, as the one who is taking leave is still there; also a real estimate of what one has achieved and what one has wished, drawing the sum of one's life—all in opposition to the wretched and revolting comedy that Christianity has made of the hour of death. One should never forget that Christianity has exploited the weakness of the dying for a rape of the conscience; and the manner of death itself, for value judgments about man and the past.

Here it is important to defy all the cowardices of prejudice and to establish, above all, the real, that is, the physiological, appreciation of so-called *natural* death—which is in the end also "unnatural," a kind of suicide. One never perishes through anybody but oneself. But usually it is death under the most contemptible conditions, an unfree death, death *not* at the right time, a coward's death. From love of *life*, one should desire a different death: free, conscious, without accident, without ambush.

Finally, some advice for our dear pessimists and other decadents. It is not in our hands to prevent our birth; but we can correct this mistake—for in some cases it is a mistake. When one does away with oneself, one does the most estimable thing possible: one almost earns the right to live. Society—what am I saying?—life itself derives more advantage from this than from any "life" of renunciation, anemia, and other virtues: one has liberated the others from one's sight; one has liberated life from an objection. Pessimism, *pur, vert,* is proved only by the self-refutation of our dear pessimists: one must advance a step further in its logic and not only negate life with "will and representation," as Schopenhauer did—one must first of all negate Schopenhauer. [. . .]

37

[. . .] Ages must be measured by their positive strength—and then that lavishly squandering and fatal age of the Renaissance appears as the last *great* age; and we moderns, with our anxious self-solicitude and neighbor-love, with our virtues of work, modesty, legality, and scientism— accumulating, economic, machinelike—appear as a *weak* age. Our virtues are conditional on, are provoked by, our weaknesses. "Equality," as a certain factual increase in similarity, which merely finds expression in the theory of "equal rights," is an essential feature of decline. The cleavage between man and man, status and status, the plurality of types, the will to be oneself, to stand out—what I call the *pathos of distance*, that is characteristic of every strong age. The strength to withstand tension, the width of the tensions between extremes, becomes ever smaller today; finally, the extremes themselves become blurred to the point of similarity. [. . .]

38

My conception of freedom. The value of a thing sometimes does not lie in that which one attains by it, but in what one pays for it—what it costs us. I shall give an example. Liberal institutions cease to be liberal as soon as they are attained: later on, there are no worse and no more thorough injurers of freedom than liberal institutions. Their effects are known well enough: they undermine the will to power; they level mountain and valley, and call that morality; they make men small, cowardly, and hedonistic—every time it is the herd animal that triumphs with them. Liberalism: in other words, herd-animalization.

These same institutions produce quite different effects while they are still being fought for; then they really promote freedom in a powerful way. On closer inspection, it is war that produces these effects, the war *for* liberal institutions, which, as a war, permits illiberal instincts to continue. And war educates for freedom. For what is freedom? That one has the will to assume responsibility for oneself. That one maintains the distance which separates us. That one becomes more indifferent to difficulties, hardships, privation, even to life itself. That one is prepared to sacrifice human beings for one's cause, not excluding oneself. Freedom means that the manly instincts which delight in war and victory dominate over other instincts, for example, over those of "pleasure." The human being who has *become free*—and how much more the *spirit* who has become free—spits on the contemptible type of well-being dreamed of by shopkeepers, Christians, cows, females, Englishmen, and other democrats. The free man is a *warrior*.

How is freedom measured in individuals and peoples? According to the resistance which must be overcome, according to the exertion required, to remain on top. The highest type of free men should be sought where the highest resistance is constantly overcome: five steps from tyranny, close to the threshold of the danger of servitude. This is true psychologically if by "tyrants" are meant inexorable and fearful instincts that provoke the maximum of authority and discipline against themselves; most beautiful type: Julius Caesar. This is true politically too; one need only go through history. The peoples who had some value, *attained* some value, never attained it under liberal institutions: it was great danger that made something of them that merits respect. Danger alone acquaints us with our own resources, our virtues, our armor and weapons, our *spirit*, and *forces* us to be strong. *First* principle: one must need to be strong—otherwise one will never become strong.

Those large hothouses for the strong—for the strongest kind of human being that has so far been known—the aristocratic commonwealths of the type of Rome or Venice, understood freedom exactly in the sense in which I understand it: as something one has or does *not* have, something one *wants*, something one *conquers*.

*   *   *   *   *

44

My conception of genius. Great men, like great ages, are explosives in which a tremendous force is stored up; their precondition is always, historically and physiologically, that for a long time much has been gathered, stored up, saved up, and conserved for them—that there has been no explosion for a long time. Once the tension in the mass has become too great, then the most accidental stimulus suffices to summon into the world the "genius," the "deed," the great destiny. What does the environment matter then, or the age, or the "spirit of the age," or "public opinion"!

Take the case of Napoleon. Revolutionary France, and even more, prerevolutionary France, would have brought forth the opposite type; in fact, it did. Because Napoleon was *different*, the heir of a stronger, older, more ancient civilization than the one which was then perishing in France, he became the master there, he *was* the only master. Great men are necessary, the age in which they appear is accidental; that they almost always become masters over their age is only because they are stronger, because they are older, because for a longer time much was gathered for them. The relationship between a genius and his age is like that between strong and weak, or between old and young: the age is relatively always much younger, thinner, more immature, less assured, more childish.

That in France today they think quite differently on this subject (in Germany too, but that does not matter), that the milieu theory, which is truly a neurotic's theory, has become sacrosanct and almost scientific and has found adherents even among physiologists—that "smells bad" and arouses sad reflections. It is no different in England, but that will not grieve anybody. For the English there are only two ways of coming to terms with the genius and the "great man": either democratically in the manner of Buckle or religiously in the manner of Carlyle.

The danger that lies in great men and ages is extraordinary; exhaustion of every kind, sterility, follow in their wake. The great human being is a finale; the great age—the Renaissance, for example—is a finale. The genius, in work and deed, is necessarily a squanderer: that he squanders himself, that is his greatness. The instinct of self-preservation is suspended, as it were; the overpowering pressure of outflowing forces forbids him any such care or caution. People call this "self-sacrifice" and praise his "heroism," his indifference to his own well-being, his devotion to an idea, a great cause, a fatherland: without exception, misunderstandings. He flows out, he overflows, he uses himself up, he does not spare himself—and this is a calamitous, involuntary fatality, no less than a river's flooding the land. Yet, because much is owed to such explosives, much has also been given them in return: for example, a kind of higher morality. After all, that is the way of human gratitude: it *misunderstands* its benefactors.

*   *   *   *   *

48

Progress in my sense. I too speak of a "return to nature," although it is really not a going back but an *ascent*—up into the high, free, even terrible nature and naturalness where great tasks are something one plays with, one *may* play with. To put it metaphorically: Napoleon was a piece of "return to nature," as I understand the phrase (for example, *in rebus tacticis;* even more, as military men know, in matters of strategy).

But Rousseau—to what did he really want to return? Rousseau, this first modern man, idealist and rabble in one person—one who needed moral "dignity" to be able to stand his own sight, sick with unbridled vanity and unbridled self-contempt. This miscarriage, couched on the threshold of modern times, also wanted a "return to nature"; to ask this once more, to what did Rousseau want to return? I still hate Rousseau in the French Revolution: it is the world-historical expression of this duality of idealist and rabble. The bloody farce which became an aspect of the Revolution, its "immorality," are of little concern to me: what I hate is its Rousseauan *morality*—the so-called "truths" of the Revolution through which it still works and attracts everything shallow and mediocre. The doctrine of equality! There is no more poisonous poison anywhere: for it seems to be preached by justice itself, whereas it really is the termination of justice.

"Equal to the equal, unequal to the unequal"—*that* would be the true slogan of justice; and also its corollary: "Never make equal what is unequal." That this doctrine of equality was surrounded by such gruesome and bloody events, that has given this "modern idea" par excellence a kind of glory and fiery aura so that the Revolution as a *spectacle* has seduced even the noblest spirits. In the end, that is no reason for respecting it any more. I see only one man who experienced it as it must be experienced, with *nausea*—Goethe.

49

Goethe—not a German event, but a European one: a magnificent attempt to overcome the eighteenth century by a return to nature, by an *ascent* to the naturalness of the Renaissance—a kind of self-overcoming on the part of that century. He bore its strongest instincts within himself: the sensibility, the idolatry of nature, the anti-historic, the idealistic, the unreal and revolutionary (the latter being merely a form of the unreal). He sought help from history, natural science, antiquity, and also Spinoza, but, above all, from practical activity; he surrounded himself with limited horizons; he did not retire from life but put himself into the midst of it; he was not fainthearted but took as much as possible upon himself, over himself, into himself. What he wanted was *totality;* he fought the mutual extraneousness of reason, senses, feeling, and will (preached with the most abhorrent scholasticism by *Kant,* the antipode of Goethe); he disciplined himself to wholeness, he *created* himself.

In the middle of an age with an unreal outlook, Goethe was a convinced realist: he said Yes to everything that was related to him in this respect—and he had no greater experience than that *ens realissimum* called Napoleon. Goethe conceived a human being who would be strong, highly educated, skillful in all bodily matters, self-controlled, reverent toward himself, and who might dare to afford the whole range and wealth of being natural, being strong enough for such freedom; the man of tolerance, not from weakness but from strength, because he knows how to use to his advantage, even that from which the average nature would perish; the man for whom there is no longer anything that is forbidden—unless it be *weakness,* whether called vice or virtue.

Such a spirit who has *become free* stands amid the cosmos with a joyous and trusting fatalism, in the *faith* that only the particular is loathsome, and that all is redeemed and affirmed in the whole—*he does not negate any more.* Such a faith, however, is the highest of all possible faiths: I have baptized it with the name of *Dionysus.*

*   *   *   *   *

The Antichrist:
Attempt at a Critique of Christianity

Revaluation of All Values, First Book[1] (1888) (*Excerpts*)

1

Let us face ourselves. We are Hyperboreans[2]; we know very well how far off we live. "Neither by land nor by sea will you find the way to the Hyperboreans"—Pindar already knew this about us. Beyond the north, ice, and death—*our* life, *our* happiness. We have discovered happiness, we know the way, we have found the exit out of the labyrinth of thousands of years. Who *else* has found it? Modern man perhaps? "I have got lost; I am everything that has got lost," sighs modern man.

This modernity was our sickness: lazy peace, cowardly compromise, the whole virtuous uncleanliness of the modern Yes and No. This tolerance and *largeur* of the heart, which "forgives" all because it "understands" all, is *sirocco* for us. Rather live in the ice than among modern virtues and other south winds!

We were intrepid enough, we spared neither ourselves nor others; but for a long time we did not know where to turn with our intrepidity. We became gloomy, we were called fatalists. *Our fatum*[3]—the abundance, the tension, the damming of strength. We thirsted for lightning and deeds and were most remote from the happiness of the weakling, "resignation." In our atmosphere was a thunderstorm; the nature we are became dark—*for we saw no way*. Formula for our happiness: a Yes, a No, a straight line, a goal.

2

What is good? Everything that heightens the feeling of power in man, the will to power, power itself.

---

[1] *The Antichrist* was conceived by Nietzsche as the "First Book" of a more comprehensive work to which he gave the general title *Revaluation of All Values*. It was intended to have three more such parts or "Books"; but this is the only one he completed before his collapse.

[2] The name of a mythical people conceived by the ancient Greeks to live at a great distance to the north from them, far beyond the world as it was known and familiar to them.

[3] Fate.

What is bad? Everything that is born of weakness.

What is happiness? The feeling that power is *growing*, that resistance is overcome.

Not contentedness but more power; not peace but war; not virtue but fitness (Renaissance virtue, *virtù*, virtue that is moraline-free[4]).

The weak and the failures shall perish: first principle of *our* love of man. And they shall even be given every possible assistance.

What is more harmful than any vice? Active pity for all the failures and all the weak: Christianity.

3

The problem I thus pose is not what shall succeed mankind in the sequence of living beings (man is an *end*), but what type of man shall be *bred*, shall be *willed*, for being higher in value, worthier of life, more certain of a future.

Even in the past this higher type has appeared often—but as a fortunate accident, as an exception, never as something *willed*. In fact, this has been the type most dreaded—almost *the* dreadful—and from dread the opposite type was willed, bred, and *attained:* the domestic animal, the herd animal, the sick human animal—the Christian.

4

Mankind does *not* represent a development toward something better or stronger or higher in the sense accepted today. "Progress" is merely a modern idea, that is, a false idea. The European of today is vastly inferior in value to the European of the Renaissance: further development is altogether *not* according to any necessity in the direction of elevation, enhancement, or strength.

In another sense, success in individual cases is constantly encountered in the most widely different places and cultures: here we really do find a *higher type*, which is, in relation to mankind as a whole, a kind of overman. Such fortunate accidents of great success have always been possible and *will* perhaps always be possible. And even whole families, tribes, or peoples may occasionally represent such a *bull's-eye*.

5

Christianity should not be beautified and embellished: it has waged deadly war against this higher type of man; it has placed all the basic

---

[4]I.e., free of the influence of the narcotic of morality.

instincts of this type under the ban; and out of these instincts it has distilled evil and the Evil One: the strong man as the typically reprehensible man, the "reprobate." Christianity has sided with all that is weak and base, with all failures; it has made an ideal of whatever *contradicts* the instinct of the strong life to preserve itself; it has corrupted the reason even of those strongest in spirit by teaching men to consider the supreme values of the spirit as something sinful, as something that leads into error—as temptations. The most pitiful example: the corruption of Pascal, who believed in the corruption of his reason through original sin when it had in fact been corrupted only by his Christianity.

6

It is a painful, horrible spectacle that has dawned on me: I have drawn back the curtain from the *corruption* of man. In my mouth, this word is at least free from one suspicion: that it might involve a moral accusation of man. It is meant—let me emphasize this once more—*moraline-free*. So much so that I experience this corruption most strongly precisely where men have so far aspired most deliberately to "virtue" and "godliness." I understand corruption, as you will guess, in the sense of decadence: it is my contention that all the values in which mankind now sums up its supreme desiderata are *decadence-values*.

I call an animal, a species, or an individual corrupt when it loses its instincts, when it chooses, when it prefers, what is disadvantageous for it. A history of "lofty sentiments," of the "ideals of mankind"—and it is possible that I shall have to write it—would almost explain too *why* man is so corrupt. Life itself is to my mind the instinct for growth, for durability, for an accumulation of forces, for *power:* where the will to power is lacking there is decline. It is my contention that all the supreme values of mankind *lack* this will—that the values which are symptomatic of decline, *nihilistic* values, are lording it under the holiest names.

7

Christianity is called the religion of *pity.* Pity stands opposed to the tonic emotions which heighten our vitality: it has a depressing effect. We are deprived of strength when we feel pity. That loss of strength which suffering as such inflicts on life is still further increased and multiplied by pity. Pity makes suffering contagious. Under certain circumstances, it may engender a total loss of life and vitality out of all proportion to the magnitude of the cause (as in the case of the death of the Nazarene). That is the first consideration, but there is a more important one.

Suppose we measure pity by the value of the reactions it usually produces; then its perilous nature appears in an even brighter light. Quite in

general, pity crosses the law of development, which is the law of *selection*.
It preserves what is ripe for destruction; it defends those who have been
disinherited and condemned by life; and by the abundance of the failures
of all kinds which it keeps alive, it gives life itself a gloomy and questionable aspect.

Some have dared to call pity a virtue (in every *noble* ethic it is considered
a weakness); and as if this were not enough, it has been made *the* virtue,
the basis and source of all virtues. To be sure—and one should always
keep this in mind—this was done by a philosophy that was nihilistic and
had inscribed the *negation of life* upon its shield. Schopenhauer was consistent enough: pity negates life and renders it *more deserving of negation*.

Pity is the *practice* of nihilism. To repeat: this depressive and contagious
instinct crosses those instincts which aim at the preservation of life and at
the enhancement of its value. It multiplies misery and conserves all that
is miserable, and is thus a prime instrument of the advancement of decadence: pity persuades men to *nothingness!* Of course, one does not say
"nothingness" but "beyond" or "God," or "*true* life," or Nirvana, salvation, blessedness.

This innocent rhetoric from the realm of the religious-moral idiosyncrasy appears much less innocent as soon as we realize which tendency it
is that here shrouds itself in sublime words: *hostility against life*. Schopenhauer was hostile to life; therefore pity became a virtue for him.

Aristotle, as is well known, considered pity a pathological and dangerous condition, which one would be well advised to attack now and then
with a purge: he understood tragedy as a purge. From the standpoint of
the instinct of life, a remedy certainly seems necessary for such a pathological and dangerous accumulation of pity as is represented by the case
of Schopenhauer (and unfortunately by our entire literary and artistic
decadence from St. Petersburg to Paris, from Tolstoi to Wagner)—to
puncture it and make it *burst*.

In our whole unhealthy modernity there is nothing more unhealthy
than Christian pity. To be physicians *here*, to be inexorable *here*, to wield
the scalpel *here*—that is *our* part, that is *our* love of man, that is how *we* are
philosophers, we *Hyperboreans*.

8

It is necessary to say whom we consider our antithesis: it is the theologians and whatever has theologians' blood in its veins—and that in-
cludes our whole philosophy.

Whoever has seen this catastrophe at close range or, better yet, been
subjected to it and almost perished of it, will no longer consider it a joking
matter (the free-thinking of our honorable natural scientists and physiol-

ogists is, to my mind, a joke: they lack passion in these matters, they do not suffer them as their passion and martyrdom). This poisoning is much more extensive than is generally supposed: I have found the theologians' instinctive arrogance wherever anyone today considers himself an "idealist"—wherever a right is assumed, on the basis of some higher origin, to look at reality from a superior and foreign vantage point.

The idealist, exactly like the priest, holds all the great concepts in his hand (and not only in his hand!); he plays them out with a benevolent contempt for the "understanding," the "senses," "honors," "good living," and "science"; he considers all that *beneath* him, as so many harmful and seductive forces over which "the spirit" hovers in a state of pure for-itselfness—as if humility, chastity, poverty, or, in one word, *holiness*, had not harmed life immeasurably more than any horrors or vices. The pure spirit is the pure lie.

As long as the priest is considered a *higher* type of man—this *professional* negator, slanderer, and poisoner of life—there is no answer to the question: what *is* truth? For truth has been stood on its head when the conscious advocate of nothingness and negation is accepted as the representative of "truth."

9

Against this theologians' instinct I wage war: I have found its traces everywhere. Whoever has theologians' blood in his veins, sees all things in a distorted and dishonest perspective to begin with. The pathos which develops out of this condition calls itself *faith:* closing one's eyes to oneself once and for all, lest one suffer the sight of incurable falsehood. This faulty perspective on all things is elevated into a morality, a virtue, a holiness; the good conscience is tied to faulty vision; and no *other* perspective is conceded any further value once one's own has been made sacrosanct with the names of "God," "redemption," and "eternity." I have dug up the theologians' instinct everywhere: it is the most widespread, really *subterranean*, form of falsehood found on earth.

Whatever a theologian feels to be true *must* be false: this is almost a criterion of truth. His most basic instinct of self-preservation forbids him to respect reality at any point or even to let it get a word in. Wherever the theologians' instinct extends, *value judgments* have been stood on their heads and the concepts of "true" and "false" are of necessity reversed: whatever is most harmful to life is called "true"; whatever elevates it, enhances, affirms, justifies it, and makes it triumphant, is called "false." When theologians reach out for *power* through the "conscience" of princes (*or* of peoples), we need never doubt what really happens at bottom: the will to the end, the *nihilistic* will, wants power.

10

Among Germans I am immediately understood when I say that philosophy has been corrupted by theologians' blood. The Protestant parson is the grandfather of German philosophy; Protestantism itself, its *peccatum originale*.[5] Definition of Protestantism: the partial paralysis of Christianity—*and* of reason. One need merely say "Tübingen Seminary" to understand what German philosophy is at bottom: an *insidious* theology. The Swabians are the best liars in Germany: they lie innocently.

Why was Kant's appearance greeted with jubilation among German scholars—of whom three-fourths are the sons of parsons and teachers—and whence came the German conviction, echoed even today, that a change for the *better* began with Kant? The theologians' instinct in the German scholars divined *what* had once again been made possible. A path had been found on which one could sneak back to the old ideal. The conception of a "*true world*," the conception of morality as the *essence* of the world (these two most malignant errors of all time!), were once again, thanks to a wily and shrewd skepticism, if not provable, at least no longer *refutable*. Reason, the *right* of reason, does not extend that far. Reality had been reduced to mere "appearance," and a mendaciously fabricated world, the world of being, was honored as reality. Kant's success is merely a theologians' success: like Luther, like Leibniz, Kant was one more clog for German honesty, which was none too steady in the first place.

11

One more word against Kant as a *moralist*. A virtue must be *our own* invention, *our* most necessary self-expression and self-defense: any other kind of virtue is merely a danger. Whatever is not a condition of our life *harms* it: a virtue that is prompted solely by a feeling of respect for the concept of "virtue," as Kant would have it, is harmful. "Virtue," "duty," the "good in itself," the good which is impersonal and universally valid—chimeras and expressions of decline, of the final exhaustion of life, of the Chinese phase of Königsberg. The fundamental laws of self-preservation and growth demand the opposite—that everyone invent *his own* virtue, *his own* categorical imperative. A people perishes when it confuses *its* duty with duty in general. Nothing ruins us more profoundly, more intimately, than every "impersonal" duty, every sacrifice to the Moloch of abstraction. How could one fail to feel how Kant's categorical imperative endangered life itself! The theologians' instinct alone protected it!

---

[5]Original sin.

An action demanded by the instinct of life is proved to be *right* by the pleasure that accompanies it; yet this nihilist with his Christian dogmatic entrails considered pleasure an *objection*. What could destroy us more quickly than working, thinking, and feeling without any inner necessity, without any deeply personal choice, without *pleasure*—as an automaton of "duty"? This is the very recipe for decadence, even for idiocy. Kant became an idiot. And this man was a contemporary of *Goethe!* This catastrophic spider was considered the *German* philosopher—he still is!

I beware of saying what I think of the Germans. Did not Kant find in the French Revolution the transition from the inorganic form of the state to the *organic?* Did he not ask himself whether there was any event which could be explained only in terms of a moral disposition of mankind, an event which would *demonstrate* once and for all the "tendency of mankind toward the good"? Kant's answer: "This is the Revolution." The instinct which errs without fail, *anti-nature* as instinct, German decadence as philosophy—*that is Kant!*

*   *   *   *   *

13

Let us not underestimate this: *we ourselves*, we free spirits, are nothing less than a "revaluation of all values," an *incarnate* declaration of war and triumph over all the ancient conceptions of "true" and "untrue." The most valuable insights are discovered last; but the most valuable insights are the *methods*. *All* the methods, *all* the presuppositions of our current scientific outlook, were opposed for thousands of years with the most profound contempt. For their sake, men were excluded from the company of "decent" people and considered "enemies of God," despisers of the truth, and "possessed." Anyone with a scientific bent was a Chandala. [. . .]

14

We have learned differently. We have become more modest in every way. We no longer derive man from "the spirit" or "the deity"; we have placed him back among the animals. We consider him the strongest animal because he is the most cunning: his spirituality is a consequence of this. On the other hand, we oppose the vanity that would raise its head again here too—as if man had been the great hidden purpose of the evolution of the animals. Man is by no means the crown of creation: every living being stands beside him on the same level of perfection. And even this is saying too much: relatively speaking, man is the most bungled of all the animals, the sickliest, and not one has strayed more dangerously from its instincts. But for all that, he is of course the most *interesting*.

As regards the animals, Descartes was the first to have dared, with admirable boldness, to understand the animal as *machina*[6]: the whole of our physiology endeavors to prove this claim. And we are consistent enough not to except man, as Descartes still did: our knowledge of man today goes just as far as we understand him mechanistically. Formerly man was given a "free will" as his dowry from a higher order: today we have taken his will away altogether, in the sense that we no longer admit the will as a faculty. The old word "will" now serves only to denote a result- ant, a kind of individual reaction, which follows necessarily upon a num- ber of partly contradictory, partly harmonious stimuli: the will no longer "acts" or "moves."

Formerly, the proof of man's higher origin, of his divinity, was found in his consciousness, in his "spirit." To become *perfect*, he was advised to draw in his senses, turtle fashion, to cease all intercourse with earthly things, to shed his mortal shroud: then his essence would remain, the "pure spirit." Here too we have reconsidered: the development of con- sciousness, the "spirit," is for us nothing less than the symptom of a relative imperfection of the organism; it means trying, groping, blundering—an exertion which uses up an unnecessary amount of nervous energy. We deny that anything can be done perfectly as long as it is still done consciously. The "pure spirit" is a pure stupidity: if we subtract the nervous system and the senses—the "mortal shroud"—*then we miscalculate*—that is all!

15

In Christianity neither morality nor religion has even a single point of contact with reality. Nothing but imaginary *causes* ("God," "soul," "ego," "spirit," "free will"—for that matter, "unfree will"), nothing but imaginary *effects* ("sin," "redemption," "grace," "punishment," "forgiveness of sins"). Intercourse between imaginary *beings* ("God," "spirits," "souls"); an imagi- nary *natural* science (anthropocentric; no trace of any concept of natural causes); an imaginary *psychology* (nothing but self-misunderstandings, inter- pretations of agreeable or disagreeable general feelings—for example, of the states of the *nervus sympathicus*[7]—with the aid of the sign language of the religio-moral idiosyncrasy: "repentance," "pangs of conscience," "tempta-

[6]Machines.
[7]Sympathetic nervous system.

tion by the devil," "the presence of God"); an imaginary *teleology* ("the kingdom of God," "the Last Judgment," "eternal life").

This *world of pure fiction* is vastly inferior to the world of dreams insofar as the latter *mirrors* reality, whereas the former falsifies, devalues, and negates reality. Once the concept of "nature" had been invented as the opposite of "God," "natural" had to become a synonym of "reprehensible": this whole world of fiction is rooted in *hatred* of the natural (of reality!); it is the expression of a profound vexation at the sight of reality.

But this explains everything. Who alone has good reason to lie his way out of reality? He who suffers from it. But to suffer from reality is to be a piece of reality that has come to grief. The preponderance of feelings of displeasure over feelings of pleasure is the cause of this fictitious morality and religion; but such a preponderance provides the very formula for decadence.

* * * * *

18

The Christian conception of God—God as god of the sick, God as a spider, God as spirit—is one of the most corrupt conceptions of the divine ever attained on earth. It may even represent the low-water mark in the descending development of divine types. God degenerated into the *contradiction* of life, instead of being its transfiguration and eternal Yes! God as the declaration of war against life, against nature, against the will to live! God—the formula for every slander against "this world," for every lie about the "beyond"! God—the deification of nothingness, the will to nothingness pronounced holy!

* * * * *

43

When one places life's center of gravity not in life but in the "beyond"—*in nothingness*—one deprives life of its center of gravity altogether. The great lie of personal immortality destroys all reason, everything natural in the instincts—whatever in the instincts is beneficent and life-promoting or guarantees a future now arouses mistrust. To live so, that there is no longer any *sense* in living, *that* now becomes the "sense" of life. Why communal sense, why any further gratitude for descent and ancestors, why cooperate, trust, promote, and envisage any common welfare? Just as many "temptations," just as many distractions from the "right path"—"*one* thing is needful."

That everyone as an "immortal soul" has equal rank with everyone else, that in the totality of living beings the "salvation" of *every* single individual may claim eternal significance, that little prigs and three-quarter-madmen may have the conceit that the laws of nature are constantly broken for their sakes—such an intensification of every kind of selfishness into the infinite, into the *impertinent,* cannot be branded with too much contempt. And yet Christianity owes its triumph to this miserable flattery of personal vanity: it was precisely all the failures, all the rebellious-minded, all the less favored, the whole scum and refuse of humanity who were thus won over to it. The "salvation of the soul"—in plain language: "the world revolves around *me."*

The poison of the doctrine of "equal rights for all"—it was Christianity that spread it most fundamentally. Out of the most secret nooks of bad instincts, Christianity has waged war unto death against all sense of respect and feeling of distance between man and man, that is to say, against the *presupposition* of every elevation, of every growth of culture; out of the *ressentiment* of the masses it forged its chief weapon against *us,* against all that is noble, gay, high-minded on earth, against our happiness on earth. "Immortality" conceded to every Peter and Paul has so far been the greatest, the most malignant, attempt to assassinate *noble* humanity.

And let us not underestimate the calamity which crept out of Christianity into politics. Today nobody has the courage any longer for privileges, for masters' rights, for a sense of respect for oneself and one's peers—for a *pathos of distance.* Our politics is sick from this lack of courage.

The aristocratic outlook was undermined from the deepest underworld through the lie of the equality of souls; and if faith in the "prerogative of the majority" makes and *will make* revolutions—it is Christianity, beyond a doubt, it is *Christian* value judgments, that every revolution simply translates into blood and crime. Christianity is a rebellion of everything that crawls on the ground against that which has *height:* the evangel of the "lowly" *makes* low.

At this point I do not let myself off without a psychology of "faith," of "believers"—precisely for the benefit of "believers," as is fitting. If today there is no lack of people who do not know in what way it is *indecent* to "believe"—*or* a sign of decadence, of broken will to life—tomorrow they will already know it. My voice reaches even the hard of hearing.

Unless I have heard wrong, it seems that among Christians there is a kind of criterion of truth that is called the "proof of strength." "Faith makes blessed: *hence* it is true." Here one might object first that it is precisely the making blessed which is not proved but merely *promised:* blessedness tied to the condition of "faith"—one *shall* become blessed *because* one believes. But whether what the priest promises the believer in fact occurs in a "beyond" which is not subject to any test—how is that proved? The alleged "proof of strength" is thus at bottom merely another faith, namely, that the effect one expects from faith will not fail to appear. In a formula: "I believe that faith makes blessed; consequently it is true." But with this we are already at the end. This "consequently" would be absurdity itself as the criterion of truth.

But let us suppose, with some leniency, that it was proved that faith makes blessed (not merely desired, not merely promised by the somewhat suspicious mouth of a priest): would blessedness—or more technically speaking, *pleasure*—ever be a proof of truth? This is so far from the case that it almost furnishes a counterproof; in any event, the greatest suspicion of a "truth" should arise when feelings of pleasure enter the discussion of the question "What is true?" The proof of "pleasure" is a proof of "pleasure"—nothing else: how in all the world could it be established that true judgments should give greater delight than false ones and, according to a pre-established harmony, should necessarily be followed by agreeable feelings?

The experience of all severe, of all profoundly inclined, spirits teaches the *opposite*. At every step one has to wrestle for truth; one has had to surrender for it almost everything to which the heart, to which our love, our trust in life, cling otherwise. That requires greatness of soul: the service of truth is the hardest service. What does it mean, after all, to have *integrity* in matters of the spirit? That one is severe against one's heart, that one despises "beautiful sentiments," that one makes of every Yes and No a matter of conscience. Faith makes blessed: consequently it lies.

* * * * *

57

[. . .] A right is a privilege. A man's state of being is his privilege. Let us not underestimate the privileges of the *mediocre*. As one climbs *higher*, life becomes ever harder; the coldness increases, responsibility increases.

A high culture is a pyramid: it can stand only on a broad base; its first presupposition is a strong and soundly consolidated mediocrity. Handicraft, trade, agriculture, *science*, the greatest part of art, the whole quintessence of *professional* activity, to sum it up, is compatible only with a mediocre amount of ability and ambition; that sort of thing would be out of place among exceptions; the instinct here required would contradict both aristocratism and anarchism. To be a public utility, a wheel, a function, for that one must be destined by nature: it is *not* society, it is the only kind of *happiness* of which the great majority are capable that makes intelligent machines of them. For the mediocre, to be mediocre is their happiness; mastery of one thing, specialization—a natural instinct.

It would be completely unworthy of a more profound spirit to consider mediocrity as such an objection. In fact, it is the very *first* necessity if there are to be exceptions: a high culture depends on it. When the exceptional human being treats the mediocre more tenderly than himself and his peers, this is not mere politeness of the heart—it is simply his *duty*.

Whom do I hate most among the rabble of today? The socialist rabble, the chandala apostles, who undermine the instinct, the pleasure, the worker's sense of satisfaction with his small existence—who make him envious, who teach him revenge. The source of wrong is never unequal rights but the claim of "equal" rights.

What is *bad?* But I have said this already: all that is born of weakness, of envy, of *revenge*. The anarchist and the Christian have the same origin.

*   *   *   *   *

62

With this I am at the end and I pronounce my judgment. I *condemn* Christianity. I raise against the Christian church the most terrible of all accusations that any accuser ever uttered. It is to me the highest of all conceivable corruptions. It has had the will to the last corruption that is even possible. The Christian church has left nothing untouched by its corruption; it has turned every value into an un-value, every truth into a lie, every integrity into a vileness of the soul. Let anyone dare to speak to me of its "humanitarian" blessings! To *abolish* any distress ran counter to its deepest advantages: it lived on distress, it *created* distress to eternalize *itself*.

The worm of sin, for example: with this distress the church first enriched mankind. The "equality of souls before God," this falsehood, this *pretext* for the rancor of all the base-minded, this explosive of a concept which eventually became revolution, modern idea, and the principle of decline of the whole order of society—is *Christian* dynamite. "Humanitarian" blessings of Christianity! To breed out of *humanitas*[8] a self-contradiction, an art of self-violation, a will to lie at any price, a repugnance, a contempt for all good and honest instincts! Those are some of the blessings of Christianity!

Parasitism as the *only* practice of the church; with its ideal of anemia, of "holiness," draining all blood, all love, all hope for life; the beyond as the will to negate every reality; the cross as the mark of recognition for the most subterranean conspiracy that ever existed—against health, beauty, whatever has turned out well, courage, spirit, *graciousness* of the soul, *against life itself*.

This eternal indictment of Christianity I will write on all walls, wherever there are walls—I have letters to make even the blind see.

[8]Humanity.

I call Christianity the one great curse, the one great innermost corruption, the one great instinct of revenge, for which no means is poisonous, stealthy, subterranean, *small* enough—I call it the one immortal blemish of mankind.

And time is reckoned from the *dies nefastus*[9] with which this calamity began—after the *first* day of Christianity! *Why not rather after its last day? After today?* Revaluation of all values!

[9]Day of birth.

VIII
Nietzsche on Nietzsche
(1886–1888)

The Prefaces of 1886–1888
Complete

The Birth of Tragedy
Human, All Too Human
   (Volumes One and Two)
Daybreak
The Gay Science (or Joyful Wisdom)
On the Genealogy of Morals
The Case of Wagner
Twilight of the Idols
The Antichrist
Ecce Homo

Excerpts from

Ecce Homo:
How One Becomes What One Is

TOWARD A SELF-INTERPRETATION

Introduction

Like so many authors, Nietzsche began by supposing that his books would speak for themselves, or at any rate would be understood by those kindred spirits he sought to reach. He knew that many would misunderstand him; but he persisted for more than a decade in the hope that his books would find discerning readers who would comprehend and appreciate what he was seeking to say and do in them. Not surprisingly, however, this most unconventional of philosophical writers met with one disappointment after another on this score, culminating in the dismaying silence with which the publication of his *Zarathustra* was met.

Becoming increasingly convinced that he was ahead of his time, Nietzsche then tried a new tack, in a different style, in his "Prelude to a Philosophy of the Future" *(Beyond Good and Evil)*, with a preface setting the stage for it. Another part of his response was to devote a good deal of the following year (1886) to writing a series of retrospective prefaces to new editions of most of his pre-*Zarathustra* books. In these remarkable prefaces he sought to provide his readers with guidance to their comprehension, while reflecting on their concerns, significance, and places in his intellectual and philosophical development, from the vantage point he had attained.

Nietzsche continued this new practice of providing his books with prefaces through the brief remainder of his productive life. They may have been to little avail in his attempt to make himself understood at the time; but they are of considerable value to those who seek to make sense of him today. Indeed, their worth in this respect surpasses that of *Ecce Homo* ("Behold the Man"), in which he took a last look back on all of his books, as well as on his life and work more generally. The period these prefaces span (1886–1888) is that of his philosophical maturity, during much of which the Nietzsche who addresses us was able to be more calmly reflective than he was during the final frenzied months preceding his collapse, when *Ecce Homo* was written.

The interest and significance of these prefaces for understanding Nietzsche's philosophy should be clear. He would not have supplied them if he did not believe that they would be helpful to readers trying to figure out what he is up to. His post-*Zarathustra* writings themselves show this kind of philosophy in practice. If those works are read (or reread) with these prefaces in mind, they reveal a kind of philosopher and a kind of philosophical activity rather different from the portraits often given of them by both his admirers and his detractors.

It seems appropriate, therefore, to conclude this volume with the complete texts of all of these prefaces of 1886–1888, along with selections from *Ecce Homo*. (The single earlier preface he wrote, to *Beyond Good and Evil*, appears in Section IV of this volume.) Because these prefaces have never been published in one volume in English, they are seldom read together. Indeed, some of them are seldom read at all. But they should be read by anyone who seeks to understand Nietzsche. And when read together, they make very interesting and illuminating reading, shedding considerable light on how he came to understand his own philosophical development and his efforts in these culminating years of his active life.

The selections with which this volume concludes, fittingly enough, are from *Ecce Homo*—the last book Nietzsche completed, and very nearly the last thing he wrote. He finished his revisions of it only a few weeks before his physical and mental collapse. (It was not published until 1908, nearly twenty years later.) It is in effect his last will and testament.

Commentators differ greatly in their assessment of this extraordinary book. Some consider it to be a masterpiece of great significance, while others regard it as little more than the megalomaniac ravings of one already overtaken by madness. Even its title—the words spoken by Pontius Pilate (according to the Gospel of John, 19:5) when Jesus was brought before him—is enough to make one wonder; and a good deal of what Nietzsche says about himself in it does seem to show signs of his impending insanity. Yet there also is much indicative of a brilliant mind still at work, blazing up one last time before it was extinguished.

The interpretation of himself, his writings, and his significance that Nietzsche offers in *Ecce Homo* certainly should not be accepted at face value; but neither should it be simply dismissed and ignored. When read together with his prefaces of 1886–1888, it contributes to the understanding of how he came to see the development of his thinking and its legacy for the future. As we seek to come to terms with his thought today, these texts must be among our points of departure.

The Prefaces of 1886–1888
(*Complete*)

The Birth of Tragedy
A Critical Backward Glance (1886)

1

Whatever it was that gave rise to this problematical work, of one thing there can be no question: the issue it propounded must have been supremely important and attractive as well as very personal to its author. The times in which (in spite of which) it was composed bear out that fact. The date is 1870–71, the turbulent period of the Franco-Prussian war. While the thunder of the Battle of Wörth was rumbling over Europe, a lover of subtleties and conundrums—father-to-be of this book—sat down in an alpine recess, much bemused and bedeviled (which is to say, both engrossed and detached) to pen the substance of that odd and forbidding work for which the following pages shall now serve as a belated preface or postscript. A few weeks later he could be discovered beneath the walls of Metz, still wrestling with the question mark which he had put after the alleged "serenity" of the Greeks and of Greek art; until at last, in that month of deep suspense which saw the emergence of peace at Versailles, he too made peace with himself and, still recovering from an ailment brought home from the field, gave final shape to *The Birth of Tragedy from the Spirit of Music.*

—From *music?* Music and tragedy? The Greeks and dramatic music? The Greeks and pessimistic art? The Greeks: this most beautiful and accomplished, this thoroughly sane, universally envied species of man— was it conceivable that they, of all people, should have stood in need of tragedy—or, indeed, of art? Greek art: how did it function, how *could* it?

By now the reader will have come to suspect where I had put my mark of interrogation. The question was one of value, the value placed on existence. Is pessimism inevitably a sign of decadence, warp, weakened instincts, as it was once with the ancient Hindus, as it is now with us modern Europeans? Or is there such a thing as a *strong* pessimism? A penchant of the mind for what is hard, terrible, evil, dubious in existence, arising from a plethora of health, plenitude of being? Could it be, perhaps, that the very feeling of superabundance created its own kind of suffering:

a temerity of penetration, hankering for the enemy (the worth-while enemy) so as to prove its strength, to experience at last what it means to fear something? What meaning did the tragic myth have for the Greeks during the period of their greatest power and courage? And what of the Dionysiac spirit, so tremendous in its implications? What of the tragedy that grew out of that spirit?

Or one might look at it the other way round. Those agencies that had proved fatal to tragedy: Socratic ethics, dialectics, the temperance and cheerfulness of the pure scholar—couldn't these, rather than their opposites, be viewed as symptoms of decline, fatigue, distemper, of instincts caught in anarchic dissolution? Or the "Greek serenity" of the later period as, simply, the glow of a sun about to set? Or the Epicurean animus against pessimism merely as the sort of precaution a suffering man might use? And as for "disinterested inquiry," so-called: what, in the last analysis, did inquiry come to when judged as a symptom of the life process? What were we to say of the end (or, worse, of the beginning) of all inquiry? Might it be that the "inquiring mind" was simply the human mind terrified by pessimism and trying to escape from it, a clever bulwark erected against the truth? Something craven and false, if one wanted to be moral about it? Or, if one preferred to put it amorally, a dodge? Had this perhaps been your secret, great Socrates? Most secretive of ironists, had *this* been your deepest irony?

2

I was then beginning to take hold of a dangerous problem—taking it by the horns, as it were—not Old Nick himself, perhaps, but something almost as hot to handle: the problem of scholarly investigation. For the first time in history somebody had *come to grips* with scholarship—and what a formidable, perplexing thing it turned out to be! But the book, crystallization of my youthful courage and suspicions, was an impossible book; since the task required fully matured powers it could scarcely be anything else. Built from precocious, purely personal insights, all but incommunicable; conceived in terms of *art* (for the issue of scholarly inquiry cannot be argued on its own terms), this book addressed itself to artists or, rather, to artists with analytical and retrospective leanings: to a special kind of artist who is far to seek and possibly not worth the seeking. It was a book novel in its psychology, brimming with artists' secrets, its background a metaphysics of art; the work of a young man, written with the unstinted courage and melancholy of youth, defiantly independent even in those places where the author was paying homage to revered models. In short, a "first book," also in the worst sense of that term, and one that exhibited, for all the hoariness of its topic, every conceivable fault of adolescence. It was terribly diffuse and full of unpalatable ferment. All the same, if one examines its impact it may certainly be said to have *proved* itself—in the eyes of the few contemporaries who mattered and most signally in the eyes of that great artist, Richard Wagner, whom it addressed as in a dialogue. This fact alone should ensure it a discreet treatment on my part; yet I cannot wholly suppress a feeling of distaste, or strangeness, as I look at it now, after a lapse of sixteen years. I have grown older, to be sure, and a hundred times more exacting, but by no means colder toward the question propounded in that heady work. And the question is still what it was then, how to view scholarship from the vantage of the artist and art from the vantage of life.

3

Once again: as I look at it today my treatise strikes me as quite impossible. It is poorly written, heavy handed, embarrassing. The imagery is both frantic and confused. In spots it is saccharine to the point of effeminacy; the tempo is erratic; it lacks logical nicety and is so sure of its message that it dispenses with any kind of proof. Worse than that, it suspects the very notion of proof, being a book written for initiates, a "music" for men christened in the name of music and held together by special esthetic experiences, a shibboleth for the highbrow confraternity. An arrogant and extravagant book, which from the very first withdrew even more haughtily from the ruck of the intelligentsia than it did from the acknowledged barbarians; and which yet, as its impact has proved, knew then as it does now how to enlist fellow revelers and to tempt them into secret alleys, onto mysterious dancing grounds. Both the curious and the hostile had to admit that here was an unfamiliar voice, the disciple of an unrecognized god, hiding his identity (for the time being) under the skullcap of the scholar, the ponderousness and broad dialectics of the German, the bad manners of the Wagnerite. Here was a mind with odd, anonymous needs; a memory rife with questions, experiences, secrets, all of which had the name *Dionysos* attached to them like a question mark. People would hint suspiciously that there was a sort of maenadic soul in this book, stammering out laborious, arbitrary phrases in an alien tongue—as though the speaker were not quite sure himself whether he preferred speech to silence. And, indeed, this "new soul" should have *sung*, not spoken. What a pity that I could not tell as a poet what demanded to be told! Or at least as a philologist, seeing that even today philologists tend to shy away from this whole area and especially from the fact that the area contains a *problem*, that the Greeks will continue to remain totally obscure, unimaginable beings until we have found an answer to the question, "What is the meaning of the Dionysiac spirit?"

4

How, then, are we to define the "Dionysiac spirit"? In my book I
answered that question with the authority of the adept or disciple. Talking
of the matter today, I would doubtless use more discretion and less eloquence; the origin of Greek tragedy is both too tough and too subtle an
issue to wax eloquent over. One of the cardinal questions here is that of
the Greek attitude to pain. What kind of sensibility did these people
have? Was that sensibility constant, or did it change from generation to
generation? Should we attribute the ever increasing desire of the Greeks
for beauty, in the form of banquets, ritual ceremonies, new cults, to some
fundamental *lack*—a melancholy disposition perhaps or an obsession with
pain? If this interpretation is correct—there are several suggestions in
Pericles' (or Thucydides') great funeral oration which seem to bear it
out—how are we to explain the Greek desire, both prior and contrary to
the first, for ugliness, or the strict commitment of the earlier Greeks to a
pessimistic doctrine? Or their commitment to the tragic myth, image of all
that is awful, evil, perplexing, destructive, ominous in human existence?
What, in short, made the Greek mind turn to tragedy? A sense of euphoria
maybe—sheer exuberance, reckless health, and power? But in that case,
what is the significance, physiologically speaking, of that Dionysiac frenzy
which gave rise to tragedy and comedy alike? Can frenzy be viewed as
something that is *not* a symptom of decay, disorder, overripeness? Is there
such a thing—let alienists answer that question—as a neurosis arising from
health, from the youthful condition of the race? What does the union of
god and goat, expressed in the figure of the satyr, really mean? What was
it that prompted the Greeks to embody the Dionysiac reveler—primary
man—in a shape like that? Turning next to the origin of the tragic chorus:
did those days of superb somatic and psychological health give rise, perhaps, to endemic trances, collective visions, and hallucinations? And are
not these the same Greeks who, signally in the early periods, gave every
evidence of possessing tragic vision: a will to tragedy, profound pessimism? Was it not Plato who credited frenzy with all the superlative blessings of Greece? Contrariwise, was it not precisely during their period of
dissolution and weakness that the Greeks turned to optimism, frivolity,
histrionics; that they began to be mad for logic and rational cosmology;
that they grew at once "gayer" and "more scientific"? Why, is it possible
to assume—in the face of all the up-to-date notions on that subject, in
defiance of all the known prejudices of our democratic age—that the great
optimist-rationalist-utilitarian victory, together with democracy, its political contemporary, was at bottom nothing other than a symptom of declining strength, approaching senility, somatic exhaustion—*it*, and not its
opposite, pessimism? Could it be that Epicurus was an optimist—
precisely because he suffered? . . .

The reader can see now what a heavy pack of questions this book was forced to carry. Let me add here the heaviest question of all, What kind of figure does ethics cut once we decide to view it in the biological perspective?

5

In the preface I addressed to Richard Wagner I claimed that art, rather than ethics, constituted the essential metaphysical activity of man, while in the body of the book I made several suggestive statements to the effect that existence could be justified only in esthetic terms. As a matter of fact, throughout the book I attributed a purely esthetic meaning—whether implied or overt—to all process: a kind of divinity if you like, God as the supreme artist, amoral, recklessly creating and destroying, realizing himself indifferently in whatever he does or undoes, ridding himself by his acts of the embarrassment of his riches and the strain of his internal contradictions. Thus the world was made to appear, at every instant, as a successful *solution* of God's own tensions, as an ever new vision projected by that grand sufferer for whom illusion is the only possible mode of redemption. That whole esthetic metaphysics might be rejected out of hand as so much prattle or rant. Yet in its essential traits it already prefigured that spirit of deep distrust and defiance which, later on, was to resist to the bitter end any moral interpretation of existence whatsoever. It is here that one could find—perhaps for the first time in history—a pessimism situated "beyond good and evil"; a "perversity of stance" of the kind Schopenhauer spent all his life fulminating against; a philosophy which dared place ethics among the phenomena (and so "demote" it)—or, rather, place it not even among the phenomena in the idealistic sense but among the "deceptions." Morality, on this view, became a mere fabrication for purposes of gulling: at best, an artistic fiction; at worst, an outrageous imposture.

The depth of this anti-moral bias may best be gauged by noting the wary and hostile silence I observed on the subject of Christianity—Christianity being the most extravagant set of variations ever produced on the theme of ethics. No doubt, the purely esthetic interpretation and justification of the world I was propounding in those pages placed them at the opposite pole from Christian doctrine, a doctrine entirely moral in purport, using absolute standards: God's absolute truth, for example, which relegates all art to the realm of falsehood and in so doing condemns it. I had always sensed strongly the furious, vindictive hatred of life implicit in that system of ideas and values; and sensed, too, that in order to be consistent with its premises a system of this sort was forced to abominate art. For both art and life depend wholly on the laws of optics,

NIETZSCHE

on perspective and illusion; both, to be blunt, depend on the necessity of error. From the very first, Christianity spelled life loathing itself, and that loathing was simply disguised, tricked out, with notions of an "other" and "better" life. A hatred of the "world," a curse on the affective urges, a fear of beauty and sensuality, a transcendence rigged up to slander mortal existence, a yearning for extinction, cessation of all effort until the great "sabbath of sabbaths"—this whole cluster of distortions, together with the intransigent Christian assertion that nothing counts except moral values, had always struck me as being the most dangerous, most sinister form the will to destruction can take; at all events, as a sign of profound sickness, moroseness, exhaustion, biological etiolation. And since according to ethics (specifically Christian, absolute ethics) life will *always* be in the wrong, it followed quite naturally that one must smother it under a load of contempt and constant negation; must view it as an object not only unworthy of our desire but absolutely worthless in itself.

As for morality, on the other hand, could it be anything but a will to deny life, a secret instinct of destruction, a principle of calumny, a reductive agent—the beginning of the end?—and, for that very reason, the Supreme Danger? Thus it happened that in those days, with this problem book, my vital instincts turned against ethics and founded a radical counterdoctrine, slanted esthetically, to oppose the Christian libel on life. But it still wanted a name. Being a philologist, that is to say a man of *words*, I christened it rather arbitrarily—for who can tell the real name of the Antichrist?—with the name of a Greek god, Dionysos.

6

Have I made it clear what kind of task I proposed myself in this book? What a pity, though, that I did not yet have the courage (or shall I say the immodesty?) to risk a fresh language in keeping with the hazard, the radical novelty of my ideas, that I fumbled along, using terms borrowed from the vocabularies of Kant and Schopenhauer to express value judgments which were in flagrant contradiction to the spirit or taste of these men! Remember what Schopenhauer has to say about tragedy, in the second part of his *World as Will and Idea*. He writes: "The power of transport peculiar to tragedy may be seen to arise from our sudden recognition that life fails to provide any true satisfactions and hence does not deserve our loyalty. Tragedy guides us to the final goal, which is resignation." Dionysos had told me a very different story; his lesson, as I understood it, was anything but defeatist. It certainly is too bad that I had to obscure and spoil Dionysiac hints with formulas borrowed from Schopenhauer, but there is another feature of the book which seems even worse in retrospect: my tendency to sophisticate such insights as I had into the marvelous Greek issue with an alloy of up-to-date matters; my urge to hope where there was nothing left to hope for, all signs pointing unmistakably toward imminent ruin; my foolish prattle, prompted by the latest feats of German music, about the "German temper"—as though that temper had then been on the verge of discovering, or rediscovering, itself! And all this at a time when the German mind, which, not so very long ago, had shown itself capable of European leadership, was definitely ready to relinquish any aspirations of this sort and to effect the transition to mediocrity, democracy, and "modern ideas"—in the pompous guise, to be sure, of empire building. The intervening years have certainly taught me one thing if they have taught me nothing else: to adopt a hopeless and merciless view toward that "German temper," ditto toward German music, which I now recognize for what it really is: a thorough-going romanticism, the least Greek of all art forms and, over and above that, a drug of the worst sort, especially dangerous to a nation given to hard drinking and one that vaunts intellectual ferment for its power both to intoxicate the mind and to befog it. And yet there remains the great Dionysiac question mark, intact, apart from all those rash hopes, those wrong applications to contemporary matters, which tended to spoil my first book; remains even with regard to music. For the question here is (and must continue to be), "What should a music look like which is no longer romantic in inspiration, like the German, but Dionysiac instead?"

7

—But, my dear chap, where on earth are we to find romanticism if not in *your* book? Can that profound hatred of "contemporariness," "actuality," "modern ideas" be carried any farther than you have carried it in your esthetic metaphysics—a metaphysics which would rather believe in nothingness, indeed in the devil himself, than in the here and now? Do we not hear a ground bass of rage and destructive fury growl through all your ear-beguiling contrapuntal art—a fierce hostility to everything that is happening today, an iron will (not far removed from active nihilism) which seems to proclaim, "I'd rather that nothing were true than see *you* triumph and *your* truth?" Listen, you high priest of art and pessimism, to one of your own statements, that eloquent passage full of dragon killer's bravado and ratcatcher's tricks so appealing to innocent ears; listen to it and tell us, aren't we dealing here with the confession of a true romantic of the 1830's, disguised as a pessimist of the 1850's? Can't we hear behind your confession the annunciatory sounds of the usual romantic finale: rupture, collapse, return, and prostration before an *old* faith, before the *old* God. . . . Come now, isn't your pessimistic work itself a piece of anti-Hellenism and romantic moonshine, fit to "befog and intoxicate," a kind

of drug—in fact, a piece of *music*, and German music to boot? Just listen
to this: "Let us imagine a rising generation with undaunted eyes, with a
heroic drive towards the unexplored; let us imagine the bold step of these
St. Georges, their reckless pride as they turn their backs on all the vale-
tudinarian doctrines of optimism, preparing to 'dwell resolutely in the
fullness of being': *would it not be necessary* for the tragic individual of such
a culture, readied by his discipline for every contingency, every terror, to
want as his Helena a novel art of metaphysical solace and to exclaim as
Faust did:

> *And shall not I, by mightiest desire,*
> *In living shape that precious form acquire?*

"Would it not be necessary?"—no, indeed, my romantic fledglings, it
would *not* be necessary. But it is quite possible that things—that you
yourselves—*might* end that way: "metaphysically solaced" despite all your
grueling self-discipline and, as romantics usually do, in the bosom of the
Church. But I would rather have you learn, first, the art of terrestrial[1]
comfort; teach you how to laugh—if, that is, you really insist on remaining
pessimists. And then it may perhaps happen that one fine day you will,
with a peal of laughter, send all metaphysical palliatives packing, metaphysics herself leading the great exodus. Or, to speak in the language of
that Dionysiac monster, Zarathustra:

> Lift up your hearts, my fellows, higher and higher! And the
> legs—you mustn't forget those! Lift up your legs too, accom-
> plished dancers; or, to top it all, stand on your heads!
>
> This crown of the man who knows laughter, this rose-chaplet
> crown: I have placed it on my head, I have consecrated laughter.
> But not a single soul have I found strong enough to join me.
>
> Zarathustra the dancer, the fleet Zarathustra, waving his wings,
> beckoning with his wings to all birds around him, poised for flight,
> casual and cavalier—
>
> Zarathustra the soothsayer, Zarathustra the laughing truthsayer,
> never out of sorts, never *insisting*, lover of leaps and tangents: I
> myself have put on this crown!
>
> This crown of the laughter-loving, this rose-chaplet crown: to
> you, my fellows, do I fling this crown! Laughter I declare to be
> blessed; you who aspire to greatness, learn how to laugh!

Zarathustra
PART IV, "Of Greater Men"

Sils-Maria, Upper Engadine
August 1886

[1] I.e., earthly, this-worldly

Human, All Too Human
Volume One[2]

Preface (1886)

1

I have been told often enough, and always with an expression of great surprise, that all my writings, from the *Birth of Tragedy* to the most recently published *Prelude to a Philosophy of the Future*,[3] have something that distinguishes them and unites them together: they all of them, I have been given to understand, contain snares and nets for unwary birds and in effect a persistent invitation to the overturning of habitual evaluations and valued habits. What? *Everything* only—human, all too human? It is with this sigh that one emerges from my writings, not without a kind of reserve and mistrust even in regard to morality, not a little tempted and emboldened, indeed, for once to play the advocate of the worst things: as though they have perhaps been only the worst slandered? My writings have been called a schooling in suspicion, even more in contempt, but fortunately also in courage, indeed in audacity. And in fact I myself do not believe that anyone has ever before looked into the world with an equally profound degree of suspicion, and not merely as an occasional devil's advocate, but, to speak theologically, just as much as an enemy and indicter of God; and anyone who could divine something of the consequences that lie in that profound suspiciousness, something of the fears and frosts of the isolation to which that unconditional *disparity of view* condemns him who is infected with it, will also understand how often, in an effort to recover from myself, as it were to induce a temporary self-forgetting, I have sought shelter in this or that—in some piece of admiration or enmity or scientificality or frivolity or stupidity; and why, where I could not find what I *needed*, I had artificially to enforce, falsify and invent a suitable fiction for myself (—and what else have poets ever done? and to what end does art exist in the world at all?). What I again and again needed most for my cure and self-restoration, however, was the belief that I was *not* thus isolated, not alone in *seeing* as I did—an enchanted surmising of relatedness and identity in eye and desires, a reposing in a trust of friendship, a blindness in concert with another without suspicion or question-marks, a

---

[2]Nietzsche added prefaces to both volumes of *Human, All Too Human*. The preface to Volume Two follows.

[3]The subtitle of *Beyond Good and Evil*, Nietzsche's most recent book when he wrote this preface.

pleasure in foregrounds, surfaces, things close and closest, in everything possessing colour, skin and apparitionality. Perhaps in this regard I might be reproached with having employed a certain amount of "art," a certain amount of false-coinage: for example, that I knowingly-willfully closed my eyes before Schopenhauer's blind will to morality at a time when I was already sufficiently clearsighted about morality; likewise that I deceived myself over Richard Wagner's incurable romanticism, as though it were a beginning and not an end; likewise over the Greeks, likewise over the Germans and their future—and perhaps a whole long list could be made of such likewises?—Supposing, however, that all this were true and that I was reproached with it with good reason, what do *you* know, what *could* you know, of how much cunning in self-preservation, how much reason and higher safeguarding, is contained in such self-deception—or of how much falsity I shall *require* if I am to continue to permit myself the luxury of *my* truthfulness? . . . Enough, I am still living; and life is, after all, not a product of morality: it *wants* deception, it *lives* on deception . . . but there you are, I am already off again, am I not, and doing what I have always done, old immoralist and bird-catcher that I am—speaking unmorally, extramorally, "beyond good and evil"?—

2

—Thus when I needed to I once also *invented* for myself the "free spirits" to whom this melancholy-valiant book with the title *Human, All Too Human* is dedicated: "free spirits" of this kind do not exist, did not exist—but, as I have said, I had need of them at that time if I was to keep in good spirits while surrounded by ills (sickness, solitude, unfamiliar places, *acedia*, inactivity): as brave companions and familiars with whom one can laugh and chatter when one feels like laughing and chattering, and whom one can send to the Devil when they become tedious—as compensation for the friends I lacked. That free spirits of this kind *could* one day exist, that our Europe *will* have such active and audacious fellows among its sons of tomorrow and the next day, physically present and palpable and not, as in my case, merely phantoms and hermit's phantasmagoria: *I* should wish to be the last to doubt it. I see them already *coming*, slowly, slowly; and perhaps I shall do something to speed their coming if I describe in advance under what vicissitudes, upon what paths, I *see* them coming?—

3

One may conjecture that a spirit in whom the type "free spirit" will one day become ripe and sweet to the point of perfection has had its decisive experience in a *great liberation* and that previously it was all the more a fettered spirit and seemed to be chained for ever to its pillar and corner. What fetters the fastest? What bonds are all but unbreakable? In the case of men of a high and select kind they will be their duties: that reverence proper to youth, that reserve and delicacy before all that is honoured and revered from of old, that gratitude for the soil out of which they have grown, for the hand which led them, for the holy place where they learned to worship—their supreme moments themselves will fetter them the fastest, lay upon them the most enduring obligation. The great liberation comes for those who are thus fettered suddenly, like the shock of an earthquake: the youthful soul is all at once convulsed, torn loose, torn away—it itself does not know what is happening. A drive and impulse rules and masters it like a command; a will and desire awakens to go off, anywhere, at any cost; a vehement dangerous curiosity for an undiscovered world flames and flickers in all its senses. "Better to die than to go on living *here*"—thus responds the imperious voice and temptation: and this "here," this "at home" is everything it had hitherto loved! A sudden terror and suspicion of what it loved, a lightning-bolt of contempt for what it called "duty," a rebellious, arbitrary, volcanically erupting desire for travel, strange places, estrangements, coldness, soberness, frost, a hatred of love, perhaps a desecrating blow and glance *backwards* to where it formerly loved and worshipped, perhaps a hot blush of shame at what it has just done and at the same time an exultation *that* it has done it, a drunken, inwardly exultant shudder which betrays that a victory has been won—a victory? over what? over whom? an enigmatic, questionpacked, questionable victory, but the *first* victory nonetheless: such bad and painful things are part of the history of the great liberation. It is at the same time a sickness that can destroy the man who has it, this first outbreak of strength and will to self-determination, to evaluating on one's own account, this will to *free* will: and how much sickness is expressed in the wild experiments and singularities through which the liberated prisoner now seeks to demonstrate his mastery over things! He prowls cruelly around with an unslaked lasciviousness; what he captures has to expiate the perilous tension of his pride; what excites him he tears apart. With a wicked laugh he turns round whatever he finds veiled and through some sense of shame or other spared and pampered: he puts to the test what these things look like *when* they are reversed. It is an act of willfulness, and pleasure in willfulness, if now he perhaps bestows his favour on that which has hitherto had a bad reputation—if, full of inquisitiveness and the desire to tempt and experiment, he creeps around the things most forbidden. Behind all his toiling and weaving—for he is restlessly and aimlessly on his way as if in a desert—stands the questionmark of a more and more perilous curiosity. "Can *all* values not be turned round? and is good perhaps evil? and God only an invention and finesse of the Devil? Is everything perhaps in the last resort false? And if we are deceived, are we not for that very reason also deceivers? *must* we not be deceivers?"—such thoughts as these tempt him and lead him on, even further away, even further down. Solitude encircles and embraces him, ever more threatening, suffocating, heart-tightening, that terrible goddess and *mater saeva cupidinum*[4]—but who today knows what *solitude* is? . . .

4

From this morbid isolation, from the desert of these years of temptation and experiment, it is still a long road to that tremendous overflowing certainty and health which may not dispense even with wickedness, as a means and fish-hook of knowledge, to that *mature* freedom of spirit which is equally self-mastery and discipline of the heart and permits access to many and contradictory modes of thought—to that inner spaciousness and indulgence of superabundance which excludes the danger that the spirit may even on its own road perhaps lose itself and become infatuated and remain seated intoxicated in some corner or other, to that superfluity of formative, curative, moulding and restorative forces which is precisely the sign of *great* health, that superfluity which grants to the free spirit the dangerous privilege of living *experimentally* and of being allowed to offer itself to adventure: the master's privilege of the free spirit! In between there may lie long years of convalescence, years full of variegated, painfully magical transformations ruled and led along by a tenacious *will to health* which often ventures to clothe and disguise itself as health already achieved. There is a midway condition which a man of such a destiny will not be able to recall without emotion: it is characterized by a pale, subtle happiness of light and sunshine, a feeling of bird-like freedom, bird-like altitude, bird-like exuberance, and a third thing in which curiosity is united with a tender contempt. A "free-spirit"—this cool expression does one good in every condition, it is almost warming. One lives no longer in the fetters of love and hatred, without yes, without no, near or far as one wishes, preferably slipping away, evading, fluttering off, gone again, again flying aloft; one is spoiled, as everyone is who has at some time seen a tremendous number of things *beneath* him—and one becomes the opposite of those who concern themselves with things which have nothing to do with them. Indeed, the free spirit henceforth has to do only with things— and how many things!—with which he is no longer *concerned* . . .

5

A step further in convalescence: and the free spirit again draws near to life—slowly, to be sure, almost reluctantly, almost mistrustfully. It again

[4]Wild mother of the passions.

grows warmer around him, yellower, as it were; feeling and feeling for others acquire depth, warm breezes of all kind blow across him. It seems to him as if his eyes are only now open to what is *close at hand*. He is astonished and sits silent: where *had* he been? These close and closest things: how changed they seem! what bloom and magic they have acquired! He looks back gratefully—grateful to his wandering, to his hardness and self-alienation, to his viewing of far distances and bird-like flights in cold heights. What a good thing he had not always stayed "at home," stayed "under his own roof" like a delicate apathetic loafer! He had been *beside* himself: no doubt of that. Only now does he see himself—and what surprises he experiences as he does so! What unprecedented shudders! What happiness even in the weariness, the old sickness, the relapses of the convalescent! How he loves to sit sadly still, to spin out patience, to lie in the sun! Who understands as he does the happiness that comes in winter, the spots of sunlight on the wall! They are the most grateful animals in the world, also the most modest, these convalescents and lizards again half turned towards life:—there are some among them who allow no day to pass without hanging a little song of praise on the hem of its departing robe. And, to speak seriously: to become sick in the manner of these free spirits, to remain sick for a long time and then, slowly, slowly, to become healthy, by which I mean "healthier," is a fundamental *cure* for all pessimism (the cancerous sore and inveterate vice, as is well known, of old idealists and inveterate liars). There is wisdom, practical wisdom, in for a long time prescribing even health for oneself only in small doses.

6

At that time it may finally happen that, under the sudden illumination of a still stressful, still changeable health, the free, ever freer spirit begins to unveil the riddle of that great liberation which had until then waited dark, questionable, almost untouchable in his memory. If he has for long hardly dared to ask himself: "why so apart? so alone? renouncing everything I once reverenced? renouncing reverence itself? why this hardness, this suspiciousness, this hatred for your own virtues?"—now he dares to ask it aloud and hears in reply something like an answer. "You shall become master over yourself, master also over your virtues. Formerly *they* were your masters; but they must be only your instruments beside other instruments. You shall get control over your For and Against and learn how to display first one and then the other in accordance with your higher goal. You shall learn to grasp the sense of perspective in every value judgement—the displacement, distortion and merely apparent teleology of horizons and whatever else pertains to perspectivism; also the quantum of stupidity that resides in antitheses of values and the whole intellectual loss which every For, every Against costs us. You shall learn to grasp the *necessary* injustice in every For and Against, injustice as inseparable from life, life itself as *conditioned* by the sense of perspective and its injustice. You shall above all see with your own eyes where injustice is always at its greatest: where life has developed at its smallest, narrowest, neediest, most incipient and yet cannot avoid taking *itself* as the goal and measure of things and for the sake of its own preservation secretly and meanly and ceaselessly crumbling away and calling into question the higher, greater, richer—you shall see with your own eyes the problem of *order of rank*, and how power and right and spaciousness of perspective grow into the heights together. You shall"—enough: from now on the free spirit *knows* what "you shall" he has obeyed, and he also knows what he now *can*, what only now he—*may* do . . .

<h1 style="text-align:center">7</h1>

This is how the free spirit elucidates to himself that enigma of liberation, and inasmuch as he generalizes his own case ends by adjudicating on what he has experienced thus. "What has happened to me," he says to himself, "must happen to everyone in whom a *task* wants to become incarnate and 'come into the world.' " The secret force and necessity of this task will rule among and in the individual facets of his destiny like an unconscious pregnancy—long before he has caught sight of this task itself or knows its name. Our vocation commands and disposes of us even when we do not yet know it; it is the future that regulates our today. Given it is *the problem of order of rank* of which we may say it is *our* problem, we free spirits: it is only now, at the midday of our life, that we understand what preparations, bypaths, experiments, temptations, disguises the problem had need of before it was *allowed* to rise up before us, and how we first had to experience the most manifold and contradictory states of joy and distress in soul and body, as adventurers and circumnavigators of that inner world called "man," as surveyors and gaugers of that "higher" and "one upon the other" that is likewise called "man"—penetrating everywhere, almost without fear, disdaining nothing, losing nothing, asking everything, cleansing everything of what is chance and accident in it and as it were thoroughly sifting it—until at last we had the right to say, we free spirits: "Here—a *new* problem! Here a long ladder upon whose rungs we ourselves have sat and climbed—which we ourselves have at some time *been!* Here a higher, a deeper, a beneath-us, a tremendous long ordering, an order of rank, which we *see:* here—*our* problem!"—

<h1 style="text-align:center">8</h1>

—No psychologist or reader of signs will have a moment's difficulty in recognizing to what stage in the evolution just described the present book belongs (or has been *placed*—). But where today are there psychologists? In France, certainly; perhaps in Russia; definitely not in Germany. There is no lack of reasons as to why the Germans of today could even regard this fact as redounding to their honour: an ill fate for one who in this matter is by nature and attainment un-German! This *German* book, which has known how to find its readers in a wide circle of lands and peoples—it has been on its way for about ten years—and must be capable of some kind of music and flute-player's art by which even coy foreign ears are seduced to listen—it is precisely in Germany that this book has been read most carelessly and *heard* the worst: why is that?—"It demands too much," has been the reply, "it addresses itself to people who are not oppressed by uncouth duties, it wants refined and experienced senses, it needs superfluity, superfluity of time, of clarity in heart and sky, of *otium*[5] in the most audacious sense:—all of them good things that we Germans of today do not have and therefore also cannot give."—After so courteous a reply my philosophy advises me to keep silent and to ask no more questions; especially as in certain cases, as the saying has it, one *remains* a philosopher only by—keeping silent.

Nice
Spring 1886

Human, All Too Human
Volume Two

Preface (1886)

1

One should speak only when one may not stay silent; and then only of that which one has *overcome*—everything else is chatter, "literature," lack of breeding. My writings speak *only* of my overcomings: "I" am in them, together with everything that was inimical to me, *ego ipsissimus*,[6] indeed, if a yet prouder expression be permitted, *ego ipsissimum*.[7] One will divine that I already have a great deal—beneath me . . . But it has always required time, recovery, distancing, before the desire awoke within me to skin, exploit, expose, "exhibit" (or whatever one wants to call it) for the

[5]Leisure, idleness.
[6]My very own self.
[7]My innermost self.

sake of knowledge something I had experienced and survived, some fact or fate of my life. To this extent, all my writings, with a single though admittedly substantial exception, are to be *dated back*—they always speak of something "behind me"—: some, as with the first three *Untimely Meditations*, even to a period earlier than that in which I experienced and produced a book published before them (the *Birth of Tragedy* in the case mentioned: as a more subtle observer and comparer will be able to tell for himself). That angry outburst against the inflated Germanism, complacency and beggarly language of the aged David Strauss, the content of the first *Meditation*,[8] gave vent to feelings engendered long before when I had sat as a student in the midst of German culture and cultural philistinism (I make claim to be the father of the nowadays so much used and misused expression "cultural philistine"—); and what I had to say against the "historical sickness" I said as one who had slowly and toilsomely learned to recover from it and was in no way prepared to give up "history" thereafter because he had once suffered from it. When, in the third *Untimely Meditation*, I then went on to give expression to my reverence for my first and only educator, the *great* Arthur Schopenhauer—I would now express it much more strongly, also more personally—I was, so far as my own development was concerned, already deep in the midst of moral scepticism and destructive analysis, *that is to say in the critique and likewise the intensifying of pessimism as understood hitherto*, and already "believed in nothing any more," as the people put it, not even in Schopenhauer: just at that time I produced an essay I have refrained from publishing, "On Truth and Falsehood in an Extra-Moral Sense."[9] Even my festive victory address in honour of Richard Wagner on the occasion of his celebration of victory at Bayreuth in 1876—Bayreuth signifies the greatest victory an artist has ever achieved—a work wearing the strongest *appearance* of being "up to the minute," was in its background an act of homage and gratitude to a piece of my own past, to the fairest but also most perilous period of dead calm of my whole voyage . . . and in fact a liberation, a farewell.[10] (Was Richard Wagner himself deceived as to this? I do not believe so. As long as one still loves one does not paint pictures like this; one does not yet "meditate" on one's subject, one does not set oneself at a distance in the way a "meditator" must. "Even contemplation involves a secret *antagonism*, the antagonism involved in comparison"—it says on page forty-

---

[8]The first of Nietzsche's *Untimely Meditations*, entitled *David Strauss, the Confessor and the Writer*, was an attack on the popular culture of Germany in Nietzsche's day that focused on the theologian David Strauss, whom Nietzsche considered to exemplify the tendencies of which he was so critical.

[9]Much of this essay is included in Part I of this volume.

[10]The "address" to which Nietzsche here refers became the fourth of his *Untimely Meditations*, entitled *Richard Wagner in Bayreuth*. While apparently a celebration of Wagner, it also marks the beginning of Nietzsche's turn away from Wagner that culminated in his violent attack on Wagner in *The Case of Wagner*, fifteen years later.

six of the said essay itself, in a revealing and melancholy phrase perhaps intended for but few ears.) The composure needed to be *able* to speak of an inner solitude and self-denial extending over long intervening years first came to me with the book *Human, All Too Human,* to which this second foreword and intercession too is to be dedicated. As a book "for free spirits," there reposes upon it something of the almost cheerful and inquisitive coldness of the psychologist who takes a host of painful things that lie *beneath* and *behind* him and identifies and as it were *impales* them with the point of a needle:—is it any wonder if, with such sharp-pointed and ticklish work, a certain amount of blood occasionally flows, if the psychologist engaged on it has blood on his fingers and not always only—on his fingers? . . .

2

The "Assorted opinions and maxims" were, like "The wanderer and his shadow," first published *singly* as continuations and appendices of the above-named human-all-too-human "Book for free spirits": at the same time as a continuation and redoubling of a spiritual cure, namely of the *anti-romantic* self-treatment that my still healthy instinct had itself discovered and prescribed for me against a temporary attack of the most dangerous form of romanticism. May these same writings now, after six years of convalescence, prove acceptable *united* as the second volume of *Human, All Too Human:* perhaps taken together they will teach their precepts more powerfully and clearly—they are *precepts of health* that may be recommended to the more spiritual natures of the generation just coming up as a *disciplina voluntatis.*[11] There speaks out of them a pessimist whose insights have often made him jump out of his skin but who has always known how to get back into it again, a pessimist, that is to say, well disposed *towards* pessimism—and thus in any event no longer a romantic: what? should a spirit who understands the serpent's prudent art of *changing his skin* not be permitted to read a lecture to our pessimists of today, who are one and all still in danger of romanticism? And at the very least to demonstrate to them how it is—*done?* . . .

3

—At that time it was indeed high time *to say farewell:* and I immediately received a confirmation of the fact. Richard Wagner, seemingly the all-conquering, actually a decaying, despairing romantic, suddenly sank down helpless and shattered before the Christian cross . . . Was there no

[11]Discipline of the will.

German with eyes in his head, empathy in his conscience, for this dreadful spectacle? Was I the only one who—suffered from it? Enough, this unexpected event illumined for me like a flash of lightning the place I had left—and likewise gave me those subsequent horrors that he feels who has passed through a terrible peril unawares. As I went on alone, I trembled; not long afterwards I was sick, more than sick, I was weary of the unending disappointment with everything we modern men have left to inspire us, of the energy, labour, hope, youth, love everywhere *dissipated;* weary with disgust at the femininity and ill-bred rapturousness of this romanticism, weary of the whole idealist pack of lies and softening of conscience that had here once again carried off the victory over one of the bravest; weary, last but not least, with the bitterness of a suspicion—that, after this disappointment, I was condemned to mistrust more profoundly, despise more profoundly, to be more profoundly alone than ever before. My *task*—where had it gone? What? was it now not as if my task had withdrawn from me, as though I would for a long time to come cease to have any right to it? How was I going to be able to endure this *greatest* of privations?—I began by *forbidding* myself, totally and on principle, all romantic music, that ambiguous, inflated, oppressive art that deprives the spirit of its severity and cheerfulness and lets rampant every kind of vague longing and greedy, spongy desire. *"Cave musicam"*[12] is to this day my advice to all who are man enough to insist on cleanliness in things of the spirit; such music unnerves, softens, feminizes, its "eternal womanly" draws *us*—downwards! . . . At that time I was first and foremost suspicious of and circumspect towards romantic music; and if I continued to harbour any hope at all for music it lay in the expectation that a musician might come who was sufficiently bold, subtle, malicious, southerly, superhealthy to confront that music and in an immortal fashion *take revenge* on it. —

4

Henceforth alone and sorely mistrustful of myself, I thus, and not without a sullen wrathfulness, took sides *against* myself and *for* everything painful and difficult precisely for *me:*—thus I again found my way to that courageous pessimism that is the antithesis of all romantic mendacity, and also, as it seems to me today, the way to "myself," to *my* task. That concealed and imperious something for which we for long have no name until it finally proves to be our *task*—this tyrant in us takes a terrible retribution for every attempt we make to avoid or elude it, for every premature decision, for every association on equal terms with those with

---

[12]"Beware of music!"

whom we do not belong, for every activity, however respectable, if it distracts us from our chief undertaking, even indeed for every virtue that would like to shield us from the severity of our own most personal responsibility. Illness is the answer every time we begin to doubt our right to *our* task—every time we begin to make things easier for ourselves. Strange and at the same time terrible! It is our *alleviations* for which we have to atone the most! And if we afterwards want to return to health, we have no choice: we have to burden ourselves *more heavily* than we have ever been burdened before . . .

5

It was only then that I learned that solitary's speech that only the most silent and the most suffering understand: I spoke without witnesses, or rather in indifference to witnesses, so as not to suffer from staying silent, I spoke only of things that had nothing to do with me but did so as though they had something to do with me. It was then I learned the art of *appearing* cheerful, objective, inquisitive, above all healthy and malicious—and this, it seems to me, constitutes "good taste" on the part of an invalid. A subtler eye and empathy will nonetheless not fail to see what perhaps constitutes the charm of this writing—that here a sufferer and self-denier speaks as though he were *not* a sufferer and self-denier. Here there is a *determination* to preserve an equilibrium and composure in the face of life and even a sense of gratitude towards it, here there rules a vigorous, proud, constantly watchful and sensitive will that has set itself the task of defending life *against* pain and of striking down all those inferences that pain, disappointment, ill-humour, solitude, and other swampgrounds usually cause to flourish like poisonous fungi. This perhaps offers to precisely our pessimists a signpost to their own self-testing?—for it was then that I acquired for myself the proposition: "a sufferer has *no right* to pessimism because he suffers!," it was then that I conducted with myself a patient and tedious campaign against the unscientific basic tendency of that romantic pessimism to interpret and inflate individual personal experiences into universal judgements and, indeed, into condemnations of the world . . . in short, it was then that I turned my perspective *around*. Optimism, for the purpose of restoration, so that at some future time I could again have the *right* to be a pessimist—do you understand that? Just as a physician places his patient in a wholly strange environment so that he may be removed from his entire "hitherto," from his cares, friends, letters, duties, stupidities and torments of memory and learn to reach out his hands and senses to new nourishment, a new sun, a new future, so I, as physician and patient in one, compelled myself to an opposite and unexplored *clime of the soul*, and especially to a

curative journey into strange parts, into *strangeness* itself, to an inquisitiveness regarding every kind of strange thing . . . A protracted wandering around, seeking, changing followed from this, a repugnance towards
all staying still, towards every blunt affirmation and denial; likewise a
dietetic and discipline designed to make it as easy as possible for the
spirit to run long distances, to fly to great heights, above all again and
again to fly away. A *minimum* of life, in fact, an unchaining from all
coarser desires, an independence in the midst of all kinds of unfavourable outward circumstances together with pride in being *able* to live
surrounded by these unfavourable circumstances; a certain amount of
cynicism, perhaps, a certain amount of "barrel,"[13] but just as surely a
great deal of capricious happiness, capricious cheerfulness, a great deal
of stillness, light, subtler folly, concealed enthusiasm—all this finally
resulted in a great spiritual strengthening, an increasing joy and abundance of health. Life itself *rewards* us for our tough will to live, for the
long war such as I then waged with myself against the pessimism of
weariness with life, even for every attentive glance our gratitude accords
to even the smallest, tenderest, most fleeting gift life gives us. Finally
our reward is the *greatest* of life's gifts, perhaps the greatest thing it is
able to give of any kind—we are given our *task* back.——

6

—Shall my experience—the history of an illness and recovery, for a recovery was what eventuated—have been my personal experience alone? And
only *my* "human, all-too-human"? Today I would like to believe the reverse;
again and again I feel sure that my travel books were not written solely for
myself, as sometimes seems to be the case—. May I now, after six years of
growing confidence, venture to send them off again? May I venture to com-
mend them especially to the hearts and ears of those burdened with any kind
of "past" and have sufficient spirit left still to suffer from the *spirit* of their
past too? Above all, however, *to you*, who have the hardest fate, you rare,
most imperilled, most spiritual, most courageous men who have to be the
conscience of the modern soul and as such have to possess its *knowledge*, and in
whom all that exists today of sickness, poison and danger comes together—
whose lot it is to have to be sicker than any other kind of individual because
you are not "*only* individuals" . . . whose comfort it is to know the way to a
new health, and alas! to go along it, a health of tomorrow and the day after,
you predestined and victorious men, you overcomers of your age, you health-
iest and strongest men, you *good Europeans!*——

---

[13]"Barrel": reference to Diogenes the Cynic (ca. 400 to ca. 325 B.C.), reported to have
lived in a barrel (trans.).

7

—Finally, to reduce my opposition to *romantic pessimism*, that is to say the pessimism of the renunciators, the failed and defeated, to a formula: there is a will to the tragic and to pessimism that is as much a sign of severity and of strength of intellect (taste, feeling, conscience). With this will in one's heart one has no fear of the fearful and questionable that characterizes all existence; one even seeks it out. Behind such a will there stands courage, pride, the longing for a *great* enemy.—This has been *my* pessimistic perspective from the beginning—a novel perspective, is it not? a perspective that even today is still novel and strange? To this very moment I continue to adhere to it and, if you will believe me, just as much *for* myself as, occasionally at least, *against* myself . . . Do you want me to prove this to you? But what else does this long preface—prove?

Sils-Maria, Oberengadin
September 1886

Daybreak

Preface (1886)

1

In this book you will discover a "subterranean man" at work, one who tunnels and mines and undermines. You will see him—presupposing you have eyes capable of seeing this work in the depths—going forward slowly, cautiously, gently inexorable, without betraying very much of the distress which any protracted deprivation of light and air must entail; you might even call him contented, working there in the dark. Does it not seem as though some faith were leading him on, some consolation offering him compensation? As though he perhaps desires this prolonged obscurity, desires to be incomprehensible, concealed, enigmatic, because he knows what he will thereby also acquire: his own morning, his own redemption, his own *daybreak?* . . . He will return, that is certain: do not ask him what he is looking for down there, he will tell you himself of his own accord, this seeming Trophonius and subterranean, as soon as he has 'become a man' again. Being silent is something one completely unlearns if, like him, one has been for so long a solitary mole————

2

And indeed, my patient friends, I shall now tell you what I was after down there—here in this late preface which could easily have become a funeral oration: for I have returned and, believe it or not, returned safe and sound. Do not think for a moment that I intend to invite you to the same hazardous enterprise! Or even only to the same solitude! For he who proceeds on his own path in this fashion encounters no one: that is inherent in "proceeding on one's own path." No one comes along to help him: all the perils, accidents, malice and bad weather which assail him he has to tackle by himself. For his path is *his alone*—as is, of course, the bitterness and occasional ill-humour he feels at this "his alone": among which is included, for instance, the knowledge that even his friends are unable to divine where he is or whither he is going, that they will sometimes ask themselves: "what? is he going at all? does he still have—a path?"—At that time I undertook something not everyone may undertake: I descended into the depths, I tunnelled into the foundations, I commenced an investigation and digging out of an ancient *faith*, one upon which we philosophers have for a couple of millennia been accustomed to build as if upon the firmest of all foundations—and have continued to do so even though every building hitherto erected on them has fallen down: I commenced to undermine our *faith in morality*. But you do not understand me?

3

Hitherto, the subject reflected on least adequately has been good and evil: it was too dangerous a subject. Conscience, reputation, Hell, sometimes even the police have permitted and continue to permit no impartiality; in the presence of morality, as in the face of any authority, one is not *allowed* to think, far less to express an opinion: here one has to—*obey!* As long as the world has existed no authority has yet been willing to let itself become the object of criticism; and to criticise morality itself, to regard morality as a problem, as problematic: what? has that not been—*is* that not—immoral?—But morality does not merely have at its command every kind of means of frightening off critical hands and torture-instruments: its security reposes far more in a certain art of enchantment it has at its disposal—it knows how to "inspire." With this art it succeeds, often with no more than a single glance, in paralysing the critical will and even in enticing it over to its own side; there are even cases in which morality has been able to turn the critical will against itself, so that, like the scorpion, it drives its sting into its own body. For morality has from of old been master of every diabolical nuance of the art of persuasion: there is no orator, even today, who does not have recourse to its assistance (listen, for example, even to our anarchists: how morally they speak when they want to persuade! In the end they even go so far as to call themselves "the good and the just.") For as long as there has been speech and persuasion on earth, morality has shown itself to be the greatest of all mistresses of seduction—and, so far as we philosophers are concerned, the actual *Circe of the philosophers*. Why is it that from Plato onwards every philosophical architect in Europe has built in vain? That everything they themselves in all sober seriousness regarded as *aere perennius*[14] is threatening to collapse or already lies in ruins? Oh how false is the answer which even today is reserved in readiness for this question: "because they had all neglected the presupposition for such an undertaking, the testing of the foundations, a critique of reason as a whole"—that fateful answer of Kant's which has certainly not lured us modern philosophers on to any firmer or less treacherous ground! (—and, come to think of it, was it not somewhat peculiar to demand of an instrument that it should criticise its own usefulness and suitability? that the intellect itself should "know" its own value, its own capacity, its own limitations? was it not even a little absurd?—). The correct answer would rather have been that all philosophers were building under the seduction of morality, even Kant—that they were apparently aiming at certainty, at "truth," but in reality at *"majestic moral structures"*: to employ once again the innocent language of Kant, who describes his own "not so glittering yet not undeserving" task and labour as "to level and make firm the ground for these majestic moral structures" (*Critique of Pure Reason* II, p. 257). Alas, we have to admit today that he did not succeed in doing that, quite the contrary! Kant was, with such an enthusiastic intention, the true son of his century, which before any other can be called the century of enthusiasm: as he fortunately remained also in regard to its more valuable aspects (for example in the good portion of sensism he took over into his theory of knowledge). He too had been bitten by the moral tarantula Rousseau, he too harboured in the depths of his soul the idea of that moral fanaticism whose executor another disciple of Rousseau felt and confessed himself to be, namely Robespierre, *"de fonder sur la terre l'empire de la sagesse, de la justice et de la vertu"*[15] (speech of 7 June 1794). On the other hand, with such a French fanaticism in one's heart, one could not have gone to work in a less French fashion, more thoroughly, more in a German fashion—if the word "German" is still permitted today in this sense—than Kant did: to create room for *his* "moral realm" he saw himself obliged to posit an undemonstrable world, a logical "Beyond"—it was for precisely that that he had need of his critique of pure reason! In other words: *he would not have had need of it*

---

[14]"More perennial than the air" (Horace, *Odes*, 3, 30, 1).
[15]"The founder on earth of the empire of wisdom, of justice and of virtue."

if one thing had not been more vital to him than anything else: to render the "moral realm" unassailable, even better incomprehensible to reason—for he felt that a moral order of things was only too assailable by reason! In the face of nature and history, in the face of the thorough *immorality* of nature and history, Kant was, like every good German of the old stamp, a pessimist; he believed in morality, not because it is demonstrated in nature and history, but in spite of the fact that nature and history continually contradict it. To understand this "in spite of," one might perhaps recall something similar in Luther, that other great pessimist who, with all the audacity native to him, once admonished his friends: "if we could grasp by reason how the God who shows so much wrath and malice can be just and merciful, what need would we have of *faith?*" For nothing has from the beginning made a more profound impression on the German soul, nothing has "tempted" it more, than this most perilous of all conclusions, which to every true Roman is a sin against the spirit: *credo quia absurdum est:*—it was with this conclusion that German logic first entered the history of Christian dogma: but even today, a millennium later, we Germans of today, late Germans in every respect, still sense something of truth, of the *possibility* of truth behind the celebrated dialectical principle with which in his day Hegel assisted the German spirit to conquer Europe—"Contradiction moves the world, all things contradict themselves"—: for we are, even in the realm of logic, pessimists.

4

But *logical* evaluations are not the deepest or most fundamental to which our audacious mistrust can descend: faith in reason, with which the validity of these judgments must stand or fall, is, as faith, a *moral* phenomenon . . . Perhaps German pessimism still has one last step to take? Perhaps it has once again to set beside one another in fearful fashion its *credo* and its *absurdum?*[16] And if *this* book is pessimistic even into the realm of morality, even to the point of going beyond faith in morality—should it not for this very reason be a German book? For it does in fact exhibit a contradiction and is not afraid of it: in this book faith in morality is withdrawn—but why? *Out of morality!* Or what else should we call that which informs it—and *us?* for our taste is for more modest expressions. But there is no doubt that a "thou shalt" still speaks to us too, that we too still obey a stern law set over us—and this is the last moral law which can make itself audible even to us, which even we know how to *live*, in this if in anything we too are still *men of conscience:* namely, in that we do not

---

[16]Its "I believe" and its "absurd"—a reference to the famous statement of the early Church Father Tertullian, *"credo quia absurdum est,"* "I believe because it is absurd."

want to return to that which we consider outlived and decayed, to anything "unworthy of belief," be it called God, virtue, truth, justice, char-
ity; that we do not permit ourselves any bridges-of-lies to ancient ideals;
that we are hostile from the heart to everything that wants to mediate and
mix with us; hostile to every kind of faith and Christianness existing
today; hostile to the half-and-halfness of all romanticism and fatherland-
worship; hostile, too, towards the pleasure-seeking and lack of conscience
of the artists which would like to persuade us to worship where we no
longer believe—for we are artists; hostile, in short, to the whole of European *feminism* (or idealism, if you prefer that word), which is for ever
"drawing us upward" and precisely thereby for ever "bringing us
down": —it is only as men of *this* conscience that we still feel ourselves
related to the German integrity and piety of millennia, even if as its most
questionable and final descendants, we immoralists, we godless men of
today, indeed in a certain sense as its heirs, as the executors of its innermost will—a pessimistic will, as aforesaid, which does not draw back from
denying itself because it denies with *joy!* In us there is accomplished—
supposing you want a formula—the *self-sublimation of morality.*——

5

—Finally, however: why should we have to say what we are and what
we want and do not want so loudly and with such fervour? Let us view it
more coldly, more distantly, more prudently, from a greater height; let us
say it, as it is fitting it should be said between ourselves, so secretly that
no one hears it, that no one hears *us!* Above all let us say it *slowly* . . . This
preface is late but not too late—what, after all, do five or six years matter?
A book like this, a problem like this, is in no hurry; we both, I just as
much as my book, are friends of *lento.*[17] It is not for nothing that I have
been a philologist, perhaps I am a philologist still, that is to say, a teacher
of slow reading: —in the end I also write slowly. Nowadays it is not only
my habit, it is also to my taste—a malicious taste, perhaps?—no longer to
write anything which does not reduce to despair every sort of man who is
"in a hurry." For philology is that venerable art which demands of its
votaries one thing above all: to go aside, to take time, to become still, to
become slow—it is a goldsmith's art and connoisseurship of the *word*
which has nothing but delicate, cautious work to do and achieves nothing
if it does not achieve it *lento.* But for precisely this reason it is more
necessary than ever today, by precisely this means does it entice and
enchant us the most, in the midst of an age of "work," that is to say, of
hurry, of indecent and perspiring haste, which wants to "get everything

[17]Slow(ness).

done" at once, including every old or new book:—this art does not so easily get anything done, it teaches to read *well*, that is to say, to read slowly, deeply, looking cautiously before and aft, with reservations, with doors left open, with delicate eyes and fingers . . . My patient friends, this book desires for itself only perfect readers and philologists: *learn* to read me well!—

Ruta, near Genoa,
in the autumn of 1886

The Gay Science (or Joyful Wisdom)

Preface for the Second Edition (1886)

1

This book may need more than one preface, and in the end there would still remain room for doubt whether anyone who had never lived through similar experiences could be brought closer to the *experience* of this book by means of prefaces. It seems to be written in the language of the wind that thaws ice and snow: high spirits, unrest, contradiction, and April weather are present in it, and one is instantly reminded no less of the proximity of winter than of the triumph over the winter that is coming, must come, and perhaps has already come.

Gratitude pours forth continually, as if the unexpected had just happened—the gratitude of a convalescent—for *convalescence* was unexpected. "Gay Science": that signifies the saturnalia of a spirit who has patiently resisted a terrible, long pressure—patiently, severely, coldly, without submitting, but also without hope—and who is now all at once attacked by hope, the hope for health, and the *intoxication* of convalescence. Is it any wonder that in the process much that is unreasonable and foolish comes to light, much playful tenderness that is lavished even on problems that have a prickly hide and are not made to be caressed and enticed? This whole book is nothing but a bit of merry-making after long privation and powerlessness, the rejoicing of strength that is returning, of a reawakened faith in a tomorrow and the day after tomorrow, of a sudden sense and anticipation of a future, of impending adventures, of seas that are open again, of goals that are permitted again, believed again. And what did not lie behind me then! This stretch of desert, exhaustion, disbelief, icing up in the midst of youth, this interlude of old age at the wrong time, this tyranny of pain even excelled by the tyranny of pride that refused the *conclusions* of pain—and conclusions are consolations—this radical retreat into solitude as a self-defense against a contempt for men that had become pathologically clairvoyant—this determined self-limitation to what was bitter, harsh, and hurtful to know, prescribed by the *nausea* that had gradually developed out of an incautious and pampering spiritual diet, called romanticism—oh, who could reexperience all of this? But if anyone could, he would surely pardon more than a little foolishness, exuberance, and "gay science"—for example, the handful of songs that have now been added to this book—songs in which a poet makes fun of all poets in a way that may be hard to forgive. Alas, it is not only the poets and their beautiful "lyrical sentiments" on whom the resurrected author has to vent his sarcasm: who knows what victim he is looking for, what monster of material for parody will soon attract him? *"Incipit tragoedia"*[18] we read at the end of this awesomely aweless book. Beware! Something downright wicked and malicious is announced here: *incipit parodia*,[19] no doubt.

2

But let us leave Herr Nietzsche: what is it to us that Herr Nietzsche has become well again?

For a psychologist there are few questions that are as attractive as that concerning the relation of health and philosophy, and if he should himself become ill, he will bring all of his scientific curiosity into his illness. For assuming that one is a person, one necessarily also has the philosophy that belongs to that person; but there is a big difference. In some it is their deprivations that philosophize; in others, their riches and strengths. The former *need* their philosophy, whether it be as a prop, a sedative, medicine, redemption, elevation, or self-alienation. For the latter it is merely a beautiful luxury—in the best cases, the voluptuousness of a triumphant gratitude that eventually still has to inscribe itself in cosmic letters on the heaven of concepts. But in the former case, which is more common, when it is distress that philosophizes, as is the case with all sick thinkers—and perhaps sick thinkers are more numerous in the history of philosophy—what will become of the thought itself when it is subjected to the *pressure* of sickness? This is the question that concerns the psychologist, and here an experiment is possible. Just as a traveler may resolve, before he calmly abandons himself to sleep, to wake up at a certain time, we philosophers, if we should become sick, surrender for a while to sickness, body and soul—and, as it were, shut our eyes to ourselves. And as the traveler knows that something is *not* asleep, that something counts the hours and will wake him up, we, too, know that the decisive moment will find us

[18]"The tragedy begins."
[19]"The parody begins."

awake, and that something will leap forward then and catch the spirit *in the act:* I mean, in its weakness or repentance or resignation or hardening or gloom, and whatever other names there are for the pathological states of the spirit that on healthy days are opposed by the *pride* of the spirit (for the old saying is still valid: "the proud spirit, peacock, and horse are the three proudest beasts on earth").

After such self-questioning, self-temptation, one acquires a subtler eye for all philosophizing to date; one can infer better than before the involuntary detours, side lanes, resting places, and *sunny* places of thought to which suffering thinkers are led and misled on account of their suffering; for now one knows whether the sick *body* and its needs unconsciously urge, push, and lure the spirit—toward the sun, stillness, mildness, patience, medicine, balm in some sense. Every philosophy that ranks peace above war, every ethic with a negative definition of happiness, every metaphysics and physics that knows some *finale,* some final state of some sort, every predominantly aesthetic or religious craving for some Apart, Beyond, Outside, Above, permits the question whether it was not sickness that inspired the philosopher. The unconscious disguise of physiological needs under the cloaks of the objective, ideal, purely spiritual goes to frightening lengths—and often I have asked myself whether, taking a large view, philosophy has not been merely an interpretation of the body and a *misunderstanding of the body.*

Behind the highest value judgments that have hitherto guided the history of thought, there are concealed misunderstandings of the physical constitution—of individuals or classes or even whole races. All those bold insanities of metaphysics, especially answers to the question about the *value* of existence, may always be considered first of all as the symptoms of certain bodies. And if such world affirmations or world negations *tout court* lack any grain of significance when measured scientifically, they are the more valuable for the historian and psychologist as hints or symptoms of the body, of its success or failure, its plenitude, power, and autocracy in history, or of its frustrations, weariness, impoverishment, its premonitions of the end, its will to the end.

I am still waiting for a philosophical *physician* in the exceptional sense of that word—one who has to pursue the problem of the total health of a people, time, race or of humanity—to muster the courage to push my suspicion to its limits and to risk the proposition: what was at stake in all philosophizing hitherto was not at all "truth" but something else—let us say, health, future, growth, power, life.

3

You see that I do not want to take leave ungratefully from that time of severe sickness whose profits I have not yet exhausted even today. I am very conscious of the advantages that my fickle health gives me over all robust squares. A philosopher who has traversed many kinds of health, and keeps traversing them, has passed through an equal number of philosophies; he simply *cannot* keep from transposing his states every time into the most spiritual form and distance: this art of transfiguration *is* philosophy. We philosophers are not free to divide body from soul as the people do; we are even less free to divide soul from spirit. We are not thinking frogs, nor objectifying and registering mechanisms with their innards removed: constantly, we have to give birth to our thoughts out of our pain and, like mothers, endow them with all we have of blood, heart, fire, pleasure, passion, agony, conscience, fate, and catastrophe. Life—that means for us constantly transforming all that we are into light and flame—also everything that wounds us; we simply can do no other. And as for sickness: are we not almost tempted to ask whether we could get along without it? Only great pain is the ultimate liberator of the spirit, being the teacher of *the great suspicion* that turns every *U* into an *X*, a real, genuine *X*, that is the letter before the penultimate one.

Only great pain, the long, slow pain that takes its time—on which we are burned, as it were, with green wood—compels us philosophers to descend into our ultimate depths and to put aside all trust, everything good-natured, everything that would interpose a veil, that is mild, that is medium—things in which formerly we may have found our humanity. I doubt that such pain makes us "better"; but I know that it makes us more *profound*.

Whether we learn to pit our pride, our scorn, our will power against it, equaling the American Indian who, however tortured, repays his torturer with the malice of his tongue; or whether we withdraw from pain into that Oriental Nothing—called Nirvana—into mute, rigid, deaf resignation, self-forgetting, self-extinction: out of such long and dangerous exercises of self-mastery one emerges as a different person, with a few more question marks—above all with the *will* henceforth to question further, more deeply, severely, harshly, evilly and quietly than one had questioned heretofore. The trust in life is gone: life itself has become a *problem*. Yet one should not jump to the conclusion that this necessarily makes one gloomy. Even love of life is still possible, only one loves differently. It is the love for a woman that causes doubts in us.

The attraction of everything problematic, the delight in an *x*, however, is so great in such more spiritual, more spiritualized men that this delight flares up again and again like a bright blaze over all the distress of what is problematic, over all the danger of uncertainty, and even over the jealousy of the lover. We know a new happiness.

4

In the end, lest what is most important remain unsaid: from such abysses, from such severe sickness, also from the sickness of severe suspicion, one returns *newborn*, having shed one's skin, more ticklish and malicious, with a more delicate taste for joy, with a tenderer tongue for all good things, with merrier senses, with a second dangerous innocence in joy, more childlike and yet a hundred times subtler than one has ever been before.

How repulsive pleasure is now, that crude, musty, brown pleasure as it is understood by those who like pleasure, our "educated" people, our rich people, and our rulers! How maliciously we listen now to the big county-fair boom-boom with which the "educated" person and city dweller today permits art, books, and music to rape him and provide "spiritual pleasures"—with the aid of spirituous liquors! How the theatrical scream of passion now hurts our ears, how strange to our taste the whole romantic uproar and tumult of the senses have become, which the educated mob loves, and all its aspirations after the elevated, inflated, and exaggerated! No, if we convalescents still need art, it is another kind of art—a mocking, light, fleeting, divinely untroubled, divinely artificial art that, like a pure flame, licks into unclouded skies. Above all, an art for artists, for artists only! We know better afterward what above all is needed for this: cheerfulness, any cheerfulness, my friends—also as artists: let me prove it. There are a few things we now know too well, we knowing ones: oh, how we now learn to forget well, and to be good at *not* knowing, as artists!

And as for our future, one will hardly find us again on the paths of those Egyptian youths who endanger temples by night, embrace statues, and want by all means to unveil, uncover, and put into a bright light whatever is kept concealed for good reasons. No, this bad taste, this will to truth, to "truth at any price," this youthful madness in the love of truth, have lost their charm for us: for that we are too experienced, too serious, too merry, too burned, too *profound*. We no longer believe that truth remains truth when the veils are withdrawn; we have lived too much to believe this. Today we consider it a matter of decency not to wish to see everything naked, or to be present at everything, or to understand and "know" everything.

"Is it true that God is present everywhere?" a little girl asked her mother; "I think that's indecent"—a hint for philosophers! One should have more respect for the bashfulness with which nature has hidden behind riddles and iridescent uncertainties. Perhaps truth is a woman who has reasons for not letting us see her reasons? Perhaps her name is—to speak Greek—*Baubo?*[20]

Oh, those Greeks! They knew how to live. What is required for that is to stop courageously at the surface, the fold, the skin, to adore appearance, to believe in forms, tones, words, in the whole Olympus of appear-

---

[20]*Baubo:* A primitive and obscene female demon: according to the *Oxford Classical Dictionary*, originally a personification of the female genitals (trans.).

ance. Those Greeks were superficial—*out of profundity*. And is not this precisely what we are again coming back to, we daredevils of the spirit who have climbed the highest and most dangerous peak of present thought and looked around from up there—we who have looked *down* from there? Are we not, precisely in this respect, Greeks? Adorers of forms, of tones, of words? And therefore—*artists?*

Ruta, near Genoa,
in the fall of 1886

On the Genealogy of Morals

Preface (1887)

1

We are unknown to ourselves, we men of knowledge—and with good reason. We have never sought ourselves—how could it happen that we should ever *find* ourselves? It has rightly been said: "Where your treasure is, there will your heart be also";[21] *our* treasure is where the beehives of our knowledge are. We are constantly making for them, being by nature winged creatures and honeygatherers of the spirit; there is one thing alone we really care about from the heart—"bringing something home." Whatever else there is in life, so-called "experiences"—which of us has sufficient earnestness for them? Or sufficient time? Present experience has, I am afraid, always found us "absent-minded": we cannot give our hearts to it—not even our ears! Rather, as one divinely preoccupied and immersed in himself into whose ear the bell has just boomed with all its strength the twelve beats of noon suddenly starts up and asks himself: "what really was that which just struck?" so we sometimes rub our ears *afterward* and ask, utterly surprised and disconcerted, "what really was that which we have just experienced?" and moreover: "who *are* we really?" and, afterward as aforesaid, count the twelve trembling bell-strokes of our experience, our life, our *being*—and alas! miscount them.—So we are necessarily strangers to ourselves, we do not comprehend ourselves, we *have* to misunderstand ourselves, for us the law "Each is furthest from himself" applies to all eternity—we are not "men of knowledge" with respect to ourselves.

[21]Matthew 6:21.

2

My ideas on the *origin* of our moral prejudices—for this is the subject of this polemic—received their first, brief, and provisional expression in the collection of aphorisms that bears the title *Human, All-Too-Human, A Book for Free Spirits*. This book was begun in Sorrento during a winter when it was given to me to pause as a wanderer pauses and look back across the broad and dangerous country my spirit had traversed up to that time. This was in the winter of 1876–77; the ideas themselves are older. They were already in essentials the same ideas that I take up again in the present treatises—let us hope the long interval has done them good, that they have become riper, clearer, stronger, more perfect! *That* I still cleave to them today, however, that they have become in the meantime more and more firmly attached to one another, indeed entwined and interlaced with one another, strengthens my joyful assurance that they might have arisen in me from the first not as isolated, capricious, or sporadic things but from a common root, from a *fundamental will* of knowledge, pointing imperiously into the depths, speaking more and more precisely, demanding greater and greater precision. For this alone is fitting for a philosopher. We have no right to *isolated* acts of any kind: we may not make isolated errors or hit upon isolated truths. Rather do our ideas, our values, our yeas and nays, our ifs and buts, grow out of us with the necessity with which a tree bears fruit—related and each with an affinity to each, and evidence of *one* will, *one* health, *one* soil, *one* sun. —Whether *you* like them, these fruits of ours?—But what is that to the trees! What is that to *us*, to us philosophers!

3

Because of a scruple peculiar to me that I am loth to admit to—for it is concerned with *morality*, with all that has hitherto been celebrated on earth as morality—a scruple that entered my life so early, so uninvited, so irresistibly, so much in conflict with my environment, age, precedents, and descent that I might almost have the right to call it my *"a priori"*—my curiosity as well as my suspicions were bound to halt quite soon at the question of where our good and evil really *originated*. In fact, the problem of the origin of evil pursued me even as a boy of thirteen: at an age in which you have "half childish trifles, half God in your heart,"[22] I devoted to it my first childish literary trifle, my first philosophical effort—and as for the "solution" of the problem I posed at that time, well, I gave the honor to God, as was only fair, and made him the *father* of evil. Was *that* what my *"a priori"* demanded of me? that new immoral, or at least unmoralistic *"a*

---

[22]Goethe's *Faust*, lines 3781f. (trans.).

priori" and the alas! so anti-Kantian, enigmatic "categorical imperative" which spoke through it and to which I have since listened more and more closely, and not merely listened?

Fortunately I learned early to separate theological prejudice from moral prejudice and ceased to look for the origin of evil *behind* the world. A certain amount of historical and philological schooling, together with an inborn fastidiousness of taste in respect to psychological questions in general, soon transformed my problem into another one: under what conditions did man devise these value judgments good and evil? *and what value do they themselves possess?* Have they hitherto hindered or furthered human prosperity? Are they a sign of distress, of impoverishment, of the degeneration of life? Or is there revealed in them, on the contrary, the plenitude, force, and will of life, its courage, certainty, future?

Thereupon I discovered and ventured divers answers; I distinguished between ages, peoples, degrees of rank among individuals; I departmentalized my problem; out of my answers there grew new questions, inquiries, conjectures, probabilities—until at length I had a country of my own, a soil of my own, an entire discrete, thriving, flourishing world, like a secret garden the existence of which no one suspected. —Oh how *fortunate* we are, we men of knowledge, provided only that we know how to keep silent long enough!

4

The first impulse to publish something of my hypotheses concerning the origin of morality was given me by a clear, tidy, and shrewd—also precocious—little book in which I encountered distinctly for the first time an upside-down and perverse species of genealogical hypothesis, the genuinely *English* type, that attracted me—with that power of attraction which everything contrary, everything antipodal possesses. The title of the little book was *The Origin of the Moral Sensations;* its author Dr. Paul Rée; the year in which it appeared 1877. Perhaps I have never read anything to which I would have said to myself No, proposition by proposition, conclusion by conclusion, to the extent that I did to this book: yet quite without ill-humor or impatience. In the above-mentioned work, on which I was then engaged, I made opportune and inopportune reference to the propositions of that book, not in order to refute them—what have I to do with refutations!—but, as becomes a positive spirit, to replace the improbable with the more probable, possibly one error with another. It was then, as I have said, that I advanced for the first time those genealogical hypotheses to which this treatise is devoted—ineptly, as I should be the last to deny, still constrained, still lacking my own language for my own things and with much backsliding and vacillation.

One should compare in particular what I say in *Human, All-Too-Human*, section 45, on the twofold prehistory of good and evil (namely, in the sphere of the noble and in that of the slaves); likewise, section 136, on the value and origin of the morality of asceticism; likewise, sections 96 and 99 and volume II, section 89, on the "morality of mores," that much older and more primitive species of morality which differs *toto caelo*[23] from the altruistic mode of evaluation (in which Dr. Rée, like all English moral genealogists, sees moral evaluation *as such*); likewise, section 92, *The Wanderer*,[24] section 26, and *Dawn*, section 112, on the origin of justice as an agreement between two approximately equal powers (equality as the presupposition of all compacts, consequently of all law); likewise *The Wanderer*, sections 22 and 33, on the origin of punishment, of which the aim of intimidation is neither the essence nor the source (as Dr. Rée thinks—it is rather only introduced, under certain definite circumstances, and always as an incidental, as something added).

5

Even then my real concern was something much more important than hypothesis-mongering, whether my own or other people's, on the origin of morality (or more precisely: the latter concerned me solely for the sake of a goal to which it was only one means among many). What was at stake was the *value* of morality—and over this I had to come to terms almost exclusively with my great teacher Schopenhauer, to whom that book of mine, the passion and the concealed contradiction of that book, addressed itself as if to a contemporary (—for that book, too, was a "polemic"). What was especially at stake was the value of the "unegoistic," the instincts of pity, self-abnegation, self-sacrifice, which Schopenhauer had gilded, deified, and projected into a beyond for so long that at last they became for him "value-in-itself," on the basis of which he *said No* to life and to himself. But it was against precisely *these* instincts that there spoke from me an ever more fundamental mistrust, an ever more corrosive skepticism! It was precisely here that I saw the *great* danger to mankind, its sublimest enticement and seduction—but to what? to nothingness?—it was precisely here that I saw the beginning of the end, the dead stop, a retrospective weariness, the will turning *against* life, the tender and sorrowful signs of the ultimate illness: I understood the ever spreading morality of pity that had seized even on philosophers and made them ill, as the most sinister symptom of a European culture that had itself become

---

[23]Diametrically: literally, by the whole heavens (trans.); i.e., "which is the very opposite of."

[24]*The Wanderer and His Shadow*, initially a separate short volume of aphorisms that became the second part of vol. 2 of *Human, All Too Human* (with the same section numbers).

sinister, perhaps as its by-pass to a new Buddhism? to a Buddhism for Europeans? to—*nihilism?*

For this overestimation of and predilection for pity on the part of modern philosophers is something new: hitherto philosophers have been at one as to the *worthlessness* of pity. I name only Plato, Spinoza, La Rochefoucauld and Kant—four spirits as different from one another as possible, but united in one thing: in their low estimation of pity.

6

This problem of the *value* of pity and of the morality of pity (—I am opposed to the pernicious modern effeminacy of feeling—) seems at first to be merely something detached, an isolated question mark; but whoever sticks with it and *learns* how to ask questions here will experience what I experienced—a tremendous new prospect opens up for him, a new possibility comes over him like a vertigo, every kind of mistrust, suspicion, fear leaps up, his belief in morality, in all morality, falters—finally a new demand becomes audible. Let us articulate this *new demand:* we need a *critique* of moral values, *the value of these values themselves must first be called in question*—and for that there is needed a knowledge of the conditions and circumstances in which they grew, under which they evolved and changed (morality as consequence, as symptom, as mask, as tartufferie, as illness, as misunderstanding; but also morality as cause, as remedy, as stimulant, as restraint, as poison), a knowledge of a kind that has never yet existed or even been desired. One has taken the *value* of these "values" as given, as factual, as beyond all question; one has hitherto never doubted or hesitated in the slightest degree in supposing "the good man" to be of greater value than "the evil man," of greater value in the sense of furthering the advancement and prosperity of man in general (the future of man included). But what if the reverse were true? What if a symptom of regression were inherent in the "good," likewise a danger, a seduction, a poison, a narcotic, through which the present was possibly living *at the expense of the future?* Perhaps more comfortably, less dangerously, but at the same time in a meaner style, more basely?—So that precisely morality would be to blame if the *highest power and splendor* actually possible to the type man was never in fact attained? So that precisely morality was the danger of dangers?

7

Let it suffice that, after this prospect had opened up before me, I had reasons to look about me for scholarly, bold, and industrious comrades (I am still looking). The project is to traverse with quite novel questions, and as though with new eyes, the enormous, distant, and so well hidden land of morality—of morality that has actually existed, actually been lived; and does this not mean virtually to *discover* this land for the first time?

If I considered in this connection the above-mentioned Dr. Rée, among others, it was because I had no doubt that the very nature of his inquiries would compel him to adopt a better method for reaching answers. Have I deceived myself in this? My desire, at any rate, was to point out to so sharp and disinterested an eye as his a better direction in which to look, in the direction of an actual *history of morality*, and to warn him in time against gazing around haphazardly in the blue after the English fashion. For it must be obvious which color is a hundred times more vital for a genealogist of morals than blue: namely *gray*, that is, what is documented, what can actually be confirmed and has actually existed, in short the entire long hieroglyphic record, so hard to decipher, of the moral past of mankind!

This was unknown to Dr. Rée; but he had read Darwin—so that in his hypotheses, and after a fashion that is at least entertaining, the Darwinian beast and the ultramodern unassuming moral milksop who "no longer bites" politely link hands, the latter wearing an expression of a certain good-natured and refined indolence, with which is mingled even a grain of pessimism and weariness, as if all these things—the problems of morality—were really not worth taking quite so seriously. But to me, on the contrary, there seems to be nothing *more* worth taking seriously, among the rewards for it being that some day one will perhaps be allowed to take them *cheerfully*. For cheerfulness—or in my own language *gay science*—is a reward: the reward of a long, brave, industrious, and subterranean seriousness, of which, to be sure, not everyone is capable. But on the day we can say with all our hearts, "Onwards! our old morality too is part *of the comedy!*" we shall have discovered a new complication and possibility for the Dionysian drama of "The Destiny of the Soul"—and one can wager that the grand old eternal comic poet of our existence will be quick to make use of it!

8

If this book is incomprehensible to anyone and jars on his ears, the fault, it seems to me, is not necessarily mine. It is clear enough, assuming, as I do assume, that one has first read my earlier writings and has not spared some trouble in doing so: for they are, indeed, not easy to penetrate. Regarding my *Zarathustra*, for example, I do not allow that anyone knows that book who has not at some time been profoundly wounded and at some time profoundly delighted by every word in it; for only then may he enjoy the privilege of reverentially sharing in the halcyon element out of which that book was born and in its sunlight clarity, remoteness, breadth, and certainty. In other cases, people find difficulty with the aphoristic form: this arises from the fact that today this form is *not taken seriously enough*. An aphorism, properly stamped and molded, has not been "deciphered" when it has simply been read; rather, one has then to begin its *exegesis*, for which is required an art of exegesis. I have offered in the third essay of the present book an example of what I regard as "exegesis" in such a case—an aphorism is prefixed to this essay, the essay itself is a commentary on it. To be sure, one thing is necessary above all if one is to practice reading as an *art* in this way, something that has been unlearned most thoroughly nowadays—and therefore it will be some time before my writings are "readable"—something for which one has almost to be a cow and in any case *not* a "modern man": *rumination*.

Sils-Maria, Upper Engadine,
July 1887

The Case of Wagner

Preface (1888)
Turinese[25] Letter of May 1888

ridendo dicere severum[26] —

I have granted myself some small relief. It is not merely pure malice when I praise Bizet in this essay at the expense of Wagner. Interspersed with many jokes, I bring up a matter that is no joke. To turn my back on Wagner was for me a fate; to like anything at all again after that, a triumph. Perhaps nobody was more dangerously attached to—grown together with— Wagnerizing; nobody tried harder to resist it; nobody was happier to be rid of it. A long story!—You want a word for it?—If I were a moralist, who knows what I might call it? Perhaps self-overcoming. —But the philosopher has no love for moralists. Neither does he love pretty words.

What does a philosopher demand of himself first and last? To overcome his time in himself, to become "timeless." With what must he therefore engage in the hardest combat? With whatever marks him as the child of his time. Well, then! I am, no less than Wagner, a child of this time; that is, a decadent: but I comprehended this, I resisted it. The philosopher in me resisted.

Nothing has preoccupied me more profoundly than the problem of decadence—I had reasons. "Good and evil" is merely a variation of that problem. Once one has developed a keen eye for the symptoms of decline, one understands morality, too—one understands what is hiding

---

[25]This polemic was written in Turin, Italy.
[26]"Through what is laughable to say what is somber."

under its most sacred names and value formulas: impoverished life, the will to the end, the great weariness. Morality negates life.

For such a task I required a special self-discipline: to take sides against everything sick in me, including Wagner, including Schopenhauer, including all of modern "humaneness."—A profound estrangement, cold, sobering up—against everything that is of this time, everything timely—and most desirable of all, the eye of Zarathustra, an eye that beholds the whole fact of man at a tremendous distance—below. For such a goal—what sacrifice wouldn't be fitting? what "self-overcoming"? what "self-denial"?

My greatest experience was a recovery. Wagner is merely one of my sicknesses.

Not that I wish to be ungrateful to this sickness. When in this essay I assert the proposition that Wagner is harmful, I wish no less to assert for whom he is nevertheless indispensable—for the philosopher. Others may be able to get along without Wagner; but the philosopher is not free to do without Wagner. He has to be the bad conscience of his time: for that he needs to understand it best. But confronted with the labyrinth of the modern soul, where could he find a guide more initiated, a more eloquent prophet of the soul, than Wagner? Through Wagner modernity speaks most intimately, concealing neither its good nor its evil—having forgotten all sense of shame. And conversely: one has almost completed an account of the value of what is modern once one has gained clarity about what is good and evil in Wagner.

I understand perfectly when a musician says today: "I hate Wagner, but I can no longer endure any other music." But I'd also understand a philosopher who would declare: "Wagner sums up modernity. There is no way out, one must first become a Wagnerian."

Twilight of the Idols

Preface (1888)

Maintaining cheerfulness in the midst of a gloomy affair, fraught with immeasurable responsibility, is no small feat; and yet what is needed more than cheerfulness? Nothing succeeds if prankishness has no part in it. Excess of strength alone is the proof of strength.

A *revaluation of all values*, this question mark, so black, so tremendous that it casts shadows upon the man who puts it down—such a destiny of a task compels one to run into the sun every moment to shake off a heavy, all-too-heavy seriousness. Every means is proper for this; every "case"[27] a case of luck. Especially, *war.* War has always been the great wisdom of all spirits who have become too inward, too profound; even in a wound there is the power to heal. A maxim, the origin of which I withhold from scholarly curiosity, has long been my motto:

Increscunt animi, virescit volnere virtus.[28]

Another mode of convalescence—under certain circumstances even more to my liking—is *sounding out idols.* There are more idols than realities in the world: that is *my* "evil eye" for this world; that is also my "evil *ear.*" For once to pose questions here with a *hammer,* and, perhaps, to hear as a reply that famous hollow sound which speaks of bloated entrails— what a delight for one who has ears even behind his ears, for me, an old psychologist and pied piper before whom just that which would remain silent must become outspoken.

This essay too—the title betrays it—is above all a recreation, a spot of sunshine, a leap sideways into the idleness of a psychologist. Perhaps a new war, too? And are new idols sounded out? This little essay is a great declaration of war; and regarding the sounding out of idols, this time they are not just idols of the age, but eternal idols, which are here touched with a hammer as with a tuning fork: there are altogether no older, no more convinced, no more puffed-up idols—and none more hollow. That does not prevent them from being those in which people have the most faith; nor does one ever say "idol," especially not in the most distinguished instance.

Turin, September 30, 1888,
on the day when the first book[29] of the Revaluation
of All Values *was completed.*

Friedrich Nietzsche

---

[27]This presumably refers to *The Case of Wagner,* which Nietzsche had just written.
[28]"The spirits increase, vigor grows through a wound."
[29]*The Antichrist.*

The Antichrist
Revaluation of All Values[30]

Preface (1888)

This book belongs to the very few. Perhaps not one of them is even living yet. Maybe they will be the readers who understand my *Zarathustra:* how *could* I mistake myself for one of those for whom there are ears even now? Only the day after tomorrow belongs to me. Some are born posthumously.

The conditions under which I am understood, and then of *necessity*—I know them only too well. One must be honest in matters of the spirit to the point of hardness before one can even endure my seriousness and my passion. One must be skilled in living on mountains—seeing the wretched ephemeral babble of politics and national self-seeking *beneath* oneself. One must have become indifferent; one must never ask if the truth is useful or if it may prove our undoing. The predilection of strength for questions for which no one today has the courage; the courage for the *forbidden;* the predestination to the labyrinth. An experience of seven solitudes. New ears for new music. New eyes for what is most distant. *And* the will to the economy of the great style: keeping our strength, our *enthusiasm* in harness. Reverence for oneself; love of oneself; unconditional freedom before oneself.

Well then! Such men alone are my readers, my right readers, my pre-destined readers: what matter the *rest?* The rest—that is merely mankind. One must be above mankind in strength, in *loftiness* of soul—in contempt.

Friedrich Nietzsche[31]

---

[30]The main title of the projected four-part work of which *The Antichrist* was intended to be the first book. (Nietzsche's collapse prevented him from going on to write the other three parts.) This preface would appear to have been meant as a preface to the entire work.

[31]No date is given, but a dating of September 1888 is suggested by Nietzsche's remark at the conclusion of his preface to *Twilight of the Idols.*

Ecce Homo

Preface (1888)

1

Seeing that before long I must confront humanity with the most difficult demand ever made of it, it seems indispensable to me to say *who I am*. Really, one should know it, for I have not left myself "without testimony." But the disproportion between the greatness of my task and the *smallness* of my contemporaries has found expression in the fact that one has neither heard nor even seen me. I live on my own credit; it is perhaps a mere prejudice that I live.

I only need to speak with one of the "educated" who come to the Upper Engadine for the summer, and I am convinced that I do *not* live.

Under these circumstances I have a duty against which my habits, even more the pride of my instincts, revolt at bottom—namely, to say: *Hear me! For I am such and such a person. Above all, do not mistake me for someone else.*

2

I am, for example, by no means a bogey, or a moralistic monster—I am actually the very opposite of the type of man who so far has been revered as virtuous. Between ourselves, it seems to me that precisely this is part of my pride. I am a disciple of the philosopher Dionysus; I should prefer to be even a satyr to being a saint. But one should really read this essay. Perhaps I have succeeded; perhaps this essay had no other meaning than to give expression to this contrast in a cheerful and philanthropic manner.

The last thing *I* should promise would be to "improve" mankind. No new idols are erected by me; let the old ones learn what feet of clay mean. *Overthrowing idols* (my word for "ideals")—that comes closer to being part of my craft. One has deprived reality of its value, its meaning, its truthfulness, to precisely the extent to which one has mendaciously invented an ideal world.

The "true world" and the "apparent world"—that means: the mendaciously invented world and reality.

The *lie* of the ideal has so far been the curse on reality; on account of it, mankind itself has become mendacious and false down to its most fundamental instincts—to the point of worshipping the *opposite* values of those which alone would guarantee its health, its future, the lofty *right* to its future.

3

Those who can breathe the air of my writings know that it is an air of the heights, a *strong* air. One must be made for it. Otherwise there is no small danger that one may catch cold in it. The ice is near, the solitude tremendous—but how calmly all things lie in the light! How freely one breathes! How much one feels *beneath* oneself!

Philosophy, as I have so far understood and lived it, means living voluntarily among ice and high mountains—seeking out everything strange and questionable in existence, everything so far placed under a ban by morality. Long experience, acquired in the course of such wanderings *in what is forbidden*, taught me to regard the causes that so far have prompted moralizing and idealizing in a very different light from what may seem desirable: the *hidden* history of the philosophers, the psychology of the great names, came to light for me.

How much truth does a spirit *endure*, how much truth does it *dare?* More and more that became for me the real measure of value. Error (faith in the ideal) is not blindness, error is *cowardice*.

Every attainment, every step forward in knowledge, *follows* from courage, from hardness against oneself, from cleanliness in relation to oneself.

I do not refute ideals, I merely put on gloves before them.

Nitimur in vetitum:[32] in this sign my philosophy will triumph one day, for what one has forbidden so far as a matter of principle has always been— truth alone.

4

Among my writings my *Zarathustra* stands to my mind by itself. With that I have given mankind the greatest present that has ever been made to it so far. This book, with a voice bridging centuries, is not only the highest book there is, the book that is truly characterized by the air of the heights—the whole fact of man lies *beneath* it at a tremendous distance—it is also the *deepest,* born out of the innermost wealth of truth, an inexhaustible well to which no pail descends without coming up again filled with gold and goodness. Here no "prophet" is speaking, none of those gruesome hybrids of sickness and will to power whom people call founders of religions. Above all, one must *hear* aright the tone that comes from this mouth, the halcyon tone, lest one should do wretched injustice to the meaning of its wisdom.

"It is the stillest words that bring on the storm. Thoughts that come on doves' feet guide the world."[33]

---

[32]"We strive for the forbidden."
[33]*Thus Spoke Zarathustra*, Second Part, last chapter.

> The figs are falling from the trees; they are good and sweet; and,
> as they fall, their red skin bursts. I am a north wind to ripe figs.
>   Thus, like figs, these teachings fall to you, my friends: now
> consume their juice and their sweet meat. It is fall around us, and
> pure sky and afternoon.[34]

It is no fanatic that speaks here; this is not "preaching"; no *faith* is demanded here: from an infinite abundance of light and depth of happiness falls drop upon drop, word upon word: the tempo of these speeches is a tender adagio. Such things reach only the most select. It is a privilege without equal to be a listener here. Nobody is free to have ears for Zarathustra.

Is not Zarathustra in view of all this a *seducer?*—But what does he himself say, as he returns again for the first time to his solitude? Precisely the opposite of everything that any "sage," "saint," "world-redeemer," or any other decadent would say in such a case.—Not only does he speak differently, he also *is* different.—

> Now I go alone, my disciples, You, too, go now, alone. Thus I
> want it.
>   Go away from me and resist Zarathustra! And even better: be
> ashamed of him! Perhaps he deceived you.
>   The man of knowledge must not only love his enemies, he must
> also be able to hate his friends.
>   One repays a teacher badly if one always remains nothing but a
> pupil. And why do you not want to pluck at my wreath?
>   You revere me; but what if your reverence *tumbles* one day?
> Beware lest a statue slay you.
>   You say that you believe in Zarathustra? But what matters
> Zarathustra? You are my believers—but what matter all believers?
>   You had not yet sought yourselves; and you found me. Thus do
> all believers; therefore all faith amounts to so little.
>   Now I bid you lose me and find yourselves; and only *when you
> have all denied me* will I return to you.[35]

Friedrich Nietzsche[36]

---

[34]Ibid., second chapter.

[35]Ibid., First Part, last chapter.

[36]Nietzsche did not indicate a date. The reference to his birthday in the following paragraph, which he inserted between this preface and the opening of the first part of the work itself, suggests the date of October 1888, three months before his collapse; but he may well have only begun the work then, completing it and writing the preface near the very end of that year and of his active life.

FOREWORD

On this perfect day, when everything is ripening and not only the grape turns brown, the eye of the sun just fell upon my life: I looked back, I looked forward, and never saw so many and such good things at once. It was not for nothing that I buried my forty-fourth year today; I had the *right* to bury it; whatever was life in it has been saved, is immortal. The first book of the *Revaluation of All Values*,[37] the *Songs of Zarathustra*,[38] the *Twilight of the Idols*, my attempt to philosophize with a hammer—all presents of this year, indeed of its last quarter! *How could I fail to be grateful to my whole life?*—and so I tell my life to myself.

---

[37] *The Antichrist.*

[38] Published, after Nietzsche's collapse, under the title *Dionysus Dithyrambs*, in the same volume with *Zarathustra* (Part) IV (trans.).

Ecce Homo:
How One Becomes What One Is
(1888)
(*Excerpts*)

WHY I AM SO WISE

1

The good fortune of my existence, its uniqueness perhaps, lies in its fatality: I am, to express it in the form of a riddle, already dead as my father, while as my mother I am still living and becoming old. This dual descent, as it were, both from the highest and the lowest rung on the ladder of life, at the same time a *decadent* and a *beginning*—this, if anything, explains that neutrality, that freedom from all partiality in relation to the total problem of life, that perhaps distinguishes me. I have a subtler sense of smell for the signs of ascent and decline than any other human being before me; I am the teacher *par excellence* for this—I know both, I am both.

My father died at the age of thirty-six: he was delicate, kind, and morbid, as a being that is destined merely to pass by—more a gracious memory of life than life itself. In the same year in which his life went downward, mine, too, went downward: at thirty-six, I reached the lowest point of my vitality—I still lived, but without being able to see three steps ahead. Then—it was 1879—I retired from my professorship at Basel, spent the summer in St. Moritz like a shadow, and the next winter, than which not one in my life has been poorer in sunshine, in Naumburg *as* a shadow. This was my minimum: the *Wanderer and His Shadow*[39] originated at this time. Doubtless, I then knew about shadows.

The following winter, my first one in Genoa, that sweetening and spiritualization which is almost inseparably connected with an extreme poverty of blood and muscle, produced *The Dawn*. The perfect brightness and cheerfulness, even exuberance of the spirit, reflected in this work, is compatible in my case not only with the most profound physiological weakness, but even with an excess of pain. In the midst of the torments

---

[39]Subsequently incorporated with *Human, All Too Human* as Part Two of Volume Two.

that go with an uninterrupted three-day migraine, accompanied by laborious vomiting of phlegm, I possessed a dialectician's clarity *par excellence* and thought through with very cold blood matters for which under healthier circumstances I am not mountain-climber, not subtle, not *cold* enough. My readers know perhaps in what way I consider dialectic as a symptom of decadence; for example in the most famous case, the case of Socrates.

All pathological disturbances of the intellect, even that half-numb state that follows fever, have remained entirely foreign to me to this day; and I had to do research to find out about their nature and frequency. My blood moves slowly. Nobody has ever discovered any fever in me. A physician who treated me for some time as if my nerves were sick finally said: "It's not your nerves, it is rather I that am nervous." There is altogether no sign of any local degeneration; no organically conditioned stomach complaint, however profound the weakness of my gastric system may be as a consequence of overall exhaustion. My eye trouble, too, though at times dangerously close to blindness, is only a consequence and not a cause: with every increase in vitality my ability to see has also increased again.

A long, all too long, series of years signifies recovery for me; unfortunately it also signifies relapse, decay, the periodicity of a kind of decadence. Need I say after all this that in questions of decadence I am *experienced?* I have spelled them forward and backward. Even that filigree art of grasping and comprehending in general, those fingers for *nuances*, that psychology of "looking around the corner," and whatever else is characteristic of me, was learned only then, is the true present of those days in which everything in me became subtler—observation itself as well as all organs of observation. Looking from the perspective of the sick toward *healthier* concepts and values and, conversely, looking again from the fullness and self-assurance of a *rich* life down into the secret work of the instinct of decadence—in this I have had the longest training, my truest experience; if in anything, I became master in *this*. Now I know how, have the know-how, to *reverse perspectives:* the first reason why a "revaluation of values" is perhaps possible for me alone.

2

Apart from the fact that I am a decadent, I am also the opposite. My proof for this is, among other things, that I have always instinctively chosen the *right* means against wretched states; while the decadent typically chooses means that are disadvantageous for him. As *summa summarum*,[40] I was healthy; as an angle, as a specialty, I was a decadent. The

---

[40]Overall summary.

energy to choose absolute solitude and leave the life to which I had become accustomed; the insistence on not allowing myself any longer to be cared for, waited on, and *doctored*—that betrayed an absolute instinctive certainty about what was needed above all at that time. I took myself in hand, I made myself healthy again: the condition for this—every physiologist would admit that—is *that one be healthy at bottom*. A typically morbid being cannot become healthy, much less make itself healthy. For a typically healthy person, conversely, being sick can even become an energetic *stimulus* for life, for living *more*. This, in fact, is how that long period of sickness appears to me *now:* as it were, I discovered life anew, including myself; I tasted all good and even little things, as others cannot easily taste them—I turned my will to health, to *life*, into a philosophy.

For it should be noted: it was during the years of my lowest vitality that I *ceased* to be a pessimist; the instinct of self-restoration *forbade* me a philosophy of poverty and discouragement.

What is it, fundamentally, that allows us to recognize *who has turned out well?* That a well-turned-out person pleases our senses, that he is carved from wood that is hard, delicate, and at the same time smells good. He has a taste only for what is good for him; his pleasure, his delight cease where the measure of what is good for him is transgressed. He guesses what remedies avail against what is harmful; he exploits bad accidents to his advantage; what does not kill him makes him stronger. Instinctively, he collects from everything he sees, hears, lives through, *his* sum: he is a principle of selection, he discards much. He is always in his own company, whether he associates with books, human beings, or landscapes: he honors by *choosing*, by *admitting*, by *trusting*. He reacts slowly to all kinds of stimuli, with that slowness which long caution and deliberate pride have bred in him: he examines the stimulus that approaches him, he is far from meeting it halfway. He believes neither in "misfortune" nor in "guilt": he comes to terms with himself, with others; he knows how to *forget*—he is strong enough; hence everything *must* turn out for his best.

Well then, I am the *opposite* of a decadent, for I have just described *myself*.

*   *   *   *   *

WHY I WRITE SUCH GOOD BOOKS

1

I am one thing, my writings are another matter.—Before I discuss them, one by one, let me touch on the question of their being understood or *not* understood. I'll do it as casually as decency permits; for the time for this question certainly hasn't come yet. The time for me hasn't come yet: some are born posthumously.

Some day institutions will be needed in which men live and teach as I conceive of living and teaching; it might even happen that a few chairs will then be set aside for the interpretation of *Zarathustra*. But it would contradict my character entirely if I expected ears and hands for my truths today: that today one doesn't hear me and doesn't accept my ideas is not only understandable, it even seems right to me. I don't want to be confounded with others—not even by myself. [. . .]

Ultimately, nobody can get more out of things, including books, than he already knows. For what one lacks access to from experience one will have no ear. Now let us imagine an extreme case: that a book speaks of nothing but events that lie altogether beyond the possibility of any frequent or even rare experience—that it is the first language for a new series of experiences. In that case, simply nothing will be heard, but there will be the acoustic illusion that where nothing is heard, nothing is there.

This is, in the end, my average experience and, if you will, the originality of my experience. Whoever thought he had understood something of me, had made up something out of me after his own image—not uncommonly an antithesis to me; for example, an "idealist"—and whoever had understood nothing of me, denied that I need be considered at all.

The word "overman," as the designation of a type of supreme achievement, as opposed to "modern" men, to "good" men, to Christians and other nihilists—a word that in the mouth of a Zarathustra, the annihilator of morality, becomes a very pensive word—has been understood almost everywhere with the utmost innocence in the sense of those very values whose opposite Zarathustra was meant to represent—that is, as an "idealistic" type of a higher kind of man, half "saint," half "genius."

Other scholarly oxen have suspected me of Darwinism on that account. Even the "hero worship" of that unconscious and involuntary counterfeiter, Carlyle, which I have repudiated so maliciously, has been read into it. Those to whom I said in confidence that they should sooner look even for a Cesare Borgia than for a Parsifal, did not believe their own ears.

* * * * *

WHY I AM A DESTINY

1

I know my fate. One day my name will be associated with the memory of something tremendous—a crisis without equal on earth, the most profound collision of conscience, a decision that was conjured up *against* everything that had been believed, demanded, hallowed so far. I am no man, I am dynamite. —Yet for all that, there is nothing in me of a founder of a religion—religions are affairs of the rabble; I find it necessary to wash my hands after I have come into contact with religious people. —I *want* no "believers"; I think I am too malicious to believe in myself; I never speak to masses. —I have a terrible fear that one day I will be pronounced *holy:* you will guess why I publish this book *before;* it shall prevent people from doing mischief with me.

I do not want to be a holy man; sooner even a buffoon. —Perhaps I am a buffoon. —Yet in spite of that—or rather *not* in spite of it, because so far nobody has been more mendacious than holy men—the truth speaks out of me. —But my truth is *terrible;* for so far one has called *lies* truth.

Revaluation of all values: that is my formula for an act of supreme self-examination on the part of humanity, become flesh and genius in me. It is my fate that I have to be the first *decent* human being; that I know myself to stand in opposition to the mendaciousness of millennia. —I was the first to *discover* the truth by being the first to experience lies as lies—smelling them out. —My genius is in my nostrils.

I contradict as has never been contradicted before and am nevertheless the opposite of a No-saying spirit. I am a bringer of glad tidings like no one before me; I know tasks of such elevation that any notion of them has been lacking so far; only beginning with me are there hopes again. For all that, I am necessarily also the man of calamity. For when truth enters into a fight with the lies of millennia, we shall have upheavals, a convulsion of earthquakes, a moving of mountains and valleys, the like of which has never been dreamed of. The concept of politics will have merged entirely with a war of spirits; all power structures of the old society will have been exploded—all of them are based on lies: there will be wars the like of which have never yet been seen on earth. It is only beginning with me that the earth knows *great politics.*

2

You want a formula for such a destiny *become man?* That is to be found in my *Zarathustra:*

"And whoever wants to be a creator in good and evil, must first be an annihilator and break values. Thus the highest evil belongs to the greatest goodness: but this is—being creative."[41]

I am by far the most terrible human being that has existed so far; this does not preclude the possibility that I shall be the most beneficial. I know the pleasure in destroying to a degree that accords with my powers

---

[41]*Thus Spoke Zarathustra*, Second Part, Chapter 12.

to destroy—in both respects I obey my Dionysian nature which does not know how to separate doing No from saying Yes. I am the first immoralist: that makes me the annihilator *par excellence*.

3

I have not been asked, as I should have been asked, what the name of Zarathustra means in my mouth, the mouth of the first immoralist: for what constitutes the tremendous historical uniqueness of that Persian is just the opposite of this. Zarathustra was the first to consider the fight of good and evil the very wheel in the machinery of things: the transposition of morality into the metaphysical realm, as a force, cause, and end in itself, is *his* work. But this question itself is at bottom its own answer. Zarathustra created this most calamitous error, morality; consequently, he must also be the first to recognize it. Not only has he more experience in this matter, for a longer time, than any other thinker—after all, the whole of history is the refutation by experiment of the principle of the so-called "moral world order"—what is more important is that Zarathustra is more truthful than any other thinker. His doctrine, and his alone, posits truthfulness as the highest virtue; this means the opposite of the cowardice of the "idealist" who flees from reality; Zarathustra has more intestinal fortitude than all other thinkers taken together. To speak the truth and to *shoot well with arrows*, that is Persian virtue.—Am I understood?—The self-overcoming of morality, out of truthfulness; the self-overcoming of the moralist, into his opposite—into me—that is what the name of Zarathustra means in my mouth.

4

Fundamentally, my term *immoralist* involves two negations. For one, I negate a type of man that has so far been considered supreme: the good, the benevolent, the beneficent. And then I negate a type of morality that has become prevalent and predominant as morality itself—the morality of decadence or, more concretely, *Christian* morality. It would be permissible to consider the second contradiction the more decisive one, since I take the overestimation of goodness and benevolence on a large scale for a consequence of decadence, for a symptom of weakness, irreconcilable with an ascending, Yes-saying life: negating *and destroying* are conditions of saying Yes. [. . .]

5

Zarathustra, the first psychologist of the good, is—consequently—a friend of the evil. When a decadent type of man ascended to the rank of the highest type, this could only happen at the expense of its countertype, the type of man that is strong and sure of life. When the herd animal is irradiated by the glory of the purest virtue, the exceptional man must have been devaluated into evil. When mendaciousness at any price monopolizes the word "truth" for its perspective, the really truthful man is bound to be branded with the worst names. Zarathustra leaves no doubt at this point: he says that it was his insight precisely into the good, the "best," that made him shudder at man in general; that it was from *this* aversion that he grew wings "to soar off into distant futures";[42] he does not conceal the fact that *his* type of man, a relatively superhuman type, is superhuman precisely in its relation to the *good*—that the good and the just would call his overman *devil*.

"You highest men whom my eyes have seen, this is my doubt about you and my secret laughter: I guess that you would call my overman—devil."

"What is great is so alien to your souls that the overman would be terrifying to you in his goodness."[43]

It is here and nowhere else that one must make a start to comprehend what Zarathustra wants: this type of man that he conceives, conceives reality *as it is*, being strong enough to do so; this type is not estranged or removed from reality but is reality itself and exemplifies all that is terrible and questionable in it—*only in that way can man attain greatness.*

*   *   *   *   *

[42]*Thus Spoke Zarathustra*, Second Part, Chapter 21.
[43]*Thus Spoke Zarathustra*, Second Part, Chapter 21.

Bibliography

WRITINGS OF NIETZSCHE

German Editions

The best and most complete edition of Nietzsche's writings is the first of those in the following list, edited by Colli and Montinari. It is now generally regarded as the authoritative edition for scholarly purposes. Before publication of that edition, the second of those listed (also known as the "*Grossoktavausgabe*" or "large folio edition") was the standard edition. The third has the advantages of compactness and a very useful index volume, but it has been eclipsed by the publication of a relatively inexpensive "student edition" of the main volumes of the Colli-Montinari in paperback.

Werke: Kritische Gesamtausgabe, eds. Giorgio Colli and Mazzino Montinari, 30 vols. Berlin: de Gruyter, 1967–1978.
Werke: Musarionausgabe, 23 vols. Munich: Musarion, 1920–1929.
Werke in drei Bänden, ed. Karl Schlechta, 3 vols. Munich: Carl Hanser, 1954–1956; with an index in vol. 4 (1965).

English Translations

The only comprehensive English-language edition of Nietzsche's works is the incomplete and very inadequate old edition published in 1909–1911 under the editorship of Oscar Levy. It is not clear whether or when a translation of the Colli-Montinari *Gesamtausgabe* will be made; but in any event it is not to be expected in the near future. Most of Nietzsche's works, and some of his other writings, have been published in one or more translations. Those of Walter Kaufmann and of R. J. Hollingdale are generally preferred to the rest.

The Birth of Tragedy (*Die Geburt der Tragödie*, 1872)
Trans. Walter Kaufmann, with *The Case of Wagner.* New York: Vintage, 1966.
Trans. Frances Golffing, with *The Genealogy of Morals.* Garden City, N.Y.: Doubleday, 1956.
Philosophy in the Tragic Age of the Greeks (*Die Philosophie im tragischen Zeitalter der Griechen*, 1870–1873)
Trans. Marianne Cowan, South Bend, Ind.: Gateway, 1962.
"On Truth and Lies in a Nonmoral Sense" ("*Über Wahrheit und Lüge im aussermoralischen Sinne*," 1873)
Trans. Daniel Breazeale, in *Nietzsche, Philosophy and Truth.* Edited by Breazeale. Atlantic Highlands, N.J.: Humanities Press, 1979.
Trans. Walter Kaufmann, in *The Portable Nietzsche.* Edited by Kaufmann. New York: Viking, 1954.
Untimely Meditations (*Unzeitgemässe Betrachtungen*, 1873–1876)
Trans. R. J. Hollingdale, as *Untimely Meditations.* Cambridge and New York: Cambridge University Press, 1983.
Ed. William Arrowsmith, as *Unmodern Observations.* New Haven: Yale University Press, 1990.

David Strauss, the Confessor and the Writer (*David Strauss, der Bekenner und der Schrift-steller*, 1873)
   Trans. R. J. Hollingdale, in *Untimely Meditations*. Cambridge and New York: Cambridge University Press.
   Trans. Herbert Golder, in *Unmodern Observations*. Edited by William Arrow-smith. New Haven: Yale University Press.
On the Uses and Disadvantages of History for Life (*Von Nutzen und Nachteil der Historie für das Leben*, 1874)
   Trans. R. J. Hollingdale, in *Untimely Meditations*. Cambridge and New York: Cambridge University Press.
   Trans. Gary Brown, as *History in the Service and Disservice of Life*. In *Unmodern Observations*. Edited by William Arrowsmith. New Haven: Yale University Press.
   Trans. Adrian Collins, as *The Use and Abuse of History*. Indianapolis: Liberal Arts Press, Bobbs-Merrill, 1957.
   Trans. Peter Preuss, as *On the Advantage and Disadvantage of History for Life*. Indianapolis: Hackett, 1980.
Schopenhauer as Educator (*Schopenhauer als Erzieher*, 1874)
   Trans. R. J. Hollingdale, in *Untimely Meditations*. Cambridge and New York: Cambridge University Press.
   Trans. William Arrowsmith, in *Unmodern Observations*. Edited by Arrowsmith. New Haven: Yale University Press.
   Trans. James W. Hillesheim and Malcolm R. Simpson. South Bend: Gateway, 1965.
We Classicists (*Wir Philologen*, 1875)
   Trans. William Arrowsmith, in *Unmodern Observations*. Edited by Arrowsmith. New Haven: Yale University Press.
Richard Wagner in Bayreuth (*Richard Wagner in Bayreuth*, 1876)
   Trans. R. J. Hollingdale, in *Untimely Meditations*. Cambridge and New York: Cambridge University Press.
   Trans. Gary Brown, in *Unmodern Observations*. Edited by William Arrowsmith. New Haven: Yale University Press.
Human, All Too Human (*Menschliches, Allzumenschliches*, first volume, 1878; first part of second volume, *Assorted Opinions and Maxims*, 1879; second part of second volume, *The Wanderer and His Shadow*, 1880)
   Trans. R. J. Hollingdale. Cambridge and New York: Cambridge University Press, 1986.
   Trans. Marion Faber, with Stephen Lehmann. Lincoln: University of Nebraska Press, 1984. Vol. 1 only.
Daybreak (*Morganröthe*, 1881)
   Trans. R. J. Hollingdale. Cambridge and New York: Cambridge University Press, 1982.
The Gay Science or *Joyful Wisdom* (*Die fröhliche Wissenschaft*, Books 1–4, 1882; 2d ed. with preface and Book 5, 1887)
   Trans. Walter Kaufmann, as *The Gay Science*. New York: Vintage, 1974.
   Trans. Thomas Common, as *Joyful Wisdom*. New York: Frederick Ungar, 1960.
Thus Spoke Zarathustra (*Also Sprach Zarathustra*, Parts 1 and 2, 1883; Part 3, 1884; Part 4, 1885)

Trans. Walter Kaufmann, in *The Portable Nietzsche*. New York: Viking, 1954.

Trans. R. J. Hollingdale. Harmondsworth, England: Penguin Books, 1961.

Trans. Marianne Cowan. Chicago: Gateway, 1957.

Beyond Good and Evil (Jenseits von Gut und Böse, 1886)
Trans. Walter Kaufmann. New York: Vintage, 1966.

Trans. R. J. Hollingdale. Harmondsworth: Penguin Books, 1973.

Trans. Marianne Cowan. Chicago: Gateway, 1955.

On the Genealogy of Morals (Zur Genealogie der Moral, 1887)
Trans. Walter Kaufmann and R. J. Hollingdale, with *Ecce Homo*, New York: Vintage, 1967.

Trans. Francis Golffing, with *The Birth of Tragedy*. Garden City, N.Y.: Doubleday, 1956.

The Case of Wagner (Der Fall Wagner, 1888)
Trans. Walter Kaufmann, with *The Birth of Tragedy*. New York: Vintage, 1966.

Twilight of the Idols (Götzen-Dämmerung, 1889)
Trans. Walter Kaufmann, in *The Portable Nietzsche*. New York: Viking, 1954.

Trans. R. J. Hollingdale, with *The Anti-Christ*. Harmondsworth, England: Penguin Books, 1968.

The Antichrist (Der Antichrist, completed 1888, first published 1895)
Trans. H. L. Mencken. New York: Alfred A. Knopf, 1918.

Trans. Walter Kaufmann, in *The Portable Nietzsche*. New York: Viking, 1954.

Trans. R. J. Hollingdale, with *Twilight of the Idols*. Harmondsworth, England: Penguin Books, 1968.

Nietzsche contra Wagner (Nietzsche contra Wagner, completed 1888, first published 1895)
Trans. Walter Kaufmann, in *The Portable Nietzsche*. New York: Viking, 1954.

Ecce Homo (Ecce Homo, completed 1888, first published 1908)
Trans. Walter Kaufmann, with *On the Genealogy of Morals*. New York: Vintage, 1967.

Trans. R. J. Hollingdale. Harmondsworth, England: Penguin Books, 1979.

The Will to Power (Der Wille zur Macht, a selection of notes from Nietzsche's notebooks made and arranged by his sister and others, published in several editions of increasing size in 1901, 1904, and 1910–1911)
Trans. Walter Kaufmann and R. J. Hollingdale. New York: Vintage, 1967.

Selected Letters of Friedrich Nietzsche
Ed. and trans. Christopher Middleton. Chicago: University of Chicago Press, 1969.

Nietzsche: A Self-Portrait from His Letters
Ed. and trans. Peter Fuss and Henry Shapiro. Cambridge: Harvard University Press, 1971.

The Poetry of Friedrich Nietzsche
Ed. Philip Grundlehner. New York and Oxford: Oxford University Press, 1986.

SECONDARY LITERATURE

The best-known and now-"classic" introduction to Nietzsche in English, Walter Kaufmann's *Nietzsche: Philosopher, Psychologist, Antichrist*, first published in 1950 by Princeton University Press and now in its fourth edition, is still a good place for students to start. Two other useful studies of Nietzsche's life in relation to his thought are Ronald Hayman's *Nietzsche: A Critical Life* (New York: Oxford University Press, 1980) and R. J. Hollingdale's *Nietzsche: The Man and His Philosophy* (Baton Rouge: Louisiana State University Press, 1965). George Morgan's earlier *What Nietzsche Means*, first published by Harvard in 1941, also remains useful. For a comprehensive study of Nietzsche's philosophical thought, see Richard Schacht's *Nietzsche* (London: Routledge & Kegan Paul, 1983).

Until recently, good studies of Nietzsche in English were few and far between; but the publication of Arthur Danto's *Nietzsche as Philosopher* (New York: Macmillan) in 1965 was a major event in the development of English-language Nietzsche studies and was followed by a trickle over the next twenty years that has now become a flood, to which increasingly numerous translations of German and French Nietzsche studies have recently been added. A selected list of notable books on Nietzsche—primarily written or translated into English since the mid-1960s—follows. Many more studies written in other languages remain untranslated into English, and there are others in English as well. This list should, however, be sufficient for most readers of this volume. [For a more comprehensive bibliography of the earlier literature, see the *International Nietzsche Bibliography*, compiled and edited by Herbert W. Reichert and Karl Schlechta, revised and expanded edition (Chapel Hill: University of North Carolina Press, 1968).]

Ackerman, Robert. *Nietzsche: A Frenzied Look*. Amherst: University of Massachusetts Press, 1990.

Alderman, Harold. *Nietzsche's Gift*. Athens: Ohio University Press, 1977.

Allison, David B., ed. *The New Nietzsche: Contemporary Styles of Interpretation*. New York: Dell, 1977.

Bergmann, Peter. *Nietzsche: The Last Antipolitical German*. Bloomington: Indiana University Press, 1987.

Behler, Ernst. *Confrontations*. Translated by Steven Taubeneck. Stanford: Stanford University Press, 1991.

Blondel, Eric. *Nietzsche, the Body and Culture: Philosophy as a Philological Genealogy*. Translated by Sean Hand. Stanford: Stanford University Press, 1991.

Brinton, Crane. *Nietzsche*. Cambridge: Harvard University Press, 1941; 2nd ed., New York: Harper, 1965.

Clark, Maudemarie. *Nietzsche on Truth and Philosophy*. Cambridge: Cambridge University Press, 1990.

Cooper, David. *Authenticity and Learning: Nietzsche's Educational Philosophy*. London: Routledge & Kegan Paul, 1983.

Copleston, Frederick. *Friedrich Nietzsche: Philosopher of Culture*. London: Burns, Oakes & Washburn, 1942; New York: Barnes & Noble, 1975.

Crawford, Claudia. *The Beginnings of Nietzsche's Theory of Language*. Berlin: Walter de Gruyter, 1988.

Dannhauser, Werner. *Nietzsche's View of Socrates*. Ithaca: Cornell University Press, 1974.

Danto, Arthur C. *Nietzsche as Philosopher*. New York: Columbia University Press, 1980.

Darby, Tom, et al., eds. *Nietzsche and the Rhetoric of Nihilism*. Ottawa, Canada: Carleton University Press, 1989.

Del Caro, Adrian. *Nietzsche Contra Nietzsche: Creativity and the Anti-Romantic*. Baton Rouge: Louisiana State University Press, 1989.

Deleuze, Giles. *Nietzsche and Philosophy*. Translated by Hugh Tomlinson. New York: Columbia University Press, 1983.

Derrida, Jacques. *Spurs: Nietzsche's Styles*. Translated by Barbara Harlow. Chicago: University of Chicago Press, 1979.

Detwiler, Bruce. *Nietzsche and the Politics of Aristocratic Radicalism*. Chicago: University of Chicago Press, 1990.

Fink, Eugen. *Nietzsches Philosophie*. Stuttgart: Kohlhammer, 1960.

Fischer-Dieskau, Dietrich. *Wagner and Nietzsche*. Translated by Joachim Neugroschel. New York: Seabury Press, 1976.

Gilman, Sander L. *Conversations with Nietzsche*. Translated by David Parent. New York: Oxford University Press, 1989.

Graybeal, Jean. *Language and "the Feminine" in Nietzsche and Heidegger*. Bloomington: Indiana University Press, 1990.

Grimm, Ruediger Hermann. *Nietzsche's Theory of Knowledge*. Berlin: Walter de Gruyter, 1977.

Hayman, Ronald. *Nietzsche: A Critical Life*. New York and Oxford: Oxford University Press, 1980.

Heidegger, Martin. *Nietzsche*. 4 vols. Translated by David Farrell Krell. New York: Harper & Row, 1979–1984.

Heller, Erich. *The Importance of Nietzsche*. Chicago: University of Chicago Press, 1988.

Heller, Peter. *Studies in Nietzsche*. Bonn: Bouvier, 1980.

Higgins, Kathleen Marie. *Nietzsche's Zarathustra*. Philadelphia: Temple University Press, 1987.

Hollingdale, R. J. *Nietzsche*. London: Routledge & Kegan Paul, 1965.

Hollingdale, R. J. *Nietzsche: The Man and His Philosophy*. Baton Rouge: Louisiana State University Press, 1965.

Hollinrake, Roger. *Nietzsche, Wagner, and the Philosophy of Pessimism*. London: Routledge & Kegan Paul, 1982.

Houlgate, Stephen. *Hegel, Nietzsche, and the Criticism of Metaphysics*. Cambridge: Cambridge University Press, 1986.

Hunt, Lester H. *Nietzsche and the Origin of Virtue*. London: Routledge, 1991.

Jaspers, Karl. *Nietzsche: An Introduction to the Understanding of His Philosophical Activity*. Translated by Charles Walraff and Frederick J. Schmitz. Tucson: University of Arizona Press, 1965.

Jaspers, Karl. *Nietzsche and Christianity*. Translated by E. B. Ashton. Chicago: Regnery, 1961.

Jung, C. G. *Nietzsche's Zarathustra*. Edited by James L. Jarrett. Princeton: Princeton University Press, 1988.

Kaufmann, Walter. *Nietzsche: Philosopher, Psychologist, Antichrist*. 4th ed. Princeton: Princeton University Press, 1974.

Koelb, Clayton, ed. *Nietzsche as Postmodernist: Essays Pro and Con*. Albany: SUNY Press, 1990.

Krell, David F., and David Woods, eds. *Exceedingly Nietzsche: Aspects of Contemporary Nietzsche Interpretation*. London: Routledge, 1988.

Lampert, Laurence. *Nietzsche's Teaching: An Interpretation of Thus Spoke Zarathustra*. New Haven: Yale University Press, 1987.

Love, Frederick. *The Young Nietzsche and the Wagnerian Experience*. Chapel Hill: University of North Carolina Press, 1963.

Löwith, Karl. *Nietzsches Philosophie der Ewigen Wiederkunft des Gleichen*. 2d ed. Stuttgart: Kohlhammer, 1956. Originally published 1934.

Magnus, Bernd. *Nietzsche's Existential Imperative*. Bloomington: Indiana University Press, 1978.

Magnus, Bernd, Jean-Pierre Mileur, and Stanley Stewart. *Nietzsche's Case: Philosophy as/and Literature*. New York: Routledge, 1992.

Martin, Glen D. *From Nietzsche to Wittgenstein: The Problem of Truth and Nihilism in the Modern World*. New York: Peter Lang, 1989.

May, Keith M. *Nietzsche and Modern Literature*. New York: St. Martin's Press, 1988.

May, Keith M. *Nietzsche and the Spirit of Tragedy*. New York: St. Martin's Press, 1990.

Mencken, H. L. *The Philosophy of Friedrich Nietzsche*. Port Washington, N.Y.: Kennicat, 1967. Originally published in 1913.

Messer, August. *Erläuterungen zu Nietzsches Zarathustra*. Stuttgart: Strucher & Schroeder, 1922.

Moles, Alistair. *Nietzsche's Philosophy of Nature and Cosmology*. New York: Peter Lang, 1990.

Morgan, George A. *What Nietzsche Means*. Cambridge: Harvard University Press, 1941; Westport, Conn.: Greenwood, 1975.

Nehamas, Alexander. *Nietzsche: Life as Literature*. Cambridge: Harvard University Press, 1985.

O'Brien, Connor Cruse. *The Suspecting Glance*. London: Faber & Faber, 1972.

O'Hara, Daniel, ed. *Why Nietzsche Now?* Bloomington: Indiana University Press, 1985.

Pasley, Malcolm, ed. *Nietzsche: Imagery and Thought*. Berkeley: University of California Press, 1978.

Parkes, Graham, ed. *Nietzsche and Asian Thought*. Chicago: University of Chicago Press, 1991.

Pettey, John Carson. *Nietzsche's Philosophical and Narrative Styles*. New York: Peter Lang, 1991.

Pfeffer, Rose. *Nietzsche: Disciple of Dionysus*. Louisburg: Bucknell University Press, 1972.

Pletsch, Carl. *Young Nietzsche: Becoming a Genius*. New York: Free Press, 1991.

Podach, E. F. *The Madness of Nietzsche*. Translated by F. A. Voigt. New York: Gordon, 1974.

Riechert, Herbert W. and Schlechta, Karl, eds. *International Nietzsche Bibliography*. Revised and expanded. Chapel Hill: University of North Carolina, 1968.

Rickels, Laurence A., ed. *Looking After Nietzsche*. Albany: State University of New York Press, 1990.

Sallis, John. *Crossings: Nietzsche and the Space of Tragedy*. Chicago: University of Chicago Press, 1991.

Salter, William M. *Nietzsche the Thinker: A Study.* New York: Ungar, 1968.

Sautet, Marc. *Nietzsche for Beginners.* New York: Writers and Readers Publishing, 1990.

Schacht, Richard. *Making Sense of Nietzsche.* Urbana: University of Illinois Press, 1994.

Schacht, Richard. *Nietzsche.* London: Routledge & Kegan Paul, 1983.

Schacht, Richard, ed. *Nietzsche, Genealogy, Morality.* Berkeley: University of California Press, 1994.

Schlechta, Karl. *Nietzsches grosser Mittag.* Frankfurt: Klosterman, 1954.

Schrift, Alan. *Nietzsche and the Question of Interpretation.* New York: Routledge, 1990.

Schutte, Ofelia. *Beyond Nihilism: Nietzsche Without Masks.* Chicago: University of Chicago Press, 1984.

Scott, Charles E. *The Question of Ethics: Nietzsche, Foucault, Heidegger.* Bloomington: Indiana University Press, 1990.

Shapiro, Gary. *Alcyone: Nietzsche on Gifts, Noise, and Women.* Albany: SUNY Press, 1991.

Shapiro, Gary. *Nietzschean Narratives.* Bloomington: Indiana University Press, 1989.

Silk, M. S. and J. P. Stern. *Nietzsche on Tragedy.* Cambridge: Cambridge University Press, 1981.

Simmel, Georg. *Schopenhauer and Nietzsche.* Translated by Helmuth Loiskandel, Deena Weinstein, and Michael Weinstein. Amherst: University of Massachusetts Press, 1986. Urbana: Univerisity of Illinois Press, 1991. Originally published 1907.

Sloterdijk, Peter. *Thinker on Stage: Nietzsche's Materialism.* Translated by Jamie Owen Daniel. Minneapolis: University of Minnesota Press, 1989.

Solomon, Robert C., ed. *Nietzsche: A Collection of Critical Essays.* Notre Dame: University of Notre Dame Press. Originally published by Doubleday, 1973.

Solomon, Robert C., and Kathleen M. Higgins, eds. *Reading Nietzsche.* New York: Oxford University Press, 1988.

Stack, George J. *Lange and Nietzsche.* Berlin: Walter De Gruyter, 1983.

Stack, George J. *Nietzsche and Emerson: An Elective Affinity.* Columbus: Ohio State University Press, 1992.

Stack, George J. *Nietzsche: Man, Knowledge and Will to Power.* Wolfeboro, N.H.: Hollowbrook Publishers, 1992.

Stambaugh, Joan. *Nietzsche's Thought of Eternal Return.* Baltimore: Johns Hopkins University Press, 1972.

Stambaugh, Joan. *The Problem of Time in Nietzsche.* Philadelphia: Bucknell University Press, 1987.

Staten, Henry. *Nietzsche's Voice.* Ithaca, N.Y.: Cornell University Press, 1990.

Steiner, Rudolf. *Friedrich Nietzsche: Fighter for Freedom.* Translated by Margaret Ingram Deris. Englewood, N.J.: Rudolf Steiner Publications, 1960.

Stern, J. P. *Friedrich Nietzsche.* New York: Penguin, 1978.

Stern, J. P. *A Study of Nietzsche.* Cambridge: Cambridge University Press, 1979.

Strong, Tracy B. *Friedrich Nietzsche and the Politics of Transfiguration.* Berkeley: University of California Press, 1975.

Strong, Tracy B., and Michael Gillespie, eds. *Toward New Seas: Philosophy, Aesthetics and Politics in Nietzsche.* Chicago: University of Chicago Press, 1988.

Taylor, Seth. *Left-Wing Nietzscheans: The Politics of German Expressionism.* Berlin and New York: de Gruyter, 1990.

Thatcher, David S. *Nietzsche in England.* Toronto: Toronto University Press, 1970.

Thiele, Leslie Paul. *Friedrich Nietzsche and the Politics of the Soul: A Study of Heroic Individualism.* Princeton: Princeton University Press, 1990.

Tönnies, Ferdinand. *Der Nietzsche-Kultus: Eine Kritik.* Leipzig: O. R. Reisland, 1897.

Vaihinger, Hans. *Nietzsche als Philosoph.* Berlin: Reuther & Reichard, 1902.

Warren, Mark T. *Nietzsche and Political Thought.* Cambridge: MIT Press, 1988.

White, Alan. *Within Nietzsche's Labyrinth.* New York: Routledge, 1991.

Whitlock, Greg. *Returning to Sils-Maria: A Commentary to "Also Sprach Zarathustra."* New York: Peter Lang, 1990.

Wilcox, John T. *Truth and Value in Nietzsche: A Study of His Metaethics and Epistemology.* Ann Arbor: University of Michigan Press, 1974.

Yovel, Yirmiyahu, ed. *Nietzsche as Affirmative Thinker.* Dordrecht: Martinus Nijhoff, 1986.

Young, Julian. *Nietzsche's Philosophy of Art.* Cambridge and New York: Cambridge University Press, 1992.

Chronology

1844	Friedrich Wilhelm Nietzsche is born on October 15 in Röcken, in the Prussian Province of Saxony.
1849	Father dies (at the age of 36).
1858–1864	Attends the classics-oriented boarding school Schulpforta. Begins composing music for piano and voice.
1864–1869	Pursues study of classical languages and literatures, first at Bonn, then at Leipzig.
1869	Associate professor of classical philology at Basel. Meets Wagner.
1870	Full professor at Basel. Enlists as a medical orderly in the Franco-Prussian war, contracting serious illnesses.
1872	Publishes *The Birth of Tragedy*. Close association with Wagner.
1873–1874	Publishes the first three *Untimely Meditations*, including the essays *On the Uses and Disadvantages of History for Life* and *Schopenhauer as Educator*.
1876	Writes a fourth *Meditation* in homage to Wagner, but his enthusiasm for Wagner cools.
1878	Publishes the first volume of *Human, All Too Human* (638 aphorisms). Wagner sends him *Parsifal*, and their estrangement deepens.
1879	Resigns from his position at Basel, incapacitated by his health problems. Begins spending his summers in the Swiss Engadine region, and his winters in northern Italy.
1879–1880	Writes two sequels to *Human, All Too Human*, subsequently published as the two parts of its second volume (another 758 aphorisms).
1881	Publishes *Daybreak* (575 aphorisms). Periods of depression and elation. First summer in Sils Maria, where the idea of "eternal recurrence" comes to him.
1882	The year of his intense but short-lived relationship with Lou Salome. Publishes the initial four-part version of *The Gay Science* (342 aphorisms and reflections).
1883	Writes and publishes the first two parts of *Thus Spoke Zarathustra*. Wagner dies. Estrangement from family and friends; depression. Resolves against living in Germany.

1884   Completes and publishes the third part of *Zarathustra*.
                Breaks with his sister, unable to endure her anti-
                Semitic, pro-"Teutonic" fiancee Bernard Förster.
                She marries him the next year, accompanying him
                to Paraguay, where he founded a Teutonic colony.

1885   Writes the fourth part of *Zarathustra*, but it is only
                privately printed and circulated.

1886   Publishes *Beyond Good and Evil* (296 aphorisms and
                reflections in nine parts, together with poem
                "Aftersong"). Prepares new editions of most pre-
                Zarathustra works and supplies them with prefaces.

1886–1887   Prepares and publishes an expanded second edition of
                The Gay Science, with a new preface and fifth part
                consisting of forty-one additional reflections and an
                appendix of poetry, "Songs of Prince Vogelfrei."

1887   Publishes *On the Genealogy of Morals*, consisting of a
                preface and three "essays" of seventeen, twenty-
                five, and twenty-eight numbered sections. Com-
                pletes orchestral score for *Hymnus an das Leben*. Be-
                gins comprehensive project with working title of *The
                Will to Power*.

1888   Publishes *The Case of Wagner;* writes *Twilight of the
                Idols, The Antichrist, Nietzsche contra Wagner, Dionysian
                Dithyrambs* (a collection of poems), and *Ecce Homo*.
                Drops *The Will to Power* project in favor of a pro-
                jected four-part *Revaluation of All Values*.

1889   Collapses in early January in Turin, at the age of 44.
                Never recovers, living his final eleven years in in-
                valid insanity in the care of his mother and sister.
                Twilight of the Idols is published in the same month.

1892   First public edition of the fourth part of *Zarathustra*
                appears.

1893   Sister returns from Paraguay, and—under the name
                Elizabeth Förster-Nietzsche—assists their mother in
                the management of her brother's affairs.

1895   *The Antichrist* and *Nietzsche contra Wagner* are published.

1897   Mother dies, leaving complete control of his care—and
                of his literary estate—to his sister.

1900   Nietzsche dies, on August 25, in Weimar.

1901   Sister publishes an arrangement of selections from his
                notebooks of 1883–1888 under the title *The Will to
                Power*.

1908   *Ecce Homo* is published.

1910–1911   First edition of Nietzsche's collected works is published under the supervision of his sister—including a greatly expanded edition of *The Will to Power*.

1935   Sister dies, triumphant in the knowledge that her brother had come to be regarded by Hitler and Mussolini as the philosopher of National Socialism and Fascism—a travesty that would plague Nietzsche's reception for the next half-century.

1967–1984   Publication of the *Kritische Gesamtausgabe* of Nietzsche's works, *Nachlass* (notebooks and other unpublished writings), and letters.